Date Due

DIVIDED LOYALTIES

GEORGE III

From a portrait by Benjamin West

DIVIDED LOYALTIES

AMERICANS IN ENGLAND

DURING THE

WAR OF INDEPENDENCE

LEWIS EINSTEIN

Essay Index Reprint Series

BOOKS FOR LIBRARIES PRESS

FREEPORT, NEW YORK

First Published 1933
Reprinted 1969

STANDARD BOOK NUMBER:
8369-1349-3

LIBRARY OF CONGRESS CATALOG CARD NUMBER:
78-99690

PRINTED IN THE UNITED STATES OF AMERICA

CONTENTS

v

CONTENTS

ILLUSTRATIONS

1. Benjamin West. Portrait of GEORGE III painted in 1780.
   (*The two equerries in the background are Lord Amherst and
   the Marquess of Lothian riding at Coxheath Camp.*)

   Frontispiece

   (*Buckingham Palace: reproduced by gracious permission of
   His Majesty King George V.*)

2. Portrait of DR. EDWARD BANCROFT   *Facing page*   6
   (*by kind permission of Mrs. Bancroft Vidal.*)

3. Gilbert Stuart after John Trumbull—portrait of SIR
   JOHN TEMPLE   82
   (*by kind permission of the Hon. C. Winthrop.*)

4. T. Gainsborough. Portrait of BENJAMIN THOMPSON,
   Count Rumford   124
   (*by kind permission of the Fogg Museum,
   Harvard University.*)

5. Benjamin West. Portraits of Six Royal Princes
   painted in 1777   162
   (*Princes* ERNEST, *Duke of Cumberland;* AUGUSTUS,
   Duke of Sussex; ADOLPHUS, *Duke of Cambridge,
   and the Princesses* AUGUSTA, ELIZABETH *and* MARY.)
   (*Buckingham Palace: reproduced by gracious permission of His Majesty King George V.*)

vii

INTRODUCTION

THIS is an attempt to relate the story and adventures of certain Americans, spies and secret agents, refugees and painters, who were in England during the War of Independence; of their feelings at the moment of the great rift between the two nations; of what they did and of how they lived during those years; and of curious intrigues and strange secret missions in which some of these were engaged.

The American Revolution began as a civil and ended as a national war, a fact which is plain today, but which hardly occurred to anyone until long after Bunker Hill had been fought. Even the Declaration of Independence at first was far from impressing the opinion of people on either side of the Atlantic, as being as a final rupture. In order to make the separation conclusive and to create a free nation out of thirteen colonies, it needed the victory of Saratoga and the French Alliance, although until long afterwards many on both sides of the Atlantic failed to grasp the significant sequence of these three events. The extraordinary situation in which a number of Americans found themselves during the years of suspense and war was due to their perplexity in a crisis which they did not understand as having already hardened into a final shape that left no room for divided loyalties.

The chronicle of these Americans has been separated into three parts, grouped by subject rather than by chronology. It is not easy to arrest the interest in a career after this has overlapped the span of a definite period, even if a lack of uniformity is the penalty for such treatment. This explains why no rigid method has been followed in attempting to trace the lives of men whose fortunes were in different degree affected by the struggle for their countrys' independence.

The first part of this book treats of those Americans who were in the service of the British Crown either as spies, as secret agents, or as officials. No Government was ever better served by its informers than that of George the Third, or possessed more accurate information of its enemies most hidden plans, or treated this knowledge with greater neglect. The information was in large part obtained by one who probably was the most remarkable spy of all time, the talented scientist and philosopher, Dr. Edward Bancroft, who lived in the intimacy of Benjamin Franklin, and, who while in English pay, advised the American revolutionary agents and even the French Cabinet who had sent him to Ireland to report on the possibility of fomenting an insurrection in Ulster.

Intimately associated with Bancroft was Paul Wentworth, the first American cosmopolitan and international speculator, who in order to further his social and political ambitions in England became a master spy, attempted a secret diplomatic negotiation with the American Commissioners in Paris, proposed a peace policy which George the Third and the British Ministry later adopted when the moment was already too late, and who, striving by every means to prevent the French Alliance actually precipitated its consummation. It was Paul Wentworth, also, who corrupted Silas Deane and left that ardent American patriot unaware that he had himself become a traitor.

Next is related the story of how Captain Hynson, a sailor from Maryland, was bribed by the scholarly clergyman, the Reverend John Vardill, Assistant Minister of Trinity Church, New York, who during the struggle with the Colonies had put aside theology to become an English spy, and as such successfully devised the plan to steal Franklin's confidential despatches to Congress, and was rewarded by the King for this service by being appointed to fill the newly created Regius Chair of Divinity at King's College in New York.

There is the chronicle of John Temple, a patriotic, though later a most embittered American, who became a British secret agent hoping to be made a baronet, tried unsuccessfully to conduct a peace negotiation of his own, and, after failing in his ambition to serve Congress, accomplished far more for America in London than he could have done in the United States, but who, misunderstood by his compatriots, ended by becoming the first British representative in the new Republic. Last related are certain chapters in the career of that adventurer of genius, Sir Benjamin Thompson, who after beginning as an obscure Yankee boy apprenticed to a Salem shopkeeper and refused a commission in the American Army, acted as an English spy, rose through his merits before he was thirty to be a British Under-Secretary of State, commanded a cavalry regiment against his own compatriots, and in his subsequent progress became the foremost Minister in Bavaria, a Count of the Holy Roman Empire, and ended his days as a retired British Colonel living in Paris during the Napoleonic Wars, a member of the French Institute, and a scientist, philanthropist, and egotist of international fame.

The second part treats of American Tories who went to England either just before or during the Revolution, and who were principally officers of the Crown, and refugees fleeing from danger. Outstanding among these is the tragic figure of Governor Hutchinson, who, after having been the idol of Massachusetts, became the most hated of its citizens, and died in London pining for his home at Milton to which he could never return. He was foremost among thousands, who felt in their exile that they had been stormtossed and ruined, for a crime they could not understand, because they remained true to their first loyalty amid events which long before had passed far beyond their control. Only here and there is it possible to read the tragedy of men who found refuge in England and lift the veil which hid their miserable lot. More often the anguish of proud souls went unrecorded and silence raised a barrier to hide the grief of loyalists whose feelings varied in scale from the perplexities of Colonel Saltonstall, too American to fight his countrymen, and too loyal to fight his King, till by degrees they attained the harsh bitterness of Governor Hutchinson rendered cruel by his suffering and calling for fire and sword to ravage Massachusetts and unleash the savagery of the Indian against his own beloved New England.

Among the Tory refugees in London was Samuel Curwen, a fat little judge from Salem, who disapproved of independence, but exulted in every success of his rebellious countrymen and became furiously indignant whenever he heard these disparaged. There were other Americans in England like Henry Cruger, of New York, whose vision of empire was far ahead of his time and who had tried to remain true to his country and yet be loyal to his King, and after this was no longer possible, resignedly accepted the separation. Henry Cruger sat in two Parliaments as a Whig member from Bristol, but after independence had been acknowledged, he refused to stand again for re-election, and returned henceforth to dwell in the city of his birth.

Another politician finds a place in this book for a different reason. Thomas Pownall was British born and had been a servant of the Crown. He was perhaps the greatest scholar in Parliament, he was certainly the greatest bore, for his speeches were innumerable and interminable. But in spite of obvious weaknesses and ridiculous sides his views of empire were those of a statesman far in advance of his age. Pownall regarded with indifference the question of his nationality among any English-speaking people, took immense pride in his former connection with Massachusetts, and after the Revolution thought at one time of settling in the United States.

The last part of this book concerns the Colonial artists in London. Benjamin West was already established and famous in England ten years before the Revolution. As the most prominent American in England he cherished a deep love for his native land and a real attachment to the King. Even during the War of Independence, George the Third, held him in particular esteem. The warm friendship between the Monarch and his favourite Court painter stands to the credit of both men and is easier to understand than that West should have regarded himself, and been generally regarded by the same generation which revered Reynolds and beheld Turner, as being one of the greatest geniuses of all time, who could only be compared to Raphael and Michelangelo.

Copley finds place in these pages primarily as a remarkable prophet of the Revolution as well as for the reasons, artistic and political, which induced him to forsake Boston and settle in London. His merit as an artist and his later career are merely outlined in order to help understand these phases of his life. John Trumbull, gallant patriot and former colonel on Washington's staff, with his ambition to preserve by his brush the memories of the revolution concerns us because of his strange adventures in London far more than by his talent as a painter.

The Americans residing in England during the Revolution differed in many respects, yet nearly all knew each other or about each other, and the War of Independence affected the lives of all in greater or less degree. Many of these also knew the King whose indefatigable and incredible activities are discovered in the most unsuspected directions. Whether studying the reports of his spies, following every move of his secret agents, listening to personal gossip about individuals, ingratiating himself to loyalist refugees, or sitting for his portrait to West, the royal presence is felt everywhere. In a sense, which since his day has never again been true except as a symbol, the reign of George the Third can truly be called the Georgian Age, for until insanity clouded his mind, his hand moulded the history of England. No monarch was ever more painstaking, more conscientious, harder working or better informed, none was so keen a politician and none has ever made graver errors in judgment or drawn more erroneous conclusions from his own frequently shrewd statement of the facts. Because the King had discovered that his American secret agents speculated on the Stock Exchange, he refused to believe in the seriousness of the news they gave to warn him of the impending French Alliance, which he regarded as tricks to depress the funds, and delayed until too late the concessions he later was ready to make and which, if offered in time, almost certainly would have preserved his Empire.

As events recede into the past they become both clearer and dimmer. Great results stand out, the rest is soon distorted and forgotten. The story of the War of Independence has usually been cast in a somewhat conventional mould and written pragmatically mainly with an eye to its ultimate results. Natural as is this treatment, particularly after the complete destruction of the great Tory party in America, it became unavoidable that the loyalist case should also have suffered. A lost cause makes only a slender appeal, and it is not easy on any practical grounds to justify a deep interest in past failure. Yet the tale of the Americans in England during the Revolution contains a tragedy that helps to throw many curious sidelights on the history of the great period which witnessed the birth of the United States.

The loyalists who wished to cling to the Mother Country and yet to remain American possess, especially for Englishmen, another interest which as yet has been somewhat imperfectly explored. The ties which many Tories felt binding them to Great Britain came from something far deeper than questions of commercial interest, constitutional issues about taxation, or even allegiance to a King. Up to the Declaration of Independence, most Americans, whether Tory or Whig, had regarded themselves as being fellow members of a great empire. This belief, somewhat imperfectly expressed and hazily adumbrated, altogether without official sanction, was none the less gaining ground in England when the Revolution came to arrest its development for another century, which has made of it a great British imperial ideal. Yet the fact that the seed of this idea of Empire was early sown in America has been forgotten in both countries for after the War of Independence new events which followed the final separation, inevitably brought with them an entirely different series of problems regarding the relationship between the two peoples. When George the Third was at last compelled to recognize the independence of his rebellious colonies he had solved only one great phase in the intercourse between England and America. Loyalty to a King has long ago ceased to be an issue, but the question of less tangible loyalties not only those visible, but others inarticulate, instinctive and inchoate still goes on unsolved and must always continue so long as two great nations speak one tongue.

PART ONE

*Americans in the British Service, Spies,
Secret Agents and Adventurers*

Chapter One

Spy, Master Spy and Silas Deane

I

AFTER Bunker Hill, when a disillusioned British Ministry had at last understood the gigantic effort necessary to subdue the revolted colonists and was scouring Germany to enlist Hessian mercenaries, the American leaders, apprehensive of the struggle before them, thought of turning for aid to France, in spite of distasteful memories associated with the Popery of Quebec and the savagery of her Indian allies during the late war.

In Philadelphia, on March 3, 1776, four months before the Declaration of Independence had been signed, the newly formed Committee of Congress for Secret Correspondence, composed of Benjamin Franklin, Benjamin Harrison, John Dickinson, Robert Morris, and John Jay, delivered a paper of instructions to the Honble. Silas Deane, Esq., agent for the thirteen United Colonies, who had greatly distinguished himself by his zeal and personal sacrifices on behalf of the American cause. Deane was directed to proceed at once to Paris with a view to obtaining arms and supplies urgently needed for the war against the British Crown and without which the Americans could hardly hope to keep the field for more than another year. In order not to embarrass the Court of Versailles by any premature demand for recognition, the new American envoy was advised to go abroad in the character of a merchant in the Indian trade. The following clause was also contained in his instructions, which were prepared by Dr. Franklin in the name of the Committee:

> You will endeavour to procure a meeting with Mr. Bancroft by writing a letter to him under cover to Mr. R. Griffiths at Turnham Green near London, and desiring him to come over to you in France, or Holland on the score of old acquaintance; from him you may obtain a good deal of information of what is now going forward in England and settle a mode of continuing a correspondence. It may be well to remit him a small Bill to defray his expenses in coming to you and avoid all political matters in your letters to him.[1]

"Mr. Bancroft," better known as Dr. Edward Bancroft, a native of Westfield, Massachusetts, was a man of the most versatile talents. After an adventurous youth begun as a sailor, following which he became a medical attendant on West Indian plantations and in Surinam, he had settled in England about 1765, with the intention of making London his future home. He was a discoverer in the use of dyes, and turned his knowledge of tropical plants to profitable account.[2] He had written an important work on the Natural history of Guyana, and was the author of an anti-religious novel. He became a member of the Royal College of Physicians, and in 1773 was sufficiently well-known by his scientific work to receive the coveted honour of being unanimously elected to the Royal Society, the Astronomer Royal, the King's Physician, and Benjamin Franklin figuring among his sponsors. His scientific papers are still to be found in the Society's archives.[3]

Five years later, when offering his resignation to Congress,

Bancroft called attention to the circumstances of this election and to the fact that he enjoyed a literary reputation in England and was honoured "with the friendship of many worthy and some very illustrious men." For the doctor added a political to many other interests and in 1768 had published in London a tract on the liberties of the American Colonies. He had also been employed to write the comments about American affairs for the London *Monthly Review*. This was on Franklin's recommendation, and when the Solicitor General, Wedderburn, had savagely attacked the latter for his part in making public Governor Hutchinson's letters, Bancroft had warmly defended the agent of Massachusetts and thereby acquired a friendship which he always retained. No suspicion that this confidence was misplaced ever entered Franklin's mind, and years afterwards, he described his former associate in the Royal Society, as "a gentleman of character and honour."[4]

On the eve of the War of Independence, Bancroft had visited America and almost certainly talked with the leaders in Congress, certain of whom, like Franklin, he knew already. At this time he had written from New York to his brother in Massachusetts, to try to find out the latter's views on the political situation, informing him that he would henceforth sign his letters under the assumed name of A. Stuart.[5] Soon after this, Bancroft returned to London, and, although occupied with scientific pursuits and private business ventures, he kept up his interest in politics, doubtless awaiting the invitation which he was shortly to receive from Congress.

Silas Deane, the first American diplomat, energetic and ambitious, but as ingenuous as many another since his day, on his arrival at Bordeaux wrote to request Bancroft to meet him in Paris, enclosing thirty pounds for his journey. The

Doctor left London almost immediately, and both men reached Paris within a few hours of each other.

Deane already knew Bancroft from the days when the latter had been his schoolmaster and, expansively frank, immediately took his one time pupil into his confidence. Like most American politicians, the new envoy was innocent of any real knowledge of European affairs and marvelled at the extent of Bancroft's information. From the day they met Deane saw only through the Doctor's eyes. Always generous with praise, the agent of Congress wrote to the Secret Committee that his associate was rendering the greatest services and soon would clinch an argument by adding that "Dr. Bancroft was full with me in this opinion." Deane even asked the latter to accompany him on his frequent visits to Versailles, and, although the Doctor discreetly kept away from the interviews, every particular regarding the assistance which was being secretly offered by the French to the American revolutionaries was at once repeated to him. For Count Vergennes, the Minister of Foreign Affairs, gladly promised Deane the munitions and supplies he had solicited for Washington's soldiers, although insisting that the royal arms of France must first be removed from the cannon shipped to the Revolutionary army, in order to avoid embarrassing complaints in case of their capture by the British.

Louis the Sixteenth's Minister made no secret of the fact that his purpose was to strike at England by helping the colonists, but it was necessary to proceed with the greatest caution, for he did not wish to commit his Court, unless the insurrection gave greater signs of success. Desiring also to hide from Lord Stormont, the British Ambassador, the connection between Deane and himself, Vergennes proposed to employ the services

DR. EDWARD BANCROFT

SPY, MASTER SPY *and* SILAS DEANE

of the playwright Beaumarchais as an intermediary. The American agent, who needed credit quite as much as supplies, was at first not over favourably impressed by the selection of a poet known to him as "a man of more genius than property." Beaumarchais, however, showed his real genius on this occasion by creating the fictitious firm of Hortalez and Company which made fictitious purchases from the French arsenals and sold munitions to the Americans on credits advanced by the French Ministry. It was not a bad beginning for an unknown and almost penniless agent like Deane, to obtain arms and credit for struggling revolutionaries engaged in fighting the greatest empire in the world, and how important this was became evident when French cannon and powder helped to win the battle of Saratoga.

After having followed for some weeks every detail of the secret negotiations, Bancroft announced to Deane that he was obliged to return to London owing to his private business, but would keep him posted about English affairs in the manner desired by the Secret Committee of Congress. The Doctor was then interested in obtaining a monopoly for certain vegetable dyes which later became profitable to him and had applied to the Crown for this on July 31, 1775,[6] almost the very day when he was to start on his career as a traitor. Nine years afterwards, Bancroft related what actually had happened at this time, in a document which is, perhaps, the most extraordinary self-revelation of a spy that has ever been written. In 1784, he addressed a memorial to the then Secretary of State, Lord Carmarthen, to solicit the continuance of pensions promised him by the former Secretaries, Lord North and Lord Suffolk, and he described in this the circumstances which had induced him to become an informer. It is a tribute to the force

[7]

of conscience that even the greatest villains always profess to find some justification to absolve them from the stigma of their crimes, and Bancroft discovered this excuse in his purpose to prevent American independence. Frankly admitting that he had formerly favoured certain claims advanced by the Colonies, he insisted that all his interests and convictions militated against their separation from the mother country. When he returned from Paris, he as yet knew nothing of the Declaration of Independence, and had hoped that the British Cabinet, warned by him regarding the danger of French assistance to America, might forestall this by taking the measures which would lead to a reconciliation. Although at first he could not resolve to become an informer, "Mr. Paul Wentworth having gained some general knowledge of my journey to France and of my intercourse with Mr. Deane, and having induced me to believe that the British Ministry were likewise informed on this subject, I at length consented to meet the then Secretaries of State, Lords Weymouth and Suffolk and give them all the information in my power which I did with the most disinterested views."[7] Actually he wrote out at considerable length a detailed report for the British Cabinet which acquainted the King's Ministers with Deane's instructions from the Secret Committee of Congress, and related the entire story of the latter's negotiations with Vergennes.[8]

Bancroft averred that he had intended at the time to confine himself to this communication for which he had asked no remuneration, but, as the information given regarding the relations between France and the Colonies was considered to be of the greatest importance, he had been persuaded by the Cabinet Ministers to watch the progress of these negotiations and report further to them. For this purpose he made several journeys to Paris and had maintained a regular correspondence with Deane by means of the courier of the French Government. "And in this way I became entangled and obliged to proceed in a kind of business as repugnant to my feelings as it had been to my original intentions. Being thus devoted to the service of Government I consented like others to accept such emoluments as the situation required." For the information already given he had been promised a pension for life of two hundred pounds, which as the Doctor was never bashful in his demands, was afterwards considerably increased.

When after his return to London Bancroft wrote to Deane he covered his treachery by relating that the Duke of Grafton had learned about the visits to Versailles and of the intentions of the French.[9] The Doctor also had much to say in his letter about influential English friends like Lord Camden, and Thomas Walpole, the member from Lynn, who at this time, unknown to Deane, was Bancroft's partner in speculations on the Stock Exchange as well as in certain ventures of shipping contraband to America.[10] He related odd pieces of gossip and gave titbits of London news which the ingenuous Deane swallowed as if such trivialities were important information. Bancroft kept impressing his former schoolmaster with the fact that he was achieving all that it was humanly possible for anyone to do without money and owing to the distinguished connections he possessed was accomplishing far more than others could have done who received the liberal secret allowances which European States gave to their agents.[11] And Deane, who felt proud of his friend, wrote sententiously to the Secret Committee of Congress in Philadelphia, that no one had better intelligence in England, for Bancroft was closely connected with the most respectable element in the Opposition without having made himself obnoxious to the majority, "but it costs something."

In London at this time Bancroft assumed the attitude of an ardent American patriot. He claimed to Deane that English sympathizers with the colonists had consulted him as to the measures which the Americans wished their Whig friends in Parliament to promote. He repeated his own proud answer to all similar inquiries that what might be done at Westminster made very little difference because British rule in America could never be regained and England would be better advised to relinquish this quietly and retain only commercial privileges. It was no longer possible, he wrote, for Britain to conquer the Colonies. "Though our wicked refugee countrymen still labour to encourage and instigate them to go on; but for the counsels of these wretches, things would never have gone thus far and no punishment can be sufficient for the execrable malignity with which they are still urging the destruction of our country."[12]

Bancroft writing to Deane, from London, had accused Colonel George Mercer, late Lieutenant Governor of North Carolina and supposedly a friend of the Colonies, of being really an English spy sent to Paris to watch the Agent of Congress. And Dr. Williamson, of Philadelphia,[13] although professing American sentiments, he declared was another British spy who had written from Paris to call the Government's attention to Bancroft's intimacy with his former pupil. Certainly the latter statement, and probably also the first was a gross libel, but Deane accepted their veracity and at once notified the Secret Committee of Congress that

Dr. Williamson, under pretence of being an American, was doing his country a prodigious mischief—let his name be known so that everyone be put on their guard—an expression of opinion which may help to explain some of the animosity later shown him by Congress. In his dispatch he added, "Dr. Bancroft, of London merits much of the Colonies."[14]

Was Bancroft acting the "double traitor" on these occasions and was he the "thorough American" that George the Third, who read all his reports and followed his movements, contemptuously called him when writing to Lord North? The King, as will be seen, distrusted the spy for quite different reasons, but apart from any question of scruple, the double espionage, of which he has been accused, seems most unlikely.

Bancroft did not dare to commit a real indiscretion because he was aware that he was always being closely watched by the British secret service, that his correspondence was intercepted by the Post Office, and that he was thoroughly distrusted by the Government which utilized his services. On one occasion when his mistress was leaving for Paris to meet him, another American spy, the Reverend John Vardill, of whom more will be said, arranged with the Under-Secretary of State, William Eden, to foist on her a companion for the journey in order secretly to examine the letters she carried—a performance which the clergyman regarded as being of sufficient importance to include mentioning several years later, among his other eminent services in order to justify his request for the payment of salary as Regius Professor of Divinity at King's College in New York.[15]

Bancroft had persuaded Deane that he possessed private channels of communication and claimed, with some reason, that the letters which he addressed to him from London were never intercepted by the British authorities. The basis for this claim was as follows: The Secret Committee of Congress, somewhat ingenuously, had instructed Deane to correspond with Mr. Garnier, the French Chargé d'Affaires in London, who was known to be sympathetic to the American cause, and was at this time watching with the keenest interest the progress of the revolutionary movement. As the diplomat's official position in London precluded him from writing directly to an American rebel agent in Paris, Bancroft, instead, frequently had "secret access to him at midnight hours," and not only claimed to have given him much serviceable intelligence, but also to have used the Frenchman as a channel for transmitting to the Court of Versailles information of value to the American cause.[16] With the help of Garnier, the spy was able to send his letters unopened to Paris by the simple means of enclosing these in the French diplomatic pouch. In later years Bancroft, however, mentioned among his many other services to the British Government that he had maintained "a regular correspondence with Deane through the French courier." That he should have cited this circumstance in his memorial to a British Cabinet Minister as among his claims for a pension conclusively proves that he carried on this correspondence with the full knowledge of the English authorities and that his famous midnight visits to the French Embassy had been prearranged with his real employers.

The British Secret Service found no reason to object to the trifling communications made by their spy, for what important information could Bancroft give? He knew it is true, certain members of Parliament, and was quick at picking up gossip and creating the impression that he possessed inside knowledge, but he was not in the real confidence of any Minister at this time and remained only on the outskirts of the political world. It required Deane's naïve trust to discover in the letters he received from Bancroft in London any intelligence of real value. Most of the news he gave was already public property or else idle gossip. The occasional reports he sent regarding the despatch of troops were probably made deliberately and with the knowledge of the English authorities, for all real information of this nature was guarded most carefully even from other members of the Cabinet, as the Under-Secretary, William Eden when later he became Peace Ambassador discovered to his indignation. The rumours current about Bancroft being an American spy, to which the King allowed his prejudice to give credence, doubtless originated among the loyalist refugees in London who were not in the secret, and may well have been fanned by the astute chief of the British Secret Service, William Eden.

Meanwhile, Bancroft in London kept writing every week to Deane to warn him that he could never be careful enough in guarding himself against the wiles of others. Fearful lest the agent of Congress should fall under the influence of someone else, Bancroft cautioned him that he would find himself assailed from every side and in a most difficult position and he begged for regular letters to relieve his own anxiety for his friend's safety. Curiously enough, although continually betraying Deane, there was also friendship on the part of the spy. It may be difficult to believe this of so rascally a traitor, but years afterwards when Deane, ruined in body and fortune, could have been of no further possible use to Bancroft and the latter was himself in straits he none the less showed him true devotion.

Obviously, Bancroft's value as a spy to the British Cabinet was far greater in Paris than in London. A series of steps were, however, necessary as a preliminary in order that this might plausibly be arranged. As an inducement to go, the Doctor first obtained an increase of his "pension" to five hundred pounds. Next, he prepared the ground with Deane by expressing grave doubts in his letters whether he would be allowed to remain much longer in England. He wrote, "There are so many rascals solicitous to recommend themselves to government by tale bearing that if they can get no intelligence they may forge lies and throw me out of that security in which I imagined myself to be."[17] He went so far as to have himself arrested in London, because of corresponding with Deane, and when the latter heard this, he reported distressfully to the Secret Committee of Congress: "This worthy man is confined in the Bastile of England. . . . I feel more for Dr. Bancroft than I can express—he deserves much from us. Consequently will be pursued with the utmost rigor by them."[18]

An incident occurred early in 1777 which to all appearance obliged Bancroft to leave England. A mentally deranged Scotsman, John Aitkin by name, but better known as John the Painter, recently returned from America, had gone to submit to Deane in Paris, who sent him to Bancroft, a plan to destroy Portsmouth. Soon after this the fellow set fire to the ropeyard at the Portsmouth Arsenal and was hanged for the offence. At his trial, Bancroft's connection with Deane leaked out, and every American loyalist in London except Paul Wentworth, who was alone in the secret, regarded the Doctor with the utmost suspicion.[19] The spy could have wished for nothing better. When shortly after this he left England, everyone supposed that he had been compelled to flee. Deane in Paris, with ecstatic delight, welcomed a friend who henceforth would be able to give all his time and devote his great abilities to the service of America.[20] And Deane and Franklin, who had lately arrived, invited Bancroft to stay under their roof at Passy, where he resided for a full year before setting up an establishment of his own in which he flaunted a mistress to the scandal of Arthur Lee, who at least waited till he reached Berlin before doing the same. Early in 1778, when Deane, recalled to Philadelphia, read before Congress an account of his mission to France, he praised the noble manner in which Bancroft had cheerfully sacrificed all his prospects in London for the patriot cause, and during the whole period of the negotiations with the French Court had devoted himself solely to the service of his country![21]

II

On May 2, 1778, John Adams, freshly arrived in Paris, where he had been sent to take Silas Deane's place, attended a performance of Voltaire's *Brutus* at the Comédie Française. As he stepped out of his box, a man seized him by the hand, saying, "Governor Wentworth, Sir." Adams was embarrassed, for he did not know how to behave. Wentworth had been his former classmate at Harvard and, with the sensibility of his time, the Revolutionary envoy wrote down in his *Diary* that he would gladly have clasped him with cordial affection to his bosom. But they belonged to two different nations at war with each other. Moreover, both were being watched by spies and the interview was certain to be known the following morning at Versailles. Wentworth asked only personal questions about his father and friends in America. The next day he called on Franklin, and Adams, whom Wentworth had only lately described in a confidential memorandum as being "uncouth and rough mannered,"[22] wrote that his whole behaviour was that of an accomplished gentleman and "not an indelicate expression to us or our country or our ally escaped him."[23]

Of the many strange figures of Americans in England, none was stranger than that of Paul Wentworth. He was a relative of the Governor of New Hampshire of the same name. He owned considerable land in that province, as well as a plantation in Surinam, but preferred life in Europe to the New World. He spoke French perfectly "as well as you do, and better than I," Beaumarchais declared to Vergennes, and for ten years before the American Revolution, he had passed much of his time in the cosmopolitan society of Paris, which tolerated every laxity except cardsharping and boredom. Paris in the eighteenth century was already a world capital in which strangers from every land like Law, Casanova and Cagliostro could seek their fortune. But Wentworth was no vulgar adventurer. He prided himself on his "irreproachable conduct" and on frequenting the "first people." He possessed a number of French friends, mainly in banking and commercial circles, though he also frequented philosophers like the Abbé Raynal. He maintained a French mistress, Mlle. Desmaillis, in whose house he usually entertained when in Paris, and who with time had become for him only an old friend. He was principally known, however, by his French acquaintances as a great speculator in European markets, and among his stock-jobbing correspondents was the well-known banker, Mr. Hope of Amsterdam. But he had many others also in localities as far apart as Lisbon and

Hamburg. He often gambled in stocks on a large scale and not always successfully, but his reputation for integrity stood very high and he had never been a "lame duck," as insolvent speculators were then called. It was noticed that invariably he paid his losses even when as gambling debts, these could not have been legally collected.[24] To his friends he justified speculating on the ground that this was fairer than playing *quinze* or backing jockeys at Newmarket.

Paul Wentworth had kept up a certain connection with America. He was always interested in Dartmouth College, had presented to it some valuable scientific appliances, and after the war, he was elected a trustee and thanked by the grateful and unsuspecting Board of that institution for his "liberal and disinterested exertions."[25] His early views regarding the Colonies were considered sympathetic to their rights, and Bancroft, whom he knew from Surinam, and whose services he would have been glad to employ to develop his plantation in that Colony,[26] was assisted by him to write his tract on American liberties. Wentworth had been the agent for New Hampshire in London, but resigned from this before the controversy with the Mother Country became acute. He claimed to have been offered several appointments by the Continental Congress which he declined out of motives of loyalty to the Crown.[27]

In 1774, when Congress was still forwarding useless petitions for the King to reject, one of these came addressed to Paul Wentworth, Benjamin Franklin, and Arthur Lee. Franklin and Wentworth were then on very friendly terms, the Doctor having at one time lived as a guest in his house, and Wentworth told him that without instructions from his constituents, he felt unable to sign this. In Tory Ministerial circles, however, he blamed the petitioners for their tone and the offensive expressions which they had used.[28]

Even among Tories British Ministers did not often find Americans of any standing who were not crown officials so wholeheartedly of their opinion. Two years earlier Paul Wentworth, at a time when he was still the agent for New Hampshire, had secretly entered the Government employ in a somewhat nondescript capacity.[29] He was henceforth given a salary of five hundred pounds a year, but, far more than the money, his ambition and half-promised reward, was to be made a baronet, to take a seat in Parliament, and a place in English life, and in order to earn these prizes he devoted himself body and soul to the service of the Ministry.

After hostilities had broken out in the Colonies, a new usefulness was found for Wentworth as an adviser to the Cabinet on American affairs, and as a master spy. He carried a private cipher on his person with receipts for various invisible inks. He went under twenty different names, kept as many addresses, and directed an intricate organization of espionage on the Continent. Often described as a spy himself there was no imputation which he resented more. He possessed considerable ability, with unflagging energy and audacity, and carried out his work so well that, although he never knew it, Beaumarchais, who feared him, was among his warmest admirers and regarded him as one of the cleverest men in England.[30] Save with money matters, Wentworth was entirely unscrupulous in all his dealings, and ready at any time to buy documents or steal them, and to corrupt others in order, as he curiously averred, to lay his bought information "at the feet of honour." On one occasion he described a friendly visit he had paid to Alderman Lee in

Paris. Finding himself alone in his lodgings, he walked off with a specimen of his friend's visiting card and his seal which he sent at once to the British Ambassador for possible use by the Post Office.[31] For a time Wentworth lived in considerable style in Paris at the English Government's expense, and to explain this establishment he wrote to the Under-Secretary, William Eden, "You encouraged me generally to take handsome lodgings, support them, take a mistress, induce intelligence, seduce it."[32] But no one could charge him with being mercenary and above all he prided himself on being a gentleman and on never having committed a breach of trust. He received only the stipulated salary and desired no more for services which were invaluable to the British Cabinet.[33] When he returned to London, bringing back with him information of the highest importance, the considerate Lord North wrote that he would gladly have sent Wentworth again on a secret mission, but, "as he refuses all indemnification and indeed every sort of emolument except a place, I really am distressed when I propose to him the trouble and expense to these expeditions."[34]

Under different conditions Wentworth might have risen high in the service of the State and enjoyed a distinguished career. The circumstance of his being a remote connection of Lord Rockingham, did not endear him to a Tory Government and he never succeeded in entering the charmed inner circle which then formed English political life. The Ministry appreciated his services and trusted him fully, but did almost nothing more for him, though they admitted that he deserved something better. Lord Suffolk thought that Lord North ought to give him a reward.[35] Lord North agreed that he should receive something, but left this for the King. Even the safe Government seat in Parliament when at last he obtained this in 1780, lasted only for six weeks. Paul Wentworth always remained a solitary figure, pathetically feeling the indignity of his position and the crying need to pour out his friendless soul, to the intense annoyance of his Ministerial employers, who never took the slightest interest in his personal effusions, and who, eager to use him as a tool, would quite as readily have disavowed him if, as he feared, he had been thrown as a spy into a French prison.

It was Paul Wentworth, as we have seen, who persuaded Dr. Bancroft, when the latter returned to London after having been with Deane in Paris, to relate to the British Cabinet Ministers the full story of the secret negotiations with the French. The "pension" which soon after was granted to Bancroft by the Cabinet, had been made "payable to Mr. P. Wentworth for the use of Edw. Edwards" the name under which the spy was henceforth always designated.[36] A most remarkable contract was drawn up between Bancroft and Wentworth when the latter's salary was increased to five hundred pounds as an inducement for him to move to Paris. Article after article enumerated the various subjects connected with American activities in Europe regarding which the spy undertook to report. The latter pledged himself to give full information about the progress of the treaty with France, the nature of the assistance expected by the Colonies, and the correspondence of the American Commissioners with Congress. This information, written in invisible ink under fictitious love letters addressed to a fictitious Mr. Richardson, was to be communicated to Lord Stormont, the British Ambassador in Paris. The letters were to be inserted in a sealed bottle which was hidden in the hollow of a box tree growing on the south terrace of the Tuileries Gardens. This bottle was to be called for every Tuesday evening and another substituted in its place containing any communications which Lord Stormont might wish to make to "Dr. Edwards." The British Ambassador agreed to forward all the spy's reports by messenger to Mr. Wentworth.[37]

Bancroft, now settled in Paris, was giving to outsiders the impression of being chiefly a pleasure-seeker. "Bancroft and I see none but ladies of the first quality," wrote Deane's disloyal secretary, Edward Carmichael.[38] Van Zandt, another American spy in the British service, described Bancroft as principally engaged in good eating and drinking "at which he is not a bad hand,"[39] and wrote to Eden that the Doctor was on the point of leaving Franklin and Deane's service because no salary was being paid him.[40] The latter spy who had a brother serving in the American army thought of applying himself for this post.

With magnificent impudence Bancroft, to divert suspicion, had complained about his treatment to the Committee for Foreign Affairs of Congress, and announced his wish to resign. In a letter breathing a noble but injured patriotism, he drew attention to the fact that he had been sent for from London without any solicitations on his part. In spite of the embarrassment this removal had caused him he had been glad to help his country and he then enumerated all the services which he had been able to render. Although twelve months had passed since he left England, no provision had yet been made for his remuneration. As Congress had neglected him "it seems expedient that I should turn my attention from public business to my own private concerns." He pointed out with pride that he had never chosen to practice the customary means of self-advancement, nor had he written to anyone since Mr. Deane's arrival in France, "because I would not incur the suspicion of communicating the secrets." With becoming dignity, it only remained for him to thank Congress for the honour previously done him by the Secret Committee which he would always remember with gratitude, and without ever complaining of the neglect which had succeeded it.[41]

When Lord North once more asked Paul Wentworth to leave his London home in Poland Street, and go to Paris in November, 1777, it was in order to discover, before the opening of Parliament, what the attitude of Spain was going to be toward the rebellious Colonies. Wentworth, on his arrival addressed a note to Bancroft at the American head-quarters at Passy, to tell the latter that his son had suddenly been taken ill, for the secret agent knew that the handwriting would prevent any uneasiness and that Dr. Franklin "was not to be discomposed by such a trifle." He waited for the spy in a hackney coach which conveyed the two men, by the only road Bancroft regarded as safe, to Wentworth's lodgings, where they found the British Ambassador waiting for them. Wentworth described the scene: "I called him Mr. 'Edwards,' telling his Lordship in a whisper the reason for my journey and of my design." "Edwards," turned to Lord Stormont and complained sharply of the manner in which the secret information he had given was being utilized in official correspondence. The recent British protests at Versailles and The Hague, had repeated the very words the spy had used in his reports and given the lists of cargoes for America in the exact order in which he had copied these out of the Minutes in the journals of the Commissioners. When informed of this, Franklin had remarked that such precise information must spring from a source very near him, and Vergennes advised the greatest watchfulness, pointing at Carmichael, which was the real reason why that most indiscreet young man was being sent back to America. "Edwards" had, however, suggested a track which led them to Beaumarchais' secretary, whose movements they were then watching. In spite of the suspicions aroused, Bancroft declared that he intended to be serviceable to the end and though "providing against the worst events would expect them with firmness." At the spy's request Lord Stormont agreed to keep passports made out in the name of Stoughton in readiness for him, so that there might be no delay to prevent his escape should this become necessary. If the worst should happen and he was arrested, the Ambassador promised to ask the French King's mercy.[42]

Never did Wentworth find Bancroft easy to handle, for the spy was continually bringing up fresh difficulties, perhaps the better to enhance the merit of his services. Wentworth had other agents in his pay but none were so reliable, and he always used Bancroft while despising him. On one occasion he related having found the spy "flush of money" and particularly difficult to manage. Bancroft had just then made a large sum by his speculations and offered to repay all he had ever received; a proposal which Wentworth thought due partly to fear, and partly, also, to jealous resentment at the favour shown to two other American informers. Generally the spy was only concerned with his remuneration. When late in November, 1777, Wentworth saw him, he had demanded the immediate payment of five hundred pounds and compared this amount with the greater rewards which other secret agents received for giving very inferior information. Wentworth refused to pay any more, declaring that he detested "higgling in a bargain for the King's services and the cause of my country." In spite of the denial, Bancroft told him the news he had come over for: that Spain although prepared to give temporary aid was not ready to enter into an alliance with the American States.[43]

When George the Third learned this, he wrote for once approvingly to Lord North, "Mr. Wentworth has shown great zeal and dispatch in the business he had so handsomely undertaken and ably accomplished."[44] No reward was forthcoming, but five days later Wentworth informed Lord North, "I shall this day carefully remit to Mr. Edwards the £500 Your Lordship endorsed to me for his account."[45]

There is an unsigned note in Lord North's hand among the Auckland Papers in the manuscripts of the British Museum, as to what might be done to find a suitable reward for Mr. Wentworth, which the Minister declared himself ready to propose to the King. Nothing came of this, for George the Third did not like Paul Wentworth, principally because the information he kept sending concerning French preparations to assist America was invariably distasteful, and the King was not disposed to give it the credit it deserved.[46] Bearers of ill news suffer because of the tidings they bring, and even Lord North would apologize when transmitting these reports for the necessity of being obliged to forward intelligence so unfortunate. The Minister would write to the King that he understood how unpleasant this was and felt sorry to recollect that Mr. Wentworth had been the first and also "the most important and truest informer we have had." Almost everything reported by him had since been confirmed—a circumstance which did not add to Wentworth's favour with his Sovereign.

To justify his prejudice against the man who always sent bad news, George the Third had discovered a further reason which allowed him to disregard this with good conscience. It was not enough to call Wentworth, as he did, a place hunter, for so was everyone around the Court except Lord North. The King gave a most meticulous attention to personal gossip about friends and enemies, of a kind which was usually discovered by the simple process of opening their private letters in the Post Office. He had found out that Wentworth speculated, that he was a "stock-jobber," a "dabbler in the alley," and men of his cast, as he observed to Lord North, were often credulous.[47] Some intimation of this opinion may have reached the former agent of New Hampshire, for after losing thirteen hundred pounds on the Exchange he made it known to William Eden that he would never speculate again.[48] But the harm had already been done and both Wentworth and Bancroft, who was a far more notorious "meddler in stocks," and popularly supposed to have made a fortune by "bearing" British funds,[49] suffered, because of this, in the King's estimation. Lord North, who knew the extent of the royal prejudice, also wrote to his sovereign that Bancroft was a bear on the funds which might explain his wish "to drive us to take some steps that may bring on a war."[50] The King was the more easily convinced that this was the true reason because he wished to be so convinced, and persuaded himself that no reliance could be placed in the alarming news which his spies kept sending him from Paris. He wrote to Lord North that "as Edwards is a stockjobber as well as a double spy no other faith can be placed in his intelligence but that it suited his private views to make us expect the French Court means war."[51] When commenting on Bancroft's reports, just before the French Alliance had been concluded, George the Third wrote that "every word he used on the late occasion was to deceive."[52]

If the King's prejudice against speculating had been less violent, American history might have taken a different turn. No Government has ever been so well informed of the most secret doings of its enemies as was the British Cabinet through Wentworth's and Bancroft's reports. The latter's first communication was dated August 24, 1776, a year and a half before the signature of the Treaty with France. If a generous offer by England, like the one made nearly two years later, had been proposed before there could be any certainty or even likelihood of the French alliance, this unquestionably would have divided American opinion and might have halted the Colonies in their wish for independence. In an extremely interesting and hitherto unknown letter, printed in the Appendix, which was intercepted in the London Post Office and signed J. A., who could have been no other than John Adams, writing from the Continental Congress in Philadelphia to Arthur Lee's brother, Alderman Lee in London, on October 4, 1775, more than three months after the battle of Bunker Hill, which Adams had described, in order to correct the account current in England, the following remarkable passage occurs:

> We cannot in this country conceive that there are men in England so infatuated as seriously to suspect the Congress or people here of a wish to erect ourselves into an independent state. If such an idea really obtains amongst those at the helm of affairs, one hour's residence in America would eradicate it. I never met one individual so inclined but it is universally disavowed.

Adams affirmed that even the delegates from Massachusetts, in spite of all their province had endured, had never disclosed sentiments favourable to independence. "They knew too well such an attempt would be likely to erect disunion."[53]

The American leaders had not regarded Bunker Hill as a break with the mother country, and Congress went on humbly declaring that its followers were "trying to be obedient subjects" to George the Third. Thomas Jefferson could write to a kinsman that he looked forward fondly to a reconciliation with Great Britain.[54] So late as October 22, 1775, the Rev. Jeremy Belknap, chaplain in the American camp, could still publicly pray for the King, and on Christmas Day of the same year, the Revolutionary Congress of New Hampshire officially proclaimed their disavowal of any purpose of independence.[55]

Until after Burgoyne's surrender, if Carmichael, the Secretary of the American Commissioners, is to be believed, Franklin in Paris did not give the impression of holding out for absolute independence. Practical as always in his outlook, the old philosopher was prepared to steer his course by events and not till Saratoga had been won did he feel certain of success. France's policy had too long been doubtful and the French Alliance would never have been signed without this victory of American arms. On October 16, 1777, Ralph Izard, of South Carolina, wrote from Paris, with the strict injunction of secrecy, to his London bookseller, John Almon, who as he knew sympathized with the American cause, to tell him that France wanted to avoid war while giving assistance. "Lord Stormont complains, Mr. Frith affects to bully, the French Ministry promise: but nothing to the purpose is done, this it would seem could not continue long but it has already continued long and may much longer."[56]

If George the Third had seen the situation at this time as clearly as Paul Wentworth saw it, if he had understood in the early autumn of 1777, that as soon as the French Alliance was signed, there could be no reconciliation short of acknowledging American independence, he would at once have offered the terms which Wentworth was to propose secretly to Franklin and Deane in December, 1777, and Lord North to announce in Parliament two months afterward. The King was only won over to accepting these when the moment was already too late. Yet Wentworth's and Bancroft's reports during the previous year and a half ought to have left no reasonable doubt in his mind, regarding the assistance which the French were giving, or their future intentions toward the rebellious colonies. The fact that both agents happened also to be speculators allowed George the Third with a good conscience to set aside their communications as unduly influenced by their own operations on the Stock Exchange. The royal horror of gambling helped to free America.

III

In December, 1777, Paul Wentworth by every means fair or foul was making his greatest effort to stave off French intervention. Six months earlier he had proposed to steal Franklin and Deane's correspondence with M. de Sartine, the French Minister of Marine, in order to bring about the latter's downfall, as these "letters cast great discredit on the Court and speak of the duplicity of their conduct so that their publication would cause great embarrassment."[57] In this way intervention might be delayed at least for another year. But Burgoyne's surrender, as Wentworth foresaw, would inevitably hasten the French alliance, and even Lord North, when he heard of the disaster, for once lost his serenity, and agreed that something would have to be done.

The new plan of Wentworth proposed to make "a well-timed offer of indemnity and impunity to those Cromwells (of the Congress)," and suggested to the English Cabinet that it might be possible to inveigle the Americans into a negotiation by holding out to them the bait of independence which later could easily be withdrawn. He wrote to the Under-Secretary of State, William Eden, his intention of attempting "to convince the agents by hopes of all they can wish—it can do no harm and if you are alert the business can be done either way."[58]

William Eden, who was also chief of the Secret Service, had already given his own views on this subject, for Wentworth's guidance. After explaining that he was familiar with the American attitude from his long intimacy with the famous Whig lawyer, Counsellor John Lee, who sympathized with the Colonies and was a close friend of Franklin, the Under-Secretary expressed his personal belief that further measures of force would have the support of the Kingdom so long as it was physically possible to supply these. On the other hand, the Government would be glad to effect a settlement if this was feasible, and he directed Wentworth to ascertain how far the Americans aimed at an absolute unqualified independence. "Also what proposal the colonies were likely to admit and through what channel it could best be conveyed."[59] If the colonists insisted in their demand for absolute independence, nothing less than a ten-year war could prepare Great Britain to accept this, and Eden offered his personal opinion that "As an English gentleman inheriting my share of that English pride which I never wish to lose, I could not bear to see a dismemberance of the Empire without running every hazard to prevent it."[60] Short of admitting independence, the Cabinet was now, however, ready to offer great concessions, and he added that there was some ground for hope that a settlement might not be out of the question. Lately the Under-Secretary had read a private letter which was written by Carmichael, who was with the American Commissioners in Paris, to a friend in London, and which, intercepted by the British Post Office, contained certain ideas of peace without victory. Eden quoted a passage from this—"If we could on one side lose the idea of supremacy and on the other that of dependence we might be friends by Treaty never by Confederation."[61]

If this view was correct, the mother country and her revolted Colonies could be reunited. Once again Wentworth was despatched post-haste to Paris, this time to ascertain on what basis the American Commissioners would consent to treat of peace and induce these to begin negotiations before they could conclude the French Alliance.

The secret agent arrived in the French capital on December 12, 1777, and at once wrote in the third person to Silas Deane, to say that a gentleman who already had some acquaintance with him wished to improve this; but fearing objections to an unexpected visit he asked the favour of a private interview. He announced that he would wait for him in his coach on the following morning near the Barrier leading to Passy. After this he would attend the Exhibition at the Luxemburg Gallery, and in the evening would go to the *Pot de Vin* Bathing Machine on the river, leaving a note with the number of the room engaged. He added in his letter to Deane that "In the meeting the greatest secrecy and honour is expected."

The agent of Congress answered to this that he would be at his lodgings in the Rue Royale next morning, when he would be glad to see anyone that had business with him, and that "Mr. Deane will always treat every subject with the secrecy and honour it merits." When he acknowledged this note Wentworth mentioned that he was on the point of returning to London "where you may have wishes to make me useful in which I shall be happy if they promote peace."

The two men met at dinner to try to heal a feud over a roast and began their talk by pledging themselves "to secrecy and the confidence of private gentlemen wishing well to both countries."⁶² Afterward Wentworth described Deane as showing himself on this occasion "vain, desultory and subtle." They wrangled over the table for hours about the antecedents of the conflict only to begin the same argument afresh next morning. When Wentworth called for Deane at the Café St. Honoré, he found the latter sitting at breakfast with Franklin and Arthur Lee. The two men went off together to continue a discussion in which the agent of Congress displayed a great deal of "Republican pride." This time the only point on which they were able to agree was that jealousy was the ruling feature of American character.⁶³

None the less Wentworth outlined to Deane his plan of reconciliation, which was to be based on an amnesty and a return to the situation as it stood in the Colonies in 1763. The measures he now advocated were the same as those later offered with the King's approval, by the Peace Embassy in America. Under this plan the Colonies were to be self-governing in their own affairs and Parliament was to interpose only in external matters. Wentworth also suggested an Armistice by which the British troops were everywhere to be withdrawn except from New York and the neighbouring islands. As a further incentive he proposed to the American leaders a

wholesale distribution of Privy Seals, Great Seals, local baro-
nies, knighthoods, and Governor Generalships. These blandishments, attended by a loan of thirty million pounds for
agriculture and sound currency, were "great objects in a plan
I have thought of since I have been here and leave the effect
work in their minds."[64]

This preposterous bribe, seemed at the time plausible enough
to Lord North, who recognized in this his own parliamentary
recipes, but showed how little Paul Wentworth had understood
the new revolutionary psychology. Six months later, John
Adams described the receipt of a long missive which the
American Delegation at Passy had every reason to believe was
sent to them with the approval of George the Third. A proposi-
tion couched in the most flattering terms was made in this to
govern America by means of a Congress of two hundred Peers
who were to be created by the Crown. Among the new nobility
were to be Franklin and Washington, Adams and Hancock.
"Ask your friend if he should like to be a peer," jestingly
wrote Adams, adding that if any American leader had been
foolish enough to approve, he would at once have lost all his
influence and been obliged to escape to England for protection
among refugees and loyalists.[65]

On New Year's Day, 1778, Wentworth called on Franklin
on the score of their old friendship, although the latter agreed
to receive him only on condition that no mention should be
made of any personal reward. They spent two hours together,
Wentworth confidentially reading aloud to him a letter from a
high personage whose name he did not disclose, but who, he
declared, was ready to assent to American independence. This
was Eden's letter, somewhat distorted perhaps by Wentworth
in order to suit his ends. The latter now proposed to offer

Franklin and Deane safe conducts to go to London in order to negotiate a peace, which would have had the effect of removing the two envoys from Vergennes at the most critical time. Franklin replied, however, that America would never consent to peace without independence and that he had no power to treat.

These secret negotiations had been anxiously watched by the French Ministry, which had a shrewd suspicion of what was going on. Wentworth, to his extreme annoyance, discovered that his steps were dogged by the police, his own servants spied on him, and that an attempt had been made to force open his strong box, after which he had burned all his papers and requested that those at the Ministry in London should also be destroyed. He felt himself in some danger of assassination, but more likely of being cast into prison among common malefactors.[66] Most of all he was deeply humiliated by his position, for in Paris everyone regarded him as a spy and his oldest friends now shunned him. In vain he had posed as a cosmopolitan speculator and a neutral, and had even written to his former correspondents at Cadiz and Lisbon, Amsterdam and Berlin, to take shares in speculations made in English and French funds in order, by engaging in such ventures, "to lessen the odious suspicion of being a spy." He had gone so far as to pay the premiums on these gambles at Amsterdam, and then covered himself with counter-orders. With the self-pity of moral solitude he wrote to William Eden, "I frankly confess it is not a situation for a man who aims at honour to be kept in—unavowed and neglected—regarded as a spy—suspected by friends."[67]

Wentworth thought of asking Lord Stormont to complain officially about the indecency of following a private gentleman

whose conduct during ten years in which he had frequented
the first persons in France, had always been irreproachable.[68]
In order to allay suspicion and as a mark of esteem the British
Ambassador went so far as to present the secret agent to Louis
the Sixteenth, after which Vergennes invited him to a dinner,
though without paying him any personal attention. Paul
Wentworth told a French friend that he knew he had no right
to expect greater consideration, but though he found the
Minister's banquet sumptuous and his wines exquisite, yet he
could not drink these with good taste at the thought of what
he was being taken for.[69]

The suspicions aroused at Versailles were easy to understand. Vergennes had been working feverishly and against the
most strenuous opposition at Court to arrange an alliance
with the American colonists. He had tried to conduct these
negotiations with the utmost secrecy, as the conclusion of the
treaty meant immediate war with England, and the Minister's
position was staked on the success of this policy. Wentworth's
arrival in Paris at the most critical moment had been at once
discovered by the police and promptly reported by Beaumarchais to Vergennes. The latter knew that the English agent was
in close touch with the British Ambassador who openly called
on him and that Wentworth had also conferred with Deane
and Franklin, but he could not penetrate the real purpose of
these visits. There were several possibilities. Was Wentworth
an emissary of the British Government despatched to wean
the Americans away from the French, or was his object merely
to create this impression in order to disgust the French with the
untrustworthy conduct of the Revolutionary envoys, with
whom they had been negotiating? Was he possibly an agent of
Franklin and Deane, who was there to bring pressure on the

Court of Versailles in order to hasten the alliance by holding out the fear that otherwise the colonists would come to terms with England? Or was he, what he gave himself out to be, merely an international speculator whose political sympathies remained neutral? Or did he only assume this rôle as a cover for his real purpose, which was to attempt to effect a reconciliation with the Colonies? [70]

Vergennes sent for an old friend of Wentworth's to try to discover the truth. This friend was a certain Jean Louis Favier, no less known as a clever political agent and pamphleteer, than for his own dissolute habits. As Vergennes had lately paid Favier's debts, which amounted to forty thousand *livres*, the latter fell under an obligation which was great enough to induce him most reluctantly to swallow his pride and act the spy on a friend, with the same aversion which Wentworth had felt at being taken for one. When Favier called at his lodgings Wentworth seemingly frank, made no secret about Lord Stormont's visit whom Favier had in fact just met on the stairs, or of the talks he had lately had with Deane and Franklin. He put these down to a former friendship dating from the time when he had been associated with the latter as an agent of the Colonies, and he added that after American demands had become excessive he withdrew from their cause without, however, joining the British, but that he had always retained his friendship with individuals.

In turn, Wentworth complained indignantly to his French friend about his movements being followed wherever he went. At the opera and at public balls he had been watched by police agents. He attributed these unwelcome attentions to the visit he had paid Deane. Favier to throw him off the track professed doubt as to whether his impression about being followed was correct, for Paris was then full of disbanded Polish officers who might be mistaken for agents of the police. He expressed more surprise that his friend should have dared to see Deane after the severe laws which had been passed by the late Parliament against holding any intercourse with the enemy. Wentworth replied that on account of these he did not care for this visit to be known in England, although such laws were intended principally to frighten people. He called himself a cosmopolitan whose property was at Surinam, in New Hampshire, and in his own pocket-book. He did not know if he would ever be able to recover his American estates which brought him in nothing, while he was obliged to pay out five or six hundred pounds every year to his relatives who had been ruined by the war. He had made use of the American agents to send over this money and also had tried to interest Deane in his speculations. Wentworth now offered to make Favier a partner in these without the latter being asked to put up anything and ended the talk by inviting him to a supper at the house of his mistress, Mlle Desmaillis, along with "other ladies and gentlemen."[71]

The supper table of a courtesan was a triviality which could not conceal to those behind the scene, that the moment was critical for three countries. The slightest mistake made by Franklin or Vergennes might have changed the course of history. In fact Beaumarchais was then convinced that all his work had been in vain and the Colonies would be reconciled with the Mother Country. The fear that Wentworth had inspired, and the knowledge that the British Cabinet was about to reverse its policy called for instant measures in Paris. On December 17, 1777, Bancroft had shown Franklin a letter just received from London containing information that so soon as the Parliamentary recess was over the British Government proposed to make an offer of peace and asking him in view of the close relations which he enjoyed with the Commissioners to ascertain what terms would be acceptable.[72] Franklin took this letter at once to Vergennes and also acquainted him with the full extent of Wentworth's overtures. No more honest tactics nor persuasive argument could have been used to conclude the alliance.

For some time already the French Minister had been engaged in a difficult struggle at Court to overcome hesitations which were particularly influenced by Turgot's sinister prediction that another war would spell bankruptcy for France. Vergennes could now point out that any further delay would mean allowing the golden opportunity for weakening England to slip by, and see the revolted colonists return to their former allegiance. On the same day that Franklin called to show Bancroft's letter, Vergennes despatched his secretary, Gérard, soon to sail as the first envoy to the United States, to inform the Commissioners about his Court's intention to recognize the new republic. Three weeks later, on January 7, 1778, a Crown Council at Versailles decided to conclude the American alliance without waiting to ascertain what Spain would do, and on the morrow Gérard went to see Franklin to ask what steps would be necessary to keep the American Commissioners from listening to any offers from Great Britain. A month afterward on the Sixth of February, 1778, the treaty with the United States was signed at Versailles as the astonished British Government learned to its dismay forty-two hours later by the special messenger whom Bancroft despatched with the news.

From the moment he had set foot in Paris, Paul Wentworth

had minutely described, in a number of lengthy reports, his attempted negotiations with Deane and Franklin, and the proposals which he had made as a possible basis for a reconciliation. Lord North's indolence was notorious and he admitted that he was not fond of the perusal of documents, but on reading these he had been deeply impressed. He transmitted the entire correspondence immediately to the King, adding that in spite of its verbosity he had found it most interesting, especially the narrative of the conversation between Mr. Wentworth and Mr. Deane. Lord North took the liberty of recommending His Majesty to read this through as it related to many points of great importance. "This expedition of Mr. Wentworth may very possibly end in nothing, but (as he speaks entirely for himself, Lord North hopes and believes that no mischief can arise from it), especially as he had the greatest confidence in the discretion and ability of Mr. Wentworth."[73]

The King was then in one of his most obstinate moods and returned the letters to Lord North with the scathing comment that they were more calculated to show Mr. Wentworth's knowledge than to convey much information. The correspondence, he admitted, had a "very unpleasant appearance," but George the Third could not believe that a war with the House of Bourbon was inevitable. Pressed again by Lord North, the King, writing on January 13, 1778, six days after the alliance had been agreed on, found Mr. Wentworth's "very voluminous and undigested letters" hard to wade through, and drew the conclusion that the latter had been too precipitate in looking on a declaration of war as immediate.[74]

The King's Ministers were less hard to convince. Early in January, Wentworth, still in Paris, had received a private letter from William Eden to say that if the news he gave was true about France and Spain having undertaken at all hazards to support American Independence, war was certain and virtually had already begun. But it had to be remembered that this information rested "on the single testimony of your friend [Bancroft], who according to your very just reasoning may either deceive or be deceived."[75] Even Wentworth at first had found it difficult to believe that the Court of Versailles would be prepared to enter into an alliance without reciprocal engagements which the American Congress would be called upon to ratify, but Bancroft rightly had insisted that no other condition except that of independence was demanded by the French.[76] Wentworth himself was convinced that this was true and Eden could only express his bitter regret that the communications received from the spy should be entitled to so much credit.

Manifestly a change in British tactics had become more than urgent. Writing from Paris, Wentworth recommended that Peace Commissioners should be sent immediately to America, but it was imperative for these to arrive before the Treaty with France could be concluded, even at the risk of Parliament not approving the great powers which it would be necessary to give them.[77] He thought of himself at this juncture in the light of a possible commissioner though recognizing that his greatest usefulness might still be in Paris. Wentworth had by this time won over Eden and Lord North to his ideas, and together they won over the King whose conversion, as will be seen in a later chapter, took place too late. For suddenly George the Third became as eager to make concessions to the Americans which, if offered in time, would have saved his Empire, as he had for years shown himself recalcitrant.

IV

Wentworth's negotiations in Paris brought about several unexpected results. Besides hastening the French Alliance and being directly responsible for the British Peace Embassy to America, which sailed tardily a few months later on its foregone mission of failure, indirectly, they led to the sad ending of Silas Deane's career after the splendid services he had rendered to the American cause. As little has hitherto been written about Wentworth's part in bringing this about, an account based principally on letters of George the Third, certain of which have only been discovered in recent years, may not be inappropriate. When Arthur Lee in a letter to Sam Adams asserted that Paul Wentworth from "his attempts upon me I knew to be a most subtle tool of corruption" had also seduced Silas Deane,[78] his remark was near to the truth.

After learning about Lee's probably quite unjustified suspicions of Deane's financial integrity, Congress passed a resolution recalling the man who had devoted his private fortune and his untiring energy to further independence, and who, in spite of many mistakes, had rendered the greatest services to the American cause in France. Disgusted by this ingratitude, Deane had already made up his mind to resign, as "it is too much for men to spend the prime of their lives in vexation and anxiety for nothing but to be found fault with and blamed."[79] He was heartily sick of public business and wanted to retire as soon as this could be done without loss or disgrace. On the eve of sailing for America, his intention was eventually to return to Europe and later to establish some commercial connection abroad.

For some time already Deane had been disgusted with the

treatment he had received both from Congress and in France. Van Zandt, alias George Lupton, an American spy in the British service, after breakfasting with him one day, reported a remark he had let fall that it was a pity England would not agree to independence, after which both countries could join together against the French. Lupton had heard privately that Deane would be recalled several months before the latter knew of this, and the spy advised William Eden that this would be an opportune time "to endeavour to bring him over to our way of thinking," for Deane would prove a valuable acquisition.[80] At this point Wentworth stepped in with his proposals, and offered certain personal advantages to Deane who, intending to resign from the service of Congress, allowed himself to be interested in a supposed commercial undertaking of a seemingly private nature, which was to be backed by English Government money. A month after his talks in Paris, Wentworth wrote to Lord North that Deane who had doubtless heard of his own impending recall, "looks to the magnanimity of Great Britain."[81] The Prime Minister, at this time, addressed a curious note to the King for it was the draft of a letter which, after His Majesty's approval had been signified, was to be written to Mr. Wentworth. The latter was to appear in this as the purchaser and shipper of merchandise and to fix on the consignee in New York who would send either the profits or the goods themselves to Mr. D.[eane] in Connecticut.[82] Lord North also sent to the King several papers, the most important of these being Mr. D.'s proposals, to which were added some pieces of intelligence Mr. W. had received from him.

Borrowing a leaf from his French admirer, Beaumarchais, Wentworth, now using commerce to cover politics, proposed to turn himself into a British Hortalez and Company, to fight the Americans, and from now on Deane became only a tool in his hands. The latter, revolted by his treatment from Congress, sick at heart and distrusting the French, had in view henceforth only a reconciliation for which he was ready to accept English assistance. And the King[83] signified the pleasure he felt on learning of Deane's return to America as this would allow the news of the forthcoming Peace Embassy, which was shortly to sail, to produce its effect. Later an unsigned communication of Deane accompanied several letters from Wentworth which point to the continued relations between the two men. This also was submitted to the King.[84] Much of the correspondence is missing, but two years afterward, George the Third wrote to Lord North to say:

> I think it perfectly right that Mr. Deane should so far be trusted as to have £3000 in goods for America. The giving him particular instructions would be liable to much hazard but his bringing any of the provinces to offer to return to this allegiance on the former foot would be much better than by joint application through the Congress.[85]

The most recent biographical notice of Silas Deane mentions, as very unfortunate for his reputation, that his private letters urging American submission should have been intercepted by the British.[86] It was still more unfortunate that he should have first submitted these letters to Lord North. Deane was always a prolix writer and the correspondence he desired to have "intercepted" was so voluminous that as Lord North admitted he had only then been able to read two of the letters, and in his opinion these proved too much, for there was in them so great a zeal for reconciliation that they would appear to be unduly inspired. He wrote to the King that "Mr. Deane seems in that respect to have acted fairly and put himself in His Majesty's power." But Lord North also expressed his own fear that Mr. Deane would not be able to return to America without a reunion between Great Britain and the Colonies.[87]

That day the King read only two of Deane's letters, but he also concurred in Lord North's opinion. Three weeks later, after re-reading them, these letters still appeared "too favourable to seem spontaneous," although Deane's wish for the Colonies' return to the mother country warmly appealed to George the Third, who wrote: "I confess I will never put my hand to any other conclusion of this business." The argument Deane had used that, as France could not long continue to help America it would be better to abandon the idea of independence and return to "so mild a government as the British," was balm to the Monarch's injured soul.[88]

By a strange paradox, on the very eve of victory, Deane was as forthright in his wish to give up the goal of independence as he had favoured this when the ambition appeared most dangerous and success seemed most unlikely. Even more incredible, he was as firmly convinced as ever that he was still acting the part of an American patriot. There is an element of unconscious comedy in a letter which he wrote to the traitor Bancroft, whom he never thought of as a spy, to say that he felt no interest personally in Great Britain, "though you with many of my friends have suspected it." In reality he was at this time only a nervous wreck, broken in spirit, and Franklin was correct when he described him as distressed in mind and circumstance, raving, with his character ruined.[89] Posterity finds it hard to understand how quickly revolutions use men most of all when they give unstintedly, and Deane had given all he possessed to the cause of his country, only to find himself reviled at the bar of Congress. Is it surprising that after the great work he had accomplished for America in France, stripped of his own small fortune which he had freely offered, poor, and yet treated as a thief and suspected of non-existent riches, doubts may have crept into his mind as to the wisdom of the goal for which he had valiantly toiled? The suspicions he aroused, which at first were unjustified, ended by being true, for Deane had, in fact, become a traitor to his cause. Yet he became one neither for mercenary reasons nor out of ambition. He deceived himself and suffered acutely when former friends like John Jay and John Adams would have nothing further to do with him after he had seen Benedict Arnold in London. He defended himself hotly against the charge that he was living in the latter's intimacy. When he lay ill and in distress at Ghent, misanthropic in his feelings and bitter against his native land, he turned again for aid to Wentworth.[90] But it was Bancroft who in the end saved Deane from starvation when the latter was lying sick and penniless in London, though still refusing to part with the diamond-studded gold snuff-box which Vergennes gave him as a testimonial when he had been recalled. Paul Wentworth had then left for his plantation in distant Surinam to die there suddenly in 1793. Bancroft at the time was himself in distress, with a large family to support, and was engaged in several vexatious lawsuits. Yet repeatedly in money, devotion and medical care, he helped the friend whom he had betrayed, and the latter always thought of him only with the most heartfelt gratitude.[91] When Deane died just as he was about to sail to return to America, the former spy wrote the account of his end.

Bancroft's subsequent activities must be briefly related. With all his audacity, the traitor lived in terror of discovery, always afraid lest the knowledge of his "pension" should leak out by reaching the opposition in Parliament, and furious when he found out that, in violation of the agreement, his reports had also been shown to other spies. When he despatched a special messenger to London with the terms of the Secret Alliance between France and the United States, this was on condition that not one syllable should be allowed to leak out until accounts had been obtained from other quarters, "else I am ruined." Arthur Lee, the third American Commissioner in Paris, was the only person who publicly charged Bancroft with being a spy, but, usually quite wrongly, he suspected everyone except his own secretary Thornton, who was a paid informer of the British Ministry. Lee heard some rumours about Bancroft from a sea captain who had known the doctor intimately in Guyana and who, when he called at his house in London, was astonished to learn that he had twice been with the Privy Council.[92] As Lee made no secret of these suspicions, Bancroft indignantly demanded from him the proof, which was not forthcoming. Seemingly cleared of guilt the spy wrote a letter, intercepted by the British Post Office, nobly affirming that after his vindication the dispute would cease, and henceforth the only conflict between Lee and himself would be as to who could best serve the great cause of American liberty.

Arthur Lee next accused him of writing an anonymous letter which had appeared in a Philadelphia newspaper. Bancroft's spirited rejoinder to this charge was a masterpiece. He asked Lee if it would not be "more reasonable, more manly and more becoming your station if on this and other occasions when you have thought proper to entertain suspicions of me you had openly and *directly* informed of your reasons for suspecting."[93] The feud continued between the two men without Lee ever being able to substantiate his charges. Later, when Franklin proposed that Bancroft should proceed to England to negotiate an exchange of prisoners, Lee was contrary-minded, which caused Bancroft to write him with his customary assurance, "Whether I am to be so employed or not is of very little importance to me; but it is of much importance that I should have an opportunity of vindicating my character and of ascertaining whether your particular opposition to me arises from a regard for the public good or from personal enmity."[94]

The French secret service which intercepted Arthur Lee's private message to Lord Shelburne informing him that the Treaty of Alliance had been signed,[95] was never able to discover anything against Bancroft. Although the Court of Versailles spied on all the American Commissioners and was always suspicious lest these should carry on secret negotiations with the English behind their backs, although they never forgave Arthur Lee for his violation of trust, they believed in Bancroft implicitly with a confidence which probably dated from the time when the spy had arranged with the English secret service to pay his "midnight visits" at the French Embassy in London. John Adams, who never suspected the truth, greatly admired Bancroft's "clear head and good pen," noting that he enjoyed "the confidence of persons about the Ministry," and that an excellent account he had written of the relations between France and America, was translated either by Turgot or the Duc de la Rochefoucauld—which of the two he could not remember.[96] The favour with which the French regarded Bancroft was more than could have been said about their feelings toward John Adams. That most honest and able of patriots so incensed Vergennes by employing expressions which the New Englander regarded as appropriate and the French Foreign Minister as offensive, that the latter refused to have anything further to do with him, and if the alliance had depended only on Adams, it might easily have been wrecked, an incident which contains a lesson in diplomacy that the American people have not yet altogether mastered.

Vergennes, however, gave Bancroft his full confidence, and later turned to the spy as a suitable agent to foment a rising in Northern Ireland where grievances similar to those suffered in America were actively nurtured. Advised by Lafayette, who regarded Bancroft as being the only American in Paris whom he was willing to rely on for such a dangerous enterprise, the Minister obtained Franklin's consent to send him on this important mission. Disguised as an English merchant, the American went to Ireland in 1779, with instructions to study the situation in order to advise the French Cabinet regarding the chances of starting a revolt among the Presbyterians in Ulster, who were in hearty sympathy with the Revolution. On his return to Paris, Bancroft reported that although many of the Irish cherished feelings of independence, yet they had no settled plan, were greatly divided among themselves, and nothing could be expected from an insurrection.[97] An English spy's advice on this occasion decided the policy of the Court of Versailles.

For his services, the British Government had raised Bancroft's pension to a thousand pounds so long as he should live in France. This enabled him to reside at Passy, where Deane, on his return from America, described him as "agreeably situated and much esteemed" in the world of politics, science and letters, in which he moved. Paul Jones was one of his closest friends. John Adams met the spy frequently at dinner at Lafayette's house and several years later again in London. Jefferson wrote to assure Bancroft of his "sincere and great esteem and attachment." Yet all this time and during the peace negotiations the spy furnished news to the British Government and indirectly helped to guide the views of the American Commissioners.

After the conclusion of peace in 1783, Bancroft went to America on a private mission to try to recover some money which had been loaned by the Prince of Luxemburg to the State of South Carolina. He remained for a time in Philadelphia, frequenting the political world which had gathered there. Franklin had given him a letter to Robert Livingston mentioning his previous employment in the service of Congress, and adding that he had known him long and esteemed him highly.[98] Although Bancroft, after the peace, had retained his British citizenship in preference to the American, this curious choice of allegiance on the part of a supposed patriot disturbed Franklin's tolerant indulgence for his friend as little as had the previous knowledge of his speculations or the disorder of his private life. He wrote to invite Bancroft to visit him, subscribing his letter "most affectionately."

From Philadelphia, the spy was still continuing to give news to the British Cabinet about American conditions, describing in his letters the many disbanded officers and soldiers who were crossing the Alleghanies to settle in the Ohio Valley. He wrote to London that "their leaders openly avow a determination soon to drive the Spaniards from West Florida. What relation they will hereafter maintain with the United States seems doubtful, but I think grave disorder is to be expected from the licentious ungovernable temper of all the interior inhabitants of America."⁹⁹

The spy's subsequent letters contained some original suggestions to the British Cabinet. In 1784, more than a year after peace had been concluded, and the independence of the United States formally recognized by treaty, Bancroft made the remarkable proposal that "if the view of His Majesty's Ministers extend towards a recovery of the sovereignty of the New United States or towards a dissolution of their Confederation, or of their present connection with France, these ends will be best promoted by an adherence to the system of excluding American vessels from British plantations and American shipping from the advantages of being sold and employed in this Kingdom."¹⁰⁰ Bancroft expressed as his personal conviction that twelve months after this restrictive policy, the people of New England, of North Carolina, and perhaps some other States, would clamour against the Union and press again for something like their former connection with Great Britain.

After his return to England Bancroft probably to justify the retention of his pension still advocated the policy of trying to destroy the United States. He advanced this in a conversation with Pitt, and afterwards declared that the latter appeared to be favourably impressed with the suggestion.¹⁰¹ But the new Ministry, surfeited by the American War, was no longer interested in hearing any of Bancroft's views.

The spy thereafter gave up political intelligence, for which he was no longer paid, and lived to a ripe old age busying himself with scientific investigations on the theory of colours, which he tried to put to a commercial use in printing calicoes. He died at Margate in 1821. He had lain in his grave for over seventy years before his guilt as a traitor became known. His grandson, after a most honourable military career, became a British general and, profoundly distressed that his forbear should have been a spy, unfortunately destroyed the greater part of his correspondence.[102]

CHAPTER TWO

The Great Theft

AT THE outbreak of the Revolution, there was no Churchman in America who gave greater promise of having before him a brilliant career than the Reverend John Vardill, the son of a former port warden of New York. Gifted with varied talents, he was already widely and favourably known for his learning and virtue, and in 1773, at the age of twenty-one, he became a Fellow and Professor of Natural Law at King's College, the present Columbia University. This was the time when he carried on some correspondence with George Washington about his stepson, John Parke Custis, who was one of his pupils.[1] In the year following Vardill was elected Assistant Minister of Trinity Church, New York, with every prospect of later succeeding to the rectorship of that pride of the Church of England in the New World which was already the most important of Episcopalian places of worship in America. The honour was all the greater because conferred on him during his absence in London. After the election, a contemporary who signed himself "A Real Churchman," wrote in praise of Vardill:

I need not enlarge on his abilities, for they are universally known and acknowledged. . . . I question whether America ever sent a better scholar of his age to England or one that has done her more honour. His character has been ever clear of even the suspicion of vice or levity . . . a devout religious turn of mind solely induced him to enter into holy orders.[2]

[51]

Nor was this tribute of admiration in any way exceptional. Vardill was on terms of personal friendship, at this time, with Whig and Tory leaders in New York, where partisan feeling did not yet run so high as in Boston. Ten years later, the former Royal Governor Tryon testified that the young clergyman had long been known to him as a gentleman eminent for his literary ability and distinguished for his loyalty. And Colonel Fanning, Lieutenant-Governor of Nova Scotia, who before the Revolution had been Tryon's secretary, and had known John Vardill intimately since 1771, pointed out that the clergyman "was thought pre-eminent in point of genius and literary attainments . . . he was rising in the Church and growing in the esteem and admiration of his countrymen."[3]

For his ordination Vardill had gone to England, which was then a necessity, and he had prolonged his stay in London so as to promote the grant of a charter required in order that King's College in New York might become a university. The young parson also displayed an active interest in the stirring questions of the day and, like nearly all the Anglican clergy in America, showed himself in these troubled times a staunch Tory. Already in New York he had engaged in a public controversy, which excited colonial opinion, with the redoubtable Scotsman, Dr. Witherspoon—who, as President of the College of New Jersey, took a different view from the Anglican about the relation between English universities and the American Church. The clergyman had the honour to find himself satirized by M'Fingal in the lines:

"In Vardill that poetic zealot,
I view a lawn bedizened prelate."

Under the pseudonym of "Poplicola" the Professor of

Natural Law had written several Loyalist pamphlets and composed a song for the merriment of true Tory circles in New York. Afterwards Vardill in England continued political writing under the signature of "Coriolanus," and had warmly defended the Cabinet's American policy and received the Government's thanks for his loyalty, with further promises of patronage. From London also he wrote extensively on political matters both to Tory and Congress leaders in New York. John Jay, Robert Livingston, Gouverneur Morris, and his own former pupil John Parke Custis, were among his correspondents. His pen was in the service of the Ministry, and he claimed among his achievements that he had won over to the Crown two members of Congress by promising these the office of magistrates, when their conversion was most unfortunately stopped by the fray at Lexington.[4]

For these and similar services and in order to give the New York Tories a convincing proof of the rewards to which their zeal and their loyalty would entitle them, the King had been pleased to appoint John Vardill, Regius Professor of Divinity at King's College in New York, and he himself had been directed to acquaint the authorities of that institution with this gracious instance of royal patronage in order that the new professorship might specifically be mentioned in a clause of the proposed charter.[5]

The political disturbances which took place in America at this time prevented the charter from being granted and had also suspended Vardill's appointment, which remained in abeyance so long as no royal warrant was issued actually establishing the chair. The outbreak of hostilities further interfered with the clergyman's return to New York. Meanwhile, the Government made him an allowance of two hundred pounds and promised that he would not be the loser because of his loyal services. At the end of 1783, when Vardill presented a memorial to ask for the arrears of his salary as Professor of Divinity,[6] he pointed out that having placed reliance on these promises, instead of seeking employment in the line of his profession in the Church, his entire time from 1775 to 1781 had been solely devoted to the service of the Government.

Theology having been set aside for public duties, Vardill was henceforth given an office at 17 Downing Street, close to that of the Prime Minister. In several letters which later he addressed to his new Chief, the Under-Secretary of State, William Eden, and in certain subsequent memorials to justify his claims for a pension, Vardill has made known the precise nature of the services which he rendered to the British Government. To some extent his new duties ran parallel to those of Paul Wentworth, but there were also real differences both in the goal and activities of the two men. Wentworth as his reward looked forward to gratifying social and political ambitions, whereas Vardill, far less worldly in his outlook, cared for nothing so much as the Professorship of Divinity, which was the greatest ambition of his life. Wentworth was to become a political adviser to the Cabinet, although his counsel was followed too late. With more modest pretensions and less well endowed with political foresight, Vardill spied mainly on American sympathizers in England. He himself has enumerated certain of his successes in this field. When for instance the Abbé Raynal arrived in London, bearing letters from Franklin in Paris, it was the clergyman who discovered the secret means to examine his correspondence unknown to the bearer. He did the same thing when Jonathan Austin came over as Franklin's confidential agent in order to confer with Lord Shelburne. On another occasion Vardill planted an American medical student, professedly with patriot sympathies, in the same boarding-house with a suspect whose activities he desired to watch. Once he met by accident in London an American fellow student described by him as a "Gentleman of Birth, Fortune and considerable confidence with Dr. Franklin," who admitted after much argument that he had come over on business of Congress with letters from the Doctor, and that he was about to return to Paris. Vardill persuaded this gentleman, whose name was Van Zandt, but who as a spy assumed that of George Lupton,[7] to disclose the contents of his correspondence and for "a Certain Reward" to continue his residence in Paris and furnish all the information he could obtain to Lord Stormont. The clergyman in his later memorial mentioned this service with quite particular pride, for Van Zandt often dined with Dr. Franklin, was intimate with all the American leaders in France, and in this way had obtained a list of the covering names and addresses under which the American correspondents in England received their letters.[8]

Incomparably, however, Vardill's greatest feat, which brought as its reward the hitherto withheld royal warrant of Professor of Divinity, was rendered on the following occasion. During the War of Independence there lived in London Mrs. Elizabeth Jamp, who kept a boarding-house, the pleasures of which were enhanced by the attractions of ladies whose virtue was none too oppressive to her lodgers. Early in 1777, one of the latter was a sea captain from the East Shore of Maryland, named Joseph Hynson, an uncouth and illiterate fellow, seemingly very stupid, insufferably conceited, but also easy-going and garrulous. Silas Deane was engaged at this time in fitting out privateers in the French yards. Hynson, the stepbrother of the gallant Lambert Wickes, who had brought Franklin to France,[9] enjoyed the reputation of being a good seaman, and had originally been recommended as a "strictly honest man" to Deane by his own secretary, Edward Carmichael, who was also from Maryland and possessed an extensive acquaintance in the ports. Deane was then looking for a sailor whom he could trust to convey despatches to America and thought that he had found the very man for this in Hynson, who afterwards might be given a post in the new American Navy. He wrote about him to the Committee of Congress, "I can answer for his fidelity."[10]

Deane's original intention was to have Hynson embark as a passenger on some vessel supposedly sailing for the West Indies, with secret authority to direct the captain of the ship to change his course, and try to reach Portsmouth, New Hampshire, or else make for the first safe harbour east of Rhode Island. Later this plan was altered for another one by which the sea captain was to pilot his own ship. Deane had sent him to Dover to buy a lugger which could be used as a packet. From Dover, Hynson had found his way to Mrs. Jamp's boarding-house in London, where he passed his time most agreeably in a feminine society congenial to his sailor tastes. Under the friendly wing of his landlady a young woman by the name of Isabella Cleghorn attached herself to the seafarer. Puffed up by his new consequence, and perhaps to enhance the esteem of his female admirers, the captain spoke freely and doubtless intentionally of the important mission he had. He boasted that he was deep in Franklin's confidence and that he had been sent to England on a highly confidential errand on behalf of the American Commissioners in Paris. Mrs. Jamp listened attentively to his boasting and went to repeat all he had told her to the Reverend John Vardill. The clergyman called at once to make the sailor's acquaintance and soon persuaded the latter "to unbosom himself." This was in fact accomplished so easily that Vardill felt suspicious of a trap, and began by putting Mrs. Jamp through a most thorough examination on the subject of her boarder, who had left his lodgings to return to Dover. The landlady took fright at the questioning and wrote to Hynson, in a letter which was intercepted by the Post Office,[11] strongly advising him to make friends with the parson, who was able to render him the greatest service. For Vardill had already mentioned to Mrs. Jamp that he proposed to make Hynson an offer which would be immensely to the sailor's advantage. The clergyman also had made friends with Hynson's mistress, Isabella Cleghorn, who became enthusiastic over his kindness, for blessing a companionship which had progressed so well without benefit of clergy. Vardill had said much to her about his benevolent intentions for his new friend. When next the parson called on Mrs. Jamp it was to write Hynson that he was sitting on the parlour sofa beside the landlady "and your fair Isabella," and that the sailor was a mighty lucky fellow to be so necessary to the happiness of the fair sex. The clergyman declared his own wish to crack a bottle with Hynson and that he looked forward to the coming summer when they might do a "little junketing together."[12]

A few days later, answering Mrs. Jamp from Dover, Hynson replied nobly to the advice she had given him. The sea captain admitted that he had received some advantageous offers from the clergyman, but these had come too late, and his greatest ambition henceforth was to serve his country's cause. Although Vardill had acted like a brother and had warned him of the great danger he ran if caught, he was not to be frightened away by the fear of any risk. This letter was only a blind, for, unknown to the landlady, whose usefulness was over, secret arrangements had already been made between the two men— so secret that not even the sailor's mistress was taken into his confidence. Hynson, cautioned by the clergyman about the need to hold his tongue if he expected to obtain the promised reward, wrote to tell his clerical employer of how he had lied to "my little girl that I was bound for Colchester." The little girl replied, however, to upbraid her lover for not being more frank and for engaging in an affair which must lead to their permanent separation—letters which may still be read among the Auckland Papers in the British Museum. But though the sailor's conceit was overwhelming, neither he nor his mistress could have suspected that their love letters would be found of enough importance to send to the Prime Minister[13] or that an Under-Secretary of State had prepared minutes of this affair for the King, and acquainted George the Third with the particulars of the plot arranged between the sea captain and the Professor of Divinity.

William Eden, the Under-Secretary, conveyed to his Sovereign's notice that "Vardill, an American clergyman who lives chiefly on his Majesty's bounty," had given all the necessary information regarding Hynson.[14] The clergyman at first had been extremely suspicious of his man, for Vardill prided himself on being far more circumspect in giving his confidence to secret agents than ever was Lord North. It took time and quite a few tests before he was convinced that the sea captain would play no tricks, and only after he felt certain of this did he submit his plot to William Eden to arrange for Hynson to steal the entire correspondence of the American Commissioners in Paris.

William Eden, who later became Lord Auckland, was at this time Under-Secretary of State, and was in charge of the British Secret Service on which some eighty thousand pounds a year were then being spent[15]—a phase in his career which his son, the future Bishop of Bath and Wells, when later writing his father's life, found it unnecessary to mention. Eden, whose activities were wide and scheming, had managed, with the assistance of Wentworth and Vardill, to organize an espionage service recruited mainly among Americans in London and Paris, and which was as brilliantly successful in obtaining the most secret information regarding all that Franklin and Deane were doing in France as the British armies in the field had been unsuccessful. The Under-Secretary, who had advised Wentworth to maintain a mistress in Paris, took an intimate interest in his agents, and certain of these, like Van Zandt, did not hesitate to confide in him the most secret and scandalous details about their private lives. As a further illustration of Eden's methods there may be cited a letter addressed to him by the head of the General Post Office, A. W. Todd, in reply to an inquiry by the Under-Secretary, who wished to know if it was easy to have seals imitated and handwriting forged by the Post Office. The chief of this service expressed his complete confidence in being able to accomplish the former but was less sanguine about his ability to have a very difficult hand imitated. He wrote, however, to assure Eden that though the latter might discover more skilful artists for the imitation of handwriting than his own young men, yet there were no forgers in the excellence of whose character a greater trust could be placed. He had trained them all himself to discretion and reliability and there was no fear of the matter later appearing in the Gazette.[16]

Eden, favourably impressed by Vardill's proposal, had sub-mitted the plan at once to the Secretaries of State, Lord North and Lord Suffolk, both of whom heartily approved and directed their assistant to give the greatest care to its success. The first idea was for Hynson, after he had received command of the packet which was to convey the despatches for Congress, to steer his ship to some designated point where British cruisers would lie in waiting, and at the moment of capture he could drop overboard a dummy parcel of correspondence. Lord North declared that he would ask Lord Sandwich at the Admiralty immediately to prepare two topsail vessels of sixteen guns, ostensibly for the Irish Service, but which were to be held in readiness at Plymouth to intercept Hynson's ship. At Lord Suffolk's suggestion, Lieutenant-Colonel Edward Smith, a retired officer with a taste for secret service, was detailed to accompany Hynson to France and remain there to direct him during the entire enterprise. Smith was given £800 on account and furnished with a messenger who had been selected for the reason that he was not known to the French.

With these details arranged the trio of soldier, sailor and clergyman left together for Dover, on their way to France. The Post Office, which was not in the secret, at once discovered Hynson's presence at Harvey's Ship Tavern, and asked for instructions if he was to be watched, to the consternation of Lord Suffolk, who dreaded nothing so much as an indiscretion and gave his underlings strict orders against any surveillance.

Shortly after this, Lord Suffolk received a letter from Paul Wentworth relating two interesting bits of news. The first concerned a certain Lafayette who had just sailed for America, and whose errand the French Court pretended to disapprove,

although all the ladies and particularly the Queen, applauded.
Lord Suffolk read further:

> There is one Hynson here, a simple fellow who was
> followed by Colonel Smith and Vardill, and was offered
> great rewards if he would mediate to a pacification between
> Great Britain and America and give information of the
> secrets of the latter. Of these he knows none, but is highly
> elated with the sudden importance given to him. He
> frequently sees Lord Stormont and his emissaries.[17]

Van Zandt, the American spy in Paris whom Vardill had
corrupted, and who pretended to be in France on personal
business, also wrote to Eden that Hynson met Lord Stormont's
secretary twice a week to repeat all that Deane had told him.
The current rumour was that the sea captain would be given
command of a twenty-six-gun ship, but the spy could hardly
believe this report, for he considered the sailor to be one of
the most stupid and at the same time conceited fellows living.[18]

Like George the Third, who distrusted all his American
spies,[19] Lord Stormont at first regarded Hynson with extreme
suspicion. This came from the conviction that he must be an
agent of Deane's or at least a tool in his hands, although even so
he thought that some use might be made of him.[20] The sea
captain's assertions that Deane, who was suspicious of everyone else, placed the greatest confidence in him seemed incredible to the Ambassador. In Paris, at this time, Hynson was
living in the intimacy of Carmichael, who acted as the secretary
of the American Commissioners and who Deane still trusted
implicitly. Carmichael, responsible for the sailor's original
selection to carry the despatches to Congress, regarded
himself as a kind of mentor, and warned his friend to go out as

little as possible and never to give any indication of what he proposed to do—advice which was promptly passed on to Vardill. Hynson also wrote to the latter that he possessed papers of the first importance, and boasted that no secret was kept from him by Deane. Years later, when the clergyman was pressing his claim to receive the salary of a Professor of Divinity, he enumerated among other services that through Hynson many vessels bound for America had been captured and much useful information obtained.[21]

In Paris, where he had been joined by Isabella Cleghorn, the sea captain was giving splendid satisfaction to his new employers. He was doing all he could to make himself useful, for he hoped by his treachery to become entitled to a pension and then settle in England. Far from being the honest simpleton or the "free easy fellow" he appeared, with apparent candour he made no secret to the Americans in Paris of his acquaintance with Colonel Smith, and was even advised by the bungling Carmichael to cultivate the British agent, for the latter as well as Deane, had ingenuously mistaken Smith for an official sent to discuss peace overtures and believed that Hynson might be useful as an intermediary.

The guileless Deane did not suspect the truth and continued to impress the sailor with the extreme importance of the despatches he was to carry to Congress, which were to contain full information about the negotiations at Versailles and give particulars of every vessel which was being fitted out in French ports for service as privateers or else sent to America with supplies. Hynson was repeatedly cautioned that under no circumstances was he ever to allow out of his sight the packet which contained these despatches, and in case of any mishap it was to be thrown into the sea. And the sailor promised entire obedience, for his future plans had all been made. Unknown to Deane, he had then given up the intention of sailing himself, as this meant taking an unnecessary risk. It would always have been difficult to explain why he had not thrown the letters overboard, and if he hesitated to do so, someone else might. He had planned a safer method, and displayed an extraordinary cunning in preparing this in such a way as to make his course appear plausible. Whenever a ship was being fitted out for him in a French port, Hynson would find some reason against using it, and the unsuspecting Deane would then write to express regret and implore him not to be discouraged, promising that he would obtain a better vessel, for it would never do to expose the despatches to the risk of capture—letters which at once found their way to the British Cabinet.[22]

After repeated delays from different causes, eight months passed, during which Hynson continued to give his new employers much useful information and retard his own departure by always finding fault with French ships, while Deane kept assuring him that he would end by obtaining a proper craft and that he was not to be disheartened. The details of these interminable postponements, the ingenuity of Hynson's excuses, and Deane's poignant regrets at being obliged continually to put off forwarding the despatches to America, need not be related. At last after nine months' delay, Deane sent a messenger to the Havre, who arrived bearing a packet of correspondence of the highest importance for immediate transmission to Congress. The packet came addressed to Hynson, but for reasons explained in an accompanying letter, he was directed to hand over the despatches to Captain Folger, a distant relative of Franklin, whose ship was ready to sail at once, whereas Hynson's vessel had not yet been prepared.

If for any reason Folger found himself unable to start immediately, Hynson was ordered to take command instead, but the decision for this was left entirely to him. Once more Deane advised extreme caution and enjoined him to mention to no one either about the journey or the contents of the packet.[23]

Only a few days later, a letter came addressed to William Eden from Lieutenant-Colonel E. Smith, the British agent in France, who wrote to say that "Hynson has been as eager to betray his despatches as we were to have them,"[24] and then related the particulars of what had taken place. After Hynson had received the correspondence, he found an excuse to send Captain Folger on some business to the docks, and during the latter's absence he had slipped off the string which secured the ends of the packet that contained the despatches, and removed these, substituting papers of equal length and thickness to those he had abstracted. He had then closed the ends of the bundle and passed back the same string which previously had been used to tie them. When Folger returned from the docks with another American sea captain called Moyland, Hynson put the bundle, which was well covered, into a bag, sealed this, and delivered it to Folger, in Moyland's presence, with instructions that it must never pass out of his hands unless it should become necessary to throw it overboard in case of meeting with a British ship. On the following morning, Folger sailed for America and Hynson left for Dieppe. From there he had crossed over to England carrying the packet which contained the entire confidential correspondence that passed between the American Commissioners and the French Court, from March 12 to October 7, 1777, as well as many public and private letters sent by Arthur Lee and other American officials, which were enclosed in a cover directed to the Chairman of Foreign Correspondence at Philadelphia. All these despatches and letters were handed on October 20 to William Eden, who the same day addressed a note to the King explaining that

The enclos   papers were brought a few hours ago by Lieutenant-Colonel Smith to Mr. Eden, who as soon as he was alone opened them carefully so as to preserve the covers, seal, and direction, for possible use which may hereafter occur. Mr. Eden sends them the first moment he can after placing them in convenient order for Y.M. counsel. Lieut.-Colonel Smith does not know any of their contents and is enjoined the strictest secrecy as to their being obtained, Hynson has by his conduct fully discharged his promises made some months ago. He deserves his reward therefore: but it will be attempted to make him of further use before he is discovered. It may, however, be doubted whether the man under the consciousness of having betrayed his employers will put himself again in their power.

Hynson pursuant to the instructions which had been given him filled up the packet so as to make it impossible for Captain Folger to miss the Despatch, and if the vessel should be chased the packet will be thrown overboard, in which case the loss of these original papers will never be known unless it should hereafter become material to make use of them . . . at the worst the transaction cannot be ascertained for some months and till the rebel agents hear from Congress after the arrival of Captain Folger.

N.B.—P.[aul] W.[entworth] gave Hynson at my desire £200 and the promise of £200 a year. He was an honest rascal and no fool though apparently stupid.[25]

[65]   F

The connection between historical events cannot always be traced, but there was no mistaking the connection between the theft of the correspondence of the American Commissioners in Paris and the appointment to the Royal Chair of Divinity in New York. The Reverend John Vardill was at last to obtain his long-desired reward for the brilliant services which had drawn on him, as he declared, "the hatred of many of his countrymen, especially the Trimmers and false loyalists." William Knox, Under-Secretary of State for the American Plantations, wrote to Eden that in accordance with the latter's wishes he proposed to see Vardill and concert with him as to the best way of making the appointment to the Chair of Divinity which had been the one great ambition of the clergyman's life. The previous nomination he had received for this professorship had, under the terms of the charter of King's College, not been legal, and at first this had appeared to be an insurmountable obstacle. But Vardill discovered a precedent in a Chair of History which George the Second had established at Oxford, and Knox asked that a search be made for the draft of this appointment and "then I think we shall finish the business."[26] And finished it was within three months of the purloining of Franklin's papers, for on January 8, 1778, the royal warrant was issued, signed by the King, and countersigned by Lord George Germaine, which stated that

Whereas we have received a good report of the ability, loyalty, prudent conduct and sober conversation of our Trusty and Well beloved John Vardill . . . we have therefore appointed him to be our Professor of Divinity in the said College.[27]

With becoming gratitude, Vardill wrote to Eden, who had arranged this reward, to say that the latter had laid him under a perpetual obligation by obtaining for him the great object of his ambition. Incidentally he asked for the salary of his professorship.[28] When Eden soon after left on his peace mission to America, Vardill wrote to caution him that, as religion exercised a great influence in the Colonies, the Ambassador must be careful not to give the appearance of contemning it by any neglect of public worship,[29] which appears to have been the only reflection of a spiritual nature recorded of a Clergyman who became Regius Professor of Divinity during his extended association with the British Government.

Returning once more to Hynson, the latter, who was obliged to explain his sudden journey to London, wrote to Deane that he had gone there to obtain some financial backing and offered his services as a spy. Deane, still without suspicion of the robbery, believed that the despatches were safe on their way to America, and that only Hynson had deserted. He replied, with a dignity wasted on the scoundrel:

> I do not write to reproach you for the ungrateful and treacherous part you have acted. I leave this to your own reflections, but as you have had the assurance to write to me and to propose the betraying your new Patrons in the manner you have wickedly but in vain attempted to betray your former and with them your country, I must tell you that no letters from you will hereafter be received by Silas Deane.[30]

To his friend, Franklin's nephew, Jonathan Williams, who was in charge of American shipping at Nantes, Deane wrote sadly:

This wrong-headed conceited fool has at last turned out one of the most ungrateful of traitors and instead of going to Nantes as he wrote me, has fled into England, there to help himself by selling all and much more than he had any knowledge of. It is fortunate for us he knows nothing but this will not prevent his pretensions to knowing everything.[31]

Several months were to pass before Deane learned the whole sad truth. Captain Johnson, who commanded the *Lexington*, sailed a few days after Folger, carrying duplicates of the despatches for Congress with identical orders to sink these in case of capture. His ship was taken by the English and soon after it was reported in London that the despatches on board had fallen into the hands of the British Cabinet. From time to time hints of their contents were given to the Press by William Eden, in a manner which greatly alarmed the American Commissioners in Paris. Deane discovered Hynson's treachery only when Captain Johnson, after having made his escape from a ship in the Thames, called on him in Paris. The first question Deane put to him was why he had not sunk the despatches, which Johnson answered so convincingly that it was impossible any longer to ignore what had taken place.[32]

On the Twelfth of January, 1778, the Committee of Foreign Affairs then in session at York, near Philadelphia, wrote to the American Commissioners in Paris to express surprise at not having received any communication from them since the preceding May 26. They had been sincerely chagrined on discovering that the despatches brought by Captain John Folger contained only blank paper, "which had been put in the place of an enclosure probably very interesting sent with the public ledgers." Except for this there were merely a few letters altogether devoid of any political interest. On questioning Folger, they had arrived at the opinion that, though he was far from discreet, yet they could not connect him with the robbery of the packet. They proposed to continue their efforts to find out if the theft had been committed after Folger left France, but depended on the Commissioners to trace the circumstances of what had occurred from the time the packet was sealed to when it was embarked. A warning was added as to the necessity for caution with regard to the character of all persons confidentially employed by the Commissioners.

Next there followed a detailed account of the examination of Captain Folger regarding circumstances of which he himself knew little. He declared that he had lived in the same lodgings with Hynson at the Havre, and had never mentioned to anyone else having the packet in his possession. When he received this, he had locked it in his trunk and had no reason to suppose that it had been tampered with while there. He had given a receipt to the messenger who brought him five different packets. One of these, marked "despatches," was wrapped in brown paper sealed in two or three places and tied with a string; but no wax was over the string and no impression was on the seals. While on his way to deliver this to Congress, he had met Governor Caswell, of North Carolina who, on learning that he was the bearer of despatches, broke the seals, and when he saw the blank paper, expressed surprise and said he did not know "the service of sending clean paper so far. The examinant answered he was surprised and did not know he had clean paper under his care."[33]

As the result of this examination, Folger was confined partly in prison and partly on parole, for nearly five months, but when nothing could be discovered against him, he was released.

[69]

Poor Deane, however, found himself most unjustly accused by
his enemies, who suspected him of having connived at the theft.

In London, the stolen correspondence served principally to
corroborate Bancroft's reports regarding the assistance rendered by the Court of Versailles and the imminence of French
intervention. When on the top of this came the news of
Burgoyne's surrender, Paul Wentworth was dispatched to
Paris to attempt his peace negotiations with Deane. Tom
Paine, the pamphleteer, pointed out with malicious pleasure
that the British Cabinet reversed its tactics, planned conciliatory measures and sent over Peace Commissioners to America
only after they had discovered the extent of French assistance.[34]

Hynson, ordered to Paris once more to continue his spying
career before the full news of his treachery had come out, met
this time with no success. Deane declared that no American
would speak to him,[35] not knowing that his own secretary,
Carmichael still went on seeing the traitor against his orders.
The latter at the time was ignorant of the true facts and
thought that Hynson had been badly treated, though even so
nothing could excuse his conduct, adding sententiously, "You
see what it is to recommend." Yet the indiscreet Carmichael
let out to Hynson, who at once reported this to London, that
there was a division of opinion among the Commissioners on
the subject of independence, and that Franklin was no longer
so insistent in demanding a complete separation.

This was the impression created on the British Cabinet
before news had come of the victory of Saratoga. Hynson
himself conveyed the first report of Burgoyne's surrender
to Lord Stormont, and afterwards virtuously blamed the
Ambassador for not at once sending a messenger to London,
which would have prevented much gambling in stocks.

The sailor, far too uncouth to be a successful spy, nobly declared, "It is a character I heartily despise." He felt lonely in Paris, where he feared arrest and lived confined to his room.[36] Vardill wrote to inform Eden that the sea captain, who was beginning to bluster and threaten, had become a nuisance, and suggested that some method be found to take care of "so rash and mercenary a man who seemed to have little attachment to Government." Hynson, ill at ease, also asked to be relieved and Eden offered him a fresh reward if he should be able to capture Deane and Carmichael on their return to America.[37] As he was of no further use in the secret service, he was given a small post in the British Navy and disappeared from the scene.

Vardill through the War continued in the employ of the British Cabinet. When William Eden left for America, the clergyman gave him letters of introduction to his former friends, John Jay, Robert Livingston, James Duane, and Gouverneur Morris, which the Ambassador was never able to present. In spite of Vardill's service, the Government ended by doing little for him, and in 1784 even the promise of a life salary of £200 which he was to receive as occupant of the Chair of Divinity had remained unfulfilled. Later, a small provision was made. He was given the living of Skirbeck and Fishtoft in Lincolnshire, and in 1807 he was still in receipt of a Treasury allowance.[38] When he died in 1811, at the age of fifty-nine, the *Gentleman's Magazine* printed as an obituary notice that "he was a rare example of splendid talents devoted to the purest philanthropy."[39]

CHAPTER THREE

Sir John Temple, British Secret Agent and American Patriot

I

WHEN Franklin's stolen despatches, Burgoyne's surrender, and Paul Wentworth's secret reports had at last convinced even George the Third that the danger of French intervention might be imminent, the King decided that the time had come for a change of tactics. The unfortunate Lord North, blamed for the American war of which he disapproved, and actually the least intransigent member of his party, had found himself in the position of many another politician since his day, who, with deeper insight than his followers, is obliged to respect their prejudices even when he discerns the peril. The royal opinions regarding the rebellious colonists, far from being peculiar to the King, had been typical of most of the Tory Party, but in December of 1777, even George the Third began to have glimmerings that the old policy had failed. The education derived from warnings and events came, however, too late. In the history of nations there are moments when a decision to be successful must be immediate and the time for this was already over before the King had understood the necessity to yield.

After the Declaration of Independence had been signed, it is an open question if any offer made by Great Britain, unaccompanied by some impressive success in the field, could have achieved a reconciliation with America on any other basis than that of recognition. After the victory of Saratoga had brought about the French Alliance, the question ceased to be doubtful, though neither the King nor most of the Tories had as yet discovered this platitude.

When the news came of Burgoyne's surrender, everyone knew that conciliatory proposals would shortly be offered. Beaumarchais in Paris was so convinced of this, and so frightened of the success of Wentworth's overtures, that he wrote despairingly to Vergennes that his work to help the Revolution had been all in vain and that peace would now be made. The playwright made only one mistake in this calculation. He knew human nature, but nothing about the nature of George the Third, who obstinately refused to swallow the bitter pill, and was still deluding himself with the belief that Wentworth and Bancroft's alarming news was coloured by their speculations. The King hoped always for some victory which might convince Americans of the uselessness of continuing the struggle, and the Under-Secretary William Eden, eager to curry favour at Court and already scheming to be a Peace Ambassador, had prepared a royal speech to have ready "on the supposition of goodish news," from which the following eloquent passage deserves to be quoted:

> Whenever the unhappy multitude shall recover from the delusion which interested or ambitious men have brought upon their minds and shall return to their allegiance, they will soon be convinced that the Parliament of Great Britain never had, never can have any view but for their true interests, Protection and Prosperity.[2]

The King was doubtless correct in believing that English opinion was not ready to submit to acknowledging American

independence. He had been all the more stubborn in refusing
to consent to this, because firmly convinced that recognition
would lead to the disintegration of his realm, George the Third
dreaded that the West Indies, whose interests depended
on the American Colonies, would also follow along the
same path, and that Ireland would then break away, after
which he prophesied that manufacturers would abandon
England for the New Empire, and, as he wrote to Lord
North, the Kingdom would then become a "poor island
indeed."[3] In order, however, to prevent the French
Alliance, the King was disposed suddenly to concede everything which the colonists had ever demanded until the moment
when they declared for independence. Offered two years
earlier, the royal proposals would have been enthusiastically
acclaimed in America and the Revolution would have subsided with its objects completely attained. In February, 1778,
with the prospect of victory assured by French aid, the moment
had passed when similar concessions could any longer be
regarded as sufficient.

The alliance between the new State and France had been
signed in Paris on February 6, 1778, and was known forty-
two hours later in London by Bancroft's message. Only
after this did the King discover as he wrote to Lord North,
that the news which Mr. Wentworth had conveyed made it
desirable that there should be no further delay in bringing
forward the American propositions after communicating
these to the leaders in the House of Commons.

Six weeks were already over since Paul Wentworth had
suggested to Silas Deane, as the basis for a reconciliation
that Parliament should no longer tax the colonies and had
proposed a return to the same situation as existed in 1763,

before the Stamp Act. This offer had been made without any real authority, but it was gladly accepted by Lord North and the King. George the Third's sudden desire for peace on this basis, with his former subjects, even at the cost of rescinding his previous measures came from the fact that he intended, in case of war with France and Spain, to withdraw most of the troops from America in order to employ these against the enemy's colonies. As Beaumarchais remarked to Vergennes, peace with America meant in good English, war with France. According to the view taken by the British Cabinet it would not even be necessary for the Colonists to disavow their Declaration of Independence. That act in the royal belief was illegal and it would automatically be rescinded through the conclusion of the new treaty.[4] Another fortnight had still to pass, however, before, on February 17, 1778, Lord North made his remarkable speech in Parliament asking for the immediate and unconditional repeal of all the obnoxious measures against the Colonies, and proposing the appointment of peace commissioners who were to be given vast powers to negotiate with Congress. He announced that the States would not be asked to abandon their independence until the treaty with Great Britain had been agreed upon and ratified. It was impossible more publicly, to disclaim the policy which had driven America to revolt.

Paul Wentworth's advice had all along been to make peace if necessary, by accepting independence, for recognition could later be withdrawn after the purpose which was solely to prevent the French Alliance had been attained. But eleven days before Lord North made his famous proposal, the alliance had already been signed. The cause for delay, which wrecked any chance of success, must be looked for only in George the Third's unique powers of self-deception and obstinacy. David Hartley, the future English Peace Commissioner in Paris, nine months before had already advised recognizing American independence as a free gift,[5] and then as well as later did his utmost to convince the Government of the folly of retarding its proposals. When he addressed the "Letters on the American War" to his constituents at Hull, Hartley pointed out that, if the Cabinet had really been sincere in its professions, the bills might have passed both Houses and received the royal assent even before the preliminaries between France and Spain with the Colonies had been set on foot.[6] That George the Third ever had any real intention of observing the concessions which Lord North announced in Parliament is doubtful, and possibly the delay which ruined any chances of success ought also to be regarded as a measure of the royal scruples.

In times of crisis, new ideas, however strange, suddenly seem roads to salvation. A Tory Prime Minister, in the interest of peace, had indicated his willingness suddenly to reverse every previous measure he had taken. The wildest rumours now filled the air of London and even so staunch a loyalist as Governor Hutchinson now expected independence to be recognized. A month later, in March, 1778, Israel Mauduit, hitherto known as a Ministerial hack, published his famous "Handbill," which urged the recognition of American independence on the ground that, as it was no longer possible to retain the Colonists as subjects it would be preferable to regain them as friends sooner than to see them fall under French influence. The pamphleteer insisted that this was only his personal opinion, but many at the time regarded it as having been written under the Government's inspiration.

In England all hopes were now pinned on peace. For sometime it had been known that the King was at last persuaded to adopt the suggestion made by Wentworth about sending an embassy to negotiate with the Americans. When at last the bill for this was introduced into Parliament, the Duke of Richmond proposed, though without success, that the Commissioners should also be given power to admit the independence of the Colonies if this was desired.[7] The Peace Embassy was to be composed of three Commissioners, with instructions "to treat, consent, and agree upon the means of quieting the disorders," and it was accorded full powers to proclaim a cessation of hostilities, treat with Congress to negotiate a peace, grant pardons, and suspend the operations of all Acts of Parliament relating to the Colonies passed since February, 1763.

The selection of the Peace Envoys was, however, on a par with the delay in their dispatch. The first of these was Lord Carlisle, an amiable and cultivated peer who was also an intimate friend of William Eden, since they had been schoolboys together at Eton. As an envoy sent to negotiate peace his choice was peculiar, for everyone remembered that in the beginning of the Revolution that nobleman had publicly denounced the Americans as traitors and rebels, and Horace Walpole, when he learned of the appointment, remarked caustically, that Carlisle was very fit to make a treaty that will not be made.

The second Commissioner, George Johnstone, was a former Governor of Florida and was then a Member of Parliament. He was appointed because of his supposed popularity with Americans, but, in the negotiations which he secretly attempted, he was to show himself as unskilful as he was unscrupulous. The third member who had been mainly

[77]

responsible for engineering the plan was the Under-Secretary of State William Eden, who was also the most familiar of the three with American affairs, though personally almost unknown in the Colonies. Ambitious and grasping, this appointment meant for him another profitable step in his career, and he noted with satisfaction in a private memorandum preserved among his papers, that as Ambassador he would be entitled to receive 5,893 ounces of white plate, and 1,066 of gilt, thereby adding a silver to a public service; and that the value of the plate due to him in his new office was nearly £200 more than he had stated in a note to the King.[8] He was also entitled to other allowances, and before leaving on his mission he asked to be given the rank of a Privy Councillor. But this George the Third absolutely refused, though granting him a thousand pounds to prepare for the American Mission. Not without reason, the King regarded Eden, who kept a foot in both camps, as an intriguer, and particularly resented the fact of his being on very friendly terms with the "Jesuit of Berkeley Square," as the Monarch called Lord Shelburne.

Eden now began seriously to prepare himself for his peace mission. He studied the confidential memoranda submitted by Paul Wentworth, who, unfamiliar with fresher developments, retailed old gossip about Washington being averse to Republican principles and jealous of the New England group.[9] For his benefit the Reverend John Vardill drew a series of somewhat unflattering portraits of the patriot leaders in New York and New Jersey, and offered sound advice to see as little as possible of the loyalists so as not to offend these by disregarding their counsels. With the same lack of comprehension as Paul Wentworth had displayed in failing to understand the new conditions in America and the democratic spirit of the Revolution, Vardill recommended, as a measure of settlement, creating a Colonial Parliament which was to be "composed of an order of Nobles or Patricians" as well as a lower House of Delegates. The purpose of this remarkable body was to moderate the leaders whose hereditary influence would thereby be handed down for the benefit of their posterity.[10]

The entire plan of reconciliation worked out in London by the British Cabinet showed, in fact, a most astonishing ignorance of the real American situation. Many offered advice and among other helpful suggestions came an interesting one from the Exchequer Baron Sir John Dalrymple, who proposed that Washington should be made a duke in order to repeat the part of General Monk.[11] Lord North himself remained somewhat sceptical, and although he accepted the plan of peace, which Eden had engineered, he doubted success even before the Commissioners had sailed. Rightly he feared that nothing short of independence would any longer satisfy America.[12] The loyalists found themselves disregarded by the Cabinet in their offer. Like many another politician, Lord North was prepared to sacrifice friends in order to win over enemies. The Tories in America and the American refugees in England felt a stab in the back. The latter, dumbfounded when they learned the news of the Peace Envoys, were "irritated to the highest degree." Jonathan Sewall wrote from Bristol that "my stormy and angry countrymen here seem to think that everything is given up and cry we are undone."[13] Only Governor Hutchinson, exiled in London, with better understanding of the temper of the United States than British Ministers, who no longer consulted him, kept his temper and merely thought that the proposal was an "infatuation."

At the moment of sailing for America, William Eden wrote to his brother that he had no personal opinion as to the chances of his mission. Some cool-headed men were sanguine about it, others believed it would fail. The three Commissioners, enjoying the rank and pay of Ambassadors, left in the middle of April, 1778, accompanied by a staff of secretaries, some twenty footmen, and with instructions sent General Howe to supply the mission with secret service money out of army funds. Lord North remarked that he was not sure that this was legal, but, as peace was the first object of the military force employed in America, he did not think he could be blamed.[14]

Early in June, the Ambassadors arrived at Philadelphia, which Eden described as being "an immense opulent village rather than a metropolis," though he foresaw that only a few years of peace were needed to make of it a magnificent city.[15] They had the ill luck to come at a moment when everything was in the greatest confusion, for Lord Howe, hearing the news that d'Estaing with a powerful fleet was on his way to America, had wisely decided at once to evacuate the place. The British army was on the point of leaving for New York, taking with them three thousand miserable loyalists far too frightened to stay behind. All this came as a painful surprise to the Peace Commissioners, who were furious at the inauspicious circumstances which they found on their arrival, and blamed Lord George Germaine for not giving warning in time of the proposed evacuation. Eden wrote to his intimate friend, the Attorney General Wedderburn, that it was impossible, after seeing what he had seen of the grandeur of America, not to go nearly mad at the long trail of mistakes by which England had lost her Colonies.[16]

The Ambassadors next went to New York, where they lingered in idleness, unable to accomplish anything owing to the blockade of the French fleet and the refusal of Congress to enter into relations with them. In vain the Commissioners proposed an immediate cessation of hostilities, offered thereafter to keep no military force in America without the consent of Congress, pledged self-government to the Colonies, and made the revolutionary suggestion that the latter should send their agents to have a seat and a voice in the Parliament of Great Britain. Similar concessions, as Governor Trumbull of Connecticut declared, would once have been accepted with joy and gratitude, but that day was irrevocably past. The proposals were in fact, regarded in America as an attempt to divide the country, and Congress skilfully countered their effect by publishing them, along with their own adverse report, and proclaiming that any man or body who presumed to make a separate convention with the Commissioners would be treated as an enemy of the United States.[17]

Unknown to his two colleagues, Governor Johnstone had attempted to carry on some private negotiations of his own, not without the suspicion of bribery. These were reported to Congress, which at once passed a resolution that it was incompatible with its dignity to hold any correspondence or intercourse with the said George Johnstone. Lord Carlisle and Eden felt it necessary to disavow their colleague's methods and publicly declared that they had no knowledge of the conversation referred to, a rebuke which led to the Governor's withdrawal. The Ambassadors, however, could make no headway in their attempted peace negotiations, and Lord

G

Carlisle, apart from refusing to fight a duel with Lafayette who sent him a challenge because of the English nobleman's aspersions on the King of France, found nothing more important to do in New York than to expatiate on the beauty of the Hudson scenery and complain about the unbearable heat of the torrid summer of 1778.[18]

After having been unable to talk to a single American of prominence, and issuing a final blast threatening that the war would henceforth be waged in a more savage way, which provoked the indignation of Liberal peers at Westminster, who vainly besought the King to disown this declaration,[19] the Commissioners returned somewhat ignominiously to England, after narrowly escaping capture by the French fleet. The Peace Embassy had ended in a miserable failure, though Eden, still undaunted, tried in vain to induce George the Third to employ him as a private negotiator with Franklin, and for this purpose began to cultivate the latter's English friend, Dr. Priestley.[20]

II

This brief account of the unfortunate Peace Embassy is a necessary preliminary to the less-known mission of John Temple which accompanied and followed it. No man illustrates better than Temple those divided loyalties which then confused the heart and judgment of so many. The failure he met with as a British secret agent sent to arrange a peace and his own subsequent misadventures were due both to his inability to understand the situation which had developed in the Colonies and to the fact that events themselves had already passed beyond the power of any individual to alter.

SIR JOHN TEMPLE
From a portrait by Gilbert Stuart, after John Trumbull

As a former British official who regarded himself as an American and possessed strong American sympathies, John Temple enjoyed a unique position. His father had crossed the ocean to establish a Scotch-Irish Settlement on the Kennebec. An accident of birth—for he was born in Boston in 1732—had made a New Englander out of the son, instead of an English Whig though his real Americanism came from the heart, for no one ever wished more ardently to be a patriot. John Temple had been sent to England for his education and was kindly treated there by the Grenville family to whom he was nearly related and who were then all-powerful. Helped by his kinsman Lord Grenville, of whom it has been said, that he lost America because he was the first British Minister ever to read the despatches from the Colonies, in 1760, Temple obtained the appointment of Surveyor General of the North American Customs. Later he became a Lieutenant Governor of New Hampshire and sat on the Council Board of five provinces. He had returned to New England, as he said, "not to make a fortune, but to make a character," and in spite of Tory slanders, he proved himself to be a capable and honest official[21] who did his utmost to suppress contraband, "the disgrace of America," and looked forward to his services entitling him to future favours "at home," for like other Americans he still called England "home."

In Boston, John Temple had married the daughter of James Bowdoin, and, unlike other British Crown officials, he formed warm friendships with the patriot leaders in Massachusetts. His intimates were then men like James Otis, who were the staunchest supporters of the American cause. Possibly he exaggerated his influence among these and

mistook a personal friendship, which was remarkable in view
of the Crown appointment he held, for a real position in their
councils. His active sympathy with patriot views was, however,
well known, and he freely criticized the Stamp Act as an
economic blunder, on the ground that whatever it brought
in would be so much taken away from the colonial importation
of English goods, freely expressing the opinion that "our
people are extravagantly fond of show and dress and have no
bounds to their importation of British manufactures but their
want of money."[22]

Temple's Whig convictions had brought on him the savage
enmity of the Tories and particularly of "that rascal Bernard,"
as he called the then Governor of Massachusetts, whom he
compared to the highwayman, Jonathan Wild. The Crown
appointees in the Colonies, carefully chosen to carry out
Ministerial orders and furious because one of their number
should have dared to take the opposite side, accused Temple
of having falsified Government accounts,[23] succeeded in
obtaining his recall, and insisted that he must not return to
America in any official capacity. Twenty years later, even
after independence had been recognized, this old charge led
to his arrest in London,[24] though he was once more cleared. It
is hardly surprising that Temple henceforth felt himself
to be a victim of the American cause. He knew that he had
acted in a conscientious way, manifestly against his own interest,
for with his Grenville relations then in power, it would only
have been necessary to fall in line with their ideas, as so many
others had done, in order to obtain advancement. He had
preferred to take the American side, and had been punished
for his sympathies. On his departure from Boston, to return
to England, after his recall as Surveyor of Customs, he

expressed a bitter regret at leaving "my native country which I sincerely love."[25] Yet there was pride in carrying away with him the warm friendship of the leaders who regarded him as a brother in their struggle for liberty.

Once in England, Temple was cleared of the charge against him and received as compensation a lucrative office in the Customs,[26] which he held for two and a half years while awaiting an Irish Commissionership. Then came out his connection in the affair of the purloined political correspondence of Governor Hutchinson of Massachusetts with a Government official in London which caused an immense sensation at the time. How Temple obtained these letters was never explained. To his dying day he would only say that they were given to him by a subordinate whose name he could not divulge. But he always insisted that he had obtained them in a perfectly honourable way, though Chief Justice Oliver and other Tories called him a thief for the part he had taken in this affair. The letters, were handed by Temple to Franklin, who sent them to Boston, and their publication led to a furious controversy and a sensational duel fought in Hyde Park by Temple, who pinked his opponent, the banker, Whateley, of whom it was said that he had never before held a sword in his hand. The King, furious at the scandal, ordered Franklin's and Temple's dismissal, on the same day, from the service of the Crown. The latter professed to find consolation at the thought that the sacrifice had been made for his country, yet felt his dismissal acutely, both as a personal blow which left him in pecuniary straits and because he understood that George the Third's American policy would lead to disaster.

Lord Dartmouth was at this time Minister in charge of the

Colonies, and Temple pleaded with him that it had been his earnest wish to prevent matters from reaching their then alarming state. He foresaw what would happen and the dismissed official complained that he had been made to suffer for having tried to prevent those greater evils which were fast approaching. Over and over again he expressed his feelings on the subject. He wrote: "I love America; it is my native country; but I never had the most distant wish for its advancing to a state incompatible with the honour and prosperity of this its parent country."[27] To his brother-in-law in Boston, he sadly foretold that the two lands would never harmonize, and though the British might crush the Americans, for a time, they would end by understanding the error of coercion.[28]

Temple's position at this period was similar to that of many other Whigs in both countries who regarded themselves as being citizens of one great empire and believed that American liberty was to the real interest of Great Britain. Of independence there was still no thought, and Liberal hopes were centred on a change of policy towards the colonies. Meanwhile Temple, who had retired to the country in order to reduce his living expenses, was trying to obtain another official appointment.

Governor Hutchinson, lately arrived in London, noted in his *Diary* on August 8, 1774, that Temple had made friendly overtures to him and expressed a wish "for any place in my government" that would support him, as his own fortune was insufficient to live upon. But no Tory would then have considered employing one whom the King regarded as his enemy, and the Secretary of State, Lord Suffolk, remarked to the already prejudiced Hutchinson, that Temple was a man with whom it was best to have no connection.[29]

Sir John Temple

After hostilities had broken out in America, the dismissed official remained unoccupied in England, although he had obtained permission to return to Boston. From his own point of view to stay on was a great mistake and this circumstance was later brought out forcibly against him. Doubtless, he looked forward to a turn of the wheel which would again bring his Whig friends into power and allow him to play a leading part in the reconciliation. The calculation was not unreasonable, though his expectations were gratified in a different way. After the war dragged on, as its unpopularity became more evident and the French Alliance brought fresh danger to England, his political enemies, who suddenly had altered their tactics and were now prepared to make concessions to end the war, believed that they had discovered in John Temple the very man they needed. His birth, his known sympathies, his previous record, and his connections, all seemed to designate him as the most suitable person to assist the work of the peace embassy which the King and Lord North were on the point of sending to America. When Temple agreed to become a secret emissary to assist the Commissioners, he did not feel that he was thereby engaging in a task contrary to his American loyalty for seven years earlier, when he had left Boston, the offer of autonomy which the King was now prepared to make would have been joyfully acclaimed by all the Colonies as giving entire satisfaction to the popular demand.

It is always difficult from afar to follow the growth of an idea, and John Temple's absence from America during a very critical period had kept him from understanding the full force of the wish for independence that had developed with sudden violence during the winter of 1776. He regarded this mainly in the light of a tactical move to allow the colonists to trade where they liked, instead of merely with the Mother Country. His second mistake was in supposing that the personal friendships which he had enjoyed in New England meant that he possessed any real political influence or that it was possible, at this time in America, to carry on an important negotiation behind closed doors, in the way in which the patriot leaders in Boston, when they were still in the opposition, had been accustomed freely to discuss their most secret plans before him. John Adams, probably with this in mind, remarked later that Temple prided himself upon a knowledge of government which he did not possess, and that his notions of the springs of public opinion were confused.[30] He was now to furnish a striking proof of the accuracy of this criticism.

In accordance with the current political practice of the time in England John Temple began to prepare for his mission by making secret terms with the British Ministry. An unsigned and undated memorandum in William Eden's handwriting, preserved among his papers, explains the agreement which was entered into early in April, 1778, between the two men, and the stipulations on both sides:

Mr. Temple is to proceed with all possible despatch to North America on such ship or vessel as the Ministers shall think proper and pledges his honour that he will then faithfully exert his utmost influence in assisting the Commissioners now going out to bring about a reconciliation or reunion between the Colonies and Great Britain. In consideration of which and his former faithful services under the crown, Mr. Temple is to have £2,000 immediately paid to him and is to be authorized to draw on the Treasury

(provided the said Commissioners shall approve his conduct) for £2,000 more—and is to be made a Baronet of
Great Britain, the Patent for the same to be sent out to
him by the Commissioners—and independent of the success
of the Commission he is to have a pension for life of
£2,000 per annum (subject to such deductions as Governor
Hutchinson and other like persons are subject to), provided
the said Commission now going out to America shall
approve his conduct in that country.

Explanatory note given to him at the time. We will with
real pleasure engage Mr. T's services for the honourable and
important object in question—but think that two of the
expressions in the paper are indefinite. By the words "shall
approve his conduct" His Ld. understands that the approbation must be in writing signed by the Commissioners
now going from England and must accompany any application made by Mr. Temple subsequent to the £2,000 now
to be given; and by the word "conduct" His Ld. understands that a mere negative conduct not exposed to blame
is not the conduct in question, nor what the Commissioners
would think proper to certify; there must be an active
assertion of notoriety and weight sufficient to engage the
observation of the Commissioners.

By the words "independent of the success of the Commission" His Ld. does not understand "supposing the
Commission" to fail totally but "supposing the Commission not to have a complete success satisfactory to this
Country."

Does not desire to name the ship as Mr. T. will of course
make it his object not to lose a moment.

A copy of this was given to Mr. T.[31]

There follows a memorandum from the Treasury to William Eden, dated April 10, 1778: "Enclosing banknotes for £2,000 for Mr. T. as ordered." There were also a few lines addressed to the Commander-in-Chief at New York "to suffer Mr. Temple and family and Dr. Berkenhout to pass the line at King's Bridge."

Governor Johnstone had desired Temple to go out with the Commissioners, who sailed in the middle of April. But perhaps for reasons of prestige the others refused to allow this[32] and the secret agent left in the least secret way in July after causing the London papers to be fully informed about his important mission of peace. Governor Hutchinson venomously suggested that Temple was going over to obtain some of the loyalists' confiscated estates,[33] and pettily noted in his *Diary* that, when he arrived on board the ship with his carriages and an enormous amount of baggage, he, with his family, took up all the cabin accommodation, while Lord Bute's son and other officers of rank were obliged to travel in the steerage.

Temple had courted this publicity and made no secret of his mission. He also took with him letters from Governor Pownall to the latter's friends in Boston. These he had first shown to Lord North, who, though disapproving of their tenor, did not want to prevent their transmission, a circumstance which, better than anything else, marks the complete change of tactics on the part of the Ministry.

When, late in August, 1778, Temple arrived in New York, giving to everyone he met the impression of his self-importance, he wrote at once to Sam Adams, who was then in Philadelphia, that, after seven years' absence, he had returned with his wife and family to his native land, and asked for permission to pay his respects to the Congress. Adams read this letter before that body, adding as a personal comment that John Temple, formerly an officer of the Crown, had given great offence to Governors Bernard and Hutchinson "by his attachment to those who espoused the liberties of America." Since his return to England he had been living privately, out of favour with the Court, and his Boston connections had long ago expected his return to his native country.

Temple's arrival in New York, largely by his own intention, had caused no little sensation. The reports about his mission printed in the London newspapers did the rest and Congress, alarmed by the fear of creating the impression that it was in a mood for an intrigue, by an overwhelming majority, which Sam Adams and the other Massachusetts members thought it wise to join, refused to give the permission asked for on the ground that Temple might be a secret emissary from the British Court. The Secretary of Congress was directed to inform Temple that, if he intended to reside in any one of the United States, it would be necessary to signify such intention to the State in question and obtain its approval.[34] After this refusal, Sam Adams thought it wise, however, to explain to James Bowdoin that he regarded this procedure to be in the real interest of his son-in-law, for the suspicious jealousy of people would have made the latter's stay in Philadelphia very uncomfortable.[35] Just about the same time a well-intentioned meddler named Dr. Berkenhout had arrived from England, on a self-imposed mission of peace. He had called to see Richard Henry Lee in Philadelphia on the strength of having once been a fellow medical student of his brother William, though he brought no letters from the latter. Berkenhout impressed Lee as being, what he actually was, an honest bungler with strong sympathies for American independence, but owing to a paragraph which had appeared in a London gazette about his mission, he was thrown into prison at Philadelphia as an English agent, though soon afterward released for want of proof.[36] Sam Adams stated, doubtless with reason, that if Temple had arrived at this time, owing to the newspaper notices in London, he would also have shared Berkenhout's fate.[37]

James Bowdoin, however, was visibly annoyed when he learned about the curt treatment extended to his son-in-law. He answered Adams that although approving of the need for caution on the part of Congress about admitting strangers into the United States, as there were British emissaries employed "to corrupt the virtue of Americans," an indiscriminate refusal to see anyone also meant cutting off much valuable information. He ignored in what capacity his son-in-law had arrived, though he thought it was private; but even if he had come in the employ of the Ministry, he would act as a man of honour and his talks with members of Congress might lead to a solid peace founded on American independence. Certain recent debates in the House of Lords, as well as Mauduit's pamphlet, had given Bowdoin the impression that the English Ministry was now inclined to accept this.[38]

After Congress' refusal Temple had left for Boston, where he met with a warm welcome from relatives and friends. Bowdoin took particular pleasure to inform Sam Adams that his son-in-law had been received with the cordiality due to a man who had given the fullest proof of his attachment to his country's liberties, adding that Temple was desirous to render service to America either here or in Europe. "In what way he can do so you can best judge." His father-in-law expressed as his personal opinion that the latter's conduct ought to entitle him to the assistance of his countrymen, for patriotism had cost him an office which brought in a thousand pounds a year. Temple, himself, believed that he could render the best service to America in England, where he would be able to represent things in their proper light, instead of allowing people to accept as true the accounts which they read in the New York newspapers, about Americans being tired of the war and disapproving of Congress rejecting the British Commissioners' proposals. Bowdoin detected merit in this idea of his son-in-law. If a suitable person could be found, he might be able to rectify English misconceptions about America and pave the way to negotiating a peace which would "secure our independence and yet be not inconsistent with the late treaty with France."[39]

In no way crestfallen by his rebuff from Congress, Temple was once more building up his former connections in Boston, not without some swagger. He advised John Trumbull, who had lately resigned from a colonelcy on General Gate's Staff, and wished to become a painter, to go to London and study art under West, offering to arrange this for him.[40] Temple's intention in making this proposal apart from the wish to oblige the son of his friend the Governor of Connecticut, and perhaps also to display his own influence in England, was by friendly intercourse to promote whatever might be conducive to a reconciliation. Trumbull, who afterwards became warmly attached to Temple, mentions in his autobiography that the latter was regarded as a neutral and occasionally permitted to pass from one side to the other.[41] Even his friends, therefore, did not look on Bowdoin's son-in-law as being altogether an American. The circumstances in his case were in fact so peculiar that, probably in his own interest, he was asked to appear before the friendly Council of Massachusetts, where he explained, to its satisfaction, the reasons which had induced him to return and cited Lord Chatham as the channel through whom he had obtained permission. After this examination, Jeremiah Powell, the President of the Council, could write to tell Henry Laurens, the President of Congress, that the Board, having taken into consideration Temple's conduct as an official of the Crown, his good offices while in England at the risk of his life, and his loss of a profitable post, saw no reason to doubt that he had retained "the warmest affection and regard to his country" and recommended him to the notice of Congress. The Council of New Hampshire did likewise.

A spate of further endorsements obtained with a view to influence Congress followed this certificate of good conduct. James Warren wrote in praise of Temple's personal character and invited the invariable attention to his past sufferings as a patriot.[42] Dr. Winthrop, Professor of Philosophy at Harvard, addressed voluminous letters to both the Adamses, praising Temple's patriotism in the warmest terms and expressing the hope that Congress would give him further opportunity to exert his great abilities in the public service. Governor Trumbull of Connecticut also contributed his mite by describing Temple as a man who "hath done and suffered much for the cause of this his native and much injured country" and, being well acquainted with public men and measures in England, "he appears a warm and real friend to our American liberties and independence." Chancellor Livingston of New York added his personal endorsement, and even George Washington, prompted by James Bowdoin, wrote to say that, although Temple was personally not known to him, yet he felt convinced that he was a man of "warm attachment to the rights of his country for which he appears to have suffered greatly" and that he had "some application to be made to Congress."[43]

Armed with all these letters, Temple set out, in December of 1778, for Philadelphia, conferring on his journey with the notabilities of all the towns through which he passed and giving the utmost publicity to his mission. After his arrival in the capital his first call was on Sam Adams, who as delegate from Massachusetts at once accompanied him to the house of Henry Laurens, the President of Congress, where he left his recommendations. After his earlier mishap, the visit was sensational and immediately caused the wildest rumours to circulate. A Philadelphia newspaper described Temple as being a British emissary and Adams read, to his consternation, that he had listened to his proposals. After the Boston leader had done everything he could think of to keep Bowdoin's son-in-law away from Philadelphia, this accusation was hard to bear. Sam Adams felt not only uncomfortable as a man, but frightened as a politician, and wrote to his wife that, though personally prepared to believe that Temple was an honest American, yet the circumstances in which he had left England made people suspicious, and his "residence at the Court of America if I may so express it" for Philadelphia even to a radical politician like Adams, seemed like a Court, gave those who were malicious-minded a chance to say that Congress, notwithstanding its public statements, was secretly treating with the British Ministers through Temple.[44] All the recommendations the latter had brought with him were not sufficient to assure his welcome. The company he came with from England had more than balanced these endorsements, and it was pointed out that his connections in Boston, and his former record in that city, made him the most appropriate agent of the British Ministers. Whigs regarded him as an English emissary and even the Tories shared the same opinion. "Thus Mr. Temple had the misfortune to be spoken of ill both by the friends and enemies of the Public." Adams insisted to his wife that personally he did not distrust him, but frankly admitted that he could not afford to risk having his own conduct questioned. For most people in Philadelphia believed that Temple came as a tool of the British Court and they expressed surprise at the recommendations he had obtained.[45] And Adams was frightened lest, if he appeared to be on terms of intimacy with Temple, a similar doubt would be cast on him as on Arthur Lee, who was suspected, with good reason, although the Boston leader did not know this, of having communicated the secret negotiations with France to Lord Shelburne.

Sam Adams merely expressed common doubts about the impossibility of the letters which Temple had addressed to him, from New York, passing the British lines without General Clinton's inspection, nor would they have been sent "unless they had been adapted to his views"—suspicions which were certainly not unreasonable.[46] There was, however, another cause to explain Adams' wish to keep aloof from Temple. The demagogue shared a weakness common in every age among many politicians and was just then highly flattered to be on friendly terms with the newly arrived French Envoy M. Gérard, who had been profuse with assurances of the very special admiration with which he professed to regard the Boston leader. Adams entertained an illusion, often found reciprocally among politicians and diplomats, about each holding the other in a most particular esteem.[47] If it had been possible for him to read the French envoy's confidential correspondence with his own Ministry, he would have better understood the profound distrust which Gérard felt at this time regarding the sincerity of Adams's enthusiasm about the alliance.[48] When the new envoy from the Court of Versailles called on the delegate from Massachusetts it was to point out that Temple's residence so near to Congress might create an unfortunate impression in the minds of people abroad, and he mentioned also that Silas Deane in Paris had already warned him against Temple's mission and remarked that the latter was all the more dangerous as a mediator because he enjoyed the rights of a citizen. The French diplomat left with a nervous feeling as to whether Congress actually would feel disposed to take suitable measures against the suspected agent.[49] His next visit was on President Laurens in order to remind him that so long as England, encouraged by the freedom extended to Temple, believed that she could carry on separate negotiations with her former colonies, it would be difficult to obtain that full recognition of American independence which was so greatly desired; for the latter's presence in Philadelphia compromised both the dignity and reputation of Congress.

The Envoy remembering how anxious his chief had been only twelve months before when Paul Wentworth was in Paris, wished to leave no stone unturned, and followed this visit with an official note calling attention to his personal embarrassment at being obliged to inform his Court about the presence of a suspected British emissary. Congress, he suggested, ought of its own accord, to allow him to disabuse the Ministry at Versailles, as well as all friends of the United States in Europe, concerning reports of this nature, which were all the more dangerous because they afforded hope of separating the two countries and of nullifying the Treaty of Alliance.

Laurens reassured the French Minister on this point. Not one member of Congress, its President asserted, would listen to Temple, and he gave the Envoy reason to hope that the latter would shortly depart.[50] Monsieur Gérard felt quieter after he discovered for himself that Congress shared the same opinion about Temple, but owing to the recommendation given by the Council of Massachusetts, the delegates felt chary of taking any measures against him. Certain of these, however, went so far as to consult the French Envoy as to the best means of getting rid of the suspected British agent, and proposed to ride him out of town.[51] The diplomat after this urged John Jay to advise Temple to leave the city of his own accord and, in case he refused to go, stronger measures would then become justified. The suggestion met with approval in Congress, and Temple, taking the hint from a man who afterwards became his warm friend, left Philadelphia on the following day with his mission admittedly a complete failure.

When Gérard next wrote to Versailles, he mentioned that he had good ground for believing that Temple had hoped to be employed to conduct American foreign relations either at home or abroad, and then to steer these towards a reconciliation.[52] Strange as this may seem, the latter did not find anything amiss in secretly receiving British pay and yet planning to handle American diplomacy. Even his friend, Dr. Winthrop, who knew nothing about the confidential arrangements in London, expressed the wish that a man of

SIR JOHN TEMPLE

Temple's great experience might be asked to direct the external relations of Congress. Preposterous as this appears to-day, and astounding as it seemed to Gérard, who had guessed the plan, Temple's idea was far from strange to eighteenth-century standards of diplomacy which caused Talleyrand to find nothing amiss as a Foreign Minister in receiving pay from other countries in order to expedite their affairs. Temple's expectation was less reprehensible. Fresh from London, the secret agent had not yet understood that the French Alliance made the break with England final and that he was himself in the pay of a country with which his own was at war. With his mind still shaped by the immediate past, Temple had until then believed that it was possible to be at the same time an American and a British subject, without there being anything incompatible in this. His avowed aim had been to bring England and America together, as he was convinced, for their mutual advantage, and he accepted a secret remuneration only for attempting to carry out what had always been his goal.

Sam Adams felt immensely relieved when Temple had left Philadelphia. He wanted to keep his influence in Congress and yet avoid giving offence to prominent citizens of Boston. He could afford now to be complimentary and wrote to his friends in Massachusetts that several gentlemen of character, whom he was careful not to mention by name, had formed a more favourable opinion of Bowdoin's son-in-law than they had before he left and now expressed themselves as satisfied regarding the uprightness of his intentions.[53] But there was one delegate of Congress who pointed out that the key to Temple's entire procedure could be found in "All is vanity,"[54] and an exaggerated estimate of his own powers had been at the bottom of the British agent's mission.

[99]

After this rebuff, Temple went to Boston and lived quietly in that city for several months. At last he had understood that a reconciliation which stopped short of independence was impossible, nor, to his credit, did he ever again attempt this, although he maintained some correspondence with General Gates, who also was favourable to the idea of peace. Temple's ambition was henceforth to be displayed in a very different way, and far more usefully, although it brought no reward and ended by causing him untold anxiety and bitter humiliation. Instead of remaining unnoticed in Massachusetts for his mission to be forgiven and forgotten, he felt attracted by the lure of an unofficial and private Embassy which he was now to create for himself. Having failed as a British agent in America, he thought he might be more successful as a self-appointed American agent in England. In the spring of 1779, he announced to General Gates his intention of sailing for Holland and going to Spa, where he proposed to see the Duke of Richmond, Lord Camden, and other influential friends known to be sympathetic to America, in order to persuade these that England could gain nothing by continuing the war and that the only alternative to accepting was "dying in the last ditch."[55] He did not ask for any authorization to go, which certainly would have been refused, although later he claimed to Franklin that when he left Boston it was with the warm approval of his father-in-law, of Dr. Winthrop, and Dr. Cooper, etc., all of whom believed that his testimony about American opinion could only be helpful in London.[56] Before sailing, Temple had an attestation drawn up and signed by James Bowdoin, Sam Adams, and other notables, which related the circumstances of his career, and certified to the fact that Mr. Temple had "rendered a most important service to his country" when he helped to destroy the influence of those who plotted against its liberties, that this had turned to his own loss and distress, while the services of many others, and notably Dr. Franklin, had been rewarded with honours and emoluments. So long as Mr. Temple "retained that fidelity and affection to his country which in every instance that has come to our knowledge he has hitherto manifested," the signatories regard him as having a claim to compensation.[57]

This paper was probably drawn up at the instance of James Bowdoin, whose name appears first on the list. The wording suggests that, in order to obtain the desired signatures, it may have become necessary to qualify the endorsement by a proviso which dwelt on Temple's continued retention of faithful affection for his native country, and implied the possibility of further facts existing of which the signers remained in ignorance. If his own relatives and friends in Boston could produce nothing more enthusiastic at a time when he was about to return to Europe to work for the recognition of independence than to express so qualified a confidence in his patriotism, it goes far to explain the treatment from which he was later to suffer.

In his own interest as an American, John Temple would have been better advised to have attempted a less arduous mission than that of a self-appointed ambassador which inevitably exposed him to suspicion from both sides. His second great mistake was, instead of remaining on the Continent, to return to England, although from all accounts he made no secret of where lay his sympathies and boasted of having dined with Washington. In London, he called at once on Hutchinson to give him news of his daughter, whom he had seen in Boston. The Governor's son, Thomas, Jr., writing about Temple to his brother, found him "a favourer of the American Cause" more than he would have supposed, for the latter had told him that the Colonies would never be conquered and also that he had a licence to return whenever he liked.

For John Temple to express such a conviction to the son of the leading American loyalist in England, after his own mission had proved a complete failure, implied at least sincerity and some courage, for the mood of conciliation of the year before had passed in England ever since the failure of the Peace Embassy. Temple claimed to have told Lord North, after he had returned, that the colonies would never be subdued. In spite of his influential friends, the freedom with which he expressed his opinions exposed him to the hatred of the Loyalists and to risking the consequences of what he not inaptly called the Attorney General Wedderburn's "extraordinary talents at constructive treason."

A man of Temple's sociable instincts found residence in London far from distasteful even during a war in which all his sympathies were on the other side. He took pleasure in the society of Whig dukes who called themselves the friends of America, although much of their friendship was based on hostility to the King. His own convivial view of life resembled that of an English contemporary of Fox and Burke, far more than of a violent associate of Sam Adams. His loyalty always remained in America, but he found, like many others have done since, that, particularly in times of crisis, there was a personal satisfaction to be derived from the self-appointed task of representing his country in England. During this period he frequented a congenial circle which included men like the

Dukes of Rutland and Richmond, the two Hartleys, Edmund Burke, Dr. Price, and Counsellor Lee,[58] who were always prepared to chat about American affairs over their port. The outspokenness of his opinions in behalf of independence appeared in his own mind to be the most convincing proof of his patriotism, and he was proud to take this risk in his country's behalf.

About this time, James Warren, President of the Provincial Congress of Massachusetts, received an enthusiastic letter from his son in London warmly praising Temple and mentioning that the latter was once more desirous to return to America, but doubted if he would be allowed to leave, as he was being closely watched by the Ministry. Young Warren had twice been arrested and examined in the expectation of discovering letters from the suspect.[59]

When Henry Laurens, on his way to The Hague as American Envoy, at the moment of his capture off Newfoundland by a British cruiser, had thrown his papers overboard they were fished out of the sea. The English gazettes, describing the incident, had reported that the correspondence recovered seriously incriminated Temple for his treasonable activities. The latter, therefore, found it desirable to publish an unsigned statement in the London *Courant*,[60] describing his activities particularly as the previous account given of his mission to America had contained, as was alleged, some serious prevarication. The same might, indeed, have been said of the account Temple now drew up which neglected to mention certain trifles like the baronetcy and the pension promised him in case of success. According to this anonymous newspaper statement, Mr. Temple had gone to America without commission or instruction of any kind, but before he left England he understood that the British Ministers were disposed to make peace on the basis that *the Colonies should legislate for themselves and trade where they pleased,* only a nominal sovereignty attaching them to England. Mr. Temple, it was said, at the time was in ignorance of the treaty between France and America, and believed that the Americans might consent to negotiate on these terms, although it is difficult to understand how he could have been ignorant of a treaty which was public property and had been signed five months before he had sailed. It was also explained that he had very little knowledge of the Commissioners' doings, which was not very plausible, for they had all been together in New York. Temple affirmed that he had seen Lord Carlisle and Mr. Eden only on one occasion and then for a short time. If, as some people had suggested, bribery and corruption were any part of their business, Mr. Temple was an entire stranger to this. He had been no negotiator for the Commissioners, but had gone to America as an avowed friend of his country and returned to England with precisely the same feelings. He had most earnestly wished for peace and was glad when he had been informed that *"fair and honourable"* terms were going to be offered to the Congress. He had asked to precede the Commissioners, and it was regrettable that he had been unable to do so, as such terms might, in that case, have had a chance of success.

The statement in the Press went on to say that Mr. Temple, although American by birth and principle, was no enemy of England. He only hoped to be instrumental in some measure in bringing the war to an end. On the first day of his return from America, he had assured Lord North that, notwithstanding all he might hear to the contrary, the American people

11111

were united in their determination never to return to English rule, and there was no likelihood of British arms effecting this object.[61]

In 1780, soon after this statement had appeared in the Press, the painter, John Trumbull, was arrested in London, and a letter found on his person to his father, the Governor of Connecticut, and read as evidence in court, referred to Temple, who expected to leave at this time for America and hoped to be received as a "deserving friend to his country." Trumbull had written this in order to refute "every insinuation" regarding his friend, who was then being reviled from opposite sides. The painter stated emphatically that Temple's residence in London had been eminently serviceable to the American cause. Later, after his release from Bridewell Prison, Trumbull wrote to his father to praise highly Temple's work in defeating the misrepresentations of the loyalists regarding the state of opinion in America, and also for his untiring efforts to convince both parties in Parliament as to the necessity of admitting independence and ending the war. The artist added that if ingratitude was not to be the characteristic American vice, Temple ought to be rewarded in his ambition, which was later to return to England in some public capacity.[62]

The change which was taking place at this time in the British attitude toward independence was not altogether caused by military events, for operations then at a standstill in the North dragged on inconclusively in the Carolinas. The pressure of individuals as well as circumstances can alter opinion, and Bowdoin's son-in-law was one of the men who helped to induce Englishmen to accept the inevitable. At at ime when Silas Deane, who originally denounced

Temple's mission of peace, had proclaimed his own conversion to the idea of abandoning independence, and when signs of increasing war weariness in America were giving revived hope to the loyalist refugees, Temple was labouring in London to obtain the recognition of the United States. It is the penalty of working as a private individual behind the enemy's ramparts, that no proof of loyalty, no assumption of risk nor mark of success will ever stave off suspicion. Temple in England might be the most patriotic of Americans. When he wrote to Governor Trumbull, in order to give news of his son, the future British Consul-General spoke of his expectation for a speedy peace "founded upon what principally concerns *independence of the United States and perfect freedom of the Ocean*," however distasteful the pill might be "to that insane kingdom now fallen never more to appear in the first rank of nations, may such the consequence of their perfidy and wickedness be a warning."[63] Few Americans knew of the risk he took, by expressing similar opinions, or cared for what he thought or did. A rumour, however, was circulated through Congress in 1780 that Temple would shortly again return to the United States bringing with him proposals to acknowledge American independence, except for South Carolina, Georgia, and Maine, on condition that the Republic remained neutral in the war between Great Britain and Spain.[64] To Americans the former British agent could be nothing else.

Before returning "to my own country," Temple had desired to visit Franklin in Paris. The latter wrote him in all frankness to mention the suspicions aroused by his continued residence in England. Temple, greatly offended, gave up all idea of the visit and hotly replied to the Doctor that this suspicion covered

everyone alike, even himself, compared it to the Salem
witchcraft, and suggested that it had been instigated by British
agents in their hope to spread distrust among the friends of
America. He insisted that it had never been in his power, after
hostilities began, to return home with his family any sooner,
and that he had always supposed that his country would compensate him for his pecuniary losses. "My other sufferings it
was not in their power to compensate." He was then on the
point of "going home, where I hope to lay my bones without
ever seeing Europe again."[65]

Instead of Paris, Temple went to Amsterdam, where for the
first time he made the acquaintance of John Adams, then
Minister at The Hague. The latter knew him well by reputation
as a man of "honour, integrity, and attachment to his native
country," who had been extremely serviceable to the American
cause. He did not pretend to vindicate Temple for having
remained so long in England. The purpose of a letter which
Adams now wrote on his behalf to the President of Congress
was not to recommend him for office, but to prevent suspicion
of his conduct. Adams remarked that Temple had fallen from
his high rank merely because he would not join in hostile
designs against his country. "This I think should at least
entitle him to quiet enjoyment of the liberties of his country
and to the esteem of his fellow citizens provided there are no
just grounds of suspicion against him . . . and after a great deal
of the freest conversation with him I see no reason to doubt his
intentions."[66] To Temple himself, then on the eve of sailing,
Adams mentioned the distrust which others entertained for
him. He hoped that the man might meet with a friendly
reception at home, but felt unable to assure this and could only
wish him success.

Trouble began in October, 1781, as soon as Temple arrived at Boston. He had returned without permission and the moment was singularly ill-chosen and unfortunate, for feeling at this time was extremely bitter against anyone suspected of having had English attachments. It was his misfortune to arrive just when hot passions, stirred by years of war, had risen to a degree of violence no longer tempered as before by any fear of compromise or defeat. Three years earlier he had been welcomed, at least in Massachusetts. His old friends still remained faithful to him, and Governor Trumbull wrote from Connecticut to congratulate James Bowdoin on the safe return of his son-in-law and quote to him his own son's praise for Temple's patriotism. The latter, however, was summoned once more before the Council of Massachusetts to explain what had been his conduct in London. John Trumbull, lately returned from England, appeared before the Legislative Committee and testified warmly in Temple's defence. The painter left, convinced that the investigation would turn out to his friend's interest, and wrote to cheer him with the hope that nothing else was wanting "to give you that high place in the esteem of your country which your services and sufferings have merited."[67] Governor Hancock, none the less, required Temple to provide a bond of three thousand pounds that he would give no intelligence to the enemies of the United States. In vain the latter protested indignantly against this humiliation. The question became political, the better element in the State sympathizing with Temple and feeling that he had been badly treated. The State Senate, however, requested the Governor to order John Temple to leave Massachusetts and not to return again without permission from the General Court. Next day this resolution was reconsidered for another one somewhat less offensive, asking the Governor to ascertain if the public welfare permitted John Temple to remain any longer in the Commonwealth.[68]

The bitter animosity displayed against Temple not unlikely was also a means used for attacking his father-in-law, James Bowdoin. Both men were reviled by the same enemies, one of whom was James Sullivan, whose knowledge, a contemporary wrote with indignant humour, was confined to the dry study of the law, and Governor Hancock, "who is acquainted with no branch of science at all, not even government."[69] Sullivan was baiting poor Temple "as though he were a British spy,"[70] while the latter's friends found that he was cruelly used and scoffed at these pretenders to patriotism who were endeavouring to blast a character far above their own reach. Meanwhile, the injured man suffered acutely. In vain he demanded that if he had offended against the laws, these should be put into force against him, but if not, and if this is to be "the fruits of our glorious revolution and no remedy or redress is to be found from the laws, I for one, Sir, would very soon relinquish my birthright and seek residence in some other country."[71]

After this outburst, the Massachusetts Legislature resolved that Temple could be discharged from his bond without harm to the Commonwealth, especially as the reasons for this had ceased with the termination of the war. The Attorney-General prudently expressed the opinion that the question of his citizenship was political and beyond his own competence. During all this time poor Temple drank deeply from the dregs of bitterness. If he had acted wisely or unwisely, if he had been led astray by ambition or the lure of office, or merely by the pleasure of congenial society, whatever he did never altered the fact that his sympathy and loyalty were unquestionably with America, and that his dearest wish had been to serve his country. That he had once acted as a British secret agent was not so discreditable as it may appear to-day. Great Britain and America, for him as for many others, were then different branches of one tree, and at the time of his mission in 1778, it was far from conclusive, particularly to one who had lived in England, that they had separated for ever. This he understood only after he had failed in Philadelphia. He had then abandoned all expectation of a British career which would have been far more profitable than anything he could hope to receive in a new country. Yet his motives had been impugned, his character blackened, his citizenship questioned, and grave doubts had been cast as to whether he would even be tolerated as a resident in his own birthplace. American democracy is often terribly harsh in its treatment of whoever is unwilling to conform to its particular pattern. John Temple had tried to follow a line of his own and although the suspicions he had aroused were natural enough no one can say that he had not accomplished a work infinitely more valuable for his country by going to London than by the negative existence he probably would have led in Boston, if he had remained there after the failure of his mission.

It was beyond any doubt that the opposition against Temple would always be too strong to allow any hope of his obtaining preferment in the United States. His friends now tried to help him in a different way. No greater American patriot lived than Governor Trumbull of Connecticut, but even he encouraged Temple to become again a British subject, and wrote a personal letter on his behalf to Lord Dartmouth, with whom he had corresponded in former years. The Governor began by deploring the bloodshed and treasure lost in the War. He recommended his son as a painter to His Lordship's notice;

but the real purpose of his letter was to mention that Franklin and Temple had been the only Crown officers of rank dismissed from office for refusing to fall in with the misrepresentations of those officials who had deceived Great Britain. Franklin had since been honoured in America, while Temple had been left "singular in his sufferings." The Governor suggested that it would please Temple's American friends if some reparation could be made him.[72] For, disgusted by his treatment in Boston, the latter had again left for England.

In London once more, where Temple accompanied John Adams on the occasion of the American Minister's first attendance at the King's Levee,[73] Temple tried to obtain compensation for his losses of property, as a farm which he possessed in Massachusetts had been most wantonly destroyed by the Americans. The late agent asked also to have reparation for the injustice done him by the late Minister "in his mad career of ruining the Empire." Publicly he now declared that he felt no insuperable objection to again becoming "a servant of the Crown of England,"[74] and would be glad for an opportunity to return to the United States as a British official. Meanwhile, he was advising the Council of Trade against taking unwise measures toward America, on the ground that the first impression created on a new nation was of enormous importance, and that the French were doing everything to foster closer relations with the young Republic.

In March, 1785, Mrs. Temple wrote to tell her father how delighted she was at her husband's new appointment as the first British Consul-General to the United States. They were sailing in a few weeks and Temple was bringing over as a gift to his father-in-law a little writing-table that had belonged to Lord Chatham. As he was about to leave for his post in New York, the former American patriot asked the new Foreign Secretary, Lord Carmarthen, for George the Third's portrait in order that "the Picture of my sovereign might again appear in the United States when it had in the course of an unhappy war been destroyed in almost every state." He looked forward to be instrumental during his mission in "renovating that veneration and respect that was once happily entertained for my sovereign and his flag."[75]

When John Adams heard the news of Temple's appointment, he wrote to James Warren, who was the Consul-General's closest friend, in order to offer some useful advice. If the new duties which Temple was about to assume depended only on a "genteel behaviour," no one, wrote Adams, would be better qualified than the incumbent. But he feared that the new Consul General could also do much mischief unless properly advised. If he were to bring on needless controversies with Congress, or its members, with States or Governors, or the consuls of other nations, he would soon destroy himself.

> He is now an Englishman and a servant of his king. Let him make no pretensions as an American because they will not be admitted and will only expose him. He must proceed slowly, softly and smoothly. . . . He is now on the right road. He was the servant of the King and should always have looked to him and him alone for service unless he had renounced his service more decidedly and engaged more clearly than he did against him.[76]

How far this excellent counsel may have influenced Temple for his good is not known, but Warren replied that he would seek an early opportunity to impart it.

Sir John Temple—for shortly after this he succeeded to the family baronetcy—was the first British official sent to the United States. He carried out with success an important task, but his later career does not enter within the scope of this study. He became an intimate friend of John Jay. During his residence in New York, where he principally lived, he exercised a bountiful hospitality congenial to his taste and which the other consuls envied. He was known as a man of warm heart, though with an impulsive temper.

He died at his post on November 17, 1798.

I

CHAPTER FOUR

The Adventurer of Genius, Benjamin Thompson,
Count Rumford

I

NO MAN was ever less of an adventurer by temperament or
rendered more so by the circumstances of his life than Benjamin
Thompson, the future Count Rumford. In outward incident
and accomplishment, he enjoyed, perhaps, the most varied
experiences of any American who has ever lived. Of patriotism
he had none, of national feeling as little, though in middle
life he professed to have acquired a certain attachment for the
United States. He cannot be called a traitor, though he fought
against his country. Nor, properly speaking, was he a loyalist,
for there was barely profession of loyalty in the service he gave
to George the Third. At the first opportune moment he left
Great Britain, and as a retired colonel in the English army, with
a military reputation and still of military age, he lived in Paris
during the Napoleonic Wars. Wherever he went he gave the
best of service and no master ever regretted having employed
him. He proved himself to be an excellent soldier in the field
against his own countrymen in the only actual fighting he ever
saw, and at one time it seemed as if he would follow a military
career, for which he showed great promise. But his tastes ran
to science and social welfare and to act the reformer and the
benevolent tyrant in a country where he had arrived as a
tourist. With a fine scorn for humanity, he enjoyed European

fame as a humanitarian, and became a forerunner in applying large-scale practical philanthropic measures to improve the condition of the poor. This penniless and obscure Yankee refugee, by his own unaided talents, pursued a career which made him successively a British Under-Secretary of State, a Bavarian Minister who was invested with powers of a dictator, a Count of the Holy Roman Empire, and an eminent member of the French Institute, known internationally by his work for the betterment of mankind, but always remaining the most consummate of egotists.

There is nothing remarkable to discover about Thompson's early years. Samuel Curwen, the refugee, remembered him when he was still a good-natured lad apprenticed to a small shopkeeper at Salem. As a boy he felt ambitious enough to try a trade in salt cod for the West Indies. He learned some French in a night school and took a course in mechanics at Harvard. Like so many New Englanders he taught school when himself hardly out of one. As a youth, he was tall, with handsome features, blue eyes, and dark auburn hair, and his comely appearance, attracted the notice of a widow of means and position considerably older than himself. Before he was twenty, they had married and settled on a farm at Rumford, the present Concord, New Hampshire. His new position brought him worldly advantages, but did not make him any more popular. His neighbours resented the commission in the militia which Governor Wentworth, a friend of his wife's family, had given him and criticized his manners as being over-courtly, an unforgivable sin in a rural community, though many years later in Paris, when Thompson had become a distinguished personality, his colleagues found him boorish.

To his dying day Thompson always maintained that he had never been unfriendly to the American cause which was probably true, for no political convictions ever troubled his conscience. A certain fondness for mingling with the mighty had led him, however, to carry on a correspondence with General Gage, regarding the return of two deserters from the British army in Boston who had been employed on Thompson's farm. Prejudiced neighbours used this incident as proof that he was a Tory at heart, for deserters were regarded as possible drillmasters by the Americans. His fellow townsmen demanded a public confession of his guilt, but he refused either to admit this or to accept the humiliation. Some of the ideas cherished by the "Sons of Liberty" in New England who in the name of freedom pried into their neighbours' affairs, bore an uncomfortable resemblance to tyranny. In the summer of 1774, Thompson was summoned before a self-constituted committee at Concord charged with being unfriendly to his country's cause. The indictment was dismissed, but not long after this, his house was surrounded by a threatening mob and he was forced to flee to escape violence. He went to Woburn, where he was arrested and imprisoned on a similar charge. A partial exoneration left him indignant. He offered his services to the American army which was being organized, but met with no success it is said, owing to the opposition of his neighbours.[1]

This was the last straw. Democracy is often intolerant and always suspicious of whatever is not in its own image. Undoubtedly Thompson was entirely wanting in patriotic fervour and frankly preferred the society of the British "oppressor" to that of his rustic neighbours. The young farmer with social aspirations had felt flattered by the friendly relations unexpectedly enjoyed with English generals and Tory governors. In his heart he was politically indifferent to both parties and solely interested in bettering his own position. His real value as a man was, however, misunderstood by the Whigs, and the services he might have rendered to his country, if he had been differently treated, were never asked, though American history would have been the richer for the use of his talents. Profoundly wounded in his pride, branded by suspicion and the slur of aspersions, not all of which were fair, he made up his mind to stand no further humiliation and fled to Boston, where he became a British secret agent.

A letter which he wrote to Timothy Walker, his father-in-law, explains the more avowable part of his conduct, and his own embitterment with the consequences which followed.[2] After describing the petty incident of the return of the deserters, in whom he professed to have taken no other interest than one of ordinary humanity, he complained that this had been distorted into a crime to injure his country while he was represented as being an enemy to the American cause, and as such deserving the severest punishment. When he stood trial, his own brother-in-law, who had approved of what he had done, did not dare to testify on his behalf. Friends had urged him to leave Concord until the storm abated, for his fellow townsmen, under pretence of defending their liberties, were depriving individuals of freedom in ways which "an Eastern despot would blush to be guilty of."

Thompson expressed the hope soon to be out of reach of his "Cruel Persecutors" and to find the peace and protection denied him by his native country in foreign lands and among strangers, for he refused any longer to submit to the insults daily offered him.

The crime which is alleged against me (viz: being an enemy to my country) is a crime of the blackest dye—a crime which must if proved against me inevitably entail perpetual infamy and disgrace upon my name. . . I never did nor (let my treatment be what it will) ever will do any action that may have the most distant tendency to injure the true interests of this my native country.[3]

This letter was written by a man whose pen ran more easily to facts than to feelings, and whose bitterness was more convincing than the assertion of his patriotism. It is hard to reconcile, however, with his lately discovered secret connection with General Gage—which favours the opinion that he acted as a spy. The question might never have arisen without the recent examination of the Gage papers. Mr. Allen French, to whose kindness I owe the information, has discovered among these an unsigned letter, presumably from Thompson, written three months earlier than the one to his father-in-law. From behind the American lines, using sympathetic ink underneath another letter which served as a blind, Thompson gave the British commander secret military information.[4] If this letter was actually written by Benjamin Thompson, which Mr. French regards certain both from internal evidence and other circumstances, how is it compatible with his offer of service to the patriot army unless this was made to allow him to act the spy. This supposition would explain the careful survey he undertook of the strength and position of the Whig forces which later, he described in a detailed memorandum given to Lord George Germaine. Yet it is possible that he became a spy only after he had been humiliated by the denial of a commission on the Whig side, and with his own indifference to either cause gave to the

British the benefit of the observations he had made of the American army. Links are still missing in the chain of evidence and positive conclusions are difficult to draw. Thompson's subsequent career was never blackened by any suspicion of treachery, which creates a certain presumption in his favour. At the worst one can surmise that there may have been greater reason than appeared for his neighbours' distrust. His remaining behind the American lines and his correspondence with General Gage place an unpleasant construction on what he did. Little creditable as may have been his actions at this time the military information which he obtained undoubtedly placed him on the road to success.

Seemingly without any regret Thompson abandoned his family. He was never again to see his wife, and he only met the daughter, whom he had left as an infant, when she had grown to womanhood. For the next few years military affairs were to occupy his interest. Well received by the British officers in Boston, he was selected to command one of the proposed loyalist battalions which Brigadier-General Timothy Ruggles was attempting to raise, and for which he had enrolled a few hundred Tory merchants.[5] Nothing came of this effort, although it kept Thompson occupied until he sailed for England on the frigate *Scarborough* and conveyed to Lord George Germaine the first report of General Gage's evacuation of Boston.

It is hardly conceivable that the bearer of such unpleasant news should have carried no other introduction of a nature to explain his being offered at once a place in the British War Office. Probably no suitable berth could be found for Thompson in Boston after the idea of a loyalist battalion had fizzled out, and General Gage may not have been averse to sending a clever young American to acquaint the military authorities with the peculiar difficulties of his position. How Benjamin Thompson, at the age of twenty-two, still an unknown Yankee, obtained his first official post in London and began his great career is an unsolved mystery, although a plausible conjecture may be offered. In spite of many warnings which had been largely disregarded, the gravity of the rebellion in America took the British Ministry completely by surprise. The military authorities had begun by refusing to believe that the rebels would fight, for professional opinion, always scornful about the colonists, expressed the view that "five hundred men with whips would drive all Americans before them."[6] Confronted by the thunderclap of Lexington and the slaughter of Bunker Hill, the War Office found it hard to understand how untrained farmers should have been able to dig proper entrenchments and resist British regulars. Lord George Germaine was himself as ignorant as were most of his subordinates regarding the extent of the Colonists' resources, but he was as intelligent as he was indolent, and very far from being the incapable nonentity he is often represented. In the presence of a crisis, the gravity of which he had never anticipated, it was natural to seek information. When Thompson arrived in London fresh from Boston, he possessed first hand knowledge in the most recent form and the news he gave was practical, thorough, and helpful. He had already written out a detailed report about the American army which was besieging Boston and had included in this a minute description of its means of transport, its munitions, where these were located, and how they could be destroyed. All this had been submitted to the War Office, probably sent to London before his own arrival. The months he spent around Boston had been employed in making this survey, which had made his name known to the Minister and is docketed Number Five among Lord George Germaine's papers.[7]

Except for an ornamental commission held in the New Hampshire Militia and his intended selection to command a non-existent battalion of loyalists in Boston, Thompson had never been a soldier. But in the memorandum given to the Secretary of State he described, like a professional, the American artillery, and sharply criticized the army which had just acquitted itself with credit at Bunker Hill. He drew a picture of the men as wretchedly clad; promised coats, as a kind of bounty for enlisting, and very angry because Congress had not given these. They were in his words "as dirty a set of mortals as ever disgraced the name of soldier." With no washerwomen in camp, the men allowed their shirts to rot on their backs sooner than to clean these themselves. They suffered from epidemics which he attributed to their dirt as well as eating too much meat, for Thompson was already a critic of diet. The American leaders had taken the greatest pains to conceal the truth, but so severe were the ravages of illness that, in July, 1775, out of 4207 men stationed at Prospect Hill, only 2227 were returned fit for duty, with a mortality all the greater because so many medicines were unobtainable.

In this report can be detected Thompson's future interest in questions of public health and his method of statistical presentation of facts. The amateur took a solely professional point of view of military affairs and displayed an unbounded scorn for the volunteer. He brushed aside as being too negligible to mention any enthusiasm for a cause or of patriotic devotion to duty. When he described the feelings of the American soldiers, it was only to say that in general they were heartily sick of the service and with the greatest difficulty could they be prevailed upon to serve through another campaign. He foretold, however, that Congress would do its utmost to persuade them to re-enlist, as their political existence depended upon the existence of the army.

Thompson noted that General Washington had met with great obstacles in introducing discipline among raw levies, for the doctrines of independence and rebellion had been so effectually sown throughout the country and so imbibed by all classes of men that it would be hard to induce the soldiers to obey orders. Many leading Americans lamented the fact that the same spirit which caused the common people to take up arms to resist British authority would also make them refuse obedience to their own officers and prevent them from ever becoming good soldiers. Another reason which made it impossible to introduce proper subordination was due to the great degree of equality of fortune and education. Officers and men were nearly on a par in birth and means, and in certain regiments were generally neighbours and old acquaintances, which made it all the harder to introduce discipline for "men cannot bear to be commanded by others that are their superiors in nothing but in having had the good fortune to get a superior commission." A further cause which stood in the way of unifying the army were the jealousies between the different Colonies. The Massachusetts contingent complained about Washington having court-martialed many of their officers, supposedly, to fill their places with his Virginian friends. Worst of all in the army were the boasted riflemen, for "there never was a more mutinous and undisciplined set of villains that bred disturbances in any camp."

This report submitted to the Secretary of State may help to explain the reason for Thompson's immediate success. Lord George Germaine, not without cause the most reviled of politicians, gave at once to an unknown Yankee the opportunity which had been denied him by his own countrymen. Soon he became the Minister's confidential man, placed by him in charge of American affairs and responsible for many of the practical duties of equipping and transporting the British forces. Also, he became Lord George's closest friend, sharing all his meals in an intimacy which gave rise to the most scandalous rumours. Governor Hutchinson records hearing Thompson described as "that scoundrel" and felt astonished at the freedom of malicious gossip current about the relations between the two men. Even Hutchinson expressed surprise that Lord George Germaine should trust so much of the King's conversation to a not over-discreet youngster.[8]

Scurrilous conjectures at the sudden rise of many men from insignificance to fortune are not peculiar to any age or country and the written word is far from being evidence of their veracity. The probability was that Lord George Germaine, surrounded by enemies more than most public men, had discovered a remarkably able young secretary whom he could trust all the more readily, because Thompson, without any connections of his own in England, owed his official existence entirely to his new chief. The Minister, aware of his unpopularity and rendered cynical by his misadventures, had found in the Yankee a helpful aide a devoted friend and an agreeable companion; and Thompson flattered by his intimacy with the Cabinet Minister, for once in his life was grateful to the man who had rescued him from obscurity and placed him on the highroad to preferment. Never weighed down by any sense of obligation, he always retained this gratitude and remained attached to his patron probably by the only true friendship he ever felt. Ten years later, when he had become a powerful dignitary in Bavaria, enjoying wealth and honours, Thompson wrote from Munich to his former chief who, then retired in the Upper House with the title of Lord Sackville, had ceased to be politically influential, a letter which, except for the one to his father-in-law, already mentioned, is perhaps the most human and certainly the most remarkable expression recorded of a man who later gave his services to humanity. After having described the influential position which he then occupied and his relations with the Elector of Bavaria, he added:

"I certainly stand well with my Master and I think I have nothing to fear from his successor . . . . Rank, titles, decorations literary distinctions, with some degree of literary and some small degree of military fame, I have acquired (through your availing protection) and the road is open to me for the rest. No man supports a better moral character than I do and no man is better satisfied with himself." Yet even so the wish expressed by this child of fortune was "to enjoy once more the society of my best my only friend . . . . Look back for a moment my dearest friend upon the work of your hands, *Je suis de votre ouvrage.* Does it not afford you a very sensible pleasure to find that your child has answered your expectations?"[9]

Ten days after this letter had been written, Lord Sackville was dead.

Benjamin Thompson's road to honours had been opened to him by Lord George Germaine. Through the Minister he met the King, to whom he made a present of a volume of original letters written by Governor Pownall, and from his patron he learned the intimate gossip of the Court. In 1780, the man, who

BENJAMIN THOMPSON, COUNT RUMFORD

From a portrait by Thomas Gainsborough

five years before had been a farmer in Concord, had become an Under-Secretary of State for the Northern Department which was in charge of the Colonies. He was then inspector of all the clothing sent to America and held a commission as lieutenant-colonel of a regiment of Horse Dragoons stationed in New York. He had been elected a member of the Royal Society, for he was already becoming known by his scientific experiments. The loyalist refugees in London envied him an income which they estimated, with some exaggeration, at seven thousand pounds a year. He held, however, certain lucrative posts like the Secretaryship of Georgia which brought him in several hundred pounds, and which he administered through a deputy.[10]

Thompson acted as the link between the Ministry and the loyalist refugees in London whom he assisted on the numerous occasions when they prepared their petitions for relief. Samuel Curwen mentions his reputation for being "peculiarly respectful to Americans that fall his way," although the favourable impression which at first he made on the refugee soon wore off. The Under-Secretary had acquired an official manner that rasps so many Americans, and Curwen resented what he described as his courtier's smile and his uncommunicative way.[11] Later, John Trumbull attributed his own arrest in London to Thompson, and felt bitter towards him although the latter was probably merely carrying out his duty without any personal animosity towards the painter. Expressions of dislike on the part of those who came into contact with him, whether Americans or English, are not surprising. As an important British official, he handled his business with the coldly polite detachment of a man whose character slipped easily into an impersonal bureaucratic groove which magnifies the self importance of the vain. Although in charge of American affairs he saw little of his own countrymen outside of official intercourse and made friends with none. He lived too close to the Minister to care for any lesser society, and the same taste for associating with the great, which had formerly made him seek the company of British generals in Boston, now kept him aloof from the refugees.

After the failure of successive American campaigns, feeling ran very high in England against Lord George Germaine, who was blamed for the lack of success and whose unfair treatment of Burgoyne for carrying out orders which led him to Saratoga, added to the Minister's unpopularity. Thompson, with shrewd foresight, understood in time that if he remained in London he would suffer with his chief, and might even be used as a means to attack the latter. His rise had been too sudden not to make for him many enemies, and for success to be forgiven, his only chance lay in the field. He resigned from the comfortable office of Under-Secretary before the storm had broken and asked to take effective command in New York of the regiment of dragoons of which he was already the titular colonel. The move was wise and the prospect of battling against his own countrymen did not for an instant disturb him. He felt merely a professional interest in the struggle, and no pretence of any greater loyalty than might be expected from a man who was eating the King's bread. The soldierly instinct caused him, however, to welcome war for its experience and he knew that only in the field would he be able to extricate himself creditably from a difficult situation. He sailed as soon as he was able to on a transport bound first for Charleston, bearing a letter from Lord George Germaine to Sir Henry Clinton, the British Commander-in-Chief in New York, full of admiration for his friend's spirit in leaving an agreeable and profitable situation in order to take the field.[12]

During the sea journey to America, Thompson had suffered from attacks of fever brought on characteristically by sitting up all night on deck in order to take lunar observations. On his arrival in Charleston, after having been informed that there was no early intention of the vessel proceeding further, he went ashore. He discovered to his consternation, a few hours later that the ship had sailed without him, and felt convinced that he had intentionally been left behind. An ordinary man would have fumed unavailingly. Thompson fumed, but went to offer his services at once to the local commandant, General Leslie, who placed him at the head of some weak squadrons of horse and a "Sepoy" troop, *gens de couleur* as their commandant called them. He was not unhappy in this command, for his duties were novel, he found the South Carolina climate heavenly, and he revelled in the sight of orange trees and hedges of myrtle.[13]

This was his first practical experience as a soldier. From Charleston he wrote to his patron to describe his military life, ending his letter with a flamboyant note that "the trumpet sounds to boot and saddle." In action he acquitted himself well and, supported by a company from a line regiment, some Irish volunteers and sixty *Jägers*, he nearly destroyed a body of American cavalry and later dispersed some of Marion's horse men in the desultory fighting which went on along the Santee River.[14] The professional instinct came out in the contemptuous opinion which the late New Hampshire farmer expressed for the revolutionary cavalry, whom he represented as being no better than children, and riding horses much too fat for a long march would knock out half of them. Marion's exploits in the Carolinas have become legendary, but Thompson boasted that he was perfectly ready to attack the whole American cavalry with his hundred and fifty loyalists, who were excellent soldiers, brave to the last degree, and requiring only a little discipline.[15] His opinion of the Indians was also most unfavourable and he wrote that little could be expected from them as friends nor were they formidable as foes.

These Charleston letters contain not a trace of any regret at the fact that he was an American fighting other Americans when he might have been on their side, or that before he had offered his services to the patriot army and had pilloried bearing arms against his country as "a crime of the blackest dye." He wrote in a coldly detached way to describe the campaign, as if cause and enemy alike were personally indifferent to him. There is no expression of any feeling other than military pride at what he was doing or any profession of loyalism at serving his King. Why his compatriots should be killing each other in a struggle which had become futile did not concern him. He, the soldier of a few hours, wrote as if he had been a veteran professional who cared nothing about the flag under which he risked his life and who despised Marion's cavalry in the same way as he had despised the American riflemen when he was still a civilian. As a soldier, however, his duty was admirably performed, and General Leslie wrote from Charleston to Sir Henry Clinton in New York that several detached corps of cavalry incorporated under Lieutenant-Colonel Thompson had become really efficient owing to the unwearied and diligent efforts of that officer.[16] Thompson had disciplined his men, gained their confidence and even affection, and General Leslie concluded his report by saying, "I much regret to part with this enterprising young officer who appears to have an uncommon share of merit and zeal for the service."[17]

At the first opportunity, Thompson left Charleston for New York, eager to find his own regiment, the King's American

Dragoons. And when he had taken over their command, he noted, with the particular pleasure he always found in social distinctions whenever these accrued to his advantage, that all the officers were gentlemen of the first families in America. He was proud to be at their head, and noted with satisfaction that one of his underlings, Captain Phillips of New York, possessed the means to give five hundred guineas to the regimental fund. His dragoons he claimed were the crack corps of the British army in America. And Prince William Henry, later to be the Sailor King, had presented them with their standards and complimented Thompson on their appearance, telling him that his regiment could easily be mistaken for one on the regular British establishment, and that the troops were good enough to parade in Hyde Park. Their colonel felt delighted. Thompson was then in high spirits, taking enough exercise "to kill a dozen wine lubbers," and the splendid health he enjoyed by his careful diet convinced him that drink and overeating were the causes of most disorders incident to "these hot climates," as he described New York.[18]

George the Third's recognition of American independence came as a sad blow to dash this soldier's paradise. The loyalists were in a wild frenzy when they heard the news. In New York many of them refused to serve any longer, and posted papers in the streets inviting Sir Guy Carleton to take command of the army and forcibly oppose the new government, promising him the assistance of thousands of their number. Thompson had previously been given the command as well of an irregular body of loyalists known as the "Queen's Rangers," whose depredations have left a most unsavoury memory in the revolutionary annals of New York. Quartered with these men as their colonel at Huntington, Long Island, Thompson is said to have horrified the inhabitants by forcing them to pull down their own church, utilizing the timbers in order to build a blockhouse and barracks in the middle of the cemetery, and to have made use of the tombstones for fireplaces, so that loaves of bread as they came out of the ovens bore their reversed inscriptions on the lower crust.[19] While the peace negotiations dragged on, the Commander of the Queen's Rangers on Long Island was engaged in carrying on what he called a little war of his own—the only one still permitted—against the American whaleboats which swarmed in the Sound, fighting the rebels with their own weapons, and using one whaleboat to catch another.[20]

When peace was concluded the future "benefactor of humanity" appears to have had no thought for the wife and child he had left nine years before, and who at the time were living at Woburn while he was in New York. There is no record that he made any attempt to see them or that he even wrote to them. His interest was exclusively in his cavalry regiment, which he offered at once for service in the West Indies or in any other part of the globe where they might be employed. Officers and men, he declared, were all "passionately fond of the army, desired to remain in it" and had lost hope of ever returning to their American homes.[21]

As a regimental commander, Thompson was now solely ambitious for a military career. Back in London once more in June, 1783, looked up to by the other loyalist officers as their leader he wrote to invite Lord North's attention to the distressing situation of the Americans who had served in the British army, had sacrificed everything to their loyalty, lost their property, and could not return to their homes. As the representative of these officers, he petitioned Parliament for half-pay with the recognition of their rank, and showed himself indefatigable in approaching the politicians to obtain this.[22]

The loyalist officers' request was granted without objection, but Thompson was less successful when he attempted to have his own regiment placed on the regular British establishment. He had asked for himself the rank of full colonel,[23] which he would have been entitled to if the regiment had been sent to the West Indies. The favour, as he wrote to Lord North, was trifling in itself, "but to me it is of infinite importance as my views are to a foreign service."[24] The significance of the rank was for its recognition abroad, and also the higher rate of half-pay to which he would have a right, was an object for one who had little else to depend on. The King, began by raising some objections, but finished by recommending him for a full colonelcy.[25]

There was no prospect of Thompson's finding any further employment in England. The war was over, regiments were being rapidly disbanded, and the military establishment drastically cut down. At one time he had thought of Bombay, but the East India Company was sending home some British regiments and felt overstocked with officers for whom they could no longer find use. With hopes aroused in another direction he wrote to a friend to announce that he would soon hear of a dash taking everyone by surprise. Russians and Turks were then on the eve of war and "on one side or another I am determined to have a hand in it."[26] Perhaps if he had reached Russia the Empress Catherine appreciative of those graces which later endeared him to Munich Countesses might have lifted his career to still more dazzling heights but he found no need to seek his fortune beyond Bavaria.

Thompson's plan was to travel on the Continent before returning to England, and in case war should break out in any part of Europe, he intended to take part, "as I would not miss such an opportunity of improving myself in my profession." Otherwise he would return to London, "which I mean to make my home." During his absence, Lord George Germaine had consented to remain in charge of his personal affairs. Their intimacy was as close as ever and Thompson left behind all his papers with full legal powers to his friend to open letters and act for him in everything.[27] After these arrangements had been completed, the late Under-Secretary set out on his journey, finding as fellow passengers on the Channel packet Henry Laurens, whose dispatches he had examined when the former President of Congress was a prisoner in the Tower, and the historian Gibbon, who jotted down in his diary the presence on board of "Mr. Secretary, Colonel, Admiral, Philosopher, Thompson attended by three horses."

II

Thompson's life from this point is almost outside the scope of this work and requires a study of its own.[28] This brief and fragmentary account of certain chapters in his career may help to explain personal sides of the man and throw light on his feelings toward America. A chance meeting on the Rhine was then to alter the course of his entire life. Prince Max of Zweibrücken, the future King of Bavaria and father-in-law of Eugène Beauharnais, was in 1787 a colonel in the French army enjoying at this time as he used later to say, the happiest years of his life. He commanded the royal German regiment of Deux Ponts which had just come back from service in America. On the parade ground at Strassburg, the Prince noticed an officer in a foreign uniform well mounted on a fine English horse. There are different versions of what took place, but the only thing of consequence is that, after the two men had met at the regimental mess Prince Max became sufficiently interested in Thompson to recommend him to his uncle, the Elector of Bavaria, who invited him to enter his employ, in order to introduce certain reforms in the army.

Benjamin Thompson, a retired British colonel drawing half-pay, was obliged to return to England and obtain the King's permission to take service under a foreign prince. This was promptly granted, a knighthood was conferred upon him by George the Third, and the former New Hampshire farmer obtained the right to use the arms of "the antient and respectable family of Thompson of York." At a moment when other loyalists were struggling to begin life afresh in the forests of New Brunswick, or eking out a wretched existence on a Government pittance as refugees in London, Thompson alone basked in fortune. How his regimental friends were impressed by this amazing luck may be judged from a letter written by Edward Chipman, paymaster of his former corps:

> Thompson is one of the wonders really of the Age . . . by some strange good fortune has been so introduced to the Duke of Bavaria, Elector Palatine, one of the first Courts in Germany, as to be appointed his principal Aide-de-Camp and Adjutant General; has jumped across to England to get the King's leave to go into foreign service; has obtained it retaining his rank and pay in the British service, has been knighted as a testimony of the royal approbation and recommendation and Sir Benjamin Thompson is now preparing to figure at the Court of Manheim with one of the most splendid equipages in Europe.[29]

And the loyalist, Edward Winslow, who received this letter in Halifax, replied, "Well done, Sir Benjamin! The next news we hear will probably be that he has mounted a Balloon—taken his flight from Bavaria—and is chief engineer to an Aerial Queen."[30]

At the age of thirty two a Yankee, who as the great Cuvier remarked many years later in his eulogy at the French Institute, had "just emerged from the forests of the New World," entered the service of a reigning Prince who made him colonel of a cavalry regiment, major general, Privy Councillor, and gave him a palatial residence in Munich. He received the order of the White Eagle and of Saint Stanislaus, and was elevated to the dignity of a Count of the Holy Roman Empire, when he assumed the name of Rumford, which Concord, New Hampshire, where he had lived, had originally been called. In his duties he united the offices of a Court Chamberlain with those of Minister of Police and of War. He soon enjoyed the entire confidence of his new Master. Years later during the Revolutionary Wars, when the French, under Moreau, marched across Bavaria against the Austrians, the Elector fled to Saxony, turning over the full charge of his State to Count Rumford, who, with admitted spirit, succeeded in keeping both belligerents out of Munich.

At the Bavarian Court, Thompson discovered the opportunity to apply his cherished ideas of enlightened despotism. The former Salem shop lad had in him enough of the old World courtier to persuade the Elector to adopt these views, enough of the Eighteenth-century spirit to carry out social reforms in the name of philosophy and enough of the Yankee left in him to reduce all his philosophy to methods of practical ingenuity. Originally the Prince had merely asked him to introduce a new system of discipline and economy into the army. Thompson explained that it might appear extraordinary for a military man to undertake a work so foreign to his profession, but his aim had been to train a standing army which should do the least possible harm to the population and make soldiers out of citizens and citizens out of soldiers. This idea, somewhat of a platitude to-day, at that time appeared like a daring innovation. Thompson simplified military exercises, dropped obsolete usages, and gave the greatest attention to the neatness and cleanliness of barracks in order that the men might be made as comfortable as possible.[31] All this seems elementary, but in South Germany at the end of the eighteenth century the novelty appeared startling. The new minister established schools in every regiment, in which soldiers along with the children of the neighbourhood were taught to read and write and given copy-books provided for them out of the Elector's bounty. Characteristically, he remarks that the paper used in these served afterwards to make cartridges, so that nothing was wasted. Also he employed private soldiers as labourers for public works under their own officers, who acted as overseers, and while they toiled, military bands played for their diversion. He made the men cultivate vegetable gardens and introduced the then unknown potato into Bavaria. When soldiers left on furlough, they were given flower seeds, and before long the head of the army had the satisfaction of watching small gardens spring up in every part of the country. The least sentimental of men looked forward with pleasure to the time when no farmer's cottage would be without its flowers, and those who have travelled along Bavarian country roads and admired pots of yellow begonias adorning the windows of every peasant's dwelling may discover the origin of this taste in Thompson's love for flowers. In Munich, the splendid park known as the English Garden, which he laid out and in which stands his statue, is also his monument.

America had long ago become for Thompson the distant memory of an obscure past. England was half forgotten, and the military career which at first he coveted had now lost for him most of its attraction. Every day that passed made the Yankee feel less of a soldier and more of a social reformer who scientifically experimented with humanity. Thus, his handling of the beggars, who had long made the streets of Munich intolerable, was a measure of public welfare carried out in his benevolently autocratic manner. When he related how he had accomplished this, he explained sententiously that "to make vicious and abandoned people happy it has generally been supposed necessary first to make them *virtuous*. But why not reverse this order? Why not make them first *happy* and then virtuous?"[32] He described the procedure. After his preparations at Munich were complete, he had made use of the military to round up all the beggars. Then, accompanied by the Chief Magistrate, he went into the streets and told the first mendicant who asked him for alms that begging was henceforth forbidden and he would be severely punished if caught again. The city was in fact thoroughly cleaned, and after this not a beggar could be found in the streets. Those arrested were taken to the Town Hall, registered, and ordered to appear next day at the new workhouse which he had in readiness to receive them, where they were given a warm dinner, comfortable quarters and work to do.[33] Later, he had the satisfaction to find that the poor of Munich gave him a touching proof of their gratitude. When he lay ill, they went in solemn procession to the Cathedral to pray for his recovery, and with justifiable pride he records this tribute to "a private person! a stranger! a Protestant."

Under a benevolent despotism, Thompson's position was less anomalous than appears today. In Naples at this time, the Irishman, Acton, enjoyed a similar power and made use of it far less wisely. In an absolute State, where everything depends on the Prince's favour, the sudden rise to fortune of an unknown stranger cannot but lead to intrigue against him and a jealousy all the greater in proportion to his merits. The fact that Thompson's reforms were largely directed to improving the conditions of a feudal peasantry which had hardly emerged from serfdom meant a corresponding diminution in the privileges of the landowning nobility who surrounded the Elector. A foreign Protestant adventurer could not expect to meet with long-continued favour in an old conservative Catholic country.

Thompson passed nearly fifteen years in an influential position in Munich. Yet the intrigues around him and the knowledge that his situation was becoming increasingly precarious induced him at last, for the third time in his career to seek a suitable exit before disgrace had befallen him. The Elector of Bavaria, perhaps somewhat wearied by his chamberlain's masterful personality, perhaps to give satisfaction to the latter's enemies by his removal, and yet get rid courteously of the man who had served him so well, in 1798 appointed Thompson as his Minister to the Court of Saint James. This, however, was too much for George the Third, who flatly refused to receive, as the accredited envoy of a foreign prince whom he was subsidizing at this time, a British subject of American origin, formerly an Under-Secretary in his Government whom he himself had knighted, and who still drew pay as a retired colonel in the English army. All these circumstances, wrote the Foreign Secretary in declining to accept the man as Bavarian

Minister, made Count Rumford's appointment "peculiarly improper and objectionable."[34]

Thompson felt acutely the King's refusal. His military and political careers he understood were at an end and his scientific and humanitarian services were henceforth solely to occupy him. With Munich no longer holding out advantages he now thought of settling in America. As men grow in years they hark back to their early associations and in spite of Thompson's brilliant career, in his middle age he may have felt occasional pangs at the thought that he was only a rootless exile.

To his old friend, Colonel Loammi Baldwin, of Woburn, with whom as a boy he had trudged on foot to Harvard to attend Professor Winthrop's lectures on mechanics, and who since had served with distinction under Washington when Thompson fought on the British side, he wrote:

> You would hardly conceive the heartfelt satisfaction it would give me to pay a visit to my native country. Should I be kindly received? Are the remains of Party Spirit and political persecutions done away?[35]

This was written in 1793. Eighteen years before Thompson had fled, leaving his wife and child behind. The former was now dead and his daughter had since made her home with Colonel and Mrs. Baldwin at Woburn. The exile had attained high honours abroad, but how would his country regard a man who had been a refugee and had then taken arms against her? The confiscation papers made out in 1781, of Benjamin Thompson absentee, late of Woburn, published that he had "fled from his habitation to the enemies of the United States." Two years afterwards his fellow townsmen had voted to exclude and prevent the return of all absentees.[36] Yet the hatreds which followed the War of Independence had by this time largely subsided, and Baldwin wrote to say that he could freely return and would enjoy a hearty welcome from his old friends and citizens in general.[37]

A correspondence went on between the two men, for Thompson wrote to announce his then intention of visiting America, partly to prepare a "little quiet retreat" to which he could later retire to spend the evening of his life. He thought of purchasing from forty to a hundred acres of good land in some tranquil spot outside Cambridge, and proposed to reside there in the character of a German Count who had renounced all political activities and devoted himself solely to the pursuit of literature and science. Perhaps with a view to ingratiating himself, he made certain donations to the American Academy of Sciences, and was elected a corresponding member of the Massachusetts Historical Society. When he acknowledged this honour, he was careful to express the admiration he felt for his compatriots' moderation in success, and their prudence in the use of independence. He declared that "I have ever loved my native country, with the fondest affection,"[38] and averred that his greatest wish henceforth was to be useful to America, finishing this letter with an offer to present all his books on war to the projected military academy.[39]

Men who attain an eminence which is outside politics and entertain no desire for office find their past easily forgiven, and few in America thought any more about Thompson's early relations with General Gage in Boston, or that he had once encamped the Queen's Rangers in a Long Island cemetery. His reputation was now solidly established as a humanitarian philosopher occupied with the benefit of mankind and Americans took pride in his achievement. At this time John Adams who was President, wrote to his Secretary of War, McHenry, to say that for many years he had been attentive to Mr. Thompson's career and had formed an esteem for his "genius, talents, enterprise and benevolence" which would secure for him, in case of his return to his native country, a reception as kind as lay in his power, but he added, "You know the difficulties these gentlemen have who left the country as he did either to give or receive entire satisfaction."[40]

The Secretary of War, authorized by the President, offered the Bavarian Count his choice between a commission of lieutenant colonel and inspector of artillery, or to appoint him first superintendent of the proposed military school. Rufus King, American Minister in London and Thompson's personal friend, conveyed this offer to him, but it was wisely refused, with an expression of genuine pleasure at receiving so flattering a mark of esteem which showed better than anything else that the past had been forgotten. The British colonel on half-pay felt pleased to be invited to enter the service of the American Government, although Count Rumford, major general in Bavaria, and Chamberlain of the Elector, must have suspected that Benjamin Thompson would not be very happy as a lieutenant colonel in the United States army. The thought of going to America was, however, active in his mind in 1799 though whether for a visit or to settle was uncertain.[41]

Thompson now wrote to explain the reasons why he was obliged to delay his return. He was under obligations to the Bavarian Government, and had considerable work before him in connection with the new Royal Institution in London, which he then was helping to found and for which he remarked with some pride that he had enlisted the support of several ducal subscribers at fifty guineas apiece.[42] He was planning a similar institution for Munich and the Elector had assured him that he would appoint him to be the President. His own life was then so busy publishing his works that when a friend asked to call on him the only moment he could give was between seven and eight in the morning.

The *Political, Economical and Philosophical Essays* of Count Rumford appeared at the very end of the eighteenth century with special copies on wove paper for presentation to sovereigns in Germany.[43] Other copies were specially printed for the Royal Family in England, and a dozen more, to be bound in the best manner and contain his portrait, Thompson thought appropriate to take with him on the prospective journey to America.[44] Also, he had just bought a house in the Brompton Road in London, where his daughter would be able to lodge whenever she was in England. For suddenly he remembered that he had a daughter called Sally, whom he had not seen since she was a baby and who was already in her twenty-second year.

The philosopher arranged for his offspring to leave Woburn, where she had made her home with Mr. and Mrs. Baldwin ever since her mother's death, in order to meet him in London. He left Munich to greet her, and was delighted to find on their reunion that Sally was an "unaffected cheerful pleasing amiable good girl."

After the novelty of the first meeting between father and daughter had passed, the daily life together of two people each with marked personality who had been strangers for so long became a somewhat trying experience, even if the curious situation which developed in their common relations interested both. Sally's impression of her newly-discovered parent, which she imparted in letters to Mrs. Baldwin, is the more interesting of the two for Thompson had no confidant and his knowledge of feminine nature was never penetrating. During the years of her girlhood the daughter had formed a somewhat romantic idea of what her father was like from her mother's accounts of him, as well as from a small profile portrait which she had always treasured. In spite of the outrageous way he had acted toward his family, she felt proud of his reputation as a soldier and of his high military rank, and having expected, as she said, to find a dashing warrior with a martial glance, was just a little disappointed at the humdrum reality of the philosopher. She tried her best to overcome this feeling and to persuade herself that she not only ought to be proud of him, but also to love the dry egotist who happened to be her father. Silently and furtively observant, each tried to penetrate into the character of the other with an invisible fencing which in the circumstances was inevitable. Sally possessed quite as decided views as her father, but with a keen sense of humour in which he was completely lacking. She soon discovered for herself that the great man was "no enemy to a little deserved renown," and also that he was somewhat alarmed by her,[45] and deeply mortified at the inadequacy of her knowledge of social usages to which she was profoundly indifferent. She was immensely amused at the terrible embarrassment she caused him in London when, by mistake, she had curtsied to a housekeeper.

Thompson took his daughter back with him to Munich, where residence in a "really magnificent" palace impressed the girl, fresh from living in the simplicity of a small New England town. In Bavaria, Sally was at once made a Countess in her own right, and her father obtained the Elector's permission to have two thousand dollars a year, which was half his own pension, conferred upon his daughter for her life.

Thompson now tried to prepare her to assume the dignity of her new position. Every morning he ordered a hairdresser to arrange her *coiffure* for the Court ceremonies. She was persuaded by him to take up French, Italian, and music, of which her father was passionately fond, but for which she showed as little glimmer of talent as she did for languages. It was far easier for Thompson to govern Bavaria than to make of Sally a lady of the Elector's Court; and to his despair she showed neither taste nor aptitude for the life he had been so proud of. To the Count's dismay, the poor girl was little impressed by the grandeur of royal proximity and felt desperately homesick for life in Woburn. Her only solace was a mild flirtation carried on while out riding with his aide-de-camp; but as her father disapproved of this, without more ado he dispatched the young officer and his entire regiment to a far-away garrison.

The joy of finding a daughter had worn away with Thompson. The great man realized that she did not fit into his scheme of existence. Sally also understood that their lives had been too different to admit of close companionship. His daughter had noticed that he was not without having formed other attachments at the Bavarian Court and that his interests were far from being exclusively confined to science and affairs of state. At times her father would go off for weeks to tour the country with a lady whom she described as "a beloved Princess." Sally discovered also that little Sophy, the child of a Countess Baumgarten, was her own half-sister, though the chaste New England virgin never showed the least perturbation because of any knowledge she had gained of her father's gallantries. She dearly loved the child and always kept Sophy's picture with her to her dying day. In after years, during which she passed her time at Woburn playing billiards and whist, Sally adorned the rooms of her American home with portraits of all the different Munich Countesses whom she knew had once accorded their favours to her father. Such souvenirs and her own title of Countess, which she continued to use in Massachusetts, were in fact all that she retained of her experiences at the Court of Bavaria. At her death she left a large part of her own fortune to another later-born natural son of Thompson who lived to become a French officer of distinction.

Count Rumford was now a great international figure, and the young Czar Alexander of Russia, with a tender wish to benefit humanity after humanity had benefited him by his father's murder, invited the philosopher to visit St. Petersburg. But without roots anywhere and interested principally in whatever pursuit for the moment occupied him, Paris seemed to be the natural home for a man of Thompson's reputation, and in spite of the wars with England the retired British colonel went to live on the banks of the Seine. By this time he had quarrelled with many of his old associates at the Royal Institution, and one of these, the physician, Sir Charles Blagden, wrote regretfully to Countess Sally whom he once had wanted to marry, that her father's "residence at Paris this winter whilst we were threatened with an invasion is considered by everyone as very improper conduct and his numerous enemies do not fail to make the most of it."[46]

The London house was still kept open for his daughter and some occasional friends. When he expected any of these to stay, the Philosopher would write from afar to give the most precise directions to his housekeeper, of how best to administer to his guest's comfort; "one blanket on each bed with the white coverlid should be enough" were his instructions sent from abroad, and if the guests were to ask the house-keeper to have breakfast with them, he ordered her to thank them politely but to refuse.[47]

In Paris, Thompson had been elected a member of the Institute of France, and regularly attended the sessions, often seated beside General Bonaparte, who took a most active part in the technical discussions. He describes Napoleon listening with the utmost attention to arguments opposed to his own and after the discussion stating the problem so clearly that all difficulties seemed to be removed. For once even the philosopher was impressed. Before the Institute Thompson periodically reported his scientific experiments on heat and moisture. He wrote lengthy dissertations on the salubrity of warm rooms and how to construct proper fireplaces, and gave personal instruction to a firm of bricklayers in the system he had devised. He affirmed that with the waste of London smoke he would undertake to warm every house and to cook all the food used by its population.[48] The benefactor of humanity now busied himself with questions of fuel economy and proved conclusively that the coal necessary to cook a dinner for a thousand persons, provided it was burned in a heater of his own invention, ought not to cost more than nine cents. He gave the most elaborate directions how to build a kitchen for a foundling hospital in Dublin, but the workmen misunderstood him, and he was obliged to go to Ireland again and have this pulled down and rebuilt, all within two days.[49] He designed a dripping pan and devised the "Rumford Roaster" which simultaneously could roast and bake. The great edition of his *Philosophical Essays* appeared, embellished with engravings to illustrate all the cooking utensils which his inventive genius had designed. The preparation

L

of food became of consuming interest to the philosopher, who discovered in this a subject which seemed to his mind quite as important as agriculture to support a population. He wrote enthusiastically on such topics as the proper preparation of coffee and the nutritive quality of macaroni, and described a dinner given to 927 persons in Dublin which had cost under a penny a head and might have been served for even less.

Thompson now enjoyed an international fame as a professional benefactor of mankind, and busied himself in his cold statistical way with scientific plans of how to improve the condition of the poor by establishing innumerable soup kitchens in which there would be no waste. The bad meals served in these philanthropic establishments were popularly called "à la Rumford," but the philosopher felt delighted when he learned that at Geneva the City Fathers had engraved his portrait on the soup tickets.

Economy in food was suitable for the poor. The Count was himself the most fastidious and daintiest of eaters, who was shortly to find a further grievance against his new wife because of the "scraps" she had served him at table. For Thompson had embarked on the last and most amazing of his adventures, and the lady in question was Madame Lavoisier, a woman of remarkable personality and wealth, widow of the distinguished chemist who had perished on the guillotine during the French Revolution. Unhallowed companionship may either preclude matrimony or else lead to this. An old friend of Thompson, who wrote to enlighten his daughter about her father's *liaison* at first did not anticipate anything more binding for the couple. They had toured Switzerland together, seemingly without further complications, and few of his friends supposed that their intimacy would end in a legal ceremony.[50]

[146]

Just before the wedding took place in October, 1805, the Count at last wrote to apprise Sally of his intention. More accurate in his observations of science than of women he described the bride as being a creature of "goodness itself" and possessing the further merit of considerable wealth and receiving in her house all the first philosophers and eminent men of the age. Moreover, she was settling an income on him and would provide for Sally's future, though she did object to having a stepdaughter living under her roof. Somewhat oddly, she had insisted on retaining her first husband's name and calling herself Madame Lavoisier de Rumford. When the new Elector of Bavaria heard the news of the marriage he wrote to congratulate his Yankee Chamberlain, announced that he would increase his pension, and approved of Thompson settling in Paris, perhaps not altogether displeased at the idea of the latter leaving Munich for good.

The couple purchased a house with a large garden in the Rue d'Anjou, in the best residential quarter of Paris. The Count furnished it with his own money and now looked forward to passing the remainder of his life in agreeable ease, as a reward for many services he had rendered to mankind. Soon after the wedding he wrote with satisfaction to his daughter that their style of living was really magnificent. Madame Lavoisier de Rumford was well-known for maintaining a *salon* in the fashion of the eighteenth century, which, with that of Madame Récamier and Madame de Boigne, were almost the last left of their kind in Paris. The former Concord farmer was not a little proud that his wife should receive "all the great and wealthy such as the philosophers, members of the Institute, Ladies of celebrity, &c." Every Monday she gave dinner parties, though her husband found it somewhat less agreeable that he should be expected to live "on bits the rest of the week"; and every Thursday evening she offered tea and fruit to their guests. When Sally, reading her father's letters learned that few nights passed without their receiving company, she made a note on the margin "just what the Count hated"; but when she heard about the tea parties she jotted down her reflection that "these were enough to kill the poor Count."[51]

Not many months after the marriage, Thompson wrote to his daughter, who, from afar, had become his only confidant. "Between you and myself as a family secret, I am not at all sure that two certain persons were not wholly mistaken in their marriage as to each other's characters."[52] Perhaps he had been a better lover than a husband for daily the quarrels of the couple became more violent, and the lady who before marriage he had described as being "all goodness" after she became a wife, seemingly had been turned by matrimony into a "female dragon." He did not mind her entertainments except for having to live indefinitely off the scraps left by her eminent guests, but resented her inviting the people whom he most disliked, for the sole purpose, as he supposed, of annoying him. Even a philosopher could not stand this treatment. The climax came when the exasperated benefactor of humanity gave orders that no guest should be admitted for the next dinner. The Rumford house was situated in the centre of a walled garden, and, although the porter had been instructed by his master to allow no one in, in order to make certain that his orders would be obeyed, Thompson took away from him the keys. When at the dinner hour the company arrived before the barred entrance, Madame, on one side of the high garden wall, was obliged to explain to her guests, who were standing in the street, the sad reason why they had been locked out, but after these departed, she revenged herself by pouring boiling water over her husband's favourite flowers.

It was impossible for relations to continue in this way and a separation had become inevitable. "I only wish it well over," Thompson wrote to his daughter, though even so there was balm for his wound when he received a letter from the King of Bavaria that he ought to bear his misfortune like a man who had nothing to reproach himself with.[53] The Count now hoped soon to be free from that "unfeeling tyrannical woman—for lady I cannot call her,"[54] and they were separated not without some more unpleasantness over the settlements. Thompson departed into solitude while Madame Lavoisier de Rumford continued to give her Monday dinners, with her friend Madame de Bassanville, telling all her guests that Count Rumford, although a theoretical Liberal, was in practice, a domestic tyrant who had made life unbearable for his long suffering wife.

Thompson now retired to a house at Auteuil, near Paris, in which formerly had resided the philosopher Helvetius and the physician Cabanis. His means were just sufficient to live on but he was no longer well off, for, owing to the wars, he remained without his Bavarian pension and his English colonel's half-pay. He lived almost alone, seeing few friends, playing solitary billiards, indulging in scathing remarks about the French, and no longer attending any more the sessions of the Institute. He still continued to conduct his experiments on the propagation of heat, and incidentally propagated another infant who lived to meet a soldier's death in the trenches of Sebastopol.

Thompson died after a three-day fever, in 1814. His friend

the great Cuvier, Secretary of the Institute of France, delivered the funeral oration with all the kindly malevolence of an intimate, and with words which find in the French tongue the most exquisite vehicle of ironical expression. Cuvier dwelt in his eulogy on the high esteem in which the Count had been held by foreigner and Frenchman alike. Nothing would have been lacking to the perfect enjoyment of his life, "if the amenity of his manners had equalled his ardour in promoting public welfare." Always tendering services to his fellow men, Thompson had felt for them no real love. He was embittered against human nature and in his opinion, mankind was quite incapable of looking after its own happiness. The Government of China seemed to him to be the most perfect, because the Chinese were ruled by educated Mandarins who rose in office by virtue of their learning. His own ideal of a State was one which could be administered like a barracks or a poorhouse, declared Cuvier with an unkind thrust at the Count's reforms in Bavaria. The great naturalist explained in his oration how Thompson had relied on a rigid system for the exercise of his benevolence without understanding the difficulty of inducing men to act only like the "arms" of a body and he compared the latter's views of humanity to those of a plantation owner who possessed Negro slaves. Everything had to be done entirely by direction from above. The philosopher's own wants and pleasures were as precisely arranged as his experiments, but this system which had helped him to devote his energies to good works, did not make him agreeable in the society of his equals. And the great Cuvier, who had risen to fame by classifying the different orders of the animal world, in the climax of a eulogy over his dead friend, extolled as a human virtue the practice of a little more *abandon*.

PART TWO

Sufferers in a Cause—Loyalists and Refugees

CHAPTER FIVE

Governor Hutchinson's visit to London

I

THE tragedies of history oftener than not remain unrecorded unless they contain spectacular elements. More numerous is the tragic fate of men who have found their lives shattered through no delinquency of their own and whose suffering is caused because, like in the Greek drama, they are caught in a mesh of circumstances which they cannot control and from which they cannot escape. Many have gone down to the grave too proud to complain, unwilling to give vent to their feelings before those sudden and devastating reverses of fortune which seize their victims out of previous security, and send them unexpectedly as outcasts from their homes in reviled and impoverished exile.

The last royal governor of Massachusetts, Thomas Hutchinson was the victim of such a tragedy. Of outward incident there was never any in his career except once in Boston when he fled before a savage mob. His drama was acted entirely within the depths of his own soul for easy as was his pen and eloquent his talk, he was sparing in the New England way of outward sign of emotion. No one could possibly have foretold his fate. His life had always been patriarchal, his family relations exemplary, his tastes scholarly, his intercourse kindly and he felt tolerant even toward those whose opinions differed violently from his own. He was a lover of his country, the best

American historian of his time and the ablest financier in Massachusetts. With inherited wealth which he had considerably increased, his integrity and his ability in the many public offices which he occupied were admitted even by his enemies. His virtues stood out for general esteem and the fact that unlike most British officials in America he was born in the Colony, descended from the earliest Puritan Stock and was not a member of the Church of England had added to his early popularity.[1] Before the struggle with Great Britain began he was regarded as the most eminent New Englander of his time who enjoyed the affectionate admiration of most of his fellow citizens, and had been revered in Massachusetts, if the hyperbolic description of his arch enemy John Adams is to be believed, as "the greatest and best man in the world . . . a sort of apotheosis like that of Alexander and that of Caesar."[2]

Yet Thomas Hutchinson who in his ambition cared more for the esteem of his fellow citizens than for anything else in the world ended a long and distinguished public career, brokenhearted in exile, impoverished with his property confiscated and held up to the execration of his compatriots and regarded as a traitor by the country he loved.

The general admiration long entertained for Hutchinson had never quite descended to the masses in the Province. A quarter of a century earlier, he had rid the Massachusetts currency of a vast amount of paper money with its consequent hardship on the debtor class. Popular dislike of a man who for many years had been prominent in the public eye by his position and wealth had simmered under the surface until after the passage of the Stamp Act in 1765. Hutchinson, who was then Chief Justice, found himself wrongly accused of having favoured this measure, although he stated under oath that he had done all in his power to prevent its enforcement. His supposed support of the Act was however enough to cause his house in Boston to be sacked and gutted by a mob, which tore off the wainscot and hangings, split the doors to pieces, scattered priceless historical manuscripts which he had collected for thirty years, stole the plate and family pictures, laid flat the garden, and destroyed the very trees.[3]

Four years later, Hutchinson had been unwise enough to accept the Governorship of Massachusetts. Was he induced by love for power as his enemies alleged, or by a high sense of duty to take office under the Crown at a critical moment when he knew that acceptance would arouse the ire of many of his countrymen? His opponents charged him with acting solely from ambition and the wish to be on the winning side. Partisan feeling had run so high in the Colonies that men could discern only the vilest motives in the conduct of their adversaries, and refused to admit that the latter might also feel a solemn duty. Most of the merchants of standing, the magistrates, many of the clergy, and not a few of the smaller people, tradesmen and yeomen, in Massachusetts, had long looked up to Hutchinson as their leader. If in the years of bitter struggle before hostilities broke out he had suddenly withdrawn from public life merely because a responsible Crown appointment made him unpopular with the Whigs, many of his followers would have regarded this as a desertion and thought him to be unworthy of their trust. However bitterly he may later have regretted accepting the Governorship, he hardly could have acted otherwise. That he took office with open eyes stands to his credit and he justified himself with the belief that this was done for the real advantage of the men who were endeavouring to bring about his ruin.

Nor did Hutchinson's confidence in the superior power of

Great Britain contain anything discreditable. His own devotion
went whole-heartedly to Massachusetts, to New England, and
to America, but like all Tories and nearly all Whigs at this
time, he was convinced that the prosperity of his countrymen
was intimately bound up with their continuing to remain within
the British Empire, that "it would be the ruin of both the Kingdom and Colonies to separate them,"[4] and that in any struggle
the latter were certain to be worsted. It was his firm conviction
that conditions in America were not ripe for independence, that
they could not be ripe for another fifty years, that it was folly to
attempt to overthrow British rule and impossible for a revolt to
succeed. He had never been impressed by the Whig argument
that in a few years time the natural increase in the Colonies
would make America strong enough to throw off all subjection.[5]
His conviction on this subject was contained in a single sen-
tence which explains his policy: "As to us, I think it is not yet
in our power and it cannot be for our interest to attain to such a
separation." Governor Hutchinson, pilloried by his countrymen as an arch-loyalist sold to the Crown and slavishly carrying out the royal orders, had never indulged in any undue professions of loyalty or in more than his formal respect and duty
towards the King. He never felt himself to be an Englishman,
but always and solely an American who believed that the policy
he urged was also the one most beneficial to his own country.

The Governor's plan of administration had been to
recognize the ultimate authority of Parliament as being
supreme in America, but to grant the largest powers of self-
government to each colony and leave these to rule themselves
in all but strictly imperial affairs. This was the accepted policy
of most Tory leaders, who felt themselves no less American
because they were prepared to admit this slender degree of

control. The intense personal animosity against the Governor which he liked to attribute to his theory of administration came, however, from another cause. As leader of the Tories, Hutchinson was enough of a politician to employ the weapon of patronage somewhat ruthlessly. By the lure of office he had won over a number of Whigs to his side and "seduced," as John Adams called it, three of the latter's most intimate friends who had previously been as staunch patriots as Adams himself.[6] Resentment against Hutchinson needed only a spark and this was provided by the *Letters.* In 1773, the bitterest feeling was unscrupulously aroused against the Governor by the publication of certain letters which he had written to explain his political views to officials at the Ministry in London. The correspondence which fell into John Temple's hands was given by him to Benjamin Franklin, and sent to Boston, with the shrewdly imposed condition that it was not to be published and only to be privately circulated among a very few Whig leaders. Nothing could have contributed more effectively to their publicity than this provision of secrecy. Actually the letters contained little not already known regarding Hutchinson's opinions. But the mysterious and sensational circumstances under which they had been obtained, and the political consequences which attended their publication, allowed their contents to be grossly distorted to fit the demands of partisan rancour. The Governor henceforth suffered under the stigma of having attempted to betray his country's liberties. Sadly, he declared that he never had but one plan for the government of America, which was not to abandon the supremacy of Parliament, but his advocacy of this had lost him his popularity and brought upon him all his troubles.[7] Even to himself Hutchinson did not wish to admit that the real loss of his popularity came from being the King's representative and acting as the head of the Tory "machine" in Massachusetts. Although disapproving of many of the decrees of the British Ministry, it became his duty as agent of the Crown to enforce these. The Governor submitted often against his own better judgment, for he knew that the principal sufferers must be the loyal element in the colony, who would be the only ones with any scruples to disobey the royal acts. After the dumping of the tea into Boston Harbour had been followed by a still more foolish batch of punitive royal decrees, Hutchinson, dismayed by their absurd inappropriateness, determined to go to London, in order to try to obtain an alleviation of these measures with a view to effecting a settlement. As the Crown authority in Massachusetts had then passed to the military, he met with no difficulty in securing the King's permission for an extended leave and on June 1, 1774, the very day on which the British Government shut the port of Boston as a punishment for the destruction of the tea, the Governor sailed for England aboard the hundred-and-eighty-ton *Minerva*.

Perhaps to strengthen Hutchinson's hand in the representations which he proposed to make, as well as to offer a mark of their esteem, many Boston merchants presented the Governor on his departure with an address commending his "wise, zealous and faithful administration." The barristers of Massachusetts offered him a similar testimonial of his "inviolable attachment to the real interest of this your native country." The inhabitants of Salem and of Marblehead and many of his fellow townsmen at Milton, both Whig and Tory, also sent him addresses. When he acknowledged these, the Governor, with no inkling of the violence of the storm so soon to burst and that neither he nor his children would ever again see their beloved home, expressed the hope shortly to return and spend the evening of his life in peace and quiet among his neighbours. Even his well-wishers at Milton were soon obliged to retract their friendly words on his departure. Four months afterwards, at a town meeting held on the public green, the latter admitted their offence and humbly made amends by declaring that "Since the temper of the times is such that what we meant to please has eventually displeased our neighbours, we who desire to live in peace and good will with them are sorry for it."[8]

The Governor's son and his daughter Peggy, a lively young lady just out of her teens, had insisted on accompanying their father to England. Peggy was the only member of the family who left Boston with unfeigned delight, after having felt the strain of what she described as "running from a mob ever since the year sixty five but soon do I hope to be out of their reach."[9] Hutchinson himself departed with not a few misgivings regarding the utility of his mission, and, perhaps, greater fears than he was willing to admit even to the privacy of his *Diary*. He felt doubtful if he would be able to accomplish anything in London; and, if he were to fail, would not his position become far worse? In spite of long political experience he did not understand that events were fast outstripping anything he could do and was still trying to persuade himself that he was undertaking this journey as a kind of debt to his children at a time when all his personal inclinations would have led him into retirement. From ages immemorial a supposed preference for the quiet life has always been a foible of public men, which deceives only themselves. Hutchinson liked to think that he was making a real sacrifice, although not even his own daughter believed this. His fondness for political life in spite of the tribulations it had brought him amazed her, for with instinctive comprehension, she knew that the slightest excuse would have led him at any time to accept any mission.

The journey across the ocean passed without incident for the Hutchinsons, and the Governor's first visit in London was to Lord Dartmouth, who, before Lord George Germaine, was in charge of the American plantations. The Minister was an amiable, pious man, full of the most kindly intentions which he had little opportunity to carry out. In the cynical political atmosphere of that age, Dartmouth was generally regarded as boringly over-sanctimonious, and at a time when Massachusetts was ablaze with revolt he still took a marvellous interest in the state of New England piety and expressed hope that this had not worn off as in the Mother country, "where it was a reproach to a man to be a serious Christian."[10] The Hutchinsons, accustomed to conversational relaxations of this order, were delighted with the welcome they received in the intimacy of the Dartmouth home which reminded them of their own family life at Milton. Later on they met there many of the Minister's friends who felt similar preoccupations like the dissenter Countess of Huntingdon, with her particular sympathy for pious Americans. Even Peggy Hutchinson, usually somewhat critical, became enthusiastic whenever Lord Dartmouth's name was mentioned, called him the most amiable man she had ever met, and as the poor girl had little opportunity to penetrate into circles of less solemn virtue wrote to her sister-in-law that if he had not been married and not been a lord "I should be tempted to set my cap at him."[11]

Hardly had the Governor set foot in London before Lord Dartmouth took him to see the King who, contrary to custom, received him at once, graciously dismissing every apology offered by Hutchinson for his sober New England dress and for not being in a fit state to be presented. George the Third, so insistent on royal prerogatives, was in privacy entirely careless of etiqutte. The King was then most impatient to hear the latest news from Boston and amazed the Governor by the intimate knowledge he displayed of personal details which were unknown to Hutchinson, who had never heard, for instance, that John Hancock's notes were protested in the City. During an audience of two hours the Monarch asked innumerable questions, relevant and irrelevant, regarding the American leaders. The Governor admitted the personal integrity of his enemies and described Sam Adams as a kind of New England Wilkes. Incidentally, Hutchinson also took occasion to speak to the King about his beloved home at Milton and expatiate on the beautiful view from the top of the hill. The audience ended by George the Third assuring Hutchinson of the entire satisfaction he felt with the latter's administration and writing to Lord North that the late Governor of Massachusetts had owned to him that the Bill for shutting the Port of Boston was "the only wise and effectual method" for bringing the colonists to a speedy submission.[12] Hutchinson's *Diary* contains a lengthy account of the audience, but has nothing to say about this. Kings have a way of construing silence into assent and distorting the opinions of their subjects to confirm what they wish to hear. Convinced as the Governor was, that the Port Bill was a grave error and prepared to argue this with Lord North if given the opportunity, he would hardly have dared to tell his Sovereign at a first audience that his own most cherished measure was a terrible mistake. His silence on the subject, or possibly a very qualified assent, was interpreted by the King as signifying approval.

Years later, when John Adams was Envoy in London, he pettily collected some bits of gossip about courtiers laughing at Hutchinson at the Court Levee when he ransacked his pockets for letters to read to the bored King.[13] Real satisfaction by George the Third with the Governor's administration was shown, however, when he signed a warrant to continue Hutchinson's salary while in London, and offered him also a baronetcy, which was then the highest dignity conferred on colonials, but which the latter declined on the ground that his means were insufficient to provide also for his younger children. More likely the refusal was meant to prove to his fellow-citizens that he was personally disinterested and that the only reward he desired was to win their approval. The Governor wrote home about this time: "I hope to leave my bones where I found them and that before I part with them I shall convince my countrymen I have ever sincerely aimed at their true interest."[14]

Settled in London, in novel surroundings the Hutchinsons tried to keep up their New England ways, and sent home for cranberries and cheeses to offer to friends. The children carried on lively discussions among themselves as to whether Old England or New was the better country, Peggy Hutchinson always favouring her home. Her sister-in-law wrote to her from Milton, to draw a flattering picture of an imaginary young nobleman as a suitor for her hand, but the girl answered that she had met no one faintly resembling this portrait, and familiar with little else than the solemnities offered by Lord Dartmouth's pious friends still thought "New England was the only place for pretty fellows."[15]

Peggy was put in charge of the household and had persuaded the Governor to change his first London residence to better

PRINCES ERNEST, AUGUSTUS, ADOLPHUS, AND PRINCESSES
AUGUSTA, ELIZABETH AND MARY

From a painting by Benjamin West

lodgings in Bond Street[16] where later Nelson lived, and send to America for his old silver coffee pot to exchange for a new one in a more fashionable style. Like her father, Peggy possessed powers of observation with a sense of humour which he lacked, and, if anything, a still more passionate love for her native land. Her sprightly letters to her sister-in-law, who had remained at Milton, enliven the somewhat dreary record of their exile. The girl refrains from making political comments enough to allow one to suspect that her sympathies were not unreservedly on the Tory side, though loyalty made her wish for her father's success. He felt proud of her and she accompanied the Governor on occasions when he attended the Court, though complaining that the strain of being presented was next to that of getting married. She had enough vanity not to relish being thought provincial and learned to her delight, that the Queen had found her "genteel" and looking like a woman of fashion.[17] After the Court ceremony, Peggy, with American curiosity wishing to see everything, insisted on going into the royal nursery, where she kissed "the little pudsey hands" of baby Prince Ernest, and watched with unmeasured amusement dukes and duchesses making their compliments to the eight-year-old Princess Royal who responded "very prettily."

Governor Hutchinson had gone to England with a definite goal before him. When he arrived in London, he was regarded as being, after Franklin, the most eminent American of his time and, unlike Franklin, Englishmen knew him to be a loyal servant of the Crown. The Governor therefore began his self-imposed mission of reconciliation with a recognized position which was useful to his purpose to see as many influential people as possible. Naturally inclined to social intercourse, he talked in London as he had talked at home, when he tried to win men over to his point of view. To his friend James Murray he wrote, "I have advantages here beyond most of the Americans as I have a very extensive acquaintance with the best people."[18] Welcome everywhere, invitations were showered upon him and his opinions regarding the difficulties in Massachusetts were attentively listened to. Public affairs are often best prepared by personal intercourse, and private relations affect the success of measures more than is suspected. The Governor persuaded himself that by his social connections he was helping to accomplish a task the nature of which he had not yet understood was impossible. His real failure was in his mistaken estimate of the change which had come over popular feeling in America.

For many years the Governor had been the foremost man in New England whose word within the Tory Party carried a weight of its own. Arriving in London, he found himself treated like a distinguished colonial official, with friendliness and great courtesy, but none the less as a Crown servant whose opinions, even when heard with respect, could hardly be supposed to change the views of the Cabinet. Hutchinson tacitly accepted this inferiority. He stood no longer on his own soil and, as he had always maintained the King's authority in Boston, it was difficult for him, when near the royal presence to question any of the royal decisions. Unconsciously he found himself relegated to membership in that wide circle which exists in London more, perhaps, than in any other capital, and is seemingly close and yet very remote from the real centre of power. The most eminent of Provincial Governors was welcome everywhere as a guest, but he freely admitted to himself his own small importance within that greater world of London.

Perhaps a certain courtier's instinct, a reluctance to displease and too great deference to those in authority, tended to obscure Hutchinson's better judgment and induced him unconsciously to misrepresent the actual conditions in Massachusetts. It requires courage to say unpleasant things and courage to see them. The Governor's greatest error lay in minimizing the danger of revolt and in not pointing out, what many Englishmen foresaw, that armed insurrection would be the consequence of following the King's policy. It was the further misfortune of American Tories that their criticism was so restrained as to produce little effect. They felt obliged out of loyalty to remain submissive before the Crown's decisions even when they understood how mistaken these might be. For it seemed ungrateful to criticize measures which the Government in its wisdom was taking against Whig enemies. Hutchinson also underestimated and disparaged the colonists' power of resistance even when he advocated sending sufficient force to crush this. Later, when British reverses showed how glaring were the Governor's errors, the proof did not affect his friendly personal relations. Long after all curiosity to hear his opinions had ceased, he was always treated as a friend in several great houses.

The Governor, with Tory misreading of the situation, could think of no other way to obtain milder treatment for Massachusetts than through an act of royal grace. Lord Dartmouth had suggested a plan to him by which the principal citizens of Boston were to address a petition to the King declaring their desire always to remain part of the Empire, yet to enjoy their liberties as British subjects. Relief might be obtained in this way as a gracious concession from the Throne, for it was notorious that the Cabinet was determined to enforce its decrees and there could no longer be any room for half-measures. The legal luminaries of the Crown, Lord Chancellor Bathurst, and the Chief Justice, Lord Mansfield, had both assured Hutchinson that the Government would never recede from its position to maintain at any cost the supremacy of Parliament.

By this time the Governor was convinced that unless British authority was prepared to assert itself with more vigour in Massachusetts the anarchy must increase. He counselled dispatching at once sufficient military forces to make the King's government possible and resistance impossible, for he was still persuaded that with this display there would be no open rebellion. To recommend the use of soldiers against his countrymen was logical and from the standpoint of the British Crown no other policy short of submitting to the Whig demands was any longer feasible, but as soon as this advice became known in America it added more fuel to the hatred against Hutchinson.

Manifestly the situation in Boston had become too dangerous to be protracted and the Governor felt at a loss to understand Lord North's unconcern at what was taking place, or "at least he appears unconcerned." This seeming apathy to the crisis in the Colonies was an attitude which the Prime Minister usually assumed to all save a few intimates. Lord Hillsborough, after having called to see him to discuss American affairs, left indignant, and told Hutchinson that Lord North would only talk to him about the gossip of Almack's and the Pantheon. Lord Suffolk, who was the Prime Minister's own colleague in the Cabinet, bitterly complained about his "inattentions and rude behaviour."[19] Lord North's enemies attributed this attitude of indifference to his horror of public business and to the fact that he was kept from resigning by love of money and until all his numerous connections had been provided for with offices.[20] They did him grave injustice. We now know from George the

Third's letters that Lord North wished repeatedly to resign, deeply concerned with what went on in the Colonies, and disapproving of the King's measures, which a feeling of loyalty and obligation made him carry out. But he hid his real feelings from nearly everyone and encouraged a false impression of apathy on his part under a very British surface of seemingly sceptical detachment which no American politician has ever been able either to understand or to condone. Doubtless Lord North felt little personal sympathy for Lord Hillsborough's former hectoring policy toward the Colonies or for Hutchinson's too ready subservience to his own ministerial orders, and as he blamed both men for many of the disturbances which had occurred in Massachusetts, he did not trouble to enlighten either as to what his real opinions were. By a strange paradox, the King's principal Minister and the King's representative in Massachusetts, each concealing his real thoughts from the other, unknown to each other, were in virtual agreement as to the utter unwisdom of the policy it had been their duty to enforce. The one kept silent out of loyalty to the King, the other out of deference and Tory loyalty. The question, however, was now no longer one of desisting from a mistaken policy, but concerned the maintenance of British authority in America, and Lord North declared to the Governor, the first time he saw him, that sooner or later order would be restored in the Colonies and meanwhile they were hurting only themselves.[21]

After the Continental Congress in Philadelphia had passed the boycott measures, the Prime Minister remarked to Hutchinson that, if the Colonies refused to trade with Great Britain, Great Britain would take care that they should trade nowhere else.[22] The Governor went away unconvinced by this remark, carrying with him a most unfavourable impression about Lord

North's seeming indifference. How could Hutchinson guess the truth or that the Prime Minister was personally opposed to the very measures which a misplaced deference to his Sovereign caused him to apply.

In other quarters the Governor now tried to pursue his self-appointed task of seeking a reconciliation which he hoped might be based on some concessions from the Cabinet. He endeavoured to persuade the Attorney General to have the duty on tea removed, but was sharply answered that this was impossible, as no one would any longer believe that the Crown was in earnest. An obstinate King who had blundered into shutting the Port of Boston was in fact afraid to rescind his own order lest this look like weakness. At last even Hutchinson had understood that it was beyond his power to dissuade the Government from its mad purpose and centred his efforts on attempting to prevent further humiliation from being imposed on the colony. Fallen between two stools, the Governor had failed to remove a single one of the grievances, yet he still went his daily round visiting high officials, peers, and merchants, and persuaded himself, though only for a brief moment, that he was succeeding. He was taking little account of the rapid change occurring in Massachusetts. A man who has grown old in the public service finds it hard to estimate the strength of sudden new forces and Hutchinson was completely out of touch with popular opinion in his own State.

Every ship brought more distressing news of the growing spirit of resistance in the Colonies and left reconciliation always more difficult to obtain. But it was impossible for any government to abandon measures, wise or unwise, in the face of threats, and Hutchinson, with every wish to stand half-way between London and Boston, was more and more impressed by the ideas he listened to in government circles. He now felt it had become his solemn duty to acquaint his people with the true state of British opinion and wrote home that all parties were united in disapproving of the open denial of Parliamentary authority in Massachusetts. Chatham, and even Burke, he explained had condemned the excesses in the Colony and this unanimity made the Crown very strong. None the less the Cabinet earnestly wished to see America at peace and was disposed to indulge the colonists on every point so long as they remained a part of the British Empire.[23] Writing to friends in Boston he tried to persuade these that, instead of English Ministers seeking to deprive Americans of their liberty in order to introduce despotism, which people at home believed, he saw an administration prepared to concede every claim consistent with union to the Kingdom and striving solely to prevent a separation.

Like other public men who talk only to those who agree with them, the Governor had been led astray by hearing the echo of his own words. English opinion at this time, although violent enough among the Tories in and out of Parliament, was far from being so unanimous as Hutchinson at first supposed, and there were circles high and low into which he never penetrated who held very different ideas from those of the Crown. Almost to a man the dissenters sympathized with the colonists, as did the great Whig Dukes, Grafton, Rutland, and Richmond, although love for America was also hatred of the Government. The Corporation of London openly favoured the colonists because of English trade, and even Hutchinson was compelled to realize at last that, if the revolt was to be suppressed, "I believe a check must be given to the abetters of it in the Kingdom."[24]

During the years of his exile, and particularly after Lord Dartmouth had withdrawn from the Government, Hutchinson was to see a great deal of Lord Hardwicke, an able and enlightened politician who, unwilling to accept a Ministerial position, was none the less in the full confidence of the Tory Party whose leaders often held their meetings at his house. Hardwicke was keenly interested in American affairs and had personally opposed taxing the Colonies, foreseeing the consequences.[25] Except for possessing greater foresight, his political views were not unlike those of Hutchinson who attached himself to his person and regarded him as a kind of chief to whom he unbosomed his opinions with a frankness which, even a century afterwards, his great grandson, when publishing his *Diary and Letters*, found it discreet to omit.

The Governor after misrepresenting the benevolent intentions of the British Cabinet to his friends in Boston, was misrepresenting America to the British Cabinet. When the news of the resolutions of the Continental Congress reached London, Hutchinson insisted that these had been passed only because the American leaders were convinced that Great Britain would be intimidated and must submit to all their demands.[26] Three weeks later he wrote: "It is certain an enthusiastic spirit spreads through the Province. I cannot yet think they will either attack the King's troops or stand against them."[27]

Unconsciously, Hutchinson was acting as a most dangerous firebrand for he was now disparaging his own compatriots and urging the British Government to resort to force. Early in January, 1775, he described the training of the militia which at

that time was going on with immense enthusiasm in all the
Colonies:

> Some of my friends speak with great contempt of all their
> doings and say that upon the appearance of a sufficient force
> the greatest heroes among them will skulk . . . one sensible
> gentleman writes me that the true reason why the people go
> to such lengths without terror is because never anything which
> has been threatened from England has been executed and
> therefore they rely upon it that no other thing ever will be.[28]

Shortly before this, M. Garnier, the French Chargé d'Affaires
in London, who was following the American situation with
the keenest interest, had called on the Governor to ask
for news, and with polite hypocrisy profess hope for a
reconciliation, and express the wish that there might be no
hostilities. But by November of 1774, even Lord North understood that makeshifts were no longer of use and that the
province was in actual rebellion and had to be subdued. He told
Hutchinson that Hessians and Hanoverians were to be employed for this purpose if necessary, although he did not think
that this would be the case.[29]

The Governor, after having long tried to delude himself,
suffered acutely when he understood finally that a conflict was
imminent. Sadly he noted that his pen and his books, which
before used to afford him so much pleasure, had become only a
burden. Night and day his thoughts were a thousand leagues
away in New England. Could nothing be done to save his
beloved home from the destruction which he foresaw as inevitable? Lord Dartmouth's brother-in-law, Mr. Keene, had
remarked to him that he would wish Americans to be allowed to
go on in their mad way until every Briton would be ready to

pronounce them rebels. The Governor learned with amazement that so many influential Englishmen expressed themselves as willing to break off all connection with the Colonies were it not for the fear that these might fall to France and Spain. From his loyalist standpoint, British inertia meant disaster to his own American Tories, and Hutchinson argued in London that, if England continued any longer to appear indifferent, everyone in the Colonies would end by joining the movement and even the supporters of the Government in America must give in. He pleaded for, and yet dreaded the dispatch of British troops to Boston.

One night, while Hutchinson was dining at the Lord Chancellor's when the Attorney General also was a guest, a discussion arose between the two lawyers as to the measures which ought to be taken in America. The Governor was still unwilling to admit that things were so bad as they seemed. He remarked that, in 1745, no one ever maintained that Scotland had rebelled, and the most that could be said now was that a rebellion had broken out in Massachusetts Bay. After urging the use of force the very idea became abhorrent as soon as he understood that soldiers were going to fight against his own people, for the New Englander inside him was already fighting the Crown official. The Lord Chancellor blamed General Gage for not employing the army to suppress the riots, and for not putting a stop to military drill at Faneuil Hall, whereupon Hutchinson stumped him by asking if the fact that persons met in London for manual exercises could be regarded as an offence. Not long after, Judge Auchmuty, whose staunch Tory opinions were shortly to drive him into exile, wrote to the Governor from Boston to say that General Gage's conduct had met with universal approval.[30]

At the eleventh hour Hutchinson was still trying to find excuses for Massachusetts, and leaned to the opposite side. He argued that the colonists ought not to be condemned because of the disorders, and that under similar conditions the English would behave in quite as unruly a way. He condoned those "Mandamus Councillors" living in the country districts who for safety's sake had resigned their commissions, and he bore no ill-will to his neighbours at home even after these had joined the revolutionary movement. Tolerant towards his enemies he wrote: "I know the nature of the contagion. It is more easy to keep the small-pox from spreading when the whole air is infected."[31] He tried to persuade himself that he bore malice to none, for his great ambition was to live and die among his own countrymen and recover their esteem. The painful feeling that he had accomplished nothing of all he had set out to do made absence seem to him the severest of punishments. He longed to be back in Milton, yearning more than ever for the peace of his own home and the society of his neighbours. In the great world of London he felt himself only an exile from Massachusetts who preferred a humble cottage on Milton Hill to the palace at Richmond.[32] When he wrote to his brother it was to say that New England was written in his heart in as strong characters as Calais was upon Queen Mary's.[33]

The military preparations which were beginning to be made in earnest to suppress the revolt filled Hutchinson with increasing dismay. General Howe, who was on the point of sailing, came to have breakfast with him and talked lengthily about American affairs. To the Governor it seemed madness for the colonists to resist, and he only hoped that there would be enough reason left in time to understand this folly. Pining to go back, he wrote that if he could be of any service he was prepared to return either as governor or, should popular feeling against him still be so great, then in a private capacity and the more obscure the better.[34] The politician spoke these words, for in the intimacy of his heart he must have understood how impossible this was.

With many of his Tory friends at home, Hutchinson long ago had convinced himself that if only sufficient force were sent "the courage of our people will soon abate and in a short time be totally extinguished,"[35] but he was now obliged to admit to Lord Hardwicke that the latter's fears of resistance were only too well grounded.[36] After the news of Lexington he wrote sadly, "America is now in such a state as I imagined that one time or another it would be but I did not expect to live to see it."[37] Without one word of comment he noted only in his *Diary* on June 10th, 1775, that a collection had been made in London for the widows and orphans of "the brave Americans inhumanly murdered by the king's troops because they preferred death to slavery."[38]

Self-deception was no longer possible, after the storm had burst. Dr. Peter Oliver, the Chief Justice's son, and a connection of the Governor by marriage, soon to become himself a refugee, wrote to his kinsman in London that there was no mistaking the temper of the Colonies and, from Florida to Halifax, they were determined to resist England. "I am in no doubt you will be able to conquer America at last but a horrid bloody scene will be opened here as never was in New England before."[39]

About this time Hutchinson, at the house of Sir Sampson Gideon, the son of the well-known Jewish financier, whom he had known through the latter's connection by marriage with General Gage, had been interested in meeting

in "a large company of nobility and gentry," the famous
Corsican leader, Paoli. The exile observed to the Governor that the Americans had begun their struggle half a
century too soon and thereby put themselves back from fifty
to a hundred years, but that in another century they would
certainly become a great empire. Three years later, when
Hutchinson had ceased to hope, they met again at court and
the Queen talked to both. The thought came to the Governor
that unconsciously she connected in her mind two men who
were now exiles, one for rebellion and the other, as he sadly
reflected, for refusing to rebel against his Sovereign, "yet
perhaps neither of them culpable."[40]

In 1775, Hutchinson was still confident of British success,
though persuaded that his advice to send greater strength, if
taken in time, would have prevented an open revolt. Long
before the patriot leaders he had understood that there was no
more any alternative between forcibly suppressing the
rebellion and leaving the Colonies to their complete independence.[41] The Governor had always regarded the patriot professions of loyalty to the King as insincere. Nine months before
the Declaration of Independence, when hardly anyone in
America as yet thought of a final rupture, Hutchinson had
foreseen that the Colonies were determined to continue till
England was tired out and willing to separate. Only by strong
measures could this be prevented; but whereas the year before
ten thousand soldiers would have been enough, thirty
thousand were now needed.[42] He no longer expected to see
America reduced unless England exerted herself with far
more vigour, and the news of Bunker Hill, reported in London
as a great success, failed to elate him, for he wrote, dejectedly,
"A few such victories would ruin us."[43] When Lord Hardwicke

expressed surprise at the skill displayed by the colonists in making their entrenchments, Hutchinson replied, "I have had this opinion of Americans that, although we never rise to the top in any art or science, yet we attain to a mediocrity with as great rapidity as any people whatever."[44]

The hospitable Lord Hardwicke had invited the Governor and his daughter to spend a few days at his country seat, but Hutchinson declined on the ground that his anxiety was such as to make him fit only to remain in his own house. He was worried over his children whom he had left behind and also greatly concerned about his property. In June, 1775, came the news that his home at Milton had been seized. After the Boston house had been gutted by the mob ten years before, Hutchinson had moved all remaining belongings to his country place which was now also in the hands of his enemies,[45] who once more were to make an unscrupulous use of his official papers. From Medfield, near Boston, the Reverend Charles Chauncey wrote shortly after this to Dr. Richard Price, the friend of Franklin, in London, to relate that Hutchinson had been "so infatuated" as to leave in his house at Milton a trunkful of correspondence which, by a remarkable Providence, had fallen into the hands of the Provincial Congress. These letters were being printed in the newspapers and shed such a light on "the perfidy, treachery and villainy of the man that his once best friends now give him up as a traitor to his country."[46]

This seizure lay heavy on the Governor, for his papers of the most private nature were maliciously exposed to the misrepresentations of his enemies.[47] In the heat of civil strife any loyalist argument spelled treason to the patriots and the fury of partisan hatred now made possible the expropriations of

Tory property. There is enough that is noble in the Revolution
to make it unseemly to associate together the heroes of Valley
Forge and the soldiers who trudged barefoot behind Greene
through the Carolinas, with the profiteers who stayed in their
houses to grow rich by spoiling their compatriots. The confiscation of loyalist property is not a chapter in the War for
our Independence of which Americans can feel proud.
Revolutionary legislatures, it is true, followed unconsciously
the example of Henry the Eighth, who found support for the
Reformation by handing over monastic property to greedy
lawyers. But the seizure of Tory estates meant the spoliation
also of many whose only crime was loyalty to the crown,
usually for the enrichment of patrioteers able to buy these at
a greatly reduced value. When the Revolution broke out,
Governor Hutchinson had probably been the wealthiest man
in New England. Four years later, he was reduced almost to
penury by the precipitate passage of the Act of 1779, "to confiscate the estates of certain notorious conspirators against the
Government and liberties of the late Province." This measure,
introduced on the ground that the sale of these estates would
defray the cost of the War for a year, had been approved with
an unseemly haste.[48] Hutchinson's first intimation of his own
impoverishment came only when he read in a Boston paper
the advertisement of sale of all the property that he possessed
in America. In his *Diary* on August 16, 1779, he noted only,
"I hope the ingratitude as well as the extravagant cruelty of
this Act will hereafter appear for the benefit of my posterity."
His estate was sold for £98,121 in the then depreciated
currency, probably far below its real value. Even the family
sepulchre was not to be respected by the new purchaser. The
bones of his ancestors, who for generations had been

prominent in the history of the Colony, were dispersed and the name of the new owner was carved upon the tomb.[49]

For some time a feeling of bitterness against his countrymen had taken root in the old Governor's heart. At first the depth of this rancour surprised his daughter when she heard her father express resentment, in the privacy of his family. Soon he talked openly, no longer caring to restrain his feelings. He welcomed the efforts which British diplomacy was then making at St. Petersburg to induce the Empress Catherine to hire out Russian mercenaries for service against the Colonists.[50] When he heard that Indians had attacked a small party of Americans, killed their leader Captain Parker, and sent his head to Montreal, he hoped for good consequences from this outrage. Still more incredibly he was pleased when learning about attacks by the savages on the settlers, he wrote to Lord Hardwicke on September 26, 1776:

> Ten years ago I should have felt for the poor inhabitants of Virginia if I had heard that the Creeks and Cherokee Indians had fallen upon them, but I have lost those feelings now and rather was pleased to read the account. I hope your Lordship will think me excusable. Those inhabitants contribute greatly to the distress brought on me and mine and 100,000 more, and I see no way of redress but by bringing distress on them and it seems to me indifferent whether it is brought on by white man or copper coloured.[51]

After General Carleton had sent away his Indian auxiliaries, who could not be kept from scalping, with the remark that he would sooner forgo their assistance than make war in so cruel a manner, Hutchinson wrote: "If he imagines that men capable of such an unprovoked rebellion can be conquered by laxity and kindness, I have no great opinion of his judgment."[52]

In all ages civil war has aroused violent passions, and the Governor felt a savage vindictiveness, which he did not conceal, towards the men who had crushed his friends, despoiled him of his possessions, and pilloried him as a traitor to his country. Suffering had driven the iron into his soul, and the former love for his countrymen and the ambition to win back their esteem now had turned into fierce hate. Every ship from America brought news of fresh persecutions of the loyalists. Peter Oliver, his son's brother-in-law, robbed of all his property and forced to flee from his home in Middleborough, cried out his hope that, after the damage had been made good, "hang all the Massachusetts rebels by dozens if you will."[53] Powerless, the Governor in London was eating his soul, in solitude with the bitterest hatred against the men who had destroyed his life-work.

In the early days of the War, loyalists in England had maintained their spirits by expecting the daily collapse of the Revolution. They heard with pleasure the report that Washington had died of camp fever and gloated over the rumours which reached them regarding the wretched condition of the American army. After the battle of Long Island, Lord Percy, forgetting his sympathy for the colonists and remembering only that he was a soldier, wrote to Hutchinson describing a bayonet charge, adding boastfully that the rebels would never again dare to withstand his men.[54] The Governor was convinced at this time that if Howe could possess himself of both New York and Philadelphia, the rest of the country would be unable to hold out for another year,[55] an opinion shared by not a few members of the Continental Congress, who feared they lacked the strength to continue the war unaided for any longer period without French assistance. During the terrible winter of suffering at Valley Forge, the refugees in London heard only rumours of dissatisfaction with Washington, and loyalist gossip reported him as spending his nights in gambling and dissipation.[56]

The disillusion only came after Burgoyne's surrender at Saratoga, which was followed by the alliance with France. An unknown "ungenteel" stranger had accosted Hutchinson one day in the park to tell him that America would never be subdued. The Governor had always foretold that, so long as Washington kept the field no Colony would give up the fight.[57] With new expectations of success, which their recent victory had given them, Hutchinson felt convinced that Franklin and Adams were determined to exclude Great Britain for ever from America.[58] He now wished to see Clinton's army strike in New England, whose Colonies had provided the mainstay of the Rebellion and as yet had felt nothing of the burdens of war. These States, on the contrary, had gained enormously by privateering, and he pointed out that many of their ships were manned by British seamen. To strengthen his argument he drew a picture of farming in New England carried on with the help of prisoners captured from Burgoyne's army who were employed at very low wages. After pointing out that this could only make the Revolution more popular, Hutchinson now declared that if a British force could lay waste their cornfields it would bring the war to an end. With a poor opinion of his fellow citizens, the Governor insisted that the New Englanders would never petition Congress to stop the struggle till they suffered more than they had gained.[59] The old puritan God of Vengeance was speaking. The dearest wish felt by a man who had once cared most in life for his country's praise was to see Massachusetts turned into a desert and for his compatriots to expiate their crimes in anguish.

Sadly Hutchinson admitted to himself that he looked in vain for the soldier to win victory which would make possible this dream of revenge. Nothing had proved a greater disappointment to him or to the other loyalists than the incapacity of the British command. The Governor expressed what was in everyone's mind when he clamoured for an Anson or a Hawke by sea, a Marlborough or a Wolfe by land. "Such Admirals and such Generals with half the force which has been employed the last two years would have put an end to the Rebellion."[60] During the summer of 1779, when the French and Spanish fleet rode off Plymouth and the danger of another Armada threatened England, he looked in vain for the temper which had formerly prevailed although this aspersion was hardly fair to the thousands who were then enrolling in the militia. Toward Britain's enemies, like many other Americans, Hutchinson felt himself also a Briton, and old as he was he yearned to serve.[61]

Long before this, the Governor had been sadly disillusioned by the incapacity of the Ministry. Hardly ever venturing to make any personal comment of his own, even in the privacy of his *Diary*, he repeated Lord Huntingdon's ironical description of a Cabinet meeting at which George the Third acted as his own Premier, assigning tasks to the other Ministers who, as soon as the King's back was turned, would spend an hour or two repeating scandal of how "Lord such-a-one keeps such a mistress, and Lady such-a-one has such a gallant," after which the Cabinet all dined together and late in the evening set their clerks to do the work.[62] For a man like Hutchinson it was heart-breaking to have to watch the wreck of all his life-work had stood for, ruined by the incompetence of the Government he had served. Nor could he understand Englishmen expressing pleasure at the defeat of the King's forces. On every side he witnessed dismay, destruction, and disaster. He did not dare to reveal his thoughts even to his own children and finished by recording events as if they were mere incidents in a chronicle of indifference.

Nothing is more depressing to the man whose life has been devoted to public affairs than the feeling that he is powerless. Unconsciously adding to the Governor's sadness was the fact that he was entirely unoccupied and had gently but firmly, been pushed aside. He was still invited to Court ceremonies and his salary, which was regularly paid, relieved him of material anxieties. But from the day that hostilities began, Hutchinson was no longer consulted. Accused in America of having misrepresented his countrymen, in England he was blamed, and with reason, for having failed to give warning of their intention to revolt. When Lord Hardwicke on one occasion asked to see him at a convenient hour, he replied with pathetic humour that there was nothing so like an old almanac as an old governor, and that his own time had now become of little consequence. It is rare that a man who has fallen from eminence ever regains complete satisfaction with life. Hutchinson's tragedy was concealed, though he tried to occupy himself in an effort to fill the many vacant hours. Always a welcome guest in several great houses, he remarked with some astonishment as did also his kinsman, the painter Copley, that he was treated with more respect and esteem in Old England than had ever been shown him in the

New. When the Governor called on the Archbishop of Canterbury at Lambeth, he was surprised to be received "like a person upon a level with him than one who is so much inferior."[63] When he stayed at Lord Hardwicke's country seat cf Wimpole, he noted that nothing could be more polite than his entertainment by that nobleman.

The description he has left of days passed in a great English country house contains a picture of the more intimate sides of ceremonial life in that age in which outward pomp often hid the emptiness beneath. The Governor, accustomed to the simpler but sharper New England intercourse with his neighbours, found the sameness of entertainment in an English nobleman's mansion monotonous, however magnificent the setting and dignified the tone. He noted in his *Diary*:

> The first appearance of my Lord and Lady is in the breakfast room at 10. Breakfast is over at 11. Everyone then does what they please till 3.30, when all meet at dinner. Between 5 and 6 the ladies withdraw the gentlemen go into the library, some chat others read. At 8 a call to one of the drawing rooms for tea or coffee, after that cards, conversation or reading. Exactly at 10 the sideboard is laid with a few light things if anyone is disposed to have supper, and exactly at 11 as many servants as there are gentlemen and ladies, come in with each of them, two wax candles and in procession we follow to the gallery at the head of the great staircase and file off to different rooms. . . . This is high life; but I would not have parted with my humble cottage at Milton for the sake of it.[64]

With no more pressing occupation than to look after the loyalist refugees, Hutchinson made a deliberate effort to distract his thoughts from events in America. He took interest in everything in England, sights, and people, observing, describing, and only rarely commenting, explaining his fondness for old castles on the ground that America had produced no work of art more than a hundred and fifty years old,[65] and taking pleasure as a scholar in Etruscan vases and mediæval manuscripts. The interest he found in manners, made him notice the new fashion to wear shabby clothes which caused some members of the nobility to be mistaken for domestics. At certain country houses he remarked what he called a "mean custom still kept up" of paying a shilling a pack for cards when these were brought in of an evening, and to the Bishop of London, who asked him what would be said in New England if a Bishop played cards, the Governor replied that the prejudice against these had largely worn off.

One evening, dining with the Chief Justice, Lord Mansfield, the Governor observed a black girl called Dido who was treated as a member of the Judge's family. The latter was heart and soul for Abolition, and mentioned a decision he had just given by which a slave could not be compelled by his master to go into a foreign country. Hutchinson at once took occasion to say that all Americans who had brought Negroes to England relinquished their property in them and paid them wages.[66] His own scathing comment after reading the Declaration of Independence was to ask how this could be reconciled with depriving one hundred thousand slaves of their right to liberty and the pursuit of happiness!

Occasional distractions might help to while away the time, but could not keep from him the knowledge that he was a ruined man. His life-work was destroyed, his party shattered, his friends exiled and he was reduced to living on royal bounty. Wealth, influence, ambition, all had turned to ashes, and he could see only devastation around him. Family unhappiness now added to the Governor's trials. His daughter Peggy, on the brink of consumption, could never get used to the English climate. At first she had complained that the weather in August was as cold as November in Massachusetts. With the progress of her illness, all her early gaiety had disappeared. In the summer of 1777, the Governor gave up his house in Bond Street, paying the rent in full and jotting down in his *Diary*: "Nothing can be more uncertain than my present state. My daughter continues to decline. What will be the state of America?" Private sorrow and political grief mingled with him in a common affliction. A month later, Peggy died in her twenty-third year. "A distressing day for me," is all that Hutchinson noted with the dry restraint which always characterized his outward expression. He was not unfeeling, but his cup of sadness long ago had overflowed. He rented another house in Sackville Street, attended the King's Levee, and within a month went to a dinner at the Duke of Grafton's.

On March 19, 1778, four weeks before the Peace Embassy sailed, on its futile errand, Hutchinson wrote down in his *Diary*: "Should not wonder if this afternoon the Americans were acknowledged Independent. . . . After all, I shall never see that there were just grounds for this revolt. I see that the ways of Providence are mysterious." Three days later, alluding to Israel Mauduit's famous pamphlet which favoured the recognition of American Independence, he remarked that never had there been such an instantaneous conversion of a whole kingdom, and about this time Gibbon the historian also noted that the vast majority in Parliament earnestly wished for peace.

The Governor failed to understand the crumbling of his world. It is the tragedy of history that the worthy are often crushed by the ruthlessness of events and their virtues add only to their misfortune. A less rigid character than Hutchinson might possibly, years before, have shaped himself to the situation in New England. As soon as the forces set in motion by the Revolution had swept over America, his elbowing had become inevitable. The inability to understand the change which had come over the minds of his countrymen, or to reconcile events with any sense of justice, was only human. He had remained a shattered wreck in a world of dissolving values when everything around him had altered, and he was left a broken man crushed by events which still seemed like a nightmare. When he looked back to recall that only a few years before he had owned one of the best houses in Boston, the pleasantest place at Milton, and one of the finest estates in Rhode Island, that he was free from debt and an affluent income allowed him to make handsome provision for each of his children, he failed to understand the reason for his punishment. He had become an impoverished exile with no longer a foot of land of his own, his personal fortune reduced to about seven thousand pounds, and depending on the bounty of a Government for a pension which, although enough for his simple needs, was none the less precarious. Even so he felt that he was more fortunate than relatives and friends and had cause to be thankful to Providence.

Without other occupation in London, Hutchinson passed his time revising, with an astonishing detachment, the last volume of his *History of Massachusetts* to the end of his own administration. Adversity and a deep religious feeling bowed him down into submission. He had given up the struggle as hopeless, and after he admitted defeat even his wrath had softened and his better nature came back. He learned with deep regret about the death in Boston of his old friend, the Reverend Dr. Eliot of Harvard. That evening Jonathan Sewall, the former Attorney General of Massachusetts, who had dined with him affirmed that Eliot had gone to hell because of his duplicity in first favouring the Government and later the American cause. But Hutchinson now grown more tolerant, by long suffering, explained how this had happened, and wrote in his *Diary*, "God forbid that he or I should have our infirmities so strictly marked against us."

The exiled Governor was no longer any more of the opinion that the war ought to be continued, and asked himself why the Crown should not withdraw its forces and leave the Americans to that independence which the Ministry seemed to expect (August 1, 1778). When he heard that in Rhode Island people abused him as much as ever, he sadly jotted down in his *Diary*, "This is my misfortune, as I wished for the esteem of none so much as my own countrymen."[67] His sons could still keep up the delusion that the British cause would triumph in the end, [68] but the Governor had lost all hope. His religion caused him to pray for a mind submissive to the divine will, for now he knew that he would never again return to America or lay down his bones in the land of his forefathers. A broken man with a heart which had no room for greater grief, he was reconciled to ending his days in England and had become incapable any longer of feeling further affliction. When his youngest son Billy died of consumption, there is no trace of human sorrow in the way he records this loss. His father noted only in his *Diary* that Billy was born at Milton, where his mother, "Of all earthly objects ever known the dearest," had retired to avoid the smallpox at Boston.

Charles James Fox, in a speech made in March, 1780, had expressed hope that the salaries of the Governors in the Colonies would cease to be paid, "and above all the pension to a late Governor, Mr. H., that firebrand and source of the American disputes." Hutchinson longed to answer this but he was too ill to remonstrate. A month later the *Diary* ends abruptly. In the midst of the Gordon Riots, the Governor, first asking for a fresh shirt in order to go clean to his Maker and then resigning his soul to God, died. Not inappropriately a surviving son who knew what his father's feelings were described his death as "melancholy to us and happy to the Governor."[69] He was buried alongside of his children, Peggy and Billy, in the cemetery of Croydon Church.

After his death, Samuel Curwen, the loyalist refugee, wrote to his friend William Pynchon at Salem to say that Bernard and Hutchinson, the two great objects of American hatred, were no more. Yet rancour did not cease at the grave. John Adams, when he heard the news in Paris, wrote to the President of Congress, and although speaking highly of Hutchinson's talents remarked that he had been led to his downfall by his inextinguishable ambition.[70]

After their father's death, Governor Hutchinson's two sons lost the position he had given them and engaged in business ventures with the little capital left as their inheritance. In spite of later solicitations from relatives in Boston, who wrote that they would be "received with open arms," if they went back to America,[71] they were never willing to return.

CHAPTER SIX

The Refugees in England

I

WHEN John Adams was a very old man he expressed the opinion that at the outbreak of the Revolution, one-third of the population in the Colonies was opposed to it,[1] which is probably more accurate than if he had claimed that two-thirds were in its favour. The elimination of the influential Tory element, which formed this third, within the space of a very few years in spite of the wealth and consideration it enjoyed, particularly in the larger cities, is one of the most amazing chapters in American annals. The loyalists had outnumbered the Revolutionaries in New York, and probably equalled them in Pennsylvania and in several of the Southern States. Later, they are said to have contributed over fifty thousand soldiers to the British forces.[2] Yet they were at first out-manœuvred, and intimidated by the action of a politically skilful and daring minority, and finally so weakened by the exile of their leaders, that they ceased to exist and the great Tory party was completely effaced from the pages of American history.

The story of the loyalists lies outside our scope,[3] and only the experiences of a few refugees in England can be described. But the reasons are interesting which led so many Tory leaders to seek an asylum abroad where they could do nothing instead of remaining, as might be expected, in America.

Those who abandon their homes are often unjustly condemned. The evacuation of Boston by the British army, which brought about the first phase of the Tory migration, does not explain why men of character and standing in their community should have found it preferable to leave their belongings and go for the most part into permanent exile rather than remain among their own countrymen.

By a curious paradox the failure of the loyalists to unite for action had also been due to the handicap presented by their own party principles. American Whigs for years had enjoyed the immense advantage of being able to take their own decisions and retain the lead in their own hands, whereas their opponents, virtually without the right to assert views independent of the Government, or to carry out any policy of their own, had to look for protection, counsel, and patronage to the officers of the Crown, who depended in turn on the most ineffective Cabinet that ever ruled England. As it was impossible to be a Tory and yet to act independently of the Government, it may be said that an excess of loyalism contributed to the ruin of the British cause in the Colonies. A spirit of greater self-reliance on the part of the many Americans faithful to the King, more initiative by their leaders and more readiness, particularly in the Middle States, not to look merely for British aid, to effect a combative organization of their own, would have been far more serviceable to George the Third than the submissive obedience to Crown officials which most loyalists displayed. Actually the fault lay more with the English military authorities than with the loyalists, many of whom as they showed were eager to enlist but who were convinced that the British troops would be irresistible and that the revolution must speedily collapse. As soon as military operations began, it was inevitable for American Tories to become mere hangers-on to the King's forces and unable to survive except through the protection and assistance which the latter afforded.

A second cause which led to the exile of the loyalists, particularly those from New England, can be found in the violent personal animosity, noticed already in the case of Governor Hutchinson, which was felt by American leaders against many Tories and went much deeper than political differences. The bitterness aroused in the name of conflicting principles between men who on both sides still professed loyalty to the same king had been largely due to the lavish use made of official patronage for the most partisan purposes which had also led to the conversion to Toryism of many Whigs. Until George the Third began to apply measures of force, the principal weapon used by the British Cabinet in the Colonies had been the bribe of office. Trumbull's M'Fingal has satirized this official corruption in the lines:

> Behold the world shall stare at new setts
> Of home-made earls in Massachusetts,
> Admire arrayed in ducal tassels,
> Olivers, Hutchinsons and Vassals.

When John Adams described the decade after 1766 as the "period of corruption" which had followed an age of purer patriotism, he remarked that it would have been easy to draw up a list of prominent men who, after having been real or professed Americans, by hopes or fears, promises and threats, had become converted to the British cause[4]. Also, and particularly in Massachusetts, outstanding among the Whigs were young lawyers like John Adams and James Otis, who had been infuriated by seeing all the avenues of official preferment barred against them and royal patronage open only to those favoured ones who subscribed to the doctrines of the Crown.

John Adams never forgave three of his former intimates for their desertion to the King's side, although less unworthy motives than he attributed in the heat of partisanship may be found for certain of these belated Tory converts. Men who favour reforms often begin to hesitate as soon as they feel apprehensive about the ultimate goal. Moderates halt and run back when they fear that they are being led too far, and many American Whigs became Tories as soon as they became fearful that the end for which they had laboured would be separation and lead to an independence of which they earnestly disapproved. The motives of those who rallied to the Crown varied, of course, enormously with individuals, but the terror of civil war provided a powerful argument to deter many from proceeding any further in the American cause, and as soon as Great Britain showed her intention to fight, numbers of men of property in the Colonies at once announced their loyalty to the King.[5]

In the years before the Revolution, Americans might be Tories or Whigs, but those who were not politicians, had often been friends. A man like Governor Hutchinson, for instance, found pleasure in the cordial personal relations which, irrespective of party, he had enjoyed with his neighbours at Milton. As feeling rose higher, each side came more and more to regard the leaders of the other as creatures of the most exceptional infamy. In Tory eyes, Franklin and Sam Adams at the head of his "psalm singing myrmidons,"

were the most abandoned characters, and Chief Justice
Oliver of Massachusetts pilloried the "Sons of Liberty" for
being aided by a "set of Priests who are a disgrace to humanity
and would have been the opprobrium of even Mahometism."[6]
A man of high character like Judge Sewall, the former intimate friend of John Adams, regarded the "Patriots" as
criminals and denounced the "plotters" of the Revolution as
"the worst set of men that have ever lived."[7]

The frequent resort to violence was a means to command
the enthusiasm of the masses who found real pleasure in
persecuting the Tories, even when this led to outrages which
disgusted moderate opinion. Particularly in New England,
Tory baiting became a popular sport, and outside Boston
the loyalist minority in Massachusetts felt powerless to defend
itself. Life was made unbearable for the latter especially
in the rural districts of the Province, where the small Tory
minority, prominent but without defence, met with deliberate ill-treatment. Anyone suspected of sympathy for the
Crown had before him only the choice of humbly recanting
or of flight. Chief Justice Oliver found it too dangerous
to attend his brother's funeral in the country, which was
marked by the unseemly yelling of the mob, and he noted
in his Diary that "never did cannibals thirst stronger for
human blood."[8]

In the towns, certain popular leaders, in the name of
Liberty, deliberately appealed to the most brutal instincts
of the mob. In Boston there occurred instances of the most
savage treatment of Tory loyalists. Ann Hulton, daughter
of the British Commissioner of Customs, described how on
one of the coldest nights of winter the patriots took an old
shopkeeper named Malcolm, stripped him naked, covered

him with tar and feathers, dislocating his arm while tearing off his clothes, and dragged him in a cart, with thousands following, some of whom beat him with clubs, knocked him out of the cart and then put him back again, giving him several severe whippings in different parts of the town. This spectacle lasted for five hours, the poor fellow behaving with the greatest fortitude and refusing to curse the King. They brought him to the gallows, put a rope around his neck, and threatened to hang him. The doctor declared that he could not survive this ill-treatment, yet no magistrate dared to punish the offenders, although these were well-known.[9]

The persecution of the Tories may appear as a step necessary on the road to independence, although it began long before there was any question or desire for separation. Except for rooting out a socially esteemed but otherwise almost helpless minority in New England country districts and for the effect it produced on the indifferent, it is hard to see in what way this brutality contributed to the final victory. The only excuse possible is that in a great crisis ruthlessness may become a desirable tactic to accomplish a purpose. The processes used to-day in order to manufacture wholesale hatred were still imperfect in the eighteenth century, and a resort to violence, although it trained the masses to take concerted action, led also to disgraceful scenes and disregard of the law. Organized manifestations, however repugnant were the outrages which followed, provided none the less a popular appeal to the American cause at a time when its chances of success against Great Britain seemed most slender. The principal benefit that can, however, be claimed for these misdeeds lay in the fact that by a process which bordered on terrorism the vast majority of the indifferent who had been reluctant to take sides were induced into partisanship. In Massachusetts, the savage persecution of the loyalists provided a powerful argument to persuade many to rally to the American cause. A Salem clergyman, the Reverend Dr. Weekes, contrasted the neglect of the British for their Tory adherents with the methodical intimidation carried on by the Americans, who "hang the turbulent, imprison the dangerous, fine the wealthy. They allure the ambitious with the hopes of preferment and distribute estates to those who have lost their property for the sake of joining them, and by such means as these have strengthened their cause amazingly."[10]

Until a movement acquires its own impetus and volume, and is no longer obliged to rely on extraneous circumstances, it needs leaders who possess a rare degree of fervour and boldness, or a sense of duty which knows no fear, or vast ambition, or the wish for revenge aroused by a smarting humiliation under indignity, and often a blend of all these different causes, in order to make men ready to embark on an action by which they risk their lives and possessions for an ideal. When no compelling reason exists, and this rarely is the case in the beginning of a conflict except for a small minority, the inclination of the average individual in the presence of danger is to remain neutral, particularly against organized authority, unless obliged to take sides.

The task of leadership in the Colonies was the more formidable, and its achievement all the more miraculous, owing to the fact that a comparatively small minority, but one filled with a passionate enthusiasm for their cause, found before it the labour to break down the surfaces of native resistance and to leaven a mass, the majority of which, outside New England and Virginia, had hardly begun to feel any real fervour but did feel a great disinclination to be dragged into any serious struggle against the mother country. How reluctant citizens at first were in New York may be judged from an incident which occurred on June 25, 1775, after Bunker Hill had already been fought, when the news came of General Washington's impending visit to the city while on his way from Mount Vernon to take command of the army at Cambridge. The Royal Governor Tryon, who later achieved an unsavoury reputation by his raids against defenceless towns on Long Island Sound, had arrived in the harbour just back from England and it was uncertain which of the two men would be there first. The New York Provincial Congress felt considerably embarrassed as to how to act, for they had thrown off all allegiance to the Governor's authority, though still professing loyalty to his person, for, until the Revolution, the latter had been a popular official. In doubt they ordered a colonel so to dispose his militia as to receive "either the General or the Governor whoever should first arrive and wait on both as well as circumstances would allow." Fortunately, Washington, by coming first, saved the situation, though later Tryon received no less hearty a welcome.[11] Yet shortly after this occurrence, the rapid growth of Whig feeling in New York obliged the President of King's College, Dr. Myles Cooper, to escape from his patriotic persecutors, whom later he whimsically described as a band of drunken gentlemen disposed to show their love of liberty by cutting off his ears and slitting his nose, by climbing through a back window to seek refuge on a British man-of-war.

New England Tories, scattered in rural communities, too few to defend themselves and too frightened to stay in their homes, went for protection within the British lines to avoid consequences of which tar and feathers provided almost the least indignity. Judge Sewall related that after his house had become "a den of rebels, thieves and lice," and the pew of his Church had been turned into a pork tub, he thought it was time to go,[12] and his experience was typical of that of many others. In March, 1776, when the bombardment of Boston began and the presence of a large civilian population, many of whom had poured in from the country districts, had become an impediment to the military, General Howe gave public notice that those inhabitants who wished to leave would have transports provided for them. Some thousands embarked for Halifax, and the more favoured among these who possessed means of their own were allowed to proceed farther and seek asylum in England. This group, small to begin with, gradually increased. It derived its special significance from several circumstances which far outweighed the numerical importance of the refugees. It was estimated in 1776 that there were between two and three thousand Americans in Great Britain.[13] Many of these were already established in the country, some in trade, others were students of medicine and law. After hostilities began the first loyalists who went to England were nearly all from Massachusetts. Very few left Philadelphia until three years later, or New York and Charleston, where they were able to live under the protection of British garrisons, before the last years of the War.

Most of the Massachusetts refugees were former Crown officials or merchants of high standing in the community. They formed a group which had suffered the same persecution, passed through the same dangers, and was held together by the same opinions and interests. Many of the loyalists also had near relations on the patriot side. Thomas Flucker, banished from Massachusetts and his estate confiscated, was the father-in-law of General Knox, the American chief of artillery; Judge Sewall was the brother-in-law of John Hancock; Sir Egerton Leigh of South Carolina, was the son-in-law of Henry Laurens, President of the Congress. The brother of General Stark, the victor of Bennington, was a British colonel. Gouverneur Morris's brother was an English officer. There was hardly an American family not divided by the struggle. That the Revolution began as a civil war, which separated fathers from sons and divided families, is often forgotten in contemplating its ultimate result. Doubt as to where lay the first claim of loyalty troubled numbers of men, and family ties often added to the perplexity. Nothing caused Benjamin Franklin greater pain than the fact that his son, the last Royal Governor of New Jersey, should have taken up arms against him. The latter maintained that he had acted out of a sense of duty to his King, but the father of a natural son sharply reminded that son that natural duties preceded political ones.[14]

II

Was a man's duty to King or country? At first this question hardly arose for the Whigs long protested that George the Third had not more faithful subjects than they, and the Tories claimed to have as much solicitude for American welfare as the Whigs. But as soon as opinions had to be translated into acts and the support of one's country's cause meant resistance to one's sovereign, a divided loyalty perplexed many an honest conscience. Particularly in Massachusetts the example of John Hampden and of Cromwell was still living in men's minds and few as yet had noticed the real distinction between the two situations. During the Civil Wars in England, whichever side won left Englishmen victorious, but another century, another cause, and another continent had turned Englishmen into Americans. But even after Colonial Whigs had taken up arms many were loyal to the Crown and, like John Adams and Thomas Jefferson months after Bunker Hill, still felt that they preferred a dependence on Great Britain to independence.[15]

The sharp line of division drawn between loyalty to the King or loyalty to one's land was equally repugnant by its consequences to a third category of colonials. Colonel Richard Saltonstall, one of whose brothers was a strong Whig and the other as violent a Tory, was himself typical of the dilemma in which many other honourable men found themselves. Colonel Saltonstall enjoyed great personal popularity in Massachusetts, possessed an excellent military record, and had once calmed a patriot mob by mentioning the number of occasions in which he had risked his life for his country. He could have obtained a high command in the American army, but felt just as disinclined to bear arms against his King as against his fellow countrymen, and, unwilling to do either, went abroad never to return. Shortly before his death, he wrote to an American friend that his conscience was at ease, for he had found more satisfaction in leading a private life in England than if he had been second in command to Washington.

Isaac Wilkins, of New York, the brother-in-law of Gouverneur Morris, is another example of a man who left America because he would not oppose his Sovereign or draw the sword against his country. Those Americans, however, who were already in the King's Service when hostilities broke out, felt no such hesitation for pride in the profession of arms is nearly always sufficient to hold men to a soldier's loyalty. The two Coffin brothers fron Nantucket, one of whom won distinction as a British Admiral, and was later a warm friend of Nelson and Lady Hamilton, and the other became a British General, fought against their countrymen without a qualm, but after the War was over, showed themselves to be generous benefactors to the island of their birth.

The tragedy for many of the refugees in exile lay in the fact that in spite of loyalty to the Crown, they felt solely Americans and could never regard themselves as Englishmen. John Adams has described his own loathing, as a very young man, whenever he heard the use of such terms as "Colonies" and "Mother Country." The majority of American loyalists, forced to flee from their homes and seek refuge in England, although avoiding Adams's vehement language, were not far from sharing certain of his ideas and greatly resented the slurs attached to their supposedly lower status as colonials. Nothing is so galling to an American as to meet with any assumption of superiority, and a Tory refugee could write indignantly from London: "It piques my pride I confess to hear us called *Our Colonies, our plantations*, in such terms and with such airs as if our property and persons were absolutely theirs."[16] By a tragic paradox many loyalists who went into exile sympathized with the greater part of their opponents' aspirations and would have been happy to see a settlement which gave satisfaction to the Colonies. The commercial interests of Tory and Whig were identical, and both parties had chafed under the same restrictions, for the loyal merchants suffered even more from these hardships than "patriot" smugglers. The refugees certainly regarded themselves

as no less American because they favoured the authority
of the Crown or had fled from their country to escape persecution. None thought of themselves as Englishmen, nor did
a return to the land which many of their forefathers had left
a century and a half before to escape from persecution of
another kind possess for them any spiritual significance.
Their first loyalty was not to England, but to New England
and the impress on their hearts was altogether American.
To this day the rustic denizens of British shires still regard
settlers from neighbouring counties as foreigners. An intense
local patriotism animated the Massachusetts refugees even
when they fled from their fellow citizens. Going back to the
mother country, strangely enough, brought out few English
sentiments on the part of American Tories.

When Chief Justice Oliver of Massachusetts departed into
exile, he noted in his *Diary* that he had dropped "a filial tear
into the urn of our country" and bade adieu to shores on
which he never wished to tread again "till the greatest of
social blessings," an established British Government, should
once more exist.[17] The Chief Justice was frankly glad to
escape from what he called the "harpy claws" of rebellion,
but England meant nothing more to this high official
of the Crown than the fact that it paid him a salary
and that he still felt confidence in its ability to suppress a revolt
which had driven him from his home. Tory hatred of their
rebellious fellow citizens far exceeded in fact the bitterness
felt against these by Englishmen. The puzzled and hesitant
attitude which in the early stages of the Revolution
characterized the British authorities, both civil and military,
could also be attributed in part to their unwillingness to engage
too violently in a quarrel in the Colonies which seemed to

them also local and partisan. Alike in their attachments
and aversions, the loyalists were Americans and nothing
else. When Judge Oliver visited the Tower of London,
and noticed that the lions kept in the moat had lost some of
their alarming traits, the only thought he noted was to
ask himself "if the omnipotent American Congress were
caged in the same manner, would their diabolical ferocity
subside?"[18]

The feeling of loyalty to the Crown was balanced in
the minds of the refugees with a far greater consciousness
of the differences between themselves and the English.
The physical circumstances of the lives which they led while
in London were little calculated to bridge these over. The sudden
uprooting from their homes, the hurried and painful departure, the discomforts of exile, and the strangeness of novel
surroundings, intensified such distinctions. London for most
of them meant damp and friendless streets. Loyalists with
straitened means, residing in lodgings, without occupation,
pining for all they had left behind and eating their souls,
became aware by their residence in a strange city of how
intensely American they felt, for, contrary to the prevalent
idea, expatriation usually strengthens national feeling by
heightening its self-consciousness.

Later proscriptions, the confiscation of their estates, and
the sentences of death suspended over their heads, made the
exiles feel not one whit less American. Love for country
has little in common with self-interest, nor does it imply
taking even a favourable estimate of one's nationals. From
Dante to Roosevelt a succession of the greatest patriots
have abundantly vilified their fellow citzens. Real lovers of
their country feel under no obligation to conceal its faults.

the REFUGEES in ENGLAND

Those who believe that the virtues of one's compatriots ought only to be exalted, should think of that charming and brilliant Frenchwoman of the eighteenth century, who explained her like affection for two young nephews because one was clever and the other a fool.

To their dying day New England retained its stamp on these exiles from Massachusetts, although a second generation, brought up on British soil like the future Lord Lyndhurst, and no longer held together by common memories, experiences, and interests, could not have preserved their Americanism. In one of his recurring visits to the scattered loyalists, Governor Hutchinson related having met near Bath a man named Middlecot, whose grandfather some eighty years earlier had left America to settle on an estate which then belonged to the grandson. The latter had a number of New England relatives and the Governor who had known certain of these marvelled that he took no interest at all in them, unable to foresee that his own descendants would also sink into the obscurity of English middle-class life and lose all touch with America.

The gravest problem faced by many of the refugees was anxiety over the fate of their children. Judge Sewall declared that his only preoccupation was to see his two boys upon their legs, not caring three farthings where he ended his own life.[19] Pride induced him to say that he did not mind his exile, and found pleasure at Vauxhall and Ranelagh, seeing Garrick at the playhouse, and hearing the opera sung at Covent Garden. The painful memories of persecution which he had carried away were in the background of Sewall's enjoyment. The old Liberal-minded Tory relished the freedom of speech and tolerance of opinion he met with in England. If he should

again return to his home he knew that he would never be
allowed to express his mind freely in the "Land of liberty . . .
though in the land of slaves my chimney sweep can condemn
the conduct of the King's Ministers, members of Parliament,
and even of the King himself."[20] The free English life formed
an agreeable contrast to the bitter experiences which Sewall
had gone through and the treatment he might again anticipate
if ever he went back. After the Confiscation Act had been
passed in 1779, the Judge made up his mind that so long as
this law remained unrepealed he would not again set foot
in the United States even if they offered to return his property
as an inducement. He wrote to a friend :

> As to Massachusetts Bay I wish it well, but I wish
> never to see it again till I return at the Millennium . . .
> the harsh conduct of my countrymen has given me a dose
> I shall never get over—God mend them and bless them—
> but let me never be cursed with a residence among them
> again.[21]

The deep impression left on Judge Sewall by his experiences
were far from peculiar to him. It is a common fallacy to
suppose that the bitterness of the loyalists against their
former countrymen, so long kept up by the many thousands
who afterwards settled in Canada, arose from any excessive
fervour in their fidelity to George the Third. The real cause for
the hatred maintained came from harsh memories of the savage
persecution which they had experienced and still more from
the spoliation they were to suffer. Usually men forgive the
death of their nearest more easily than they do the seizure
of their property. Most Tories would have been glad to
remain quietly in their homes had they been permitted to,

and later would have accepted the change of Government and have become excellent citizens of the young Republic. The vast majority would have gladly returned after the peace, if their estates could have been given back to them. The aversion felt by so many long after the War emanated far less from a dislike of the new institutions or from any abstract loyalty to the King than from the rankling feeling of injustice at the humiliating and confiscatory treatment to which they had been subjected.

Samuel Quincy, who had been Solicitor General of Massachusetts, offers another example of a man who in spite of real patriotism had been too deeply offended ever to wish to return. The other members of his family were all fiery Whigs, and, although they had hitherto been singularly united, with the shallow explanation by which near relatives often love to diminish their kinsmen, they pettily attributed his loyalism to his wife's preference for the superior social attraction of the British officers. Quincy was really a moderate, whose sympathies and loyalties were divided, and who, unable to take sides, found himself torn from the rest of his family, which, before the Revolution, had been closely united. His sister, Mrs. Lincoln, ablaze with patriotic ardour, was at this time consumed by a fierce hatred of England, while he could feel antipathy for neither side. It is the tragedy of those who stand half way and are caught in a storm which they are powerless to escape from, that they have to suffer without true faith. They form part of a residue of intelligence, ability, and often of real virtue, which like civilization itself runs to waste in every crisis, for, with too much character to appear to conform to violence without conviction, they are still not partisan enough to take sides at a moment when the excess of party feeling makes of moderation a crime. Samuel Quincy found himself proscribed in Massachusetts, his estate was confiscated, and, most mortifying of all to him, his law library was taken away. Obliged to live in exile in London, left with only scanty means, he tried to steel himself in adversity. In spite of his affection for his country, his pride had been far too deeply hurt by the humiliations heaped upon him, and he made up his mind never to go back to New England "until I am convinced that I am as well thought of as I know I deserve to be. I shall ever rejoice in its prosperity, but am too proud to live despised where I was once respected."[22] How many other men of character and cultivation did such political intolerance cause America to lose for the same reason? Quincy never returned. After the Revolution he received the post of Attorney to the Crown in Antigua, which he held to his death.

Refugees continued to arrive in England.[23] Tory Massachusetts seemed to be transplanted to London, and St. James's Park was said to present an appearance not unlike the Exchange in Boston.[24] Those able to bring with them enough of their property were not badly off, but the majority, who expected to be reimbursed for the losses they had suffered, besieged the British Treasury with petitions for help. Everyone complained of the cost of living in England, which was so much higher than in America, and many of the refugees, by continually shifting their residence, only made matters worse for themselves.

The Massachusetts loyalists at first saw little of the exiles from other Colonies until, later, they were brought together for the defence of common interests. Pride and local associations make for clannishness. Few of them ever had any

English friends. They lived mainly among themselves, frequenting the New England Coffee House in Threadneedle Street, and meeting at the home of Governor Hutchinson, for all looked up to him as their leader and they gathered frequently around his hospitable board. Twenty-one of the refugees founded a New England Club and agreed to meet for weekly dinners at the Adelphi. Without regular occupation they hardly knew how to pass the time with nothing in the world to do save sightsee and gossip. Some wandered around auction rooms or frequented the play to admire Garrick's acting.[25] The greater number found that the gnawing tedium of exile would have provoked Job himself. Without home or work, the refugees became increasingly depressed by the rootless solitude of their lives. Reading newspapers at the Coffee House, meeting at tea to exchange gossip, was poor compensation for all they missed. They felt as if their lives had been left shapeless and unfulfilled. One of their number meditated bitterly that once he had supposed health with virtue and a competence would be sufficient to enjoy happiness, but experience had taught him that more than this was necessary, for "without something in pursuit, rightly or wrongly estimated worthy, life is insipid."[26] In his mood of depression, unable to emancipate himself from his lethargy, the refugee understood in his exile that he was only dreaming the blank of years.

Many of the loyalists who brooded over their lot became obsessed by the fear of being buried in England and longed, even dead, to return to their homes. Andrew Jolly, who had been a boarding-house keeper in Boston, died in London, expressing the wish that when the War was over, his remains should be taken back for burial. Another exile,

Charles Paxton, a former Commissioner of Customs, was ready to offer a hundred guineas so that he might afterwards be laid beside his parents in Boston. To console him, Governor Hutchinson remarked that, though he could not help feeling the desire for his own remains to rest by those dear to him in life, yet, if he had a bad leg or tooth, would he care what became of it, and why should he be more concerned with his other bones?[27]

It was inevitable that instances should occur when the moral solitude of the refugees induced despair and suspicion which led to some tragic results. There were cases of suicide, and one duel, all the more regrettable because of the high character of its victim, Lloyd Dulany, of Maryland, who had been a former intimate friend of Washington and a man of whom it was said by English admirers that he would do honour to any country. When families with great estates were divided in their loyalty as had happened in England during the Civil Wars, and in Scotland in Jacobite days, suspicion became inevitable. Another refugee, the Reverend Bennet Allen, a graduate of Oxford, and former rector of All Saints' Parish, in Maryland, had written in the *Morning Post* that, whereas part of the Dulany family remained in America to secure their property from confiscation, other members sought refuge as loyalist sufferers in England in order to save their vast possessions, whichever side was victorious. Lloyd Dulany felt the affront, and challenged the Maryland clergyman at this aspersion on his loyalty.[28] The Reverend Bennet Allen, like the Reverend Henry Bate, the so called "fighting parson" and bruiser, who then edited the *Morning Post*, in which this slander had appeared, stood his ground, and in a duel, which took place in Hyde Park, inflicted a wound on Dulany from the consequence of which he died.

Neither indifference nor negativeness spares men in a crisis and a great convulsion like the Revolution necessarily affected the life of every American although with consequences far from uniform. The former orthodox belief that all colonists, except for a few traitorous Tories, were from the beginning of the struggle solidly arrayed against the British oppressor and continued to wage a heroic warfare until victory had rewarded their sacrifices, need no longer be maintained as a patriotic lie. If such union could have been possible the Revolution in fact would have been successful far sooner and have met with far fewer difficulties to overcome. In a protracted and inconclusive struggle, bitterly contested, it was unavoidable as the fortunes of war wavered that doubts should arise on both sides. Many repressed these perplexities or waited for opportunities which never came, but there were others who openly changed their views. After the early Revolutionary enthusiasm had worn off, some who at first had been most zealous in the cause became lukewarm or worse. It is customary to hold the latter up to contempt and attribute their conversion solely to the most ignoble grounds, when a deeper insight into motives which cannot always be fathomed might lead to a more generous tolerance. It is no simple matter for instance to explain the case of the Reverend Jacob Duché, of Philadelphia, who had been the most eloquent and popular preacher of his time in America, and was the brother-in-law of Francis Hopkinson, a signer of the Declaration of Independence. When Congress elected him as its chaplain, he had prayed to invoke the divine blessing "on these our American states who have fled to Thee from the root of

the oppressor." John Adams, thrilled by this sermon, enthusiastically praised the preacher's patriotic eloquence. But after
General Howe had entered Philadelphia, the clergyman suddenly changed his views, offered prayers for the King, and
addressed an extraordinary letter to General Washington in
which he exhorted him to resign his command, force Congress
to abandon the Revolution, rescind the Declaration of Independence, and negotiate for America at the head of his army.[29]
Washington at once turned this letter over to Congress and
Duché was banished, his estate confiscated, and he went into
exile, to become chaplain of an orphan asylum in London and
continue to deliver eloquent sermons before large congregations
which later Mrs. Adams went to hear.

No more than with Silas Deane is it possible to explain
Duché's suddenly forsaking the American cause merely for interested motives. After the Revolution, when the clergyman appeared before the British Claims Commissioner, he testified that
he was opposed to independence and accepted his position as
Chaplain only because he feared that otherwise his Church
would suffer. He had resigned when he discovered that there
was no idea of reconciliation. Samuel Shoemaker, the former
Mayor of Philadelphia, who had known Duché from
his infancy, gave evidence as to his high character and expressed
the opinion that originally the preacher had been influenced
by his wife's family, who were all "rebels."[30] Any explanation
of the motives which led to his conversion is inadequate,
yet a likely reason may be offered. A movement so rapid and
unforeseen as the one for Independence when this suddenly
developed during the winter of 1775–6, exercises different effects on different individuals. Most men, whether
they approved or not of the new State, were able, sooner or

later, to fit their convictions to the novel circumstances, but it was inevitable that some also should later slip back and repudiate all previous professions. A highly emotional preacher like Duché may have been less of a time-server and more of a neurotic weakling than certain of his contemporaries believed and it is unfair to attribute his change of sides merely to self-seeking. Perhaps Elbridge Gerry understood human failings of this kind when he proposed the banishment of the Tories on the ground that "prisons we have not a sufficiency and they are not worth hanging."[31]

Except for Silas Deane, the principal political convert gained by the Crown during the Revolution, was Franklin's former friend, Joseph Galloway, who deserves a more extended treatment than is possible in this brief notice. As the leader of the popular party in Philadelphia, he had been the author of a plan of union for the Colonies which called for a confederation with rights of home rule, and, supported by John Jay, was lost by a single vote. Galloway had signed the different boycott measures taken against British trade. Yet he abandoned the American cause and in 1778 migrated to England to become the most embittered of loyalists. Like so many others the Pennsylvania politician explained his action by his disapproval of independence[32] which, along with the French Alliance, were the two motives given invariably by turncoats. The general belief among the refugees in London was that conviction had little to do with a change of front which ended by making him the most rabid of diehards. Even after the Howe brothers and Lord Cornwallis had formally expressed their opinion in Parliament that the conquest of America was impracticable, Galloway, with word and pen, still asserted the contrary, and insisted that

Congress did not represent one-tenth of the community and had merely usurped a despotic power over the remainder.[33] His ideas ably and energetically expressed, were not without exercising some influence on Lord North and strangely enough, even on Lord Shelburne. The latter when he became Secretary in 1782 occasionally transmitted the refugee's memoranda to the King, who found them "very curious" and recommended that he be shown "some civility." John Temple, with good opportunity of judging, described the Pennsylvania loyalist as a continual source of misrepresentation in England and as being responsible for persuading the Cabinet that the Revolution was always on the point of collapsing and that four-fifths of the Americans were prepared to accept British rule.

Under Galloway's inspiration there had appeared anonymously in London in 1779, the *Considerations upon the American Enquiry*, with the argument that not one-fifth of the people of America had at any time supported the Revolution from choice. The die-hard kept insisting that the Middle Colonies were tired of the struggle and ready to return to their former loyalty, although the accuracy of this statement left even Governor Hutchinson sceptical. In their hearts many loyalists hated Galloway for his unceasing efforts to continue the War. His own bitterness became so intense that the refugee hardly knew whether more to blame the ungrateful Americans whom he was attempting to save, or the folly and wickedness, as he called it, of the generals who were mishandling the British cause. His advice, so far as it was followed, did the gravest injury to both countries and to his own partisans. The acts of confiscation of loyalist property were considered as answers to the senseless depredations

committed in America by the British Army which caused so
much harsh feeling on both sides and occurred principally
during the last three years of the war. If peace had come,
as it should have in 1778, instead of four years later,
many of the worst evils of the struggle would have been
avoided, to the immense advantage of both England and
America.

III

Few of the refugees have left any record of their trials,
and the occasional evidence obtained from letters or diaries,
when these have survived, suggests little more than the outward circumstances of their lives. The inner heart-
burnings of a taciturn race like that of New England are
hardly ever expressed. The feelings and hopes of the loyalists
underwent, moreover, many changes during the frequent
crises they traversed in their exile. Such glimpses as are
afforded of their life in England can be found principally
in a few somewhat bare recitals.

Among the thousands who left America, every one was
to pass through different trials and it is difficult to single out
the experiences of any man as having been either typical
or unique. Yet one record stands out from among the others
owing to the interest and extent of its observations, its very
human quality, and most of all by the feeling of real
Americanism on the part of a Tory refugee.

A fat little Judge of Admiralty at Salem, Samuel Curwen
by name, during the years of his exile kept a journal which
deserves to find a higher place in the literature of the Revolutionary Era than is commonly assigned to it. As an official

of the Crown, Curwen had been induced to subscribe to the address presented to Governor Hutchinson when he left for England and local feeling at Salem had been roused in consequence with some violence against him. The judge refused to recant and felt alarmed at the rising tide of indignation against all moderates who without distinction were being pilloried as enemies to their country. In order to escape from insult and, perhaps, with some curiosity to go abroad, he made up his mind to leave for England. He admitted that his self-designation as a loyalist sounded somewhat pompous, for his wife called him merely a runaway. Whether political differences led to conjugal disagreements or the reverse, the Curwen family then separated, for Mrs. Curwen, as her husband complained, was more terrified by the prospect of an ocean passage than by a mob, and refused to accompany the Judge in his exile abroad. The rift between the two was to be prolonged beyond the grave, for Curwen left instructions that they were to be buried apart, on the ground that he would feel not a little deranged to find her rising by his side on the Day of Judgment.

Except towards his wife the Judge's views were never ungenerous, and he felt neither bitterness nor hatred on leaving his home. It is part of the price of any struggle that only after the fatigue which follows contest has lowered the fury of enmity and led to relaxed feelings that there is room again for tolerance. After Curwen had escaped from the violence of partisanship, nothing impressed him more, in England, than to observe that political disputes could be carried on without abuse and that it was, in fact, unfashionable to differ too violently. The doctrine of respect for other men's opinions he found was far better practised in London than in America, "otherwise there would not be such numbers of unhappy exiles."[34]

Curwen had arrived at a time when nearly everyone in England still believed that the Revolution would speedily be over. As soon as the British Government began to make serious military preparations, few of the loyalists thought that the Colonists would be able to resist. Judge Sewall wrote at this time from London, to a friend in Boston, that if he could only form an idea of the wealth and power of the British Empire he would tremble "at the foolish audacity of your pygmy States"—an opinion which was also then shared by not a few patriotic Americans in and out of Congress. Like the other refugees, Samuel Curwen was at first convinced of British victory. He lacked the confidence in the Massachusetts Militia entertained by some of his Whig friends at home, and, although believing that civil war eventually made good soldiers, he felt certain that the immense inequality would end the struggle long before this had become possible. "In any case America must be ruined."[35] The recollection of the indignities he had suffered from the Whigs still rankled, and Curwen desired British success because he believed that the welfare of America depended on the ability to restrain the outrages of "unprincipled men who run riot against all the laws of justice, truth and religion."[36] He explained his feeling against independence partly owing to a dislike for the popular leaders, and partly because he feared this would lead to an even greater oppression and tyranny from the mob than by allowing royal pretensions. This confidence in British success underwent a change after Curwen had discovered a fact, which exiles like Governor Hutchinson who moved in higher circles took much longer to notice, that although most of the English upper classes supported the Government, it was otherwise with those of middle station. Curwen, who spent much of his enforced leisure seeing the country and meeting people of all kinds at inns and in stage-coaches observed that English dissenters sympathized with the colonists.[37] At Newbury, where there were four dissenting chapels, he discovered that the inhabitants were "avowed friends of American liberty and disavowers of the war." Afterwards, when he had supper at an inn with some chance companions of the road, these passed the evening "talking treason and justifying American independence."[38]

A curious change was to come over the little Salem judge so imperceptibly that he did not altogether understand its nature. With his Tory convictions he still desired, or believed that he desired, a British victory, but any aspersions on America and particularly any disparaging remarks made against his countrymen, although they were enemies, aroused his anger. He became indignant when he heard a British officer, lately returned from the seat of war, describe Yankees as cowards, and would have been still more furious if he had read certain letters written after Bunker Hill, by an English official in Boston, who lamented that British soldiers should fall by the hands of "such despicable wretches as compose the bandits of the country; among whom there is not one that has the least pretension to be called a gentleman. They are a most rude, depraved, degenerate race and it is a mortification to us that they speak English and can trace themselves from that stock."[39] Absence from home only increased Curwen's sympathy for his rebellious countrymen, and he eagerly looked forward to the despised Americans convincing these conceited islanders, "by some knock down argument that even without a regular army they could produce brave soldiers and skilful commanders. Not till then may we expect generous or fair treatment."[40]

The American in Curwen was fast getting the better of the Tory, although he neither realized nor would have been willing to admit this. He was just then beginning to feel an immense pride in the Revolution, and to discover that he was far more of a patriot in England than he had ever been in Massachusetts. The news of the defeat at the battle of Long Island was a keen disappointment, until cheered by reading in a letter from a British officer, that the Americans had fought courageously. Like most of the exiles, his dearest wish was for bloodshed to cease and for Congress to accept any reasonable proposal. When he heard Bishop Keppel preaching a sermon that this was a *Civil War* and calling the Americans *our unhappy fellow-subjects*, without otherwise attempting to justify British measures,[41] Curwen listened with unfeigned delight.

The refugee's thoughts kept running home and caused him to regret his foolishness in having emigrated to escape from a few insults. A dress of tar and feathers and the rabble's rough treatment would be preferable, he thought, to the distress of mind he was daily suffering in London. Country, family, and friends, he had abandoned all, on as foolish and fantastic grounds, so it now seemed to him, as the crusaders, though these had gone to fight and he to avoid fighting. His purse was nearly empty, and he saw only the prospect of poverty ahead suffered by a man unaccustomed to its hardship. One cheering piece of news came when his friend Judge Sewall accompanied him to the Treasury, where he was given a hundred pounds, and promised as much every year during the troubles in America, an arrangement which henceforth saved him from material anxiety.

Unlike most of the refugees who clutched at any bit of gossip, Curwen never believed that the Americans were almost ready to abandon their fight. Loyalist papers read at the New England Coffee House were then full of wild reports about the supposed death of Washington and other rumours which left the Judge sceptical as having been "prepared by Court cookery in the Gazette."[42] After Burgoyne's surrender he was convinced that nothing less than independence would satisfy America. His own feelings were still mixed because of the fear that his countrymen's victory might mean for him perpetual banishment. Yet he thrilled with pride whenever he learned of the success of the "raw undisciplined beggarly rabble," and wrote exultingly to his friend, the former Harvard instructor Isaac Smith, to ask what he now thought of the boast that five thousand British troops could march from one end of the continent to the other. When in 1778 George the Third was about to dispatch the Peace Embassy, Curwen's only comment was that "the sun of Britain is past the meridian and declining fast to the West and America is for ever emancipated from the legislative authority of this once potent Empire. Alas, no more so."[43]

At a time when British success appeared to be most certain, Curwen had felt only the more American. Later, when he believed no longer in an English victory, a curious change came over the man. He was proud when his countrymen had beaten the English, but, like most Americans, did not relish their being defeated by anyone else. When a French and Spanish fleet rode the Channel in sight of Plymouth, whose inhabitants spread terror by their flight, he noted indignantly the thoughtless levity which engrossed the upper ranks, the middle classes, disregarding national danger, only intent on their selfish gain, while the *canaille* remained stupidly unconcerned by events. His heart bled for Great Britain, though he had never thought of himself as an Englishman, and was without a single English friend. His remarks about the upper classes came only from hearsay, for in common with many Americans he was ready to condemn the great world although knowing nothing about it. He indulged in no profession of loyalty to the King, but long residence had made him think of England as another mother country which now held the second place in his affection, and he saw with dismay the want of preparations made to meet the peril.

Judge Sewall, with no suspicion of the struggle which then was going on within the recesses of Curwen's heart, tried to cheer him with good news, and to persuade him that the situation was becoming better once more for British arms in America. The Judge felt particularly elated just then, because the time-serving Chief Justice Smith of New York, of whom Trumbull had written:

> Smith's weathercock in veers forlorn
> Could hardly tell which way to turn,

along with several other influential men, hitherto on the fence, had at the end of 1778 gone over to the English side, which seemed to the refugees a clear indication that the Revolutionary cause must be in a bad way.[44] Owing to the tyranny of Congress and their "sub-devils," the distress of the people, and the general dislike felt for the French Alliance, many loyalists were at that time convinced that the Union of the States was on the point of dissolution, and that only one more effort would be necessary to crush the rebellion.[45]

Curwen, long ago, had ceased to expect a British victory,

and believed that the successes gained in the Southern campaign merely delayed an inevitable result. Like Charles James Fox and Horace Walpole, who saw in Yorktown the end of the War, Curwen also rejoiced at the news of Cornwallis's surrender, "perhaps the first of the kind that ever befell this haughty America-despising people." The Salem Judge wrote ironically that the British garrison in New York could now return to their "useful employment of dancing, card playing, acting farces."[46] Most of the loyalists had been stunned by the final disaster to their cause and little faith was henceforth attached to the efforts still periodically announced to protract the struggle.[47] The King's recognition of independence came, however, as the final tragedy to many of the refugees. One, in his despondency, after eating a hearty dinner cut his throat, which caused a grim jest to circulate among the loyalists that Americans were beginning to adopt the English custom of taking leave. James Murray, the friend of Governor Hutchinson, expressed only what many others believed, when he wrote:

> Poor Britain! How much like Babylon and Carthage in her fall and how nearly will she resemble them in her fate; the owl and the bittern may soon take possession of her palaces.[48]

Even before the peace preliminaries were ratified or hostilities had ceased, an American ship, with her thirteen stripes flying, laden with whale oil, sailed into the Thames from Nantucket by way of Ostend. Others arrived shortly after, and in the words of a loyalist refugee their crews were "caressed" by the Londoners,[49] who felt delighted that the War was over. City merchants were in a hurry to resume the former trade, and within a few days after the preliminaries had been published, the names of a dozen vessels were posted up in the coffee houses advertised for carrying freight to Boston and New York.[50]

Many Americans also were beginning to arrive. Peter Oliver, Jr., wrote that his former friend, John Jackson, had called and "several others of that class of wretches who deserve the halter . . . he bragged here of being a Member of Congress."[51] When at last John Adams came to take up diplomatic relations, his arrival in London caused consternation among the refugees, who remembered the harsh remarks on their score which he once had made. But John Adams, with a more statesmanlike tolerance, and mellowed views, announced that he had buried all his old animosity with the War and the refugees discovered that they could only criticize the first United States Minister for his wish to be a "plain American Republican, his garb plain without a sword," which seemed to them like carrying transatlantic ideas a little too far. The Envoy of the new Republic even renewed certain of his friendships with Tories, and in one of her letters from London, Mrs. Adams describes dining with the loyalist, Mr. Hallowell, who had been the King's Customs Commissioner at Boston, and still lived handsomely, though not with his former splendour.

Five years had passed since Curwen had received news from his home. When at last letters came, the correspondence gave him all the more pleasure because he had attributed the silence of his friends to partisan feeling. The description of life in Salem which he received was, however, not very alluring. Former leaders and men of wealth had been reduced to poverty and lived glad to remain unnoticed. New people, violent in their republican principles, had become *horriblement riches*, while the old ones were still exposed to insult and plunder. Curwen was asked what his own feelings would be if he had lost all his business, had then been driven to sell his house and land, and the rest of his property had depreciated fifty per cent, and, thus reduced, he could not walk through the streets safely—"a just picture, I fear, of American popular liberty."

No picture, however sombrely painted, could put off a man who for years had longed for his home. But before going back he wished to know more about the temper of the inhabitants towards those who had fled into exile. Had the spirit of persecution abated so that "they be restored to reason and I to my native country?" His desire to return was so great that at times he felt as if he could throw himself on the mercy of his fellow-citizens, but fear and a dislike of humiliation still restrained him. He had read in the American newspapers that refugees who returned to the United States were threatened with death, and, although his name had never been included on the proscribed list, Curwen still hesitated. Was it wise to go back? How would he be received in the "land of purity, sanctity, and liberty?"[52] Would it be prudent to leave his safe shelter for a country where he feared the excessive power of the narrow-minded and intolerant lower classes? In spite of his friends' persuasion he still dreaded a revival of popular dislike and lest he, advanced in years and in feeble health, should no longer enjoy even his British pension of a hundred pounds which allowed him to live at least in comfort if not in affluence.

Friends in Salem reported to him that they saw no prospect of the laws against absentees being repealed, yet they did not anticipate any danger for Curwen. In Rhode Island, and in certain parts of Connecticut, the refugees who had returned had been cordially received, and they hoped for a similar temper in Massachusetts.[53] In fact, there had recently been a great change of feeling towards the late enemies. Everyone who could was now crossing the Atlantic to buy British goods, and "going to England is now as formerly called *going home*." Also towards the exiles opinion had suddenly changed, and Curwen then learned certain things which his friends at first had carefully kept from him. At the time their original inquiry was made as to how he would be treated, they were told that the exiles would first have to go down on their knees before the General Court, then do the same before the Committee to ask forgiveness of their townsmen, after which they might be allowed to stay, provided they behaved themselves. Fortunately, this kind of insolence was already a thing of the past.[54]

At last Curwen was persuaded that he could return safely, but before leaving England he wrote to acquaint his old friend, Judge Sewall, with his intention. The latter understood the reason, and gave him some private letters to take with him, always provided he felt no objection to being the bearer of correspondence "from an alien traitor by law, *vide* Act of 1779." The parting meant farewell for two friends who knew that they would probably never see each other again in this world. "God only knows what kind of one the next will be, whether more or less dirty," wrote the embittered former friend of John Adams.[55]

Before departing, there were still some necessary calls to make; the most important being on the Commissioners of American Claims, where Curwen found their door besieged by "a score of mendicants like myself." His petition, which was readily granted, after reciting the facts in his case, stated that if he could not safely reside at Salem he proposed to go to Nova Scotia, and asked that an agent might be authorized to receive his allowance for so long as it should be continued. He paid a last call on Mr. Copley and visited once more the Tower of London. From the ramparts he saw for the first time the Stars and Stripes flying on eight vessels anchored in the Thames.

In September, 1784, Curwen arrived in Boston after an absence of nine years and five months, "occasioned by a lamented Civil War excited by ambitious selfish men here and in England."[56] Only after his return to Salem did he begin to understand the extent of the social revolution which had taken place. Those whom he had known affluent had fallen from their former station. Others of lowly origin occupied their places, and he was but one among many who were left to lament the wreck of their departed wealth. Discouraged by the spectacle of his losses, he entertained some idea of moving to Nova Scotia, but time in the end reconciled him to his former abode and he lived at Salem until he died a very old man, in 1802.

On the death of Thomas Flucker, Curwen had recorded that the late Secretary of Massachusetts was the forty-fifth of the refugees from his State to die in England. When Curwen left, Judge Sewall noted that twenty-eight others from Massachusetts would still remain in exile. Some of these returned later, like Edward Oxnard; Colonel Pickman, who was proscribed and banished in 1778, went back in 1787, after the Legislature had restored his citizenship and part of his confiscated estate. Many others emigrated to New Brunswick, as did Judge Sewall, who, tired of doing nothing in England, left to become a Judge of Admiralty in the new Province which then was rapidly being peopled by loyalists principally from Massachusetts. Other refugees found new employment under the Crown in Bermuda and the British West Indies, and only very few remained permanently in Great Britain.

CHAPTER SEVEN

Great Britain Compensates the Loyalists

WHEN fear of violence had forced Massachusetts loyalists to leave their homes, the belief which they cherished in British victory and the expectation of an impending triumphant return long prevented them from understanding the true nature of their exile. The refugees had fled from America before what appeared, at the time, to be a temporary necessity, the tragedy of which was obscured by a natural error of judgment. The majority of these men had lived hitherto in affluent circumstances and regarded the straitened means of their existence in England as a hardship which they could the more easily endure, because of their conviction that it would be of short duration.

Until the news of Burgoyne's surrender they had felt certain of victory, and the opinion held by Washington's former friend, the Reverend Jonathan Boucher, who wrote, after his arrival in London, that "America will be reduced, must be, I cannot entertain a doubt,"[1] was also typical of many others. Only by slow degrees, as disaster to British arms lessened the belief in victory, did the loyalists begin to measure the lasting consequences of exile and understand the terrible plight of their position. The pinched circumstances in which they found themselves in England had left them entirely dependent on the bounty of the British Government. It was inevitable, and in a sense true, that every American Tory should regard his own suffering as a sacrifice made to his King.

Irrespective of any antecedent causes which had brought about their misfortunes, all were affected by the same material necessities which reduced them to dependence as pensioners of the Crown.

In the summer of 1778, when the British Peace Commission was already in America, certain of the refugees in London prepared a memorial to be presented to the Council and House of Representatives of Massachusetts Bay. They had felt alarmed by the rumours of an impending peace, and, apprehending that they might be left out from its benefits, expressed the wish to be restored to the friendship and affection of their countrymen. They therefore solicited an act of amnesty and naturalization, offered to become peaceful subjects of the new State and to pay an equal proportion of the public debts, asking in return only for protection, and for their property to be restored to them. A copy of this memorial was addressed to the Royal Commissioners, who took a very sympathetic view of their case, but found it impossible to sanction any British subject renouncing his allegiance to the King.[2]

All hope of reinstatement was dashed, however, by the Massachusetts Act of 1779, which left loyalists without any legal redress unless they took an oath that they favoured independence.[3] The further confiscation of all their property, with the decree of banishment passed on the exiles, left the latter justifiably indignant, though a few believed even then that, like all excessive penal measures, these would destroy themselves, and pointed to the contradiction between their countrymen fighting for liberty, and oppressing fellow-citizens merely because of their opinions.[4]

It is a melancholy reflection of history that great causes have always had an ignoble side. There was just sufficient ground for American indignation at the senseless and savage raids, carried out in the King's name by loyalist volunteers and Indians, to provide an excuse for reprisals against the loyalists. The customary war propaganda was therefore employed to manufacture hate and the spoliation of the Tories was justified as a war measure and as a counterpart for the British army's depredations. The refugees in England, blamed in America for encouraging hostilities to go on, and whose chief sin in their bewildered fright had been to run away, woke up to discover that they were paupers. When the American Tories in London learned to their horror that their impoverishment was not merely a temporary measure, that they had been permanently banished from their homes, their property confiscated, and that they were left on the losing side, they turned in their despair for redress to Great Britain.

The loyalists who had gone to England owe not a little of their peculiar importance to the fact that they also represented the much greater majority of those who still remained behind. Many of the refugees in London before the Revolution had also been Government officials accustomed to administrative methods of procedure and skilled in the drafting of petitions and memorials. Upon these now fell the duty of submitting to the Crown a statement of the plight of all who had suffered because of their allegiance.

In 1779, when the subjection of the Colonies was no longer expected, the American loyalists in London formed an association for the protection of their interests and elected as president Sir William Pepperell, a man who was hardly second to Governor Hutchinson in the esteem of the refugees. He was the only New England baronet and grandson of the soldier who had so greatly distinguished himself at the capture of Louisburg. Before the troubles began, he had enjoyed the highest consideration from both parties, but Tory sympathies made it necessary for him also to abandon his home and go into exile. His enormous estate in Maine was confiscated, and, after having been one of the richest men in the Colonies, he found himself reduced almost to poverty. The British Government provided him with a pension of five hundred pounds which, with the sale of some personal effects, allowed him to live with comfort in his house in Portman Square in London. During the next ten years his unceasing efforts were entirely given to the furtherance of loyalist interests.

The Crown and Anchor, in the Strand, which was also a favourite resort of Boswell and Dr. Johnson, became the meeting-place for American refugees. They gathered in this tavern to consider the measures they could take, and appointed a committee, composed of thirteen members, one from each colony, to prepare an address to the King. The attention of George the Third was invited in appropriate language to the circumstance that, notwithstanding the methods of intimidation employed to compel his American subjects to abjure their loyalty to the Crown, the greater number of these had kept the firmest attachment to His Majesty's sacred person and government. Apart from their own sacrifices, the refugees made their humble appeal in the name of the sufferings of multitudes who had patiently endured all their trials, with the expectation that the blessings of royal government would again be restored to them. They appealed in the name of thousands of American loyalists serving in His Majesty's armies, who, they claimed, with some reason, exceeded in number the troops enlisted by Congress to oppose them. "Finally we make a melancholy appeal to the many families who have been banished from their once peaceful habitations; to the public forfeiture of a long list of estates; and to the numerous executions of our fellow-citizens who have sealed their loyalty with their blood."[5]

Among the signers of this address were Daniel Leonard, formerly the bosom friend of John Adams, and Thomas MacKnight, of North Carolina, who at first had been on the Whig side. An executive committee was organized to press these claims, under the chairmanship of Sir Egerton Leigh, of South Carolina, the recipient of a recently bestowed baronetcy which had profoundly disgusted Governor Hutchinson, who disapproved of Leigh's private morals. The original intention, of which little came, however, was to have a similar committee of loyalists formed in New York, to correspond on questions of mutual interest.

As the prospects of peace drew nearer, rumours became frequent that the government intended to withdraw the pensions it had been granting to the refugees. It had always been expected that, as soon as hostilities were over, the loyalists would return to their homes and no longer require allowances which, originally given for three months, con- sidered, at first, as the likely duration of the rebellion, had since been paid on a regular basis.[6]

There were probably between five and six thousand American loyalists in the British Isles[7] at the end of the Revolution and the position of the majority of these had become pitiable. Certain refugees like Dr. Sylvester Gardiner had lost by his loyalty a fortune of forty thousand pounds. Others, like Elizabeth Dumeresque, had been so impoverished that, although a woman of gentle birth, she was obliged to take service as a domestic.[8] A respected magistrate like Judge

Auchmuty, of Boston, found himself under the necessity to petition humbly for a hundred pounds. The grim suggestion facetiously advanced at this time by a London newspaper, that owing to the Government withdrawing its support to the refugees there would be no shortage of haymakers at the next harvest, was not calculated to allay their fears. All this while still more unfortunates kept arriving in England, for the British garrison when it left Charleston took with them the loyalists, who were completely destitute and felt far too terrorized to stay behind.

The situation of the Americans who were faithful to the King added enormously, however, to the difficulty which was being experienced by England in making peace with the United States. The loss of territory and the recognition of independence had for some time been accepted as inevitable, but Great Britain could not honourably desert subjects whose only crime had been one of fidelity to the Crown. Which side was now to pay for the property confiscated? The future Peace Commissioner, Richard Oswald, talked over this question with Franklin in Paris, before the actual negotiations had begun, and the latter proposed creating a fund for compensating loyalists from the sale of waste land which might be obtained by ceding Canada to the United States. This suggestion met with no favour in London, where it was pointed out that thirteen colonies were unpalatable enough to lose without adding a fourteenth to the number. Earnestly desirous as Lord Shelburne was for peace, he felt apprehensive about "the probability of the negotiation *hitching* upon the refugees, the state of whose claims was confused to the greatest degree and required to be investigated before their claims could be enforced."[9]

[231]

The instructions given to Richard Oswald by the British Cabinet for the negotiation of peace stipulated that the acknowledgment of American independence was to be made conditional on indemnifying the loyalists. At this time New York, Charleston, and Savannah still contained British garrisons and the plan was that their surrender might be proposed as a basis for compensation.[10] Against this, Franklin offered an argument which since his day has often been advanced and not always to the credit of the United States as a nation. Loyalist property, he maintained, had been confiscated under the laws of different states, and Congress was powerless to interfere against these. Whatever redress was made for losses of this nature must come from England, and in any event America would advance counterclaims for the destruction of property committed by the British forces. Bitter against his Tory son, Franklin felt little sympathy for the loyalists. Many he asserted were merely waverers, whose partisanship came from sheer opportunism and on whom there was no need to waste sympathy. Still another class, in which he tacitly included his former friend Joseph Galloway, were immensely to blame for having contributed by their misrepresentations to prolonging the war. Franklin was personally in favour of omitting all mention of the lot, as to bring up their case would cause more mischief than remedy. "After the harm they have done us it was imprudent to insist on our doing them good," the old philosopher wrote to Benjamin Vaughan, who was then acting as Lord Shelburne's secretary.[11]

The fate of the loyalists was held in anxious suspense during the long drawn out peace negotiations which followed the long drawn out war. John Adams would himself have favoured indemnifying "the wretches how little soever they deserve it,"[12] but the American Commissioners in Paris were rightly afraid, if they did this, of being disavowed by Congress, and they refused to listen to the British Envoys demand for compensation unless England also undertook to indemnify those Americans who had suffered from British ravages. The question of loyalist property, stubbornly argued by both sides, became the principal obstacle to delay the final peace settlement. In the end the English government wisely gave way on the ground that the cost of continuing the war for no purpose would be far greater than any claims they might be called upon to meet. On their side, the Americans agreed that there should be no further seizure of estates or persecution of loyalists, and that persons having rights in any confiscated property should be allowed to pursue all lawful means to regain these. Lastly, they agreed that Congress ought to recommend to the State Legislatures an amnesty and the restitution of property.[13]

These vague terms admittedly possessed no binding nature and were regarded as most unsatisfactory by the loyalists and by their British sympathizers. Lord North, then in the opposition, Edmund Burke, and other public men, united in denouncing what Sheridan called a crime, and Lord Mulgrave pilloried as "a lasting monument of national disgrace." A loyalist scribbler, hearing the news, wrote:

> The American refugees were in consternation ;
> 'Tis an honour to serve the bravest of nations
>   and be left to be hanged in their capitulations.[14]

Lord Shelburne did not even try to defend these provisions beyond declaring that the only alternative to their acceptance would have been to continue the war, and he pleaded with reason that for less than a fifth of the cost of one year's campaign, comfort and happiness could be given to the unfortunate loyalists.

In a pamphlet, written by Joseph Galloway which appeared in 1783,[15] the contention was advanced that the loyalists "were and yet are as perfectly subjects of the British State as any man in London." He argued that the latter, after having been summoned by their Sovereign to defend the rights of the nation, had confidence that their losses and sacrifices would not be borne solely by themselves. The King and Parliament had found it necessary as the price of peace to acknowledge the independence of America without securing any restitution to those colonists who had remained faithful to the Crown, but the latter regarded the British nation as bound to make compensation the total of which would cost probably less than a quarter of the amount necessary to defray for one year the expenses of war.

At this time loyalists were arriving in numbers from America to seek redress for their forfeited estates. Colonel John Harris Cruger, who had fought on the British side and was the brother of the American member of Parliament from Bristol, wrote to describe the swarms of Americans in London, grumbling and discontented, and expressed his apprehension that two or three years must elapse before these would know what compensation the Government proposed to allow for the loss of property and for services.[16] It was only natural for Parliament to wait in order to ascertain how the provisions affecting the loyalists would be carried out by the American States, and the British Government can hardly be blamed for a series of delays which now occurred and were occasioned by causes beyond its own control. Meantime, through a system of temporary grants a great deal was being done to alleviate the distressing condition of the refugees.

Peace in the United States brought only the release of the prisoners and left American Tories in a state of the greatest anxiety. The latter indignant, felt that they had been basely abandoned by the British Ministry, that their sacrifices for the King had been ill requited, and that, while a disposition prevailed in England to bury the hatchet, the loyalists had been left to the "vindictive resentment of a set of people whose tender mercies are cruelty."[17] The exiles in England also found themselves in a tragic situation. Peter Oliver, Jr., wrote in dismay to his brother-in-law:

> We are obliged to put up with every insult from this ungrateful people the English without any redress. . . . If this government does not make the refugees compensation for the losses they have sustained . . . a curse will befall them sooner or later.[18]

Other loyalists complained that they had lost everything because of their fidelity to the King and accused the British Government of doing nothing to defend them from the "relentless malice of their countrymen."[19] The poor wretches, despoiled and disowned by America, shipwrecked and stranded in England felt that Great Britain had been monstrously ungrateful in requiting their sacrifices.

The American States, unfortunately, paid little heed to the articles of peace which their negotiators had signed. In vain, the three commissioners in Paris, Franklin, Adams, and Jay, on September 10, 1783, urged the attention of Congress to the solemn duty before it to perform its obligations toward the loyalists "with the most scrupulous regard to good faith," and pointed out that the unreasonable resolutions passed against the Tories, their actual expulsion from some places, and the hostility of the sentiments expressed against them were "construed not only to the prejudice of our national magnanimity and good faith, but also to the prejudice of our government."[20]

Twelve months after peace was concluded, Congress had not yet made its promised recommendation to the sovereign States for the favourable treatment of the loyalists and even after this was done it remained without effect. The Virginia legislature declared that they would refuse to regard any such request, and passed a resolution that no private debt should be paid in England until the latter had reimbursed £500,000 for their lost Negro slaves, who had run away to the British forces. The termination of hostilities had in no way abated the spirit of persecution. Committees organized in different states were occupied passing the most violent resolutions against the loyalists and proposing instructions to the legislative bodies which were in direct contradiction with the treaties. The Worcester Resolution of May 19, 1783, stated, for instance, that it would be "extremely dangerous to the peace, happiness, liberty and safety of these states to suffer those . . . who abandoned their native land, turned parricide and conspired to involve their country in ruin and blood to become subjects and reside in this Government." The exiles who chose to return to the new Republic were to be regarded as British subjects and aliens who must be compelled to take out papers of citizenship, and the commonwealth ought to act with the greatest caution before it naturalized a set of people who had been declared "outlaws, exiles, aliens and enemies." The Resolution stated that so long as there were in America thousands of innocent people whose property had been destroyed by the British army, it would be unjust and cruel to allow estates to be restored to those who had abandoned their country.[21] The town of Lexington went so far as to pass a resolution that it was necessary for the peace and welfare of the state, and the freedom and happiness of the United States, that steps should be taken to prevent the return of the refugees and the recovery of the property that was formerly theirs.[22]

The story of hysterical hatred let loose after the war is not a creditable one in American history, for patriotism was used by many as a cloak to hide the rapacity with which they profited from the confiscated property. When, after the treaty had been concluded, a number of loyalists returned to America in order to claim their estates, as they were entitled to do under its provisions, their applications remained without effect, and some were even imprisoned and subsequently banished.[23] The refugees in England heard that in New Jersey those who had returned were naturalized with tar and feathers. Even a loyalist so inoffensive as David Colden wrote, with sad derision, that he had been condemned to death if he was ever found again in the state of New York.[24] The better element in America regarded such spoliation with disgust, but could do nothing to restrain the persecution demanded by the masses. When John Jay learned about the Confiscation Act passed at Albany, he wrote to Governor Clinton from Madrid, to say that if the news were true "New York is disgraced by injustice too palpable to admit even of palliation,"[25] nor would he himself ever purchase any land forfeited under the provisions of the law. Men like Hamilton and Patrick Henry tried in vain to obtain better terms for the returned loyalists, and the first, for a time lost much of his popularity by acting as counsel for a Tory merchant.[26] The feeling in New York, typical also of other states, was that there could be no reason to restore any confiscated property so long as the King refused to offer compensation for the destruction committed by his soldiers.

In August, 1783, six months after George the Third had recognized American independence, General Carleton, the British Commander-in-Chief in New York, informed Congress that, owing to the violences committed against the loyalists, so many of these had applied to be removed to places of safety that he was unable to say when New York would be evacuated by the English garrison, for he was determined to leave behind no loyalist who wished to go. Already over thirty thousand of the latter had been transported to Nova Scotia, to the satisfaction of American Whigs who saw them depart with pleasure, and many more were waiting at this time for ships to carry them away. The late Mayor of Albany had in person led over three thousand of these unfortunates to Cape Breton Island. In the fall of 1783, between fourteen and fifteen thousand American loyalists were landed along the St. John River, where they found at the time not so much as a roof to shelter them. The settlement of New Brunswick began, however, in this way,[27] former officers being granted two hundred acres of land, and privates fifty acres in addition to the ground they were entitled to receive as settlers. The first council of the new province, which, owing to the origin of many of its inhabitants, seemed to the exiles like another Massachusetts, contained among its members two distinguished American judges, two colonels of colonial corps, and Beverley Robinson, an old personal friend of Washington.[28]

[238]

The refugees who remained in England were left in a state of perplexity. The British Treasury, which had begun to overhaul their pensions, struck off some names as that of one fortunate loyalist who had married an English heiress; many other pensions were reduced, although a few also were raised. The eighty thousand pounds previously paid out to the refugees were now whittled down to forty-three thousand.

The original hesitation of the loyalists to pursue any independent action of their own in pressing claims had also been due to the fear of displeasing the King, who, for reasons entirely to his credit, regarded himself as being their official protector. George the Third had long felt a generous interest in their welfare, and on one occasion, when he learned of a British naval officer treating certain loyalists in America with harshness, he wrote at once to express earnest regret that the little regard shown to these faithful partisans seemed to him an even greater disaster than the destruction of his fine army, for, if their confidence were lost, he did not know how it could ever be regained.[29]

At the first opening of Parliament after the peace treaty, the King spoke most feelingly of the American sufferers who, out of motives of loyalty to the Crown, and attachment to the mother country, had given up their property and professions and he asked that a generous attention be accorded to their claims. The Massachusetts refugees held a meeting afterward and urged Sir William Pepperell to present a petition of relief to Parliament, although Lord Shelburne still considered the moment inopportune, not wishing, perhaps, too soon to discredit his own treaty. Two members of Lord North's Cabinet had in private, however, told Pepperell that in their opinion the step would be appropriate, but the latter was still somewhat doubtful about being able to obtain satisfaction before more should be known regarding the intentions of the American states to carry out the treaty provisions recommended by Congress.

When the petition of the loyalists was presented to Parliament it received the hearty support both of the government and of the opposition. The next step was to appoint commissioners to examine the claims of those "reduced to distress by the late unhappy dissensions in America." Lord Shelburne made an admirable selection in the persons of John Eardley Wilmot and Daniel Parker Coke, both lawyers, both members of Parliament, and with enough public spirit in an age of often corrupt and generally interested patronage to insist as a condition that their work should be unpaid. The latter testified afterward in a debate in the House of Commons, that although far from sympathetic at first to the loyalist claims, he had seen so much evidence of real suffering among the exiles that his feelings toward them had entirely changed.

Admittedly the new commissioners took the greatest pains in the difficult task before them. They insisted on the actual presence of the applicants, and, being lawyers themselves, they refused to allow any demands to be presented to them by other lawyers. They sent agents to Canada to inquire into the applications of those who were unable without grave inconvenience to present these personally in England.[30] During the long and inevitable delays they allowed temporary support to those in need.[31] Compensation was granted for losses of property through loyalty, for offices held before the war, and for loss of actual professional incomes. The commissioners refused, however, to countenance many of the other claims brought forward. They denied this in the case

WILLIAM PITT
From a drawing by John S. Copley

of estates purchased after the war, or for anticipated profits, losses in trade, or by depreciated currency, and in this way largely reduced the amount of the claims. James De Lancey, for instance, who acted as the representative of the New York loyalists, saw his own application to receive $390,000 for an estate parcelled among two hundred and seventy-five small proprietors, cut down to one third of this sum.[32]

In all, over two thousand claims were examined, and the memorials, preserved in their original wrappers grown musty with age, lie to-day in the dockets of the Record Office in London, to tell the forgotten tragedy of homes forsaken, of families dispersed, of careers ruined, and of suffering endured by those whose crime had been loyalty to a King. Actually more than nine million dollars were paid out by the British Crown, or somewhat less than one-fifth of the total amount which had originally been asked for. A few claims were withdrawn after South Carolina restored certain of the loyalists' estates. Some dissatisfaction was inevitable, for the commissioners were called upon to decide many knotty points. The expectations of the refugees had been over-sanguine, but the result on the whole was most satisfactory, and after years of suspense, disappointment, and misery endured by these unfortunates, the indemnities they received came as a godsend.

In 1788, after the Commissioners had finished their work and obtained the sanction of Parliament, the Board of Agents, headed by Sir William Pepperell, presented in person an address of thanks to the King for the liberal provisions made in their behalf. On this occasion, Benjamin West drew an allegorical sketch, now lost, in which Religion and Justice extended the mantle of Britannia which, with outstretched arms, receives the loyalists who throng around the Crown of Great Britain. These stand in a group representing the Law, Church, and Government, with whom are also other inhabitants of North America, including an Indian Chief who points one hand to England and the other to a widow and orphans rendered so by the civil war. A Negro with his children look up to Great Britain with gratitude for emancipation from slavery, and in a cloud on which rest Religion and Justice, are seen the genii of Great Britain and America, binding up the broken *fasces* of the two countries as emblematic of the Treaty of Peace. West included his own portrait and that of his wife in this sketch, which was used by John Eardley Wilmot as the frontispiece for his account of the work of the commission.

From a British point of view the settlement of the loyalist claims marked the final liquidation of the war. The reactions in the United States were more extended, and to the student of history are more impressive. The legislation enacted against the unfortunate Tories lasted for many years and the last repressive measures were only rescinded in the early part of the nineteenth century. The permanent effect on the American people continued beyond this, hardly suspected except by a few students of history.

The savage persecution and virtual expulsion of the American Tories may at first appear as part of the price which had to be paid for independence. Actually, not even that excuse can be found for a result which already had been secured before the persecution was at its worst. Their ill treatment was merely due to an unrestrained mob hysteria, common enough in all countries in times of war and of civil strife, which displayed its savage vindictiveness against the shattered survivors of the Tory party blamed for having helped the English to prolong the struggle and the vivid remembrance of whose former power mistakenly still seemed a threat to the new nation. Hatred against the loyalists doubtless also was deliberately fostered by those who assuming the shield of patriotism benefited by plunder taken from their fellow-citizens.

The virtual expulsion of nearly a hundred thousand loyalists, who left the United States in an ultimate emigration comparable to that of the Huguenots from France, was a crime which since has been expiated in other ways, although little more than a small fraction of the American people has ever been aware either of the enormity of the offence, the stupidity of the act, or of its real consequences upon their own national future. Mr. James T. Adams has aptly pointed out[33] one phase of this in the rapid decay in taste and cultivation which marked American history during the nineteenth century and which he has partly attributed to the disappearance of a conservative and educated class who might have helped to oppose their higher standard of refinement to the cruder influences of the frontier. Also many town-bred loyalists under the stress of necessity found themselves compelled after their exile to begin life afresh under rough conditions in Canada. The great majority of American Tories went to settle in the wilderness of New Brunswick and Ontario to become the founders of British Canada which might otherwise have been overrun by American settlers during the last century, who would then have desired to live under their own flag.[34]

Canadians point with pride to another unforeseen consequence of this migration. During the war of 1812, when most of the British Army was engaged fighting Napoleon in Spain, it was largely due to the determination shown by the children of these loyalists that Canada was successfully defended from the American invader.[35] In the intense feeling which the sons of American Tories displayed and in the stubborn resistance they put up against the forces of the United States, may also be seen a revenge for the spoliation and expulsion of their fathers. The real price paid for the persecution of the loyalists after the War of Independence lies in the lesson that without this the North American Continent might to-day have been one country.

CHAPTER EIGHT

Cruger and Pownall, M.P's

I

AT THE outbreak of the Revolution most Americans, whether
Whig or Tory, considered themselves to be fellow-members
who were possessed of equal rights in a great sea empire of
which England was the centre. Obviously, this assumption of
equality made its principal appeal to the colonists, although not
a few far-sighted Englishmen, particularly among the merchants, looked with favour on a doctrine in which may
be found the germ of modern British imperialism. As a
principle of practical administration, however, this broad view
of their relations was never accepted by the King's Government, and the divergence of opinion regarding the measures
introduced by the Crown, which grew on both sides of the
Atlantic till the controversy ended in war, arose largely as a
result of the undefined relationship between the mother
country and the Colonies.

The English commercial classes who lived in closer touch
with oversea opinion than a Tory Cabinet which derived its
main strength from the landed gentry, desired to maintain
friendly relations on which their trade depended and had done
their utmost to avert the struggle. Shortly before the outbreak
of hostilities, there had occurred several examples to indicate
the favour with which the business community in the City
regarded the growing participation of Americans even in

[245]

purely English affairs. In the election of 1775, the Virginian, William Lee, brother of Arthur Lee, the future American Commissioner in Paris, was returned on the Wilkes ticket as an alderman of the City of London.[1] Two years earlier, Stephen Sayre, a native of Long Island, and a graduate of Princeton, had been elected Sheriff of London in a campaign in which Arthur Lee took so prominent a part that his brother-in-law, Dr. William Shippen, wrote to him from Philadelphia to express amazement at these "strange impudent Americans." Later Sayre, who had been charged with high treason in an alleged plot to seize the King on his way to Parliament and overturn the Government, was committed to the Tower, henceforth to enjoy the nickname of "Tower Sayre." Arthur Lee acted as one of his counsel at this trial. Sayre was confined only for five days and the jury, disbelieving the Government's charge, awarded him a thousand pounds damages, although this verdict was subsequently set aside. After this, the late Sheriff of London continued, principally outside the British realm, his madcap career as a brainless adventurer.[2]

The centre of English intercourse with the colonies had long been Bristol. All its merchants were engaged in the American trade and not a few held mortgages on plantations in Virginia and the Carolinas. The simple provincial life of the western seaport was congenial to colonials, who felt more at home in a small town than in a capital like London. When Governor Hutchinson visited the city he noted that the manners and customs of the people were so like those of New England, that he would have been able to pick out a set of Boston selectmen from any one of their churches.[3] Bristol became a favourite residence for many of the Tory refugees, who found life far cheaper than in London, and a loyalist lady living there has recorded having as neighbours seventeen American families, "very genteel well bred people, all of one heart and mind."[4]

The essential commercial and middle-class origin of American urban life helps to explain why a New Yorker could feel at home in Bristol and be able to represent that seaport in the British Parliament during the most critical years of the Revolution. The member in question was Henry Cruger, of New York, a graduate of King's College, now Columbia University, who had gone to Bristol in 1757 to learn the family business, which consisted principally of sending English goods to New York and importing mahogany and whale oil. He became a partner in the firm of Cruger and Mallard, merchants in the American trade, and had married there the daughter of a wealthy banker by the name of Peach who added to his already considerable fortune by a traffic in slaves.[5] For a number of years Cruger had taken an active part in the public affairs of a commercial community whose interests were intimately bound up with those of America. Commerce led him to politics, and when the Stamp Act had exasperated opinion in the Colonies, Cruger carried to London a petition from Bristol for its repeal, and spent three weeks ineffectually pleading with members of Parliament as earnestly "as it were for my own life." He wrote at this time to a friend, "I am no politician, but in the matter of America and its trade I embarked body and soul."[6]

Eight years later, in 1774, "Doodle Doo," as Cruger became familiarly known in Bristol, decided to enter politics for himself. As an American he felt pleased to represent an English constituency and believed that he would be able to express the colonial point of view with advantage to both sides. "The Hibernian Demosthenes," Edmund Burke, had been invited at this time to stand for Bristol by his friend the porcelain-maker, Richard Champion, who after the Revolution moved to South Carolina.[7] On a ticket of "Burke, Cruger, and Liberty," the two men ran together for Parliament. Each candidate, however, contested the election separately with separate funds and platforms, for Cruger advocated certain reforms like a short Parliament and a bill for disabling members from holding public offices, which were impossible for a politician like Burke to relish. The latter found his revenge when he learned that the New Yorker had described himself in his campaign as the servant of his constituents not their master. This gave Burke a magnificent opportunity to assert, in often quoted words, the righteous but double-edged argument, that a member owed his electors, not merely his industry, but his judgment, and that he betrayed instead of serving these if he sacrificed his convictions to their opinion. The criticism implied of Cruger was none too fair and it is no disparagement to Burke to remark that it was his fellow-member from Bristol who in Parliament showed the greater independence of the two men.[8]

The 1774 election was hotly contested, with both candidates coming in for the grossest abuse and the most enthusiastic support. According to the custom they were "chaired" after their victory. Even in that moment of triumph their feelings for each other were hardly more friendly than those felt towards them by their late opponents, and neither did justice to his associate. In a letter, intercepted by the Post Office, Cruger had censured the "selfish and crafty action" of his fellow-member,[9] and Burke spoke of "the absurd and petty behaviour of my foolish colleague,"[10] who shortly after was to show that he was neither absurd nor petty. The latter's unsuccessful opponent, Brickdale, had ineffectually tried to prevent Cruger from taking his seat on the ground that he was an American. He continued his unscrupulous campaign and accused the new member of having written a letter to an unnamed person in Philadelphia which contained some violent abuse of England and an alleged copy of which was published in the *Bristol Gazette*. Governor Hutchinson, who disliked seeing a New York Whig sitting in a British Parliament, noted approvingly that if the contents of this letter had been known earlier Cruger would have been defeated.[11]

The story shows pure partisanship, for the new member from Bristol wrote at once after the election to his brother-in-law, Peter Van Schaack, in New York, who all along had kept him informed about the conditions in the Colonies, to say that he intended to connect himself with none of the violent parties in Parliament, and, although Lord North was convinced that he was all gunpowder, he proposed to undeceive him "if a moderate and modest speech can do it";[12] the greatest ambition of the new Whig member was to prove that in a British Parliament he could show himself to be both a patriotic American and a loyal subject to George the Third.

The New Yorker began his career as a British legislator with a remarkable maiden speech delivered at Westminster on December 16, 1774. After lamenting the enforcement of coercive measures which only widened the breach and diminished the obedience of the Colonies, he declared that every American who loved his country must also wish for the prosperity of Great Britain and the uninterrupted continuation of their union, for if the parent trunk was injured the branches would suffer. He attributed the recent punitive measures of the Crown to the still undefined nature of the relationship which existed between England and her Colonies, and ascribed to an identical cause the "violence and mistakes of America." Why, he argued, should British authority be strained so as to make submission impossible without a surrender of liberties acknowledged to be the birthright of Englishmen? Those who insisted on these measures seemed to have more in mind the hardship they would inflict on Americans than the benefits they could obtain from them. The effect would only be to increase discontent, and even if coercion forced the colonists in the end to give in, where would lie the advantage? He asked, "Will severities increase their affection and make them more desirous of a connection with and dependence on Great Britain?" Was it not more likely that such a policy would cause them to fly "to the protection of another power," he declared with prophetic foresight.[13]

Praise for this speech came from many quarters. The Reverend John Vardill, a friend of Cruger, who had just taken holy orders and not yet become an English spy, wrote enthusiastically that he seemed "to glory in being a New Yorker." Applause was plentiful for the new member, but Cruger's views counted for little in that packed Tory Parliament in which speeches might change opinions, but never votes.

Two months later, during another debate, a Tory member, Colonel Grant, who professed to possess an intimate knowledge of American character on the score of having once served in the Colonies, gave his expert opinion as a soldier that Americans would never dare to fight nor face a British army. General Wolfe had expressed a very similar judgment doubtless angered at the time by his colonial teamsters.

This was an old argument which helped to confirm the King in his obstinacy and more than any other had infuriated the colonists. Cruger rose at once to challenge the aspersion, and, while vindicating the courage of his people lost his temper, became personal, and had to be called to order.[14] Governor Hutchinson wrote in his *Diary* a burlesque account of the incident and described the House as laughing when it heard Cruger's alleged remark that although an American he lived in Parliament Street, after which the member from Bristol found himself unable to continue his speech.[15] In reality Cruger's words, though they remained without any result, were deeply impressive. The New Yorker pointed out with great earnestness that they were all living on the brink of a precipice, that the salvation of the country depended on the measures they were about to take, and he pleaded though in vain for a plan to restore harmony.

At the moment of first taking his seat in Parliament, Cruger admitted that he had felt proud to be both a British "Senator" and the first American member. He was then keenly ambitious to render service to his country and to the Empire, and it took some time before he realized how utterly impossible this had become, most of all from a novice and a stranger in politics who had entered Parliament from a business community, was without county standing of his own and who sat on the wrong side of the House. Hope gave way to discouragement as he was made to understand the futility of all his efforts. In May, 1775, a petition had arrived, addressed to Parliament by the New York Assembly, forwarded over the signature of the Speaker, who was his own uncle, John Cruger. The memorial began with a declaration expressing the warmest sentiments of loyalty and affection to the King and of attachment to his person, family and government. Only after this came a list of remonstrances presented, however, in very respectful language. The Assembly when forwarding these insisted that they harboured no thought of diminishing the power of the mother country or of lessening the dignity of Parliament, and, although they could not avoid feeling sympathy for their brethren in Massachusetts, the New York Legislature expressed its own disapproval of the violent measures pursued by certain Colonies. In particular, the petition disclaimed all desire for independence, admitted the necessity of an ultimate authority in Parliament, and gratefully acknowledged the benefits derived from the parent state. Cruger spoke most warmly in support of this memorial and drew the attention of the House to the fact that, although New York could not wholly disregard the opinion of her sister colonies, yet, in contrast with those who "rush on to civil war" the leaders were attempting to find the way to a settlement. He might have argued with the tongue of angels that policy and justice alike urged the encouragement of such a spirit, but his speech could not have prevented the petition from being contemptuously rejected.[16]

In and out of Parliament, Cruger talked, reasoned, prayed, and prophesied, always hoping to bring about a settlement and always to no purpose. John Bull just then was in one of his most truculent moods, and the answer invariably given the New Yorker was that England would neither be intimidated nor receive its laws from America.[17] Obviously the member from Bristol was merely an isolated figure in a body which looked upon him as a stranger and in which every argument he advanced only exposed him to suspicion. There are moments in politics when reason counts for nothing and words of golden wisdom fall on deaf ears. A Tory House voting under strict party discipline cared nothing for the moderating counsels of a Whig of American origin, who was a newcomer in Parliament, and without family connections in England. For a man in public life there is no more distressing situation than to foresee a danger which he knows can still be remedied, but which all his efforts leave him powerless to avert. Through his brothers and friends in New York Cruger had remained in intimate touch with American opinion, and could clearly discern the disaster ahead occasioned by the obstinacy of the King and the complacent acquiescence of a packed Parliament. But the member from Bristol shouted vainly in the wilderness and was obliged to watch with growing despair the futile efforts still attempted by the colonists to effect a reconciliation. His words and warnings all went for nothing.

The keenest understanding of the danger was then to be found among the commercial classes in England, although their way of manifesting such opinions was not calculated to further their goal. One week after Bunker Hill was fought, the Lord Mayor, Aldermen, and Livery of the City of London petitioned the King to allow Americans to enjoy peace and liberty and declared that the resistance of the Colonies was in their opinion a duty to God. Solemnly they entreated His Majesty to dissolve the Parliament which under royal biddance had sanctioned such acts of cruelty as had been practised against Massachusetts, and to settle the dispute with the colonists upon an honourable and lasting foundation. They could hardly have anticipated any favourable result. Yet George the Third was enough of a politician to receive the petitioners politely after which he continued to do as he liked.

The Continental Congress then sitting in Philadelphia was

also to make one last effort at a reconciliation, which might still have been possible, if the King had shown himself a little more conciliatory. Three weeks after Bunker Hill had been fought, on July 8, 1775, a petition was forwarded to London over the signatures of the delegates, among whom can be read the names of John Adams and Thomas Jefferson, subscribing to a memorial which reminded George the Third that his American Colonies were "attached to your Majesty's person, family and government with all the devotion that principle and affection can inspire, connected with Great Britain by the strongest ties that can unite societies and deploring every event that tends in any way to weaken them." Congress expressed its wish for the blessings of this connection to be transmitted to succeeding generations and assured the King that nothing was desired inconsistent with the dignity and welfare of the Crown.[18] But Lord Dartmouth informed the delegates who presented this Memorial that "no answer would be given to it." Soon afterward, an English political correspondent, John Lloyd, wrote to the London printer, John Almon, that the petition had been treated with contempt and was the last that would be presented by Congress. "Next summer will witness alarming events in the British Empire," and he foretold the assistance which France would extend to the struggling Colonies.[19]

Three weeks after this final attempt at reconciliation had been rejected, Benjamin Franklin addressed a letter to Lord Howe, who, a convinced Whig, had formerly been the doctor's friend, to remind him that "Long did I endeavour with unfeigned and unwearied zeal to preserve from breaking that fine and noble china vase the British Empire, for I know that once being broken the separate parts could not retain even their share of the strength and value that existed in the whole."[20]

Warnings were wasted on a sovereign who was bent on carrying out a policy which called for force. Whoever did not see eye to eye with the King had become a suspect if not a rebel. For some time Cruger had been carefully watched by the government, and his correspondence was intercepted at the Post Office and sent to Cabinet Ministers, who, if they had taken the trouble, might have read the entreaties which his brother, John Harris Cruger, later a colonel in the British army, sent him from New York, imploring the member of Parliament not to insist on taxation, and writing, "Don't let's quarrel for the shadow and lose the substance. Sheathe the sword and trust to American generosity. We will be faithful, we will be loyal, we will be just."[21]

Other intercepted letters which Cruger received at this time from New York may have better diverted the British Post Office when they read them. One friend wrote that General Washington had discovered a series of frauds in the Massachusetts and Connecticut musters by which their officers had drawn pay for a far greater number of men than they had in the field, adding: "I believe the eastward people will twig them. You know it was their practice the last war. They cannot help it, poor people."[22]

In a parliamentary debate which was held on February 20, 1776, to discuss the ill success of British arms, the member from Bristol again spoke out his mind courageously. Victory itself, he declared, would be ruinous, and he then made use of the same argument which Lord Chatham invoked eighteen months later when he foretold that, whoever was the conqueror, England would have fallen upon her own sword.[23] In that hostile assembly, Cruger boldly affirmed that the Colonies were animated by a single soul and determined either to perish or be free, and he deplored the opinion then current in England that nothing would satisfy the Americans but independence. An unfair resentment had been kindled in this way against a people who, after having repeatedly submitted their complaints in vain to Parliament and Throne, at last took up arms in their own defence. Insults on their character had been added to encroachments on their rights as citizens, and all the overtures which they made had been treated with contempt. Even admitting that in the end the colonists would be defeated, what advantages could Great Britain hope to obtain from the bare acknowledgment of the right of Parliament to tax? Yet the breach was as yet not irreparable, and feelingly he pleaded for liberal terms to be offered which would instantly lead to a settlement. No little courage on the part of an American Whig in a Tory Parliament was needed to make this speech for Cruger could have had few illusions as to its effect. He made it, so he declared, to free his own conscience by condemning the useless and painful prosecution of the war.[24] If by any miracle his advice had then been followed and if the same terms had been offered which George the Third was prepared to grant two years later, the Revolution would have ended with its objects attained and England would have been spared the humiliation of defeat and the loss of an empire.

The member from Bristol was to make one more notable effort for peace. On December 10, 1777, after British prospects of victory had been dashed by Burgoyne's surrender, and the dreaded French Alliance threatened a fresh danger which everyone except the King foresaw, Lord North, still awaiting the result of Paul Wentworth's secret mission in Paris, had admitted for the first time in Parliament that propositions for a treaty of reconciliation might become necessary. Cruger rose to express his personal satisfaction with the Ministerial declaration in which he had been glad to discover a disposition for peace. He used words on this occasion which were more calculated to enhance the merit of his former advice than to convince the Cabinet. Expressing the hope that adversity had taught the Government wisdom, he remarked that it was unfortunate that the knowledge should have been so dearly bought. He recalled the petition from the New York Assembly which had been rejected with contempt. Military operations since then had weakened England, taught the Americans war and cemented their union. What greater folly could there be, as he pointed out, than to force a people into friendly allegiance by devastating their country. "You have subdued, not their armies, but the small remains of their affection," and it was madness to expect that men who had taken up arms in defence of their liberty should after victory be induced to throw these away and submit to their conquerors. Even those who had kept their fidelity to the Crown went unrewarded and the inhabitants of New York, "for all their singular loyalty,"were forced to live under military rule with their commerce at a standstill. Once more, before it was too late, he pleaded with the Government to abandon its absurd and pernicious measures. All the reports which he had received from his American connections convinced him that independence was not yet the great object of the majority of the people, and he urged as a sacrifice to peace the abandonment of a train of acts which had proved barren and useless.[25]

S

In spite of his difficult position in Parliament the member from Bristol acquitted himself with dignity, associating with the moderates who still hoped for a reconciliation. Paul Wentworth mentions him as belonging to a club which met at the Salopian Coffee House, "an object of the fraternity being to undertake fresh Yankees,"[26] though the spy Vardill was among its members. The effect of war is to reduce all except the most violent to silence. The wisest men can do little so soon as force takes the place of reason, and Cruger's hope of a great British Empire which should include the New World was now manifestly shattered. An American member in a Parliament which was occupied in conducting war against his native land found himself in a false position which left him without utility even to the opposition. For the Whig leaders, like Fox and Burke, were not inclined to pay much attention to an outsider who did not belong to their group by birth or training. He was almost alone in a hostile assembly and had become an isolated figure who represented a past that was no more and could no longer be revived. Only on rare occasions did he speak, always as an American who remained loyal to the ideal he had cherished long after he understood how impossible this had become. When General Conway advocated a so-called peace measure, the member from Bristol rose to say that the colonists four years earlier would have indignantly rejected similar terms. The French Alliance had given them the certainty of "Empire and Independence," and it was no longer possible to persuade them to return as subjects and foolish to attach any hope to the belief that the Americans did not care for their allies. Standing in a British Parliament Cruger declared that the United States had made a treaty with France and that their rising reputation as a nation depended upon its faithful observance. Even so, he announced that he would vote for Conway's Bill solely because it was a measure to promote reconciliation, although his ballot on a similar occasion had made him "a victim to obloquy." The New Yorker invited attention to his record in always opposing the taxation of the Colonies and other obnoxious measures, while simultaneously trying to discourage the excesses of the American leaders. "In my conscience I thought I was acting right. I meant it for the good of both countries. I have no reason now to find fault with my conduct."

To accept the recognition of independence as inevitable and follow this by a reconciliation, was the policy which Cruger now advocated, and it was one also approved by many of the very members who under the lash of party whips voted against it. Few had the courage to express their views in Parliament, but numerous were the Tories who knew that independence would have to be accepted in the interest of Great Britain, and that it was a blunder to allow the new republic to increase its intimacy with the enemies of England. When the member from Bristol spoke on this subject at Westminster, he declared with great feeling: "No man's mind can possibly be more hurt than mine is at the separation between the two countries, which appears to be so unavoidable," yet gladly would he give his vote to accept independence which would alone secure peace, and thereafter attempt to conquer America by generosity.[27]

The war election of 1780, when Paul Wentworth was given a safe Government seat as a reward for his services as a master spy, brought only a momentary triumph to the Tories on a so-called patriotic issue. The Secretary of the Treasury had made a grant of a thousand pounds to the Tory candidates at Bristol,[28] and as an electioneering dodge the thirteen stripes were hoisted on many of its churches in order to incense the voters by making them believe that the New Yorker wished for the success of the revolted colonies. After Cruger had gone down to defeat, he addressed his supporters for a last time, to remind them that seven years before, it had been no crime to be born in America, and that as a British subject he would always show himself zealous for British liberty. He and his followers had been misrepresented as enemies to the Church and King, although His Majesty in all his dominions had no subjects more attached to his person and government. He hoped that the year would bring peace with America and expressed a prophetic wish to have one soul dominating the extensive empire. Also he looked forward to the development of future trade, and foretold that America would once more be a reservoir of wealth to all.[29]

In the year following, Cruger was elected Mayor of Bristol. As soon as peace was signed, he returned, however, to New York to attend to certain private affairs and during his absence he was again chosen candidate as "the man of the common people," and triumphantly re-elected to Parliament in 1784, over his opponent, a certain Daubeny. The latter during a venomous campaign abused him as a "rebel" and a violator of decency toward the sovereignty of his country, who had acquired American citizenship merely to preserve some landed property. Cruger's enemies tried ineffectually to have his election set aside as invalid, on the ground of his being ineligible as an American and no longer a British subject.

The question of dual allegiance still exists to perplex legal minds, but the independence of the United States offered a

novel case in politics concerning the status of a large number
of individuals. For a man like Cruger, with a genuine loyalty
to both sides, which was no longer compatible, and possessing
interests in both countries, the position had plainly become
one of extreme difficulty. The defence against his defeated
opponent's savage attack was, however, taken up by a barrister
of the Inner Temple, named Dawes, who published a tract
on this subject,[30] and with doubtful legal reasoning denounced
as absurd the charge that Cruger was no longer an Englishman
because he might have taken an oath of allegiance to Congress.
The member from Bristol denied that he had ever subscribed
to such an oath, but, even supposing this to be true, the lawyer
maintained that he could have qualified his statement so as
not to imply a renunciation of his loyalty to the King. The
question of American-born British subjects was still in suspense and the lawyer admitted as a moot point, whether the
fact of a man owning landed property in the United States at
a time when the country was under British domination, and
afterwards taking an oath of allegiance to the new Republic in
order to preserve his property, implied a renunciation of his
English citizenship. Behind the legal fiction of two nationalities
lay the fact that America was "a country like unto our own,
peopled as it were by our fellow-countrymen, who speak our
language, bear our names, profess our religion, and are
governed in a like way," and there was no reason to think
that, because America had obtained her independence by
mutual consent, she would, like France or Spain, be a natural
enemy in her laws, religion, constitution, and views. It was
more likely to anticipate that she would become "a co-oper-
ating friend under the cement of a federal union." And if this
were true, ought the circumstance of an Englishman having

taken an oath to Congress to be regarded as a renunciation of his allegiance?[31]

Odd as this reasoning may seem to-day, unsound as it is according to international law, the barrister had in mind the same deep popular belief which countless others on either side of the Atlantic at that time and since have often felt gripping their hearts. Grievances, misunderstandings, and blunders had driven the two countries wide apart and anticipated the normal and inevitable march of history by using a revolution to make an independent nation out of thirteen Colonies many years sooner and with far greater violence and animosity than the processes by which this might otherwise have come about. Legal fictions henceforth would regard two peoples as though they were strangers to each other, and a narrow bureaucracy could pick at times on controversial points to envenom disputes. But there was also something deeper and more significant than the law, something which outlasted animosity, which caused the mistakes of politicians to be forgiven, and kept Englishmen and Americans bound in a reciprocal relation towards each other, no less real because it was henceforth to be free from any quarrel over sovereignty and had to remain below the surface undefined, inarticulate, and instinctive.

An American member from Bristol sitting in a British Parliament which had just recognized the independence of his native country, torn between two sides, could hardly feel at ease under attacks which made necessary a lawyer's defence. One of his brothers, Nicholas Cruger, who was a friend of Washington, had fought as an American, the other, Colonel John Harris Cruger, had served in the British army, had seen his estate in New York confiscated and had gone to

England to live there in permanent exile. Not unnaturally, Henry Cruger's loyalties were too divided to enjoy peace of mind. Former views were manifestly no longer possible to hold, and it was apparent that every year would widen the political breach between the two countries. In 1784, he had accepted re-election to Parliament probably only to vindicate himself for his earlier defeat, but his position as a member could no longer have been comfortable. He had become an anachronism and represented an order which had ceased to exist. No more did he take an active part in the debates, doubtless feeling the anomaly of his status. Six years later, he declined to stand again and soon after this refusal moved with all his family to New York. In 1792, the former member from Bristol was elected to the State Senate at Albany. The compliment was pleasing, but it could lead to no future in his native land. After having been too American to succeed in England, he was certainly too English for American politics. He retired permanently into private life and died a very old man in New York in 1827.

Although singular in his Parliamentary position, Cruger's double loyalty as a British subject and an American had been common enough in the Colonies even after the Revolution began. When with the progress of hostilities the two became incompatible and a choice had to be made, the preference was perhaps oftener given to the native land by New York loyalists than in the New England states where partisanship from the outset had been excited to greater bitterness.

No better illustration of this readiness to accept new conditions can be found than in the case of Cruger's brother-in-law, Peter Van Schaack, of Kinderhoek, New York, who was a singularly estimable lawyer, almost over-virtuous, like another Sir Charles Grandison, and with political convictions similar to those held by the member from Bristol. Before the Revolution, Van Schaack had enjoyed the personal friendship of many American leaders in New York, and even after hostilities had broken out he was never accused of having committed any enemy act. His avowed loyalty to the Crown gave offence, however, to the patriots, who were then in no mood for half-measures. Summoned to Albany in 1776, on a charge of disaffection to the American cause, and having refused to take the oath of allegiance, he was banished at first to Boston, although allowed to return to his home at Kinderhoek in the following year.[32] His wife was then in the last stages of consumption, yet forbidden to go to New York for treatment or even to consult an English physician of repute who had been captured at Saratoga. In 1778, Van Schaack, after another refusal to swear allegiance, was sentenced to perpetual banishment by order of his own former law student, Leonard Gansevoort, sent within the British lines, and threatened with death if he returned. He sailed soon after for England, leaving his children behind and expressing the wish that his son, who was about to enter Yale, should never cross the ocean, for he desired him to have an American education even if he remained unacquainted with old world refinements.

Like most of the refugees, Van Schaack suffered from financial embarrassment during his exile. Like the others, he petitioned the British Government for a small sum to support him until able to return,[33] giving as justification the loss of his property and the restrictions imposed on the future practice of his profession. A grant of a hundred pounds had been made to him, but he learned of this only after the pension was cut down to sixty, regarded by the Treasury as sufficient for a man who had not exceeded this amount in his annual living expenses in England.[34] His great wish was to return to his home, although he expected to be debarred from resuming his former profession by an act which disqualified all persons from practising law who had not supported American independence.[35]

When peace came, Van Schaack was still living in England. His old friend, John Jay, wrote from Paris to remind him that, although the two had differed in their conscience, when all who were not with the Americans, and he among the rest, had been regarded as enemies, yet this had never kept John Jay from being the friend of Peter Van Schaack nor did he blame him for having taken the side he considered right. Jay asked for news, and, in ignorance of what were his means of support, generously offered assistance to the exile. "While I have a loaf, you and they may freely partake of it. Don't let the idea hurt you. If your circumstances are easy, I rejoice; if not, let me take off their rougher edges."[36]

Even from so warm a friend Van Schaack needed no help. He was a philosopher who wanted only to return to his home if this was possible and was already reconciled to the defeat of his side. He wrote that if America was to be happier from the Revolution, he would be first to rejoice at his side having been vanquished, and he added, "My heart warms whenever our country (I must call it my country) is the subject, and in my separation from it I have dragged at each remove a lengthening chain."[37] To his brother he declared that he now welcomed American independence from the bottom of his heart, though along with this joy there was mingled pain at the sufferings of loyalists who had sacrificed their life and fortune "to an object merely ideal."

In spite of his own exile, Van Schaack felt no sympathy

for those unreconciled loyalists who announced that they could not bear to live under the government of people they hated. As a man of moderate views and small ambition, he declared that power had no such charm as to cause him to care much who possessed it. The lesson of history showed that revolutions had taken place in all countries and that the weaker must submit to the stronger. In the belief that America would be as well governed as any part of the old world, for its inhabitants were neither more corrupt nor less sensible, he had made up his mind to be as good a subject of the new government as of the old. Nor did he see anything derogatory to his self-respect in the readiness to be loyal to the new state. If these views were acceptable to those who were in power he would gladly return. If he was unwelcome, his heart would not be broken, and he concluded a letter in which he explained these opinions with the words: "We ought now to consider ourselves in no other light than that of citizens of America . . . the affairs and concerns of England will in a little time affect us no more than those of any other state in Europe."[38]

When Peter Van Schaack arrived in New York, after the years of exile passed in London, he was met by John Jay, who went aboard his ship and took him personally to call on the Governor and the Chief Justice. The returning loyalist received a warm welcome, even from such violent Whigs as Governor Clinton.

II

Peter Van Schaack and Henry Cruger belonged to that reasonable loyalist element more numerous than it was conspicuous in the Colonies, where after the struggle had begun moderation was usually hushed into silence or frightened into partisanship. The greater distance of England from the storm centre and an older political tradition allowed more tolerance for expressions of opinion by the "friends of America." At the time of the peace negotiations, John Adams had remarked, somewhat cynically, that opposition to the Ministry was the only solid ground on which rested this friendship.[39] There was some truth in this opinion, for also Jonathan Boucher had noticed several years before that many sympathizers with the Colonies evinced their feelings "not from affection to the Americans, but disaffection to the Ministry." Yet there was more than partisan rancour in the sympathy felt for the Colonists. Men like Franklin's friend, the good Bishop of Saint Asaph,[40] the Dukes of Richmond and Rutland, and David Hartley, had always been sincere in their conviction that America ought not to be conquered even if this was possible, and believed that if British liberty was to be preserved, no body of freemen should be subjected against their will. An obscure English political correspondent named John Lloyd, at a time when John Adams had as yet no thought of breaking away from England, wrote from the provinces so early as October, 1776, to the London printer, John Almon: "The infamous system of Colonial Government has lost America, I have no doubt but her independency will be effectually established; it is not in the power of this country to make America an adequate compensation for the injuries she has sustained, therefore no reconciliation can or ought to be expected."[41]

Patriots like Adams, who until peace had been concluded looked with suspicion on everything which came out of

England, as well as loyalists like Governor Hutchinson, and later Joseph Galloway, who thought that the Revolution was only succeeding because of British support, agreed at least in finding something reprehensible about this attitude of the Whig leaders, whose American sympathy went not nearly far enough for the one and much too far for the others. In his still unpublished history about the origins of the war, Chief Justice Oliver relates that the Americans had been able to secure the friendship of the seditious in England—of merchants who were republican from interest, "but also of another set of men of no ignoble degree who having ate their cake and being turned away, cried to have their cake again, and thought that by encouraging the revolt in America they would have it. Among these though not equal in dignity was a most eccentric character who had been Governor of an American province."[42] This was Thomas Pownall.

Governor Pownall, as he is generally called, colonial administrator, politician, scholar, antiquarian, and philosophic statesman, was a man of whom it would be difficult to say if his parts or his vanity were the greater. He had foresight and possessed an intimate personal knowledge of American affairs, but his influence was negligible in a Parliament, in which he had crossed over to the Tory party without really adopting Tory opinions. Like John Temple, the Governor was an Englishman who felt himself to be also an American, and later thought of becoming one.

So far back as 1754, when Pownall was present as a spectator at the meeting held at Albany to adopt common measures of defence against the French, he had conceived the idea of a Federation of the Colonies, and many years afterwards he recalled with pride, having negotiated the first union of the forces of New York, Pennsylvania, New Jersey, and New England, for service against the French garrison at Crown Point. Soon after appointed Governor of Massachusetts, he made himself very popular in the province in spite of certain convivial tastes which did not meet with puritan approval. Sam Adams, who was indifferent to Pownall's wide scholarship, which led him to make a study of Indian picture writing, denounced the Governor as a "mere fribble" only because he gave dances "to please a few boys and girls."[43] With greater insight John Adams had admired in the student of Indian lore the most constitutional representative of the Crown ever known in Massachusetts and praised him as a friend of liberty and a patriot who considered that North America was quite as much a part of his country as was England or Scotland.[44] When Pownall resigned from his office to return to London in 1760, both branches of the Massachusetts Legislature showed their respect by accompanying the Governor to his ship.

Unable to obtain any further official preferment Pownall occupied himself with political writing, and in his famous work on Colonial Administration which first appeared in 1764, he outlined a plan to unite the Atlantic and American possessions into one dominion of which Great Britain was to be the commercial centre. The Colonies, although retaining separate administrations, were to be subordinated to a Federal Parliament in which every state was to be represented. Pownall had already the vision of the British Isles and the Colonies forming a great sea empire which ought to be united, and he foresaw that ultimately the centre of this empire might even be in America. Ideas of this kind, were of course regarded as visionary by politicians but they aroused an interest which

was not unlike that felt for certain of Mr. Wells's antici-
pations.

At a time when the Governor's brother John, who was a
permanent official in the Colonial Office, had advised arresting
Adams and the other "principal incendiaries," bringing them
to England for trial, and, if found guilty, putting them to
death,[45] Thomas Pownall's sympathies went unreservedly to
the American side. He had a friendly spar with Governor
Hutchinson, when he asked him to dinner and in his own
house implied blame on the latter for the way he had acted in
the matter of the tea.[46] The discussion on this occasion was
not pushed too far by the host, though Pownall made no secret
of his opinion that taxation without representation would bring
about armed resistance in the Colonies. Franklin always
regarded Pownall as a warm friend of America and described
a *tête-à-tête* dinner at his house in London in 1775, at which
the latter explained his reasons for most unexpectedly having
left the Whigs to support the Tory Ministry. The former
Governor hoped at this time to be employed as a commissioner
to settle the differences with America and asked for Franklin's
co-operation. With intense interest the latter listened to his
account of Lord North as personally disapproving of the very
measures he had taken and still anxious for a reconciliation,
but paid little attention to the overtures which the Governor
made to him, feeling certain that neither one would be so
employed.[47]

On one occasion Pownall had modestly asserted, in a speech
in Parliament on American affairs, that "There was nobody
at that time who knew so much about the matter as myself."[48]
It was true that he knew more about the real conditions
and feeling in the Colonies than any other Englishman of

his time, though the method he selected of conveying this superiority was not calculated to increase his popularity among fellow-members. Neither did his party approve of his opinions. After a long opposition he had unexpectedly entered the House of Commons as a Government member who held the same opinions as Cruger, even if he sat on the opposite side. Yet with similar aims, in the same Parliament, the two men remained virtual strangers to each other and there is no record of any relations between them. Ambition had turned Pownall into a nominal Tory, and not without some reason Burke despised him as a place-hunter, for the turncoat in politics is never forgiven by the side he has left and rarely more than tolerated by the party he joins. The Governor, however, had too much honesty and foresight to feel comfortable in his new affiliations or continue subservient to partisan discipline with regard to measures of which he thoroughly disapproved. His independent views soon caused the Ministers to regard him as unreliable, and later he quoted their opinion of him as being a "wild man" unfit to be employed.[49] The King with his long memory did not trust him, and found further reason for this suspicion when Benjamin Thompson, to curry favour, presented George the Third with a number of Pownall's letters written to friends in Boston and expressing his sympathy with the Colonies. Worst of all the Governor's speeches on America were extremely boring and of inexcusable length. Members yawned and crawled away from the drab delivery of Burke's solemn eloquence, but even the latter could occasionally raise the laughter of the House at Governor Pownall's expense.[50]

In spite of these small sides to his character there were some large sides to his speeches for Pownall's ideas were those of a statesman far in advance of his age. At first, when making an effort to be a Ministerial hack at Westminster, he had duly declared that he would never think of laying down arms in the face of the enemy, and that the Americans by preparing for war had set the example. Later he was reproached for inconsistency. His pretence of Tory orthodoxy was not long kept up, and on November 8, 1775, the Governor, at a time when even leaders in the Colonies would have indignantly repudiated the suggestion, foretold in Parliament that the Americans meditated, were able to establish, and would establish a Republic, and an independent state, although necessity had not yet driven them so far. The colonists earnestly wished to remain united to England, subordinate to the mother country, obedient to its sovereignty, and in his opinion peace could still be had on safe and honourable terms.[51] Two years later, on December 2, 1777, after Fox had proposed some futile measures in the hope of alluring the states to return to their allegiance, Pownall rose to tell the House that Americans would never again return to their subjection to the British Government and they had gone too far to retreat. For the first time the House of Commons heard from his lips the ominous words: "Your sovereignty over America is abolished and gone for ever." The idea of a Peace Commission was then in the wind and some intimation of the plan advanced by Paul Wentworth had already leaked out, for the Governor asked of what use were Commissioners with instructions that presupposed a domination which no longer existed. Until Parliament was convinced that the inhabitants of the United States were a free and independent people, and until they were prepared to treat with them as such, no scheme of conciliation which the House might adopt would be of any consequence, and the only treaty which henceforth could be expected with America was one of commerce between the two countries.[52] When next he spoke on this subject, in March, 1778, it was to foretell the failure of the Peace Commission which had just been appointed and allude to a letter he had lately received from Franklin in Paris, though without mention of his name, expressing the latter's hope to resume friendly relations with England on condition of acknowledging independence.[53]

A month before this speech, Lord Rockingham had read in Parliament a letter which General Gates, the British-born commander of the American army that had just compelled Burgoyne's surrender at Saratoga, had shortly before addressed to Lord Thanet. Gates invited attention to the fact that, born and educated in England, he could not help feeling for the misfortunes of his native country caused by the wickedness of the administration, and gave as his opinion that it needed a statesman like Lord Chatham to save the sinking ship and accept that independence for which the American people were ready to die. He bade Great Britain withdraw its fleets and armies in order henceforth to cultivate the amity and commerce of the new Republic. These were the sentiments, General Gates declared, of a man who did not rejoice in the bloodshed of the contest, "of a man who glories in the name of an Englishman and wishes to see peace and friendship between Great Britain and America fixed upon the firmest foundation."[54]

If there could be anything more extraordinary than the English-born commander of a victorious army, who as a young man had suffered in England from the humiliation of his lowly birth bringing about the humiliating surrender of a British force, it was to see him offer unsolicited advice for

T

a change of Government in the country with which his own was at war and for a letter of this nature to be read in Parliament by the leader of the Opposition. Nor can anything illustrate more strikingly the confusion of ideas which still prevailed in the minds of many men in both countries, who had not yet understood that, as soon as the American Revolution became a struggle for independence, it had ceased to be a civil war.

Thirty years earlier, the future independence of the Colonies had already been foretold by the Swedish traveller, Peter Kalm, [55] and in 1770 Horace Walpole prophesied the day when twenty empires and republics would form on a vast scale to cover the American continent, which was growing "too mighty to be kept in subjection to half a dozen exhausted nations in Europe."[56] After Bunker Hill, the Lord of Strawberry Hill expressed doubts if England would ever be able to conquer the Americans. But Walpole was not a politician, felt no responsibility, detested the Government, and wrote whatever thoughts passed through his mind and seemed to him appropriate for posterity to admire.

Governor Pownall's position was very different. He had been extremely ambitious for a place, had become a Tory almost on sufferance, and knew that his speech, urging the recognition of independence must give deep offence to the Government. Yet he was undeterred by the consequences of what he said. With more regard to truth than to his career he declared that the United States were willing to be friends, but never slaves. His political office, in fact, came to an end with the life of that ⌐arliament. A solitary figure in his new party, he often had his say courageously and wisely. He spoke with humanity when he denounced the use of Indians by the

British and with all the greater authority because he had himself been a witness to their atrocities.[57] But he spoke always in vain. When the Peace Embassy was to be sent over Pownall had recommended that the Commissioners should be instructed to acknowledge American independence and negotiate treaties of commerce with the United States.[58] Two years later he maintained in Parliament that America was a free sovereign power and would remain so, and moved a Bill authorizing the King to make peace with his former subjects.[59] He talked, however, as an isolated member and his opinions were only regarded as being the expressions of a "wild man." Yet they deserve to be recorded in the history of a Parliament which was notable for its servile discipline.

During the years of war the Governor had been in occasional correspondence with Franklin in Paris, exchanging such letters as he declared, "a man of honour could write to the Minister of a Power with which his country is at war."[60] As soon as the treaty of peace had been signed, he hastened to congratulate his old friend on the establishment of the Republic as an independent state. Also he published a Memorial addressed to "the Sovereigns of America" by T. Pownall, late Governor, Captain General, Vice-Admiral, etcetera, of Massachusetts, which began almost as grandiloquently as the list of his own titles with the words:

> Therefore United States and citizens of America I address you as you are: I do it under every sense and sentiment of reverence to your sovereign nation. . . . I congratulate you as Free States as founded and built upon the principles of human freedom.

After which he lavished praise for the totally novel system at the foundation of the Republic which held in esteem only whatever led to equality of rights. A wave of enthusiasm for democracy had just then swept over Europe equally felt by English Whigs and many French aristocrats. Pownall, who shared this feeling, became enthusiastic at the absence of any feudal survivals in the new land of liberty, and wrote approvingly of how the American citizen found nothing to repress or to exclude him from rising to that natural importance in the community to which he was rightly entitled.[61] Wishing also to show his friendship in a practical manner, the Governor offered Harvard a tract of five hundred acres of land with which to endow a chair of political law in order to train students to become useful members of a free state. The land had originally been a gift from the Kennebec Company, but, unknown to him, at the time had already been sold for taxes which when he learned of, he offered to pay back. Later, after great trouble and expense the college succeeded in obtaining for the property little more than three hundred dollars.[62]

It was apparent that Pownall's independent attitude in Parliament left him without any future expectation of office in England. Thoroughly disgusted by his treatment, discredited with the Tories, and unable to go back to the Whigs, he now thought seriously of becoming an American and of settling in the United States, and proposed to bring over with him several families of farmers who would be established on reclaimed soil which he intended at this time to purchase. In a letter to his old friend, James Bowdoin, written to congratulate him and the State of Massachusetts on the establishment of its political freedom, in case a former Governor's wishes were still acceptable, he announced his impending visit to see the country in its new independence and his intention "to adopt that branch of the English nation which shall adopt me." Above those foibles and vanities which obscured the man's true worth, a statesmanlike foresight can be seen in the vision which Pownall then drew of the future of the United States:

> To see the commencement of a great Empire at its first foundation is an object that no other period, no other part of the world, ever since it was a world could exhibit . . . and to one who loved that country so rising an Empire must be a source of joy.[63]

This letter of congratulation gave great satisfaction when it was publicly read before both Houses of the Massachusetts Legislature. But Bowdoin wrote to warn the old Governor that although he would receive the heartiest welcome, for there was no resentment except against refugees, the changes which had taken place in the few years since the war were as remarkable as the Revolution itself, and on his return he would find mostly new faces.[64] Bowdoin sent this message by his son-in-law, John Temple, who, after his misadventures in Boston, was on the point of sailing for England. Pownall's intentions to settle in America became more remote. Perhaps his remarriage had something to do with this. He was then an old man and may have dreaded the hardships of establishing himself in a new country. Benjamin Vaughan, who had been Lord Shelburne's secretary, afterward emigrated to Maine, but he was many years younger.

Yet Pownall retained his sympathy for Massachusetts and announced his intention of leaving by will all his printed books to Harvard, though no record exists of this donation having reached the college library. Later he acquired an interest of a different kind in the New World, for he also predicted the independence of the Spanish Colonies, acted as the political adviser in London of General Miranda, and became so enthusiastic for the latter's plan of liberation that advanced age alone prevented him from joining in the proposed revolt.

Pownall's most curious ambition has still to be made known. With the feeling that he had been badly treated by the British Government and smarting under this neglect, he asked for a strange mark of appreciation from the State where formerly he had been Governor. He reminded Bowdoin that it had once been his prerogative to bestow honours and commissions on others; now he would like to receive from Massachusetts the honorary title of a lieutenant-general, though also willing to accept one of major-general if no higher rank was granted. Having been left without esteem by his native country, his ambition was henceforth to appear in Europe "in my *American rank* which I will be proud of and will not dishonour," and he proposed, wherever he went, to wear the uniform and livery of the State that had so honoured him.[65]

Unfortunately, political reasons prevented the possibility of gratifying this quaint desire. Most tactfully James Bowdoin explained to the old Governor that major-generals in Massachusetts were limited by the law to three, and that commissions for these had already been granted. If a new rank, even honorary, were to be given, this would encourage French subjects to apply and either to refuse or to yield to their requests would lead to the most disagreeable consequences. With every wish to accord a mark of appreciation, Bowdoin hesitated to introduce a motion in the House for he feared its non-success.[66] And Governor Pownall, who in the prime of his life had failed to bring about his plan to make of Great Britain a sea empire, failed in his old age to become an honorary major-general of militia in the State of Massachusetts.

PART THREE

American Painters in England

Chapter Nine

Benjamin West, Court Painter

I

AN OLD man of over eighty years lay ill on his couch from which he was never more to rise, and, looking back on the memories of a long life, had reason to feel content. Born poor and obscure in a distant colony, he had arrived an unknown stranger in England to attain dignity, affluence, and fame. He had enjoyed the warm friendship of a king and kept this while his native country, to which he was deeply attached, was throwing over that monarch's rule. He had risen to an eminent position in British art and had formed a valuable and dearly loved collection of old masters. His family life had been singularly happy, and he could recall with satisfaction innumerable acts of kindness towards his fellow men. Success he attributed to his genius, for he felt as certain that his future fame would always be linked with the glorious names of Raphael and Michelangelo as of the immortality of his soul. And the English public which ended by sharing the painter's conviction of his own greatness had rewarded him with its munificent patronage to a degree hitherto unprecedented in the annals of art.

In the small Quaker settlement of Springfield, on the fringe of what was then the primeval forest which traversed Chester, now called Delaware County, in Pennsylvania, Benjamin West was born on October 10, 1738. His father was an Englishman

by birth, who had kept a public-house in the vicinity and did
not join Meeting till late in life. For some unknown reason his
mother had been disowned by the Community of Friends
and no record has been discovered of West ever having been
received as a Quaker.[1] Yet he always claimed youthful membership in that sect, perhaps because his origin made this seem
appropriate but more likely because of its singularity in the
annals of art. West, in his old age, felt convinced that a genius
so great as his own could not have been born without some
portent, and took delight in weaving a half-mythical legend
around his beginnings. His life had always been so regular, so
virtuous, and so uneventful, that his imaginative fancy, in
order to escape from the placid chronicle of his career, was
obliged to run back to embellished memories of early days in
the forest. The painter, at the height of his fame, found pleasure
in recalling a few childhood incidents which he believed contained already the premonitions of his talent. He was proud
of the fact that no other artist could be pointed to who had
felt equally at home in the wigwams of American savages
and the refinements of royal palaces in Europe.[2] Although
his brush was somewhat anæmic in its use of colour, he alleged
that Indians had taught him as a child how to prepare the
ochre with which they daubed their bodies. Also, he associated
the first signs of his later calling with a touching filial sentiment.
His mother, on discovering that he had played the truant from
school in order to draw his baby sister in her cradle, instead of
punishing, kissed the future President of the Royal Academy,
and that kiss to a child, West sententiously declared, "made
me a painter."

There is a legend, doubtless improved by the romantic
John Galt, who became West's official biographer, but which

the latter had related to him, that his early ambition to become an artist filled the Quakers with consternation. Solemnly, therefore, they met to discuss the propriety of allowing one of their young brethren to follow so vain an occupation. After several unfavourable opinions had been expressed an elder, highly esteemed for his virtues, declared that he discerned in the youth's artistic bent the evidence of Divine Will. His fervour at last persuaded the Friends, and gravely all the elders then laid their hands on the boy's head and the women kissed his forehead. In that small settlement in the wilderness, the future Court painter felt that he had been anointed, and, like a priest in the Temple, West knew that henceforth he was dedicated to Art and pledged to use his talents only for subjects holy and pure.

Still untaught in his future profession, and barely possessing the most elementary rudiments of an education, West at the age of eighteen left the small community in which he had grown up to begin his career as a portrait painter in Philadelphia. His demands were then still modest. Two and a half guineas for a head, five for a half-length, were the charges asked by the future Academician, who afterwards in London raised the scale of remuneration for artists to most unprecedented and astonishing heights. Life in the Quaker capital at this time was still wanting in what West later described as the "elegancies of intercourse." Fresh from sylvan surroundings, the young painter may have been less unpleasantly affected by this innocent simplicity than many years later, when, with more exacting standards of comparison he looked back to this period of his life. Even so, he found generous patrons at Philadelphia in men of undoubted cultivation like the Chief Justice William Allen who had once been a pensioner of Clare College, Cambridge, and in his brother-in-law, Governor Hamilton, at whose house West copied the first real picture he had ever seen— a Saint Ignatius of the school of Murillo, captured as booty from a Spanish prize.

The painter's next occasion to practise his art came in New York, which, according to the Tory historian, Thomas Jones, was at this time, enjoying its golden age. Many years afterwards, when West looked back on this phase of his career he contrasted entirely to the advantage of Philadelphia the cruder social usages which he remembered as having seen practised in Manhattan. But the painter had no cause to feel ungrateful with its customs for, like many future visiting artists in New York he doubled his charges and yet increased his orders. One munificent sitter presented him with fifty guineas after he had learned of the young man's ambition to study in Europe, for West had already discovered the art of interesting patrons in his talent.

Opportunity to go abroad came to the painter in a curious way. In 1759, after a complete failure of the Italian harvest, a firm of Leghorn merchants, Messrs. Rutherford and Jackson, wrote to ask their agent in Pennsylvania, Chief Justice William Allen, who, with his magistracy, combined a business occupation, to send over to them a cargo of flour. Shipments of American foodstuffs have helped to make possible the formation of many later collections in the United States, but this was the first occasion in which they led to the enrichment of American art, for the same vessel which conveyed wheat abroad also carried Benjamin West on his first voyage across the Atlantic, taking with him Allen's recommendation to the English consignees. With real kindness the merchants of Leghorn gave him useful letters for Rome, and despatched him on his journey to the capital, accompanied by a garrulous French courier who told all he met that he was escorting an American savage who had crossed the ocean solely to study art, a report which in every Italian town caused crowds to gather around the young painter.

From birth West had been endowed with an inborn solemnity which found it natural to attach a transcendental importance to whatever he did. As the first American who had gone to study art in Italy, he had discovered the finger of Fate in his mission. An eighteenth century convention obliged travellers of sensibility and taste at the moment when for the first time they gazed on the Eternal City from the solitude of the Campagna, to be saddened by philosophic meditations on the decay of the Empire that once was Rome. After this appropriate mood of melancholy had depressed the young painter, he suddenly felt elated by the thought that the progress of the arts had always been from east to west and naturally he identified with his own genius the prospect of the future greatness of America. A chance incident to confirm this opinion took place soon after this in a coffee house. A local *improvisatore*, whom the Romans had nicknamed Homer, on hearing that an American was present, sang to foretell how the New World was destined to become the refuge of arts and sciences, after these had been driven away from Europe. The impoverished bard certainly had a more immediate and more practical goal than this distant prophecy, but West remembered it always as a most remarkable forecast of his own destiny.

In the course of nearly three thousand years of history the Papal Capital had gazed with fear, amazement, or fury on many of its invaders, but an American painter was a novelty which took even Romans by surprise. The most incredible reports were circulated about the stranger and reached the ears of a British visitor on the Grand Tour, Mr. Robinson, the future politician, who later became better known for his persuasive dispensation of Tory patronage. Mr. Robinson's interest in this strange wonder from the New World came perhaps as a relief from the one he had been sent to take, in the monuments of the Old. He called at once to invite West to dinner, after which he produced him as a curiosity at a party, where among the guests was Cardinal Albani, the famous antiquarian whose touch was so marvellously delicate that, although blind, no one understood ancient gems so well. When the learned Prince of the Church heard that a young American was present, he inquired if his colour was black or white. West was then presented to the Cardinal, who, after running his fingers over the painter's features, pronounced them comely.

Rome in the eighteenth century was a capital in which amiable and cultivated pursuits still seemed an appropriate recreation with which to occupy the attention of the great and the art-loving Cardinal could barely restrain his impatience to know what impression the first sight of the great Vatican Marbles might make on the mind of an untutored but comely barbarian of whose colour he had not been quite certain. He therefore suggested an interesting experiment, which met with an enthusiastic approval from the other guests at the party, in order to test how the mind of a young American savage would react to the genius of antiquity.

On the following morning a procession of thirty coaches, filled with learned dignitaries of the Church, great nobles, and distinguished strangers, rattled over the Roman cobbles on their way to the Vatican, following behind a blind Cardinal, next to whom sat a youthful American, in order to discover what would be the latter's first impression of an ancient statue. The most perfect masterpiece of classical art was by common consent considered to be the Apollo of the Belvedere, and the Cardinal, leading his strange party to where this marble stood, ordered the keeper of the case in which it was treasured to fling ajar the doors so as to enhance the first impression. West had never before seen a nude statue, and in his astonishment exclaimed that the Sun God resembled a young Mohawk warrior. When this comment had been translated the Italians became indignant at hearing Apollo compared to a savage by a youth whom they regarded as little better. They only recovered their politeness and admitted that there might be some ground for the observation after West had explained that Indian education was directed solely to attain skill in archery and that he had often seen the red men, stretching their bows in the same attitude.

The Cardinal continued to show a friendly interest in West, and at the Villa Albani the young American met the art world of Rome. Many years later, when he was President of the Royal Academy, the painter confessed that even the greatest art at this time meant little to him. Ignorance is inclined to take easily for granted whatever it sees and the genius of old masters, whose names still conveyed nothing, made then only a slight impression on a quite untutored mind. West had not yet learned how to draw, and frankly admitted this lacuna to the painter, Rafael Mengs, although he was perfectly satisfied with his skill as a colourist when the latter asked him for a specimen of his talent. The Bohemian artist esteemed by his many admirers to be the greatest painter of his age showed real kindness in guiding his young friends' studies: Angelica Kauffmann, who was residing in Rome before her matrimonial misadventure, drew West's portrait.[3] Pompeo Batoni upon whom the young student called and whose sugary manner and vacuous forms were not without some influence in shaping his style, after learning that the American had crossed the Atlantic in order to become a painter, told him how fortunate he was to arrive at a time when there flourished so illustrious a genius as himself, and unable to restrain enthusiasm at the sight of his own works, shouted *Evviva Batoni!* For once, even West had occasion to smile at the vanity of another artist.

Life in Rome to the young student was as much an education in manners as in art. Its easy tolerance helped a man, naturally rigid and whose virtue was never endangered by any Italian allurements, to see existence with somewhat more mellowness than was customary in the wilderness of Chester County. West was still too raw to appreciate the refinement of Roman dilettantism but he gained an experience and a knowledge of men and manners which were useful to his subsequent career, and aided his position at the court of George the Third. He met people of all kinds, like the sympathetic Abbé Grant, the Scottish Jacobite priest who just then had shielded from the Inquisition a fanatical Presbyterian compatriot mad enough to shout insults against the Pope during Mass at Saint Peter's. West studied the masterpieces of art and ended by acquiring a foundation for his later connoisseurship. At the suggestion of Rafael Mengs, the young painter also spent some time in the northern Italian cities and followed the practice of the age by copying Correggio at Parma. The Grand Duke, on learning that he was an American visitor, asked to see him, and West always remembered the horror of the courtiers because he claimed to have kept on his Quaker hat during the audience.

In the course of these studies the young painter duly admired the Bolognese School and naturally neglected to notice the still unfashionable Primitives. The so-called pupil of the Mohawks soaked himself only in the most conventional standards of that conventional age. Rarely does a man who arrives from a new country have anything fresh to offer in art. Usually he accepts, without a doubt, the canons and the fashion of the land of his first studies and hardly ever brings to this any novel contribution of his own. Innovations come principally from those long enough familiar with the past to know when it can safely be disregarded. West's claims to singularity as a painter never went beyond externals, although three years of study in Italy gave him a knowledge of art which, deficient in any spark of original genius, was almost as respectable as his own character. Fragonard, who studied in Rome at the same time as West, discovered a very different vision of beauty in the tallness of its cypresses and the ripple of water splashing on its marble fountains.

After completing his Italian tour, West had intended to return to America, but he gladly complied with a suggestion made by his father first to visit England. He never forgot the date of his arrival in London, on August 25, 1763, or the White Bear Tavern where he put up, and the lodgings and painting room he found at 19 Bedford Street, near Covent Garden. As an unknown and friendless stranger he ventured to seek fortune in a great capital and, although setting to work at once with the soft touch he had acquired in Rome, the canvas on which his brush depicted the rosy seduction of an

Angelica, rested unseen on the easel of his still unvisited studio. Then in the most unexpected way came fame, wealth, and royal favour.

The winter of 1764 was particularly rigorous and the cold had become so great that London enjoyed the rare pleasure of putting on its skates. The crowd skated on the canal in Saint James's Park, those of middle station thronged the Serpentine, while rank and fashion congregated on the basin of Kensington Gardens. By an odd whim of fortune, West's previous obscurity turned out to be a blessing. The smallest order would have sufficed to keep the most conscientious of painters toiling assiduously through the few hours of wintry daylight. With nothing more pressing to do, West remembered that he was also a skater.

An unknown man, who had just admired the painter's performance on the frozen canal of Saint James's, and noticed that he was a stranger, enlightened him about the social gradations of London ice. Although West claimed attachment to a sect unfamiliar with such vanities, he was not without some knowledge of the connection between fashion and art. Profiting at once by his newly acquired information he abandoned the popular pleasures of Saint James's for the more exalted delights of skating among the higher circles who frequented Kensington Gardens. In ancient Athens, it was said that the use of a false quantity would ruin a reputation, but in London, proficiency in a sport can make one. Hardly had West begun to display his rare skill on the ice when an English officer approached him in the most friendly way, with the reminder that they last had met on the wharf of Philadelphia at the time when the painter was sailing for Italy. This amiable soldier turned out to be Colonel, afterwards General Sir

William Howe, whose pleasures, when later in command of the British army in the Quaker capital, appeared to Americans somewhat less austere than the delectations provided by a winter sport. Only a few moments before, Colonel Howe had described to his unbelieving friends the exceptional merit of American skaters, and he was delighted to offer West as an example of his veracity, upon which certain doubts had been cast. On the frozen basin of Kensington Gardens a fashionable crowd now assembled to admire a talent which London had never before seen rivalled, and watch the young American perform on the ice the intricate figure of the Philadephia "salute." One hour's display of talent as a skater was sufficient to start the artist on the road to fame as a painter. Lord Spencer Hamilton, and a whole bevy of Cavendishes, whose names after half a century were still fresh in West's memory, came up to be introduced to him. When men of rank learned the skater's profession, they were convinced that so great an artist on the ice could handle his palette with no less talent.

Fashionable London now discovered the painter's studio and enthusiastically praised his pictures. From obscurity, he awoke, like Byron, to find himself famous. Many years later, when the future President of the Royal Academy had become a very old man, laden with honours and more than ever convinced of his own genius, almost on his deathbed, he imparted the secret to his biographer, that he had received greater encouragement as a painter because of his skill as a skater than he could ever have hoped to attain by ordinary means.

There was another reason to account for West's success. His pictures were painted in a mellifluous style which he had learned in Italy, and which was still unknown in England, where the artists of that virile age delighted in depicting their subjects in a more beefy manner. West's pallid compositions created a real sensation at the Exhibition of 1764, at a time when the British public wished to pass for refined and was just beginning to take a novel interest in painting. By good fortune West had arrived at the very moment when a genuine enthusiasm for the arts was sweeping over English society, and the slim sentimentalism of his classical subjects made an appeal to the growing refinement of taste which was now in full revolt against the older exuberance. The thinness of the American's talent was preferred to the coarse ribaldry of the incomparably greater Hogarth. The art-loving public suddenly relished delicacy, and West's drooping figures, in their elegant poses carefully studied from the antique, conformed to a new taste which no longer cared for the beer-sodden rotundities of an earlier British School.

Horace Walpole's fastidious eye may have found the American painter somewhat tawdry and criticized the artist's brush for being heavy, but even he admitted that the young man possessed merit. The less discriminating crowd at the Exhibition "flocked to behold such a prodigy as a painter imported from the New World."[4] Daily, the multitude thronged around his works, his house was filled with admirers, and his servant received thirty pounds in gratuities merely to display his master's pictures. Poor West, himself, sadly in need of money, remained unaccountably without orders. The practice of purchasing the art of the day was then unknown in England, and an enthusiast, whose father had asked him why he did not buy one of the painter's pictures which he so greatly admired, replied that, except for portraits, it was impossible to hang up anything modern in his house. Much against his will, for West already suspected that portraiture was not his forte, he none the less was compelled by necessity to paint "the unmeaning faces of portrait customers." Fortunately, his full-length likeness of General Monckton, who commanded the British troops at Quebec after Wolfe was killed, met with instant success which procured for him further orders. The young American needed this piece of luck in order to remain in London. Men only transplant themselves successfully when they can discover some benefit, and the stranger who wishes to find a welcome must also bring his contribution to overcome the disadvantage of the alien.

It stands, withal, to the credit of English painters that the young stranger who had helped to introduce this innovation should have been so well received. West adapted himself easily to the world in which, henceforth, he was to live. He gave up all idea of returning to his early home, and instead sent for his father to join him. When the elder West arrived in London after an absence of forty years, he could not understand what had become of the slow-moving bewigged Englishmen of his youth who had been replaced by people "docked and cropped and skipping about in scanty clothes like so many monkeys."[5] Father West brought from Philadelphia his son's fiancée, Elizabeth Shewell, and the painter was married at once at Saint Martin's in the Fields, thereafter to lead a life of domestic felicity which calls for no comment. There was no longer a thought of returning to America, for West now regarded himself as "the adopted child of England," took his place in the world of art, began with Reynolds a friendship broken only by death, and formed part of that circle which bowed before the talk of Dr. Johnson and listened admiringly to the eloquence of Edmund Burke.

Lord Rockingham had just then built a great mansion

in Yorkshire and offered the new celebrity an engagement at seven hundred pounds a year to decorate his residence with historical pictures. After carefully considering the proposal and taking advice from his friends, the artist, perhaps scenting the King's particular aversion to that statesman, wisely preferred to make his own way. Bishops were already his warm admirers, and he found a most enthusiastic patron in Dr. Drummond, the Archbishop of York, a sensible worldly man, and much addicted to his bottle, according to the opinion of Horace Walpole. The prelate, as a liberal protector of the arts, believed that he had discovered a new genius in the painter whose morals would have done credit to any archbishop. For Dr. Drummond's pious mind had highly approved of West's æsthetic doctrine regarding the true purpose of art, which was to assist the reason to reveal virtue through beauty. According to the painter's edifying philosophy, which later he publicly expounded, the presence of virtue was of paramount importance in the life of the "elegant artist." Genius to be creative had always to be sedate, which only became possible on condition that the artist's life should also be virtuous. The historical painter, entirely regardless of historical fact, declared that the men whose talents had adorned English Annals would never have risen to eminence unless they themselves had enjoyed purity of mind.[6] Archbishops became enthusiastic when they heard this novel theory about the value of virtue in art explained by the painter who unblushingly drew his own ethical portrait.

To a stainless purity, West added a shrewd business instinct, for no artist ever sold his wares to better advantage. The Archbishop listened sympathetically to the painter's complaint that the drudgery of mere portraiture, on which he had to rely for a livelihood, made it impossible to carry out his noble ideals in art. Dr. Drummond deeply impressed by this waste of rare talent, tried to find a remedy. Gallantly, the Archbishop attempted to collect a fund of three thousand guineas for the express purpose of encouraging West's genius to soar to heights still unparalleled in representing the great events of history and of religion. The subscription failed dismally, yet failure led to a greater success, for Dr. Drummond, who had suggested that West should paint a picture of *Agrippina Returning with the Ashes of Germanicus*, arranged to have this composition shown to the King.

When the name of the American artist had first been mentioned to George the Third, the King was inclined to look with suspicion on a young colonial who, as he knew, had so nearly enjoyed the patronage of his arch-enemy, Lord Rockingham. Magnanimously the Monarch consented to overlook this indiscretion, for his curiosity had already been aroused by the prospect of having his favourite classical subjects appropriately depicted by a painter whose moral elevation had been vouched for by an archbishop. When the King consented to receive the artist he remarked to Queen Charlotte that Dr. Drummond had asked his son to read Theocritus to Mr. West, but he himself would read Livy to him, and selected for this purpose the passage describing the last departure of Regulus from Rome. The painter was commanded to represent this subject in a picture which hangs to-day at Kensington Palace. George the Third was delighted when the composition was brought to him and prince and painter soon discovered, with mutual pleasure, the many common sympathies they shared. Both men were deeply virtuous, conscientious, and industrious. The King at once understood West's lofty moral purpose, and the painter did his best to understand the King's peculiar taste in art, and even understood his conversation when he talked in German to Queen Charlotte. West's Quaker origin was also sympathetic to a sovereign whose fondness for that sect came certainly from a less scandalous cause than George the Fourth later most irreverently asserted, when he remarked that his father liked Quakers ever since "he had kept that damned little Quaker, W—."

Since Velasquez no painter had been so intimately associated with a monarch. The artist from the New World with a courtly vocabulary which he had acquired in the Old, expressed his delight in placing an admiring loyalty at his Sovereign's feet, and dilated ecstatically on that gracious royal benevolence which so encouraged genius to hover majestically over the fine arts in England. With a reverence, which his detractors were malicious enough to ascribe to less worthy grounds, West assured the King that His Majesty's virtues had long been the theme of his profoundest admiration for in his heart he cherished the conviction that the Monarch was "good from principle and austere from a sense of the beauty of virtue."

In more worldly ways West adapted himself with facility to the urbanities of his new situation. The familiar intercourse with the great which he had learned in Rome now stood him in good stead. Court manners and the appropriate Court dress were easy to his fit and he abandoned the Quaker hat worn before the Grand Duke of Parma. The King responded to this admiring homage by showing friendship to an artist who wanted no political place, whose talent His Majesty sincerely admired, whose loyalty he accepted as a due, and whose moral elevation gave him far more intimate satisfaction than he had ever obtained from a mere painter like Reynolds who George the Third knew was no less indifferent to the virtue of his sitters than he was to the ethical purpose of his art. The Monarch was particularly gratified when, by accident, one day at Windsor he discovered that his favourite artist was no ordinary plebeian, but derived an ancient lineage from the great Lord Delaware of Edward the Third's reign. West learned of this new-found pedigree with considerable satisfaction, and remarked that his own noble origin had been unknown to him in the forests of Pennsylvania, where the possession of similar advantages might have been less appreciated.

It is a regrettable fact that the best kings often possess the worst taste, but George the Third offered a singular exception to the further rule that unwise princes like Charles the First are almost always endowed with a fastidious discrimination in art. As a youth, a series of royal professors of perspective and of architecture had done their utmost to instil in their princely pupil a conviction, which the King retained, that cultivation of the arts conferred lustre on a reign. West, years later, felt obliged to admit, though not until royal favour had ceased, that George the Third, who had entertained so great an admiration for the painter's genius, was himself wanting in any real love for the fine arts. In spite of certain occasional shrewd purchases the King took a somewhat pedantic interest in painting, but he showed as meddlesome a curiosity in the gossip of artists' private lives as he did in those of politicians. Long afterwards, when West had been urged to acquaint his master regarding certain dissensions within the Royal Academy, he replied that this was superfluous, as George the Third knew to a hair the intricacies of every intrigue.

[299]

Ten years before the American Revolution broke out, there existed in London a society which was known as the "Incorporated Artists," who, in the intervals of holding public exhibitions of their works, quarrelled so exceedingly that both West and Reynolds deemed it wise to resign from their membership. This happened at a time when the King earnestly desired to promote the study of the fine arts in England and frequently invited his favourite painter to spend evenings with him at Buckingham House in order to talk over these matters. From their conversations originated the plan of the Royal Academy. George the Third personally and with the utmost secrecy drew up different articles of its constitution and deputed West to induce Reynolds to accept its presidency.

The American painter was then in high favour at Court. The King addressed him as Benjamin, and Queen Charlotte would consult him about the arrangement of her jewels at state ceremonies.[7] Royal friendship did not detract from the artist's industry. While the War of Independence was being fought, West painted the King, though unfriendly critics professed to be shocked that he should have given him the horrid features of the tyrant Domitian, maliciously comparing this portrait to a tavern sign.[8] The American painted all the English princes and a picture of Queen Charlotte surrounded by her thirteen children, which took many years to finish, for the Queen, less fond of sitting than the King, would accord the painter only brief poses, and every year brought forth another royal baby. This large group by West became a special favourite of George the Third, which he hung in his breakfast room.[9] The King commissioned another version of his family after the number of royal children had increased to fourteen. These portraits, which still hang in Buckingham

Palace, occupied the painter's brush for years. After Prince Alfred and his young brother Prince Octavius, who was his father's favourite, had died, West, with unusual warmth of colour, painted an apotheosis of the royal infants in heaven, with a fine figure of an angel clasping the children and for which he received the sum of three hundred guineas.

The Court painter's most famous picture was the *Death of Wolfe* which, reproduced in engraving and lacquered on trays, caused an immense sensation by its novelty in depicting heroes who instead of togas and laurel wreaths wore breeches and cocked hats. Critics gibed at this "coat and waistcoat piece," and, to prove its incorrectness, James Barry maliciously painted the same subject with nude figures. Even the King felt alarmed lest the dignity of the event be impaired, and Reynolds, who heard the gossip, called with Archbishop Drummond as a friend to dissuade West from attempting so daring an innovation. The artist who felt proud to be the originator in England of a practice which two centuries ago had been no novelty in Venice and which the French painters of battle pieces had continued at Versailles, insisted on what he called historic truth, and Reynolds, when he saw the painting, admitted that his criticism had been mistaken. A curious anecdote is attached to this picture. Thirty years later, just before Trafalgar, Nelson, who had met West at a dinner, told him that he could never see the *Death of Wolfe* without feeling deeply moved and asked him why he had not painted similar pictures. The artist replied that subjects of this kind were wanting, though he feared that his neighbour's intrepidity might furnish such another scene, which caused Nelson gallantly to answer that if he could be so immortalized he would wish to die in the next battle.[10]

Nearly all the painter's work at this time was undertaken for the King. West completed many canvases for the State Rooms at Windsor, some of which now adorn the back stairs of the Castle, and finished pictures of vast dimensions representing scenes from English medieval history, which, as may be fitting for subjects so remote, have been hung so high that to-day they can only be admired from a considerable distance. Back of the Court painter's mind lay a project even more grandiose. With his early recollections of saints and angels floating among clouds which waft over the lofty ceilings of Italian Baroque churches, West had once proposed to his fellow Academicians that they should offer to fill the spaces at Saint Paul's which Wren purposely left blank for similar future decoration. Reynolds, as well as several other artists, had each agreed to paint a panel, but the Bishop of London was adamant against admitting such Popery to his Cathedral. West was not easily put off. He had just at this time finished a religious picture representing the *Death of Saint Stephen* which may still be admired over a side altar in the Church of Saint Stephen's, Walbrook, which Wren had built near the Mansion House in London. He had received six hundred guineas for this altarpiece, a price which the artist regarded as being so inadequate to its real value that he remarked it was like making a gift to the Church.[11] Ambitious to paint further works of gigantic piety, he now suggested to the King undertaking an entire series of compositions in order to illustrate the progress of Revealed Religion.

The merit of this pious idea made a fervent appeal to the devout mind of George the Third, but a greater prudence than he had ever displayed towards his other American subjects caused him to apprehend that Parliament, which was so

PRINCES ALFRED *and* OCTAVIUS *as Angels*
From a painting by Benjamin West

submissive to the King's political inspiration in the Colonies, might manifest more independence over matters of faith. He remembered that under the first Charles, religious painting had been condemned at Westminster as a Popish practice. Half a dozen bishops were therefore summoned by royal command to deliberate on the propriety of adorning a house of worship. Solemnly and unanimously, the divines reported to the King that the laws of the Anglican Church would not be violated by sacred pictures and in order, perhaps, to signify their approval of the Court painter the bishops noted that even a Quaker might be edified by the contemplation of such works.

Secure on this point, the royal patron and his favourite artist could now unite together in their pious plan to shed lustre on the King's reign. In the course of the next thirty years, West by royal command was occupied in painting for Saint George's Hall, at Windsor, five and thirty compositions of gigantic size representing the progress of Revealed Religion which was to be traced from its remotest origin in the Antediluvian ages, through the Patriarchal and the Mosaical Dispensations. His many admirers were unanimous in affirming that never before had the painter's art been employed for a nobler purpose nor had his pictures attained to so lofty an elevation. When the great work was already well advanced, and had been momentarily interrupted West addressed a letter to the King to remind his royal patron to what extent he was associated in this noble task:

Your gracious protection of my pencil had given it a celebrity throughout Europe and spread a knowledge of the great work on Revealed Religion which my pencil was engaged in under Your Majesty's patronage: It is to that work which all Christendom looks with a complacency for its completion.[12]

It is impossible to-day to form any adequate idea of this monumental task. The immense labour which had cost the King some twenty thousand pounds, which in the painter's words, had crowned West with a European celebrity, and to the completion of which the whole of Christendom looked forward, has, in little more than a century, so completely disappeared from human memory that no record of it can be discovered. Five and thirty gigantic compositions, on which the painter spent thirty years of his life, and which he firmly believed assured his future immortality and conferred lustre on the reign of his Sovereign have gone from Windsor without leaving a trace. They were probably put aside during the extensive alterations carried out in the castle under George the Fourth. No record can, however, be found of the date when their removal took place, or of their subsequent fate, and nothing is known about them by the highly competent keepers of the royal collections. The vaults and cellars of the castle have lately been most carefully examined without affording any indication of their whereabouts. It is possible that the riddle of this disappearance may one day still be solved by their chance discovery rolled up in some disused storeroom. Until this happens, it is idle to express an opinion regarding the merit of a work which West regarded as his greatest masterpiece.

Genius is usually careless of the past. Michelangelo had been ruthless with Bramante's work at Saint Peter's, and West, blamed only by his enemy the Court architect Wyatt, who committed the same crime in Winchester Cathedral, destroyed a beautiful Gothic window in Saint George's Chapel at Windsor, to make way for his own painted glass later in turn put aside by the Prince Consort. The painter's work in the castle, often interrupted by what West euphemistically described as "the occasional eclipse of the King's understanding," was in fact never finished. Permanent royal insanity terminated the American's career as a Court painter. The latter, in fact, was the first person to notice the King's madness, when George the Third insisted that a lion which the painter had drawn was a dog, and drew one himself to illustrate how that animal ought to be represented. Greatly offended, West showed the Monarch's sketch to Queen Charlotte,[13] who understood the sad truth.

II

Benjamin West left Philadelphia many years before the Revolutionary movement had begun. He was without interest in politics and had lost touch with the temper of America. Personally attached to the King, from whose kindness he had greatly benefited, and historical painter by royal appointment since 1772, at the time when hostilities broke out in the Colonies, he was wholly occupied by his art. Former ties in Pennsylvania had long ago been severed and his roots were then all in England. In political matters, it was said that he tried to maintain the reserve common to those about the Court, though there was always a strong suspicion that he leaned to his native side.[14] At this time and until much later he had never thought of himself in any other light than as an American. Gulian Verplanck, who afterwards became

Speaker of the New York Assembly, and had called on the painter in 1773, describes him as "greatly partial to Americans," and very much pleased when he received visits from compatriots.[15] An example of his unfailing generosity to artists from the New World can be found in the friendly letters of encouragement he wrote to Copley long before he knew the latter personally.[16]

After the Revolution broke out, West frequently talked over American conditions with the King, and intimated that he had given certain information unobtainable through official channels. Garrulous on most subjects, West was disinclined to say much about this side of his intercourse. Years afterwards, the painter declared that Washington's original appointment had been made with a view to effecting a reconciliation with England and that the great Virginian had sent a communication with this purpose which was never formally laid before the Privy Council until six weeks after it had been received, when the time was already too late.[17] This statement seems less unlikely if one recalls certain remarks which were attributed to Washington by his Tory friend, the Reverend Jonathan Boucher. The latter claimed to have warned the General, at the moment when he crossed the Potomac on his way to take command of the army, that his mission would lead to civil war and an effort to establish independence, but Washington is alleged to have scoffed at this idea and replied that if ever the clergyman heard of his joining in such measures he had his leave to set him down for "everything wicked."[18]

The King's warm friendship for West, particularly during the Revolution, was resented by the American loyalists in London as well as by many about the Court who disliked seeing him so near to George the Third. One day Lord Cathcart, who had served in America, pointedly asked the painter, in the royal presence, if he had heard the news of the British victory at Camden, saying that he did not suppose it would give West so much pleasure as it did to loyal subjects in general. With great presence of mind the artist replied that the calamities of his native country could never give him pleasure, and the King, who overheard the conversation, remarked to West that the answer did him great honour; and then, turning to Lord Cathcart, he bade him remember that the man who did not love his native land could never make a faithful subject of another nor a true friend.[19]

When a very old man, almost forty years after the occurrence, the painter related how on one occasion, while the King was sitting for him, a messenger brought in the Declaration of Independence. George the Third, greatly agitated at first, then became silent, and at last exclaimed, "Well, if they cannot be happy under my Government I hope they may not change it for a worse."[20] West's real thoughts during the Revolution were never expressed. Probably he had few clearly defined political opinions beyond a personal sympathy for the King and an impersonal one for America. The artist lived in a world aloof from politics. Yet, when the war dragged on inconclusively for years, the painter gave the impression to those near him of regretting that the British Government should still listen to the advice of die-hard loyalists like Governor Franklin and Joseph Galloway. Many years later he related to a friend that, after the surrender of Cornwallis, the Queen had asked the painter to enter her closet, and in tears betrayed the depth of her emotion, while the King asked what Washington would do if independence should be acknowledged. West expressed as his personal opinion that the latter would then retire into private life. If he did this, George the Third exclaimed, he would be the greatest man in the world. The King also wished to know his opinion of how America would act towards England, and the artist assured him that the bad blood made by the war would soon subside.[21] The Court painter's sympathies for his country's freedom could not have been easy to express, but when the King recognized American independence in his speech to the Lords, West was noticed as sitting among the spectators.[22]

Dr. Franklin was always the painter's friend and several times wrote to him from Paris even during the War. Later, to show his admiration, West drew a sketch for a singular picture in which the Doctor, surrounded by naked boys, was represented as sitting in glory amid the clouds. At one time the artist had thought of undertaking a series of compositions to represent the principal scenes of the American Revolution, and proposed to publish these in album form and to employ for this purpose the first engravers in Europe. He wrote to his former pupil, Charles Wilson Peale, to ask for Continental army uniforms and the portraits of the Revolutionary leaders,[23] but he soon dropped an idea which would have given great offence at Court. Patriotism is less an act of volition than a state of mind, and West's feeling for his country was always of that quiet kind which was no less sincere because it called for no forceful expression. He cared very little about political domination or the physical circumstances of residence, but until towards the end of his life the painter felt quite as American, although living in London, as if he had continued to dwell in the wilderness of Chester County. In an unobtrusive way which endeared him to those who admired his virtues more than his talent, he performed innumerable acts of kindness to his countrymen. Thus he intervened personally at the Palace to obtain a pension for his wife's nephew, the Reverend Isaac Hunt, father of Leigh Hunt, who, after he had been severely handled by the mob in Philadelphia because of his loyal sentiments, escaped with his family to London, where West gave them shelter under his hospitable roof.[24]

The Quaker merchant, Samuel Shoemaker, who had been Mayor of Philadelphia and was attainted for his loyalism, has described how West arranged to have him meet George the Third. The informal audience took place in the "painting room" of Windsor Castle. The King, doubtless coached beforehand by West, and using that personal charm which he exercised occasionally and to which even John Adams responded, when he compared it with that of Charles the Second, delighted Shoemaker by greeting him with the remark that he knew him well already by reputation. The former Mayor had noticed that George the Third spoke in German to the Queen, and when the King asked him why Pennsylvania was so much further advanced than the other colonies, he answered that this progress had been due to the great number of Germans in the state. To return the compliment the King gave full credit to the Quakers and made some flattering personal remarks to the Mayor. Shoemaker left the audience enchanted, regretting only that his violent countrymen could not have enjoyed the same opportunity. He declared enthusiastically that Americans would then be convinced that George the Third had not "one grain of tyranny in his composition and that he is not, he cannot be that bloody-minded man." It was quite impossible for a man of his fine feelings, who was so good a husband, so kind a father, to be a tyrant.[25]

For thirty years Benjamin West, favoured by the King, had lived in a manner which befitted his station as a painter of the Court. From 1777 to the time of his death in 1820, he resided in London in a large dwelling at 14 Newman Street. This house has lately been torn down and replaced by a drab office building, whose show windows recently displayed the not inconspicuous poster of a Hollywood film, as if impishly to fulfil West's prophecy that the arts were destined to forsake Europe for the New World. The painter had added a gallery to this house, which was famous in its day, and was built around a grass plot and over an arcade adorned with busts of Roman Emperors. The quiet of this gallery and the high quality of the statuary and pictures in the collections left a deep impression on visitors. West was an assiduous buyer of works of art, for, like Reynolds and many other painters, he was also something of a dealer in old pictures, which was a traffic more appropriate, perhaps, than that engaged in by Titian, who in his old age, when he had returned to his birthplace, became for a time a lumber merchant, and wrangled at law with his customers. On one occasion West bought for twenty pounds a wax-besmeared Titian for which later he refused four thousand. His collections were his pride and most of his savings went to enrich these.

West's numerous visitors found the painter, usually clad in his white woollen gown, sitting at the end of the gallery before his easel, happy, as Leigh Hunt described him, because convinced that his art was in the true spirit of the great masters, and, as he was conscious of no limitations on his genius, he sincerely believed that his fame would be immortal. His appearance was courtly, and the instant he changed his gown for a coat he seemed fully dressed. His most gifted pupil,

Gilbert Stuart, has left a description of him with his powdered hair, white silk stockings and yellow slippers "looking as if he had stepped out of a bandbox." Stuart painted him more than once and with rare talent for sharp characterization his portraits set off the master's deep-set observant eyes, intelligent nose, and determined mouth, but with a chin somewhat uncouth and hands large and coarse.

West's work was marked by a continuous order and calm. No outward incident nor inward storm ever ruffled the perfect serenity of his life. One day passed like another, for his habits were as placid as his art. Like Reynolds, West received his pupils in the early morning and criticized their work before his own had begun. Usually he held a veritable levée of artists, and no one could have been kinder in imparting to others the real technical knowledge he had finished by acquiring. He gave up entire mornings to the instruction of students, and was invariably considerate and generous to struggling artists, always ready with purse and praise, to befriend those who needed his help. At one Academy Exhibition he withdrew three of his own pictures in order to make room for the works of younger men. John Thomas Smith, later to become Keeper of Prints at the British Museum, was proud to admit that he owed West the best part of his knowledge of painting, and affirmed that the latter's name ought never to be mentioned but with grateful respect, adding that there were few artists then flourishing who had not benefited by his generous aid.[26]

Americans in particular came to study under him. Charles Wilson Peale, Mather Brown, Joseph Wright, John Trumbull, and William Dunlap were among his earlier pupils. The latter has described his own arrival when, as a young student, he was greatly impressed by the gigantic pictures in West's studio, on which he gazed with all "the wonder of ignorance and the enthusiasm of youth," brimming over with admiration for the painter, who was then at work on a *Lear and Cordelia* ordered by the Empress of Russia. Gilbert Stuart, as a young assistant to whom West gave only a guinea to copy a portrait for which he himself was well paid, found this hard, but later, after Stuart understood better the size of his master's establishment, the benefits of which he enjoyed, along with his instruction, he exonerated West from any niggardliness.[27] The painter Farington, who often dined in the Newman Street house, described the cooking as excellent and noted as quite an ordinary repast the fare offered him of soup, salmon, fowls, stewed beef, tongue, a fine haunch of venison, and a boiled leg of lamb.

In 1792, after Reynolds had been interred amid great ceremony in the vault of Saint Paul's with West as one of the pall bearers, the latter was unanimously elected to succeed his friend as President of the Royal Academy. On this occasion a knighthood had been offered him, but the painter politely told the Duke of Gloucester, who conveyed the King's invitation, that in view of his own ancient lineage and the situation which he occupied among artists, only a more permanent title than that of knighthood could add dignity to his family. In his new position of prominence it would not have been unreasonable if some criticism had been levelled to question the genius of a painter who lived through the golden age of English art from Hogarth to Turner. But only a very captious few made themselves singular by any unwillingness to admire his artistic talent. The critic of *The Times* expressed in fact what he called the general opinion when he described West's

BENJAMIN WEST

From a portrait by Gilbert Stuart

picture of *Hagar and Ishmael* at the Academy as being "not unworthy the pencil of Leonardo da Vinci."[28]

One weakness, however, even his most enthusiastic admirers could never quite forgive. They were ready to overlook the dryness of the painter's brush, his lifeless compositions, the irritating calmness with which he handled the most dramatic subjects, and even the unkindly criticism of his pupil Gilbert Stuart that he was only great by the acre. But in that fastidious age, when a scholarly statesman like Lord Shelburne could suffer in esteem because accused of speaking the kind of English associated with conversation in a boarding-house, it was impossible to overlook that West's use of the language was somewhat vulgar. His nephew, Leigh Hunt, with the pride of his own letters and the double irreverence of youth and near relationship, doubtless exaggerated by insisting that West could hardly read or write and that he mispronounced words with a "puritanical barbarism," saying *haive* for *have*. The painter's grammar and spelling were unmistakably faulty, and friends recognized that his reputation suffered from the inability to express himself with any distinction. The art collector, Sir George Beaumont, admitted that a vulgar expression in conversation lowered him in general estimation, and even George the Third, as little conspicuous for any sense of humour as was West himself, and whose own English was far from being always appropriate to a king, took occasional digs at the uncouthness of the Court painter's pronunciation and laughingly imitated his peculiarity of adding an aspirate which made him pronounce *Hackademy*.

Unfortunately, West's letters lent themselves to such irreverent remarks. The painter would at times carelessly write about the "eligent arts,"[29] and grandiloquently foretell that his native city of Philadelphia, "so furnished in the materials of instruction, would in a few years be the vortext of that was neutal (mental?) in the Western world."³⁰

A jealousy which found pleasure in attaching ridicule to these minor foibles was inevitable on the part of fellow artists, not all of whom possessed the elevation of Reynolds. A competition took place for the design of a medal which was to commemorate the twenty-fifth anniversary of the Academy. West at first had intended to participate, but desisted after a remark was repeated to him, that as the Institution of which he was President had clothed him with a robe of velvet he ought not to struggle for every stripe of ermine. There was further criticism after he bought for the Academy library, Bromley's *History of the Fine Arts*, which contained a statement that he was the first living painter in the world attributed on somewhat inadequate authority to Reynolds. When he presided over the Academy sessions, certain members noticed with quite lamentable pleasure that he was continually betraying his ignorance of the bye-laws and constitution. Malice went still further when Hoppner, whom he had befriended, but who fancied after his marriage that West had maligned him to the King, attacked the Court painter anonymously in the columns of the *Morning Post*,³¹ and wrote about him ironically as being well known for his scholarship

West did not retort, nor ever talked ill of anyone except the "reptile" Tresham, and the Court Architect Sir James Wyatt, both of whom he had good reason to loathe. After the latter had curtly informed the painter that his great work in Saint George's Hall, at Windsor was suspended, West wrote nobly to the King that "the breath of envy nor the whisper of detraction never defiled my life, nor the want of morality my character."[32] Professionally magnanimous, he refused to allow a vote of censure to be passed against his enemies at the Academy even after he had signally defeated these. This surfeit of virtue and his own supermorality irritated not a few artists. When a new regulation was introduced to demand certificates of moral character from students of drawing, Reynolds's former pupil, James Northcote, remarked that the Royal Academy was not an institution for the suppression of vice and that no good would come out of this busybody spirit of dragging morality into everything.[33] Sir William Beechey, who blamed West because his pictures had been poorly hung at the Spring Exhibition, never forgave him for telling the King that Lady Beechey was not his wife and forcing him to the indignity of proving his marriage.[34]

The cumulative effect of jealousy in the end wears down even the most upright. Royal virtue, ever on the look-out for misconduct, was never deaf to gossip. Formerly West had gone frequently to Windsor, often sharing a coach with his assistant, the Italian painter, Rebecca, an inveterate practical joker whose impish delight, when employed to decorate noble mansions, was to paint cracks in the most valuable Chinese porcelains, simulate rents in the brocade of newly-covered sofas, and depict half-crowns which he would drop on the floor of the Throne Room in order to have the pleasure of watching elderly peers pick them up. It was noticed that West no longer went so much to Windsor, though he explained that his visits had become scarcer in order to prevent envy. The King's increasing lapses from sanity, reacted on the artist, who experienced great difficulties in obtaining payment for his pictures. A considerable sum was still owing him for the work on Revealed Religion, and the painter remarked that the King became shy as soon as money was touched upon. His own personal fortune of fifteen thousand pounds was then all in the royal hands and its security depended on the Monarch's life. Formerly, too, he had been able to sell between four and five hundred pounds of prints every year, but this income had dwindled almost to nothing. West had, therefore, to cut down his servants from six to three, and reduce his living expenses from sixteen to twelve hundred pounds a year. The President of the Royal Academy told a friend that, if he could obtain payment from the King, he would abandon England and return to the United States, but he could not afford to leave off painting without also selling his beloved collections.[35]

Benjamin West had traversed the difficult period of American independence without loss of favour. His shortcomings as a painter had been forgiven more easily than his use of English, but he now had to face a very damaging charge. In the days of the French Revolution, when the Academy was "under the stigma of having many Democrats in it,"[36] the Court painter's supposed Jacobin leanings were regarded as quite unpardonable, and the King, when told about these, angrily exclaimed, "Who would have thought he would have been one of them!" Royal favour now turned sternly against West, and at Windsor the famous painter could no longer be mentioned without a degrading epithet, "West is an American, so is Copley, and you are an Englishman and you can all go to the devil," the King in one of his worst humours had remarked to Sir William Beechey.[37] Queen Charlotte now frowned on him and the Princesses, whose portraits he had so often painted, spoke of him only with a feeling of disgust. Bishops, who before had been his warmest admirers did not lag behind the King in expressing their disapproval of the former favourite. One of these at Windsor, mistaking another painter's work for his, exclaimed, "Oh, do not look at those wretched things by West!" Certain clergymen in fact had come to regard the artist as if he were a heathen, and though the supposed Quaker stoutly denied any irreligion, he admitted having developed "a very philosophical turn of mind."[38] Even the friendly Sir George Beaumont was impressed by the sudden violent prejudice against a man who had been so generally admired and thought that time would be needed to do justice to the painter's merit.[39]

Such intimately connected sins as philosophy, democracy, and sympathy for France, were of course unpardonable in the most estimable Court painter. The climax came by West's own doing. To the horror of his fellow Academicians, their President could not restrain his admiration for the Corsican ogre, whose star was shining brightly across the Channel. As soon as the Treaty of Amiens made this possible, West journeyed to Paris. Charles James Fox also went over to the French capital with the lady whom he had only just married and whom he took to visit Madame de Talleyrand, much to the astonishment of the British Ambassadress who found it hard to understand why the lately married mistress of one eminent statesman should deem it so desirable to receive the lately married mistress of another. During his stay Fox found time to visit the Louvre with West and when a huge crowd had gathered around them, the painter observed with satisfaction, to his companion, how genuine was the admiration entertained for artists in France. It had never occurred to the President of the Royal Academy that the eyes of the crowd might have been fixed on the famous Whig.[40] After he returned to London, the painter blandly told everyone that he had found Napoleon's smile enchanting and that the First Consul possessed the best-shaped leg he had ever seen. He made no secret of his feelings, and after the recent rebuffs in London, was delighted to mention to friends that Bonaparte had praised his pictures, the great men of Paris had lavished attentions on him, and that Ministers of State and important notables had called at his rooms.

Enthusiasm for Bonaparte was then a sufficient crime in London to convict anyone. The artist's friends agreed that West talked in a way which could not be pleasant to the feelings of Englishmen and that he ought to be advised to desist. Farington, who was an intimate, remarked that obviously the Court painter did not possess a British mind and was only kept in the country by the income he received from the King and the fact that his sons had married there. George the Third, who listened to every whisper of gossip, was furious when he learned about the visit to Paris. This was the last straw. Could anything show better how manifestly unfit the painter was to be President of a Royal Academy. On the King's intimation, West resigned from the office and his arch-enemy Wyatt was elected in his place.

The new President imposed by royalty was no success, and sadly and gladly West declared to everyone that the Court architect was ruining the academy, his academy, for had he not been one of its original founders? Wyatt, in fact, knew that he was little suited to his position and felt no wish to continue in an office to which he had never aspired, and the former President, amid a freshly revived popularity, was triumphantly re-elected in 1805, only one dissenting vote being facetiously cast for Mrs. Lloyd, the woman Academician.

When Fuseli, no admirer of West, was taxed by a colleague for having voted for him he answered "Is not one old woman as good as another?"

Once more artistic London looked up to West's opinion in all matters of taste. Lord Elgin had then just brought the Parthenon Marbles to England and, eager to justify their merit and their price, before selling them to the nation, wrote to ask the views of the President of the Royal Academy as to how they might best serve the interests of art. West was convinced that he had already improved on the genius of Pheidias. He replied to Lord Elgin that in copying the frieze he had added female figures of his own to the *Battle of the Centaurs*, and "I flatter myself the union will not be deemed incongruous." He explained that his purpose had been to give a kind of climax to the detached figures of the Athenian sculptor and thereby he had blended art with character in nature, combining both elements so as to unite poetic fiction to historic fact. His own ability to accomplish this he modestly admitted had been due to his early acquaintance with Raphael. The Urbino master, however, had never enjoyed the good fortune of studying Pheidias, and the Athenian sculptor had not known Raphael, whereas West felt proud to have been the first who possessed the inestimable advantage of knowing both. No one before him had enjoyed this coveted opportunity and gratefully he thanked Lord Elgin for enabling him "to add my name to that of Pheidias by arranging his figures in my own compositions."[41]

In 1811 when occurred the King's final superannuation, as his permanent madness was politely called, without any other intimation, West suddenly discovered that his annuity of a thousand pounds had been stopped by the Court. His wife dejectedly declared that her husband's supposed wealth was a myth, and that his easy temper had caused her sons to be brought up improvidently. Also West obviously was getting old and looked so for the first time. His spirits were low and he seemed exhausted.[42]

Then came a miracle. In spite of his seventy-two winters, the painter rallied with a vigour which many a younger man might have envied. Dropped by the Court after having lost royal favour he now appealed to the public and undertook a fresh series of scriptural paintings on an even more gigantic scale than anything he had hitherto attempted. The size of his works—ten-acre pictures as Gilbert Stuart facetiously called them—grew with his years. His *Crucifixion* extended sixteen feet by twenty-eight. His still more monumental *Christ Rejected* filled a canvas which measured thirty-four feet by sixteen. Soon he had the satisfaction of seeing a smaller work bought for two thousand guineas by Hart Davies, a member of Parliament, who was engaged in forming a collection of modern pictures after having completed one of old masters.

A few years before his dismissal from the Court, West had been instrumental in founding the British Institution with the laudable intention to promote a spirit of patronage towards native artists among the higher classes. It was appropriate that he should be the first to reap the benefit of this idea. After the honours of the Academy had gone to the venerable painter for his *Christ Healing the Sick*, the British Institution, by popular subscription, purchased this composition for three thousand guineas, which was by far the largest sum ever given, up to that time, to remunerate the work of a living artist. The painting proved at once so popular that five-sixths of this amount went back to the donors in gate money and almost as much was made by West in subscriptions for the engravings. The exaggerated praise the picture met with and the judgment passed on it of being "the greatest performance of modern times," was long kept up in the Press, although Lawrence and other artists found such extravagant notoriety "disgusting."[43] West, however, was frankly delighted with his success, and the painter proposed to present a medal to each of the subscribing donors including one in gold for the Prince Regent. New fame had given him new life and he seemed to his friends to have become ten years younger.[44]

While Wellington was fighting Napoleon, West once more was setting the fashion in art by his religious pictures. Admiration for his talent continued to grow and the painter had the satisfaction to refuse the hitherto unheard of figure of eight thousand guineas for his gigantic *Christ Rejected*. In his old age he was enjoying the highest pinnacle of celebrity as an artist whose fame in fact, had become world-wide. The Academy of Saint Luke elected him to its membership. From Rome, from Florence,[45] from Philadelphia, came requests for his portrait. Longevity in any accomplishment offers in England a certain road to renown, and West obviously was getting very old. Little criticism was now heard against the venerable painter, apart from certain malicious lines which only the scoffing Byron could write, about:

> The flattering feeble dotard West,
> Europe's greatest dauber, poor England's best.[46]

British public opinion rendered more solemn by feeling itself to be the guardian of legality in Europe, had acquired an unexpected taste for religious pictures and reverenced the President of the Royal Academy as "a great and admirable painter, frequently grand, sometimes sublime, always moral and instructive."⁴⁷ It was impossible for men to withhold admiration from an artist who admittedly was able to account for every line and touch of his pictures on the most philosophical principles.⁴⁸ At the age of seventy-four he was still hard at work and in complete possession of all his faculties. He looked fresh and in good health enjoying a hearty appetite, although now obliged to leave off his port.

August 20, 1814, the fifty-first anniversary of the painter's arrival in England was celebrated by three of his closest artist friends, Sir Thomas Lawrence, Robert Smirke, and Joseph Farington, who united to invite him to a dinner. That same day West had gone alone to the tavern where half a century earlier as an unknown stranger he had dined just before entering London. He called for a solitary repast and looked back on the recollections of fifty years.⁴⁹ Did he remember that he had first gained fame as a painter by his skill as a skater; that he had basked in royal favour because he was virtuous, and lost this because he was a democrat; that his art had been admired and his English laughed at, until, as a very old man, he had suddenly and unexpectedly risen to an unprecedented height of prosperity and fame?

The story of West's life had in his old age become a matter of national importance and it was flattering for him to admit the debt which he owed to posterity. Of what nationality was he to describe himself? The King had always thought of him as an American, and perhaps cherished in the Court painter the last link with his former subjects. Until late in life West had so regarded himself, but after the great success attained in his old age, he had finished by assuming a different view. In a biographical note submitted to his approval, the painter remarked that after fifty years' residence in England, although born in America, yet being the son of an Englishman by birth, and he and his father having left America before that country had declared its independence, he could only be considered as an Englishman.[50]

The artist's life by John Galt, full of romantic narrative and which appeared just after his death, was, in the words of the biographer, all but written by West himself. The latter had carefully corrected the manuscript of the first part, and on his death-bed he had read nearly all the proofs of the second. Galt was as sincerely convinced as his hero that the painter's name would live forever alongside those of Raphael and Michelangelo.[51] And S. F. B. Morse, who was to prove later that he was a great inventor, although a mediocre artist, described West as a genius who bore the same relation to painting that Milton did to poetry, and could only hope to receive proper praise after death, when the lustre of his works would not "fail to illuminate the dark regions of barbarism."[52]

When George the Third died in 1820, West remarked to his son that he had lost the best friend he ever had. Artist and King were of the same age, and many years earlier, the latter had jocosely remarked to West that, whenever he himself died, the painter would begin to feel nervous. Very few weeks after his royal patron, West passed away in his old age as peacefully as he had lived, surrounded by his beloved art treasures and till the very last moment turning over the pages of an album of Fra Bartolomeo's drawings. Death came to him in its mercy just as the fashion for his art once more was beginning to wane and he had been compelled to reduce the price of his pictures.[53]

The Royal Academy voted to inter its President in the

crypt of Saint Paul's, with the same pomp as for Sir Joshua, near whose dust he was laid. The coffin, however, was first brought into the smaller exhibition room of the Academy, where "the nobility, gentry and deceased's private friends soon after arrived." Marshalmen, cloakmen, mutes on horseback and pages headed the funeral procession, and it was remarked by the press that in the coaches which followed, sat three dukes, two marquesses, many earls and bishops. The American Minister was among the pall-bearers. The gazettes explained that, "owing to the absence from Town of so many noblemen and gentlemen of the highest rank, many warm admirers of this celebrated artist were precluded from attending."[54]

Sir Thomas Lawrence, elected to succeed him at the Academy, delivered his predecessor's eulogy with high praise for West's gentle humanity. The new President expatiated on the display of his talent at so advanced an age, which combined with the sacred importance of his subjects, conferred on the artist at the end of his life a renown greater than he had ever before attained. West in fact had become "the one popular painter of his country" and his death was felt to be a national calamity.

The late President left only trifling personal property, but he possessed a number of valuable ancient paintings, including works by Titian, Rembrandt, Rubens, and Vandyck, which were sold two years later. When in 1829, his own pictures came under the hammer, they brought over twenty-five thousand pounds, three thousand being paid for his *Christ Rejected*, which it was whispered had been bought by the Duke of Orleans.

Only three years before his death, West had finished an *Annunciation* for the new Church of Saint Marylebone, receiving for this eight hundred pounds. In 1840, the same picture was put up at public sale and the auctioneer called attention to its remarkable merits and the great celebrity of the artist. As a further inducement to the purchaser he promised to throw in a particularly interesting letter written by Benjamin West to describe the special circumstances in which this pious commission had been executed by the late President of the Royal Academy. After a considerable time had passed without a single bid being made, the picture and the letter were finally knocked down for ten guineas.[55]

CHAPTER TEN

John Copley, Prophet of Revolution

I

THERE is a tendency in the United States, to exalt somewhat
uncritically the æsthetic side of American origins, and value
the feeble manifestations of early colonial art as though they
were a fitting counterpart to other more virile forms of
national expression. The gawky portraitists who flourished
in the middle of the eighteenth century have had their rustic
talent honoured beyond all deserts, and given an importance
as if they had been gifted forerunners of a great native school.
The wish is pious, and ample precedent can also be found for
similar worship in other countries. Yet it defeats its purpose,
for any over-favourable appraisal of crude æsthetic beginnings
in the Colonies rests on a misconception. If the national
instinct had run to painting instead of to more urgent forms
of expression, at a time when the United States needed to
devote all its creative energy for a far more notable work of
art, the country would hardly have grown into the great
Empire it has become. The political genius of the founders of
the Republic and the pioneering genius of men who tamed
the wilderness would, with difficulty, have been able to flourish
alongside of a corresponding artistic development among
colonial craftsmen. It is rare that the crude provincialism of
these early painters in the New World justifies much more
than an antiquarian curiosity.

[326]

American leaders in the eighteenth century were certainly under no illusions regarding the merit of native art. Benjamin Franklin had observed in 1763 that "Painting has yet scarce made her appearance among us,"[1] and later explained as a reason for this that, owing to private persons in America not being rich enough to offer sufficient encouragement to the fine arts, "our geniuses all go to Europe."[2] John Adams with real understanding of the situation disapproved of any premature development of the arts and advocated for his own generation concentrating on the homely necessities of practical education, leaving artistic pursuits for his grandchildren to cultivate.

The real penury in art that existed in Boston in the middle of the eighteenth century can be understood after mentioning a few examples which explain the requirements of the time. The first portraitist of his day in Massachusetts was the Scotsman, John Smibert, who had arrived in America with Bishop Berkeley, bringing with him a few casts and copies of old masters from which his talent does not seem to have benefited. Smibert later opened a colour shop in Boston. An obscure, though at times not unskilful London painter named Arthur Pond, who also dealt in prints and was in the habit of executing small commissions for the Colonies, had forwarded a few engravings for Smibert to sell. The leading portraitist in the leading American city, after expressing satisfaction with a view of Greenwich, and certain *Antique Ruins* after Pannini, which he had just received from London, wrote to his correspondent principally to ask for ten or fifteen shillings' worth of coloured prints, "slight and cheap for japanning."[3]

The recognition of this dearth in the arts had led to the foundation of a society for their encouragement in Boston.

In 1767, a business correspondent in London proposed to
James Bowdoin, who was a member of this society, to purchase
an important publication by Boydell, who had just completed
engraving the most famous pictures in England.[4] The future
Governor refused to subscribe to this work owing to the
prevailing spirit of economy which would not allow
Americans to import similar articles, and explained his attitude
because of British measures of taxation. In reality the political
ferment was too engrossing for any real interest in the arts
to develop in the Colonies, but politics were not the only
reason why art had remained so backward. Most Americans
still held a very contemptuous attitude towards painters.
Early in the last century when S. F. B. Morse arrived in
London, he was most impressed by the contrast between
America, where art was looked upon as "an employment
suited to a lower class of people," and England, where it
provided a constant topic of conversation.[5]

This contemptuous attitude towards artists is illustrated
by a passage from a book published in Boston in 1786, containing the statement that "Painters (particularly inside, house,
miniature and portrait painters), hairdressers, tavern keepers,
musicians, stage players, buffoons and exhibitors of birds
and puppets" rank among the unprofitable labourers in the
State,[6] a judgment which, in the opinion of Mr. James T.
Adams, from whose book on New England this passage is
quoted, reflects with some accuracy the prevalent contemporary American idea. Even Copley, in spite of the
influential connections he enjoyed, found it most mortifying
that people in Boston generally regarded art in the same way
as tailoring, shoe-making, or other trades, and remarked
that if it were not for the wish to preserve the resemblance of

particular persons, painting in the Colonies would be unknown.[7]

To one who, like Copley, caressed an ideal which he shared at this time with no one else in Boston, the slight consideration given to painting and the contempt shown for painters, were profoundly humiliating and counted among the reasons which furthered his desire to settle in England. Even highly cultivated men like Governor Hutchinson evinced few signs of the slightest æsthetic understanding. The Governor was himself related to Copley, who had married his grand niece. During the later years of exile in London, when time hung heavy on him, Hutchinson, who had sat for his portrait to the painter, saw Copley frequently and mentions him repeatedly. Yet in a *Diary* teeming with observations on persons, manners, and objects, there is not the slightest allusion to Copley's merit as an artist nor, in fact, to that of any other painter of the day.

There was another reason which explains Copley's wish to leave America. The painter had long felt a real craving to see works of art, which was all the greater because he was unable to visualize what these really were like. In Boston there were then only a few prints indifferently executed, and Copley lamented his peculiar misfortune as a painter who was obliged to live in a place where there was not a single portrait worthy to be called a picture.[8] This scathing remark has since been challenged on the ground that a number of Smiberts and Blackburns, a possible Kneller, and an impossible Vandyck, then adorned the walls of Boston drawing-rooms, better perhaps, than anything to prove the force of his indictment. A few pictures which may be traced in houses at Newport and in other American cities can hardly affect the accuracy of the charge. Nor was Copley the only one to deplore this complete dearth of works of art in America. Benjamin West was also of the same opinion, unimpressed by the fact that his first patron, William Allen, later had acquired a few copies of Titian and Correggio. An art-loving Philadelphia physician, Dr. John Morgan, who had lived abroad and had given Copley, although the latter was personally unknown to him, letters of introduction to artists and collectors in Rome, explained in these that the Boston painter had never yet seen a good picture except his own, and that history offered no other instance of a man with so little opportunity having by his own genius attained to such pre-eminence.[9]

For several years Copley's ambition to study abroad had been restrained by certain practical considerations. He was at this time earning in Boston an annual income of three hundred guineas, which he observed was as much "as the poverty of this place will admit," and affirmed that, though he were a Raphael or a Correggio, it would be impossible to gain more. His great desire to settle in England came moreover from the feeling that there was no durable fame to be gained in a land where pictures were confined to sitting-rooms and esteemed only because of the resemblance they bore to their originals.

The thin New England soil breeds some curious growths, and Copley's ambition had been almost sporadic. "Painters cannot live on art only, though I could hardly live without it," he wrote, but with Yankee practical-mindedness his ambition to study the old masters was restrained by fear that any improvement in his work after a European tour would be of no benefit to him in America either in fortune or in reputation. Although longing to settle in London he dreaded, in case of being unable to make his mark as a painter in a great capital, that he would be obliged to return to Boston and bury all he had ever learned abroad among people destitute of any understanding of the arts and with whom he would no longer enjoy the same consideration as before.

Pondering over his future, and still uncertain of what to do, his kinsman, Peter Pelham, wrote enthusiastically from the Barbados to point out the advantage it would be for the artist to leave bleak New England in order to make his home in the West Indies. This was in 1766, eight years before he actually departed, but Copley had already then made up his mind that if ever he left America it would be for Europe, as he promised himself to regale his eye with the sight of the great masters.[10] The doubt which for so long kept him back before deciding on what to do was solely the question of the ability to gain his living by his brush in case he should settle in England. It was no question of modesty on his part, but of unavoidable ignorance, for never having seen a really good picture, he had not yet been able to form an opinion about the merits of his own. As a test he sent his *Boy with the Squirrel* to London. The painting was submitted to Reynolds, who criticized its hard and overminute drawing, the absence of life and want of transparency in the shadows, but found it none the less a wonderful performance, all the more extraordinary as being the work of a young man who had never been out of New England. He prophesied that Copley might become one of the first painters in the world if he could have the advantage of example and instruction before this should come too late and his manner had been "corrupted and fixed" by working in his former little way at Boston. Generously, Sir Joshua sent Copley's picture along with his own paintings to the Exhibition, where it met with a deserved success.[11]

At this time also Copley was personally unknown to Benjamin West, but the latter as a fellow artist and compatriot wrote to offer some friendly criticism and his earnest advice to study abroad. With his invariable kindness West promised to give the Boston painter letters for friends in Italy, placed his house in London at his service, and proposed him for membership in the Society of Artists. Copley was overjoyed at this piece of good news, and wrote to express fulsome gratitude for the praise of "my countryman from whom America receives the same lustre that Italy does from her Titian and Divine Raphael"; he enquired from West about the state of the arts in Rome and asked him if the living painters were as good as the dead.

More than ever Copley felt perplexed about his future as a painter. Ambitious for success abroad, yet held back by family ties and genuine doubts regarding his own talent, he had made up his mind that if he left Boston it would be with no intention to return; but in his situation could he safely take this risk? Convinced that West would not advise him to abandon this without a fair prospect to obtain something equivalent in England, he wrote to London to beg the latter to help him reach a decision. If West, after having weighed all the arguments, should still advise him to go, the Boston painter would need yet another year in which to arrange his affairs. The change of residence was a step in the dark for one who had never been abroad and meant leaving comparative affluence for an uncertain position in a city in which the cost of living would be three times as great as in Boston. Copley threw the responsibility for making a decision on West, who was then a stranger to him, but the latter, after consulting other painters, replied that in his opinion the New

England artist had nothing to fear. Yet none the less he advised him to go first to Italy and there to study the old masters. With that unfailing kindness which helps to explain the eminent position West enjoyed among artists, the latter wrote to a man whom he had never seen to tell him that "I beg you'll make my house your home," promised him his aid, and encouraged a stranger and a possible rival by holding out to him the prospect that London was the only city in Europe in which an artist could find adequate reward for his painting.

Unexpectedly to Copley, further encouragement came at this juncture from another compatriot, a certain John Greenwood, who wrote to him also from London. The latter, the nephew of a Harvard professor, was probably the first American painter ever to go abroad. After a career which had begun in Dutch Guiana, where he is said to have painted a hundred portraits, Greenwood had gone to Amsterdam to learn mezzotint engraving, and in Holland he took up the picture trade. Settling later permanently in London, he exhibited at first his own paintings, among these a view of Boston, but most of his time was taken up as an art dealer. Commissioned by Lord Bute to form a gallery of old masters Greenwood had purchased two large collections on the Continent and was proud to have brought back some fifteen hundred pictures to London. He also held yearly sales at Christie's and had ended by giving up painting and setting up for himself as an art auctioneer. His principal convictions were a touching admiration for West whom he regarded in the light of another Raphael, and a firm belief in London as the great centre of art and a city where everyone then spoke of new pictures at exhibitions, "just as in Boston before an election, even children talked of nothing else."[12] From the specimens seen Greenwood had formed a most favourable opinion of Copley's talent and asked the latter to paint his mother, who lived in Marblehead, a portrait which was later exhibited in London. Copley, delighted with this order, expressed hope that some day the arts might reach even America, however little indication there still seemed to be of this. The painter had shortly before received two guineas from Dr. Myles Cooper, President of King's College, New York, for a small picture of a man holding a candle, which the latter proposed to present to the college library. Copley announced that he accepted the offer because he wished to see a public collection begun in the New World.[13]

A curious incident brought out at this time the connection between art and politics which had always existed in the painter's mind. One of John Wilkes's numerous admirers in Boston had named his son after his idol and commissioned Copley to paint the boy's likeness in order to send as an offering to the great demagogue. On its receipt Wilkes wrote to express admiration at the high degree of excellence which painting had attained in New England and, forgetting his own scandalous past, the author of the "Essay on Woman" unblushingly added some nonsense about "the generous sons of freedom in America who remain undebauched by the wickedness of European courts and Parliamentary prostitution."[14] Copley welcomed the praise, but felt torn between his wish to exhibit this portrait in London and the fear of its possible consequences. Cautious timidity kept him once more from making a decision for himself. Again he asked for West's advice, mentioning in his letter that party spirit ran so high in Boston that any compliment paid to the leaders of either side would be resented by the other. He himself wished to keep aloof from any suspicion of partisanship, for he understood that political strife was of no advantage to art. His only ambition was to be considered as a painter, and he begged West to withhold the picture if its subject could give offence to anyone.[15]

This letter is very typical of Copley's timid attitude towards events, for except in the privacy of his family he refrained as much as he could from expressions of personal opinion. His own genuine Whig sympathies were kept in the background, and deliberately he isolated himself from events the gravity of which he understood better than anyone. In Boston, where politics were all-important, he held aloof from a movement of which he heartily approved without ever wishing to join. After the Stamp Act, when the mob had sacked the houses of Crown officials, Copley described the outrages committed without one single word of blame. In letters which he wrote to friends, he made use of the words "we demolished" and then gave a list of the houses sacked.[16]

In an inconspicuous way the painter stood very well with the American leaders and the circumstance of the patriots regarding him as being on their side soon after proved most useful to his wife's family. Although his mother kept a small tobacco shop, Copley had married the daughter of a wealthy Tory merchant, Richard Clarke, to whom the famous East India Company tea had been consigned. After the Boston patriots had dumped this cargo into the harbour, the mob displayed its further zeal for liberty by smashing the windows of his father-in-law's house. The cautious Copley claimed after this to have cooled popular feeling against the Clarkes by speaking privately in their behalf to Whig leaders like Dr. Warren and John Hancock, explaining to these that his wife's relations had acted only as agents without assuming any further responsibility. Although there were no more attacks he advised his Tory in-laws to stay in hiding until the vessel which brought the tea had sailed and to take no further steps to justify themselves, but allow others to contradict the newspaper calumnies.[17]

This departure from his customary reticence must have been highly distasteful to the cautious painter. Against every inclination he had been forced into the open, and, though patriot leaders bore him no ill-will for his conduct, the incident left traces. Some suspicion must have lingered among the masses, for not long afterwards a howling mob appeared before his house at midnight, having learned that the Mandamus Counsellor, Colonel George Watson, was with him. Copley in fact, just before the mob appeared, had pressed Watson to spend the night in his house, but fortunately the latter had left in time and the painter could truthfully declare that he knew nothing of his whereabouts. The rabble shouted that if he deceived them his blood would be on his own head, and Copley understood that he had escaped from the terrible dilemma of being obliged to give up a friend to an infuriated mob or else having his own house pulled down and perhaps his family murdered.[18]

Looking to the future, the artist saw the political outlook ahead by the same cold light in which he painted his sitters. The course he then embarked on was neither heroic nor patriotic, if patriotism is restricted to action. Copley justified himself on the ground that, with his ambition to become the foremost American painter, civil strife would be detrimental to the pursuit of art. He foresaw that impending events would make it difficult for him to continue to paint in Boston and that it might be wiser to leave as soon as possible in order to settle in England. How far he told friends about these intentions is uncertain, for it must have been hard to keep his plans a secret, but by an odd paradox at the same time as Copley, the American Whig, was intending to expatriate himself forever from his native country, his Tory brother-in-law, Jonathan Clarke, argued with him against Americans settling abroad in a letter written to the painter from London in which the following passage occurs:

All the objection we can have to our friends travelling is that after they have been for some time abroad and much improved themselves and been used to the society of men of Literature and attached to the polite arts, upon their return they find our young country don't furnish a great number of the same relish, and therefore are obliged to seek them in older countries where it is reasonable to suppose they more abound so that our country is checked in its improvement. Now I hope better things of you than a disposition which is rather selfish.[19]

Copley, who saw his future already mapped out, was not the man to be impressed by this reasoning. He had suffered for years from the contempt shown for art and had deplored the inability of America to provide a suitable atmosphere for a painter. His conviction that the impending civil strife would make his profession impossible had led him to form plans which none of his wife's relatives could influence. His mind was already set to go abroad alone, first to Italy to perfect his skill, during which time his family were to remain in Boston

until later they could all meet in London to make England
their future home.

One week after Governor Hutchinson, Copley sailed from
Boston almost in the nick of time to realize his ambition.
From the moment he set foot in England a succession of
unexpected delights filled a man rarely given to enthusiasm.
Driving along the road to London he may have neglected to
notice the enchantment of the Kentish countryside in the first
green of early summer, for the painter's cold eye lacked
appreciation for nature. But he expressed real admiration for
the livery of the postilion who accompanied the stage-coach,
and remarked on the quality of the Hyson tea which he
drank at wayside inns, as being far superior to the Dutch
contraband found in American gentlemen's houses. His coldness changed suddenly to warmth when he praised the amenities of old world surroundings, which were still a novelty
to him.

After a night in London, passed at the New England Coffee
House, Copley had rented lodgings near West, who with
his customary hospitality gave him a standing invitation to
dinner, and presented him to Sir Joshua, in whose painting
room, for the first time, he saw pictures by other great artists.
The Boston painter was hardly able to describe a series of im-
pressions which rapidly followed each other in a mind always
more receptive to observation than responsive to feeling. He
had brought with him some letters of introduction from British
officers on General Gage's staff which described him as being
one of "the first geniuses of the age."[20] This reputation as
an artist must have counted much towards assuring him a
welcome in London, for his real personality, devoid of all
charm, was little sympathetic. Possibly the self-consciousness

of his own aridity made him appreciate all the more in others those qualities of genial intercourse which notably West possessed and in which he felt himself to be so deficient. At all events the "manly politeness" and the hospitality and kindness of everyone whom he met in London amazed him. He wrote to his wife that he was shown more civility than he had received in Boston, except from a few friends, during his whole life. Governor Hutchinson also had made much the same observation. The painter, had he chosen, might have begun on some portraits at once, but his mind was made up first to see Italy before he should again settle down to work.

II

When Copley passed through Paris on his way south, he visited the Duke of Orleans' great collection, yet cautiously forbore from making any comment, for he was still timid as to the value of his own opinion and uncertain if the paintings he had seen were really good examples of their kind. Curiously enough the manners of the strangers he met appear to have impressed him more than the examples of art. Always observant of every detail, he admired the obliging civility of both French and Italians, and wrote to his wife that by their politeness they set an example worthy of imitation for the people of Massachusetts.

The effect of Italy on a Northern mind is usually to quicken the perception of beauty, to stir emotion by giving pleasure to the eye, and warm the coldish stream of Gothic blood. Artists who come from beyond the Alps have often found their pleasure in yielding to the smile of the Mediterranean land. But Copley, like Benjamin West and Henry Benbridge, the two American painters who had preceded him in Rome, discovered in Italy no sensuous appeal to mellow the expression of his somewhat frigid art. His virtue was never endangered by any Southern blandishments. The Boston painter was then the father of a family, almost forty years of age, and the only life he had hitherto known was in the austere New England tradition from which he never departed. His personality, moreover, was unsociable and his purpose so immediately practical that in the land he had gone to visit he passed quite untouched by the spectacle of its beauty. Never for an instant did he forget the true intention of his tour, which was to see just as much and to learn just as much about his profession in as short a space of time as was possible. Italy meant for him only an education of the eye and brush, and not of the heart. His observation of trivial detail led him to comment on the cheapness of velvets at Genoa, but the greater beauty of the Latin land was hidden from Copley as in a sealed book.

The New England painter became an indefatigable sight-seer and remarked that there was a kind of habit in this, just as in eating and in drinking, which the more it was indulged in, the less could it be restrained. Above everything else he was impressed by the magnificence of Italian buildings, and wrote to his wife that if he should again be transported to Boston it would seem to him as if the people there lived only in huts. With a precise eye he had calculated that if his whole house could be placed within an Italian palace it would bear the same relation to this as a box a foot square inside his sitting-room. Painting oddly enthused Copley less than architecture. He felt that he had little to learn from living artists in Rome, and the genius of Guardi and Tiepolo in

Venice remained quite outside his ken. Even the masters of former ages appeared to him less great than he had expected. He was disappointed in their skill and with a judgment more independent than penetrating ventured the opinion that eminence in art was attained so soon as a painter went a little beyond his contemporaries, and that the difference between Raphael, Titian, and the common run of moderately good artists was less great than might be supposed from the praise which they enjoyed.[21]

The letters Copley carried with him had all alluded to the honour for America to have produced such an illustrious painter, for he was no longer under any illusion with regard to his own merit. Common nationality had caused his name to be usually associated with that of West, but Copley felt pleased when in Rome the Scottish painter and art dealer, Gavin Hamilton, who sold antique statues to Englishmen on the Grand Tour, told the Boston artist that he was "better established" than his compatriot owing to the superiority of his portraits. Copley found other Americans in Rome like the Ralph Izards of South Carolina, who had lately left their home in London and with whom he travelled to see the Greek temples of Paestum. Another companion of the road whom he met in Italy was an ill-natured painter named George Carter, who has left a malicious description of Copley bragging about the art which America would produce after she had gained her independence. The two men cordially detested each other, and it is just possible that to irritate this unpleasant companion the Boston man may have departed from his customary reserve, for otherwise the story seems unlikely. Curiously enough, Copley associated the consequences which he already anticipated from the impending struggle in the

Colonies with his own future fame as an American artist. Without a qualm for any duty left unfulfilled towards his country, he felt only a deep satisfaction at having escaped from Boston before the storm had burst. No possible doubt nor hesitation entered his mind regarding the egotism of this course or that he might deliberately have evaded the obligations imposed by his sympathies. In his own opinion, which was also the opinion generally current in that age, he remained something apart as a painter. But whereas most Americans looked with some contempt on that profession, Copley felt that he needed no other apology than the glory to which he confidently looked forward as his reward, of being a forerunner of art in the new State. The letters written during his Italian tour illustrate this complacent feeling of satisfaction at his own wisdom in leaving America and of belief in his future fame through the victory of his countrymen.

From Parma he wrote to his half-brother:

> Could anything be more fortunate than the time of my leaving Boston? Poor America! I hope the best but I fear the worst. Yet certain I am she will finally emerge from her present calamity and become a mighty Empire. And it is a pleasing reflection that I shall stand among the first of the artists that shall have led that country to the knowledge and cultivation of the fine arts, happy in the pleasing reflection that they will one day shine with a lustre not inferior to what they have done in Greece or Rome, in my native country.[22]

The painter's only concern was for his wife and children whom he had left behind in Boston. He trembled for their safety, and dreaded the impending civil war which he saw coming. Long before hostilities had broken out Copley felt convinced that the breach was impossible to heal and that America would be torn asunder first by the quarrel with Great Britain which would last until the Colonies became a separate nation, and later by civil discord till time at last settled the new State into some form of government.[23]

The letters containing these prophecies were written at a time when professional politicians like Governor Hutchinson on the one side and John Adams and Thomas Jefferson on the other, had not yet begun to understand the future which was in store. American Whigs were still indignantly protesting against any aspersions on their loyalty, and the leaders of the Continental Congress were denying, in all sincerity, any thought of independence and loudly proclaiming their unalterable attachment to the King. A mere painter like Copley aloof from politics, and at that time a visitor in a distant land, saw from afar the real significance of what was impending and drew a picture of future political events with the same cold and unemotional precision with which he painted his portraits. From Parma, where he was then engaged in copying Correggio's Saint Jerome, on August 6, 1775, before the news of Bunker Hill had time to reach him, he wrote with amazing foresight to his half-brother that the civil war in the Colonies would inevitably be carried on with extreme violence. The Americans, in the belief that England would not act, had incited the British to do their utmost. The King was obliged to carry through his policy of domination and the colonials, having gone too far to retract, yet had it in their power to baffle all that England could do against them and, although oceans of blood would be shed, they would never be subdued.

After they have with various success deluged the country in blood, the issue will be that the Americans will be a free and independent people. This may be the result of a struggle of many years during which the customary miseries of war, sword, famine and pestilence will be suffered.

At a moment when hardly an Englishman and not very many Americans believed in the success of Revolution and still thought that this must end in a rapid defeat or in some form of compromise, Copley wrote from Italy to his wife in Boston:

I cannot think that the power of Great Britain will subdue the country if the people are united as they appear to be at present. I know it may seem strange to some men of great understanding that I should hold such an opinion, but it is very evident to me that Americans will have the power of resistance until grown strong enough to conquer, and that victory and independence will go hand in hand.[24]

About the same time the painter wrote to his half-brother, Henry Pelham, urging the latter for most important reasons to leave at once for England, and under no circumstances to take any part in the conflict. Deeply attached to the boy, Copley had acted like a father to his half-brother, who was then just beginning to earn his own way. Pelham had started his career as an artist by drawing the Boston Massacre, and gave his drawing to be engraved to Paul Revere, but the latter, more scrupulous in patriotic solicitude than in his business dealings, had pirated this for his own benefit, and the young artist could only indignantly complain to him that he had acted "as if you had plundered me on a highway."[25]

Later, Pelham had taken to painting miniatures with fair success. He already had a hundred guineas' worth of work begun, but owing to the disturbances he was unable to collect a hundred farthings. He was forbidden to publish a plan of Charleston he had just drawn lest it should give information of the British entrenchments to the Americans. The boy complained that everything was being kept secret and spies and informers maligned people's characters. Even Copley's letters had proved embarrassing, and he begged his brother to refrain from making any further political reflections in writing to him and allow him to "scrabble through" as best he could. So far he had avoided blame, was still regarded as a faithful subject to "the most amiable and injured of sovereigns," and felt proud to have been invited to lunch by General Howe at whose table he had tasted fresh meat for the first time in four months.

Like many others, Henry Pelham had been reluctant to take sides, but after the first violence forced all moderates into partisanship, the young miniature painter, who felt no personal inclination to participate in the struggle and no greater obligation than his brother, had become a Tory largely out of disgust for the "lawless and outrageous rabble."[26] None the less, he regretted that anyone who was not sufficiently violent should now be branded as an enemy to American liberty. After Bunker Hill, whenever he passed the freshly made grave of the fallen Dr. Warren, whom he had known personally, the sight of this gave him a disagreeable sensation. Pelham, who only wanted tranquillity, lamented that the "patriots" should have deluded a well-meaning but credulous people with the wish for independence, though he was bound to admit that the Americans were impelled by the most surprising enthusiasm.[27] The poor boy felt miserably unhappy at the turn events had taken. His livelihood could no longer be earned in Boston and he knew that shortly he would be obliged "to abandon my native land" and seek his bread elsewhere. Saddest of all, as a result of this change in his fortunes, he wrote to his brother that it was no longer possible for him to "avow with Reputation and Propriety a tender attachment for one of the most lovely and amiable of my Female Friends—Miss Sally Bromfield." Soon after this, Pelham emigrated to England to end by becoming a land agent in Ireland.

Copley was now deeply concerned for himself lest the struggle in America should reduce him also to poverty. He then owned about eleven acres of farm land on Beacon Hill, which to his keen regret he had not sold in time.[28] It was out of the question to go back to Boston to starve, and he felt tormented by the doubt that he might not be able to earn enough in London to bring up his family in comfort. The painter made up his mind to leave Italy at once, and to begin work just as soon as possible. His wife had been in England already for a year, having settled in Islington while awaiting her husband. She, too, felt greatly worried about her family which had remained in Boston, and did not dare to express her real thoughts to them lest her letters should be read in Congress.[29] "The Americans muster very thick in England," she wrote her husband as more and more refugees kept coming over.

On her arrival in London, Mrs. Copley had called on Mrs. West, who returned her visit, but the friendship stopped there. The lady from Philadelphia and the lady from Boston had both their settled habits and these included very little readiness to make new friends. Nor did intimacy ever go much further between West and Copley, and apart from the fact that both painters were Americans, there was not a great deal to draw them together in any real cordiality. At first they saw each other frequently: West would drop in occasionally for tea[30] and Copley would take his New England friends to call on the Court painter. The latter's reputation was solidly established, while the Boston artist was still a newcomer who felt, not without some reason, that his own talent was far superior to that of the Royal Academician. On political matters it is probable that both men thought alike, but neither ever spoke to the other about their American sympathies, and caution induced each to keep his opinions to himself. West was too closely associated with the King ever to express his mind freely and Copley far too reticent to do so except within the bosom of his own family.

In many respects the eighteenth century was far more tolerant than is our age, and Copley had reason to appreciate the liberality of England in not demanding from him any open profession of loyalty.[31] With no recognized duty save to art and his family, the only course possible for him to pursue was one of silence which cost his secretive nature no real effort. It has been said that he fell under the suspicion of the British Government, though this seems most unlikely and authority for the statement is lacking.[32] Certainly he did nothing to justify distrust and gave the example of a perfect neutral during the Revolution. It stands, withal, to the credit of a man so cautious that he should have joined West in going bail for John Trumbull when the latter was released from prison.

Copley's apparent unconcern with political events was the more natural, as his wife's family and the Massachusetts refugees whom he principally frequented were all loyalists, and in the habit of visiting his studio without, however, expressing much admiration for his art. Edward Oxnard, who was a member of this group and passed his days in auction rooms, thrilled by the pictures he saw, knew Copley well, but had not one word to say in his praise as a painter. The only exception to this general seeming indifference was the whimsical Peter Oliver, who wrote to his son-in-law, Elisha Hutchinson, "I rejoice with Mr. Copley in his success, tell him not to be exalted beyond measure," and then suggested as a noble subject for his next picture depicting the shield of Æneas, which he was convinced would add immortality to the painter's fame.[33] With all his absurdities the former Chief Justice of Massachusetts was, perhaps, the only American in London who genuinely admired the artist in Copley and saw in him something more than a maker of family portraits.

Elisha Hutchinson, a cousin by marriage, mentions having been taken by the painter to call on Reynolds and West whose rooms, he observed, were principally filled with portraits of the royal family. Royalty also sat occasionally for Copley. He, too, painted the over-painted King and several other members of his family. Perhaps his greatest work is the pleasing group which hangs in Buckingham Palace of the three young Princesses, Mary, Sophia, and Amelia, playing with their pet spaniels—a carefully executed composition carried out with an unaccustomed elegance, and a little superabundance of detail, but with more grace of brush than was characteristic of his usual performance.

Copley's greatest triumph was the *Death of Chatham*, which ranks among the finest historical paintings of the eighteenth century, and is said to have brought in five thousand

PRINCESSES MARY, SOPHIA AND AMELIA
From a painting by John S. Copley

pounds in gate money and a well-merited reputation, which was burlesqued by Pasquin in the jingle:

> From Massachusetts rebel state
> When loyalty was crying,
> I ran on shipboard here to paint
> Lord Chatham who was dying.[34]

Numbers of City merchants who worshipped Chatham's memory sat after this to Copley for their portraits; while West painted the Court, the Boston painter enjoyed the favour of the business community. Always a conscientious artist, he never attained quite the first rank nor did he quite fulfil the promise of his early work. His drawing was correct and he had an eye for light and shade, but his colouring was frequently as cold as was his character. New England rarely brings out warmth in its talent, and the glow which brightens even the feeblest of Sir Joshua's canvases was usually lacking in an art which missed the latter's sacred fire.

In spite of relations broken by war, the report of Copley's fame in England soon spread to Boston, and his old friend John Scolloy wrote from there to express hope that the painter would not forget his native country and the cause it was engaged in, "which I know lay once near your heart and I trust does so still." Yet caution and coldness united to make Copley repress any sign of his political sympathies until after peace had been signed. When once more it became safe to show these, he was present with West in the House of Lords when the two painters listened to the King's Speech on December 5, 1782, recognizing the independence of the United States.

George the Third usually read his addresses in a free and impressive manner, but this time he showed marks of embarrassment and a halting delivery in his words. Elkanah Watson, an American then in London, who describes the incident in his *Memoirs*, had just won a hundred guineas at Lloyd's for a bet that Lord Howe would relieve Gibraltar, and had made use of this money to have his portrait painted by Copley. The picture was ready except for the background, which the painter and he had designed to represent a ship bearing to America the acknowledgment of independence. All was complete save the flag, which under the circumstances Copley did not like to depict. On the evening of the King's Speech, Watson, who had dined with the artist, relates that "he invited me into his studio and there with a bold hand and a master's touch, he attached to the ship the stars and stripes. This was, I imagine, the first American flag ever hoisted in Old England."

Americans had become proud of Copley and no stigma was ever attached to his departure from Boston. Nor was the fact that he should have settled in England ever held out against him. When he sent the engraving of his *Chatham* to Washington, the latter found that it was all the more admirable because of the artist's American birth. John Adams, who received the same print, acknowledged this with the words that he would preserve the engraving as a token of friendship and an "indubitable proof of American Genius." Rightly, Adams recognized in Copley the greatest of American masters, for he had long before this discerned the immense superiority of his portraits over those of West.[35] The first Envoy of the United States in London sat for him in 1783, when he was painted in a brown velvet Court dress, a picture which now hangs in the Memorial Hall at Harvard. Mrs. Adams was a frequent visitor at the artist's home, and it is said that while stitching her husband's shirts she would relate to Mrs. Copley the scant courtesy shown at Court to the American Minister.[36]

The remainder of the artist's life hardly enters within the limits of this study and will only be outlined. As a painter of established reputation, he was elected to the Royal Academy and lived in comfortable circumstances as a member of the circle of men of letters and artists which formed an important part of London at the end of the Eighteenth Century. In 1781, he moved into an "elegant and well furnished" house in George Street, Hanover Square, which has since been torn down and was only a few doors from St. George's Church in which later Theodore Roosevelt was married. Copley and his more famous son, the future Lord Chancellor, both lived and died in this house.[37]

The Boston painter was never personally popular nor was his manner agreeable. Farington relates in his *Diary* his own surprise when, for the first time in several years, Copley had accosted him civilly.[38] Even toward West the early friendship cooled and all gratitude for the former's fine generosity to the then unknown artist was forgotten after royal influence had obtained for the President of the Academy the order to paint scriptural subjects at Greenwich Hospital which Copley hoped to secure through the head of the Admiralty, Lord Sandwich.[39] There never was any open breach between the two artists, but the malicious Hoppner noticed at Academy sessions that Copley invariably was against any measures proposed by West and it was principally owing to the Boston man's opposition that a picture by the latter was rejected for exhibition on the ground that it had been shown before.[40]

Many years later when Copley's son, who had then become Lord Lyndhurst, was asked for information about his father's life, he replied that its uneventful nature provided only slight material for a biographer. This was true enough for there was little outward interest in his career beyond a few lawsuits, in one of which Copley was condemned to pay £650 compensation for his refusal to use the plate of an engraving he had ordered for the *Death of Chatham*, lest this should injure his artistic reputation.

Another litigation in which the artist acted as the plaintiff was not without its humorous side. English baronets have an unfortunate predilection for American painters which has led to unpleasantness before Whistler; Copley also went to law over a family group he had painted for a wealthy but eccentric baronet, Sir Edward Knatchbull. Originally this picture had included his second wife and his seven children, but the baronet, missing his first wife's portrait, insisted on having her added, not as an angel as the artist had proposed, but in the flesh. Some time later the baronet returned with another lady and explained to the painter that, after an accident to his second wife, he had married a third whose likeness he now wished to have included. Again Copley agreed, but this time he raised the first two wives to a suitable place in heaven. The gigantic family group, when exhibited at the Academy, with two ladies represented in the sky, provided so much hilarity that the third Lady Knatchbull insisted on her predecessors having to go. The artist painted them out, but was obliged to take legal steps to obtain payment for the portraits effaced.

In spite of real success, Copley never felt completely at ease in London. Perhaps his unsociable character did not allow this, but there were also other reasons which left him dissatisfied. After having been the first painter in America, he knew that he was far from occupying the same position in

England. The political difficulties from which he escaped had now ended in the way he foretold, and his own choice between politics and art had, perhaps, been a mistake, for with his clear foresight he might have made the greater mark in public life. Underneath his cautious reticence he still preserved hidden republican convictions, which were well known to his son. When young Copley visited America in 1796, he wrote to his father:

> I have thought ever since I set foot in this country that it was possible you might think of returning hither, that you would find your profession more profitable than in England I have no doubt; the state of Society and of Government would be more congenial to your inclinations, and nothing but the difficulty of moving seems to stand in the opposite scale.[41]

The future Lord Lyndhurst knew that after twenty years' residence in London the painter had never taken root in England.

The later Chancellor, who was then visiting his American kinsmen, has described himself as a "fierce aristocrat" very far from sharing the artist's republican convictions, and highly pleased to find that all the better people in Federalist Boston were of his opinion. "My father is too rank a Jacobin to live among them," he wrote, and by a strange coincidence of foresight, just as Copley had prophesied American independence, the son, writing in 1796, foretold the Civil War. He remarked to his family that—

> A great schism seems to be forming, and they already begin to talk of a separation of the States North of the Potomac from those on the Southern side of the river.

There was also a more material cause for the painter's unhappiness. Before the Revolution, Copley had made investments in land in what was later to become the best residential quarter in Boston. As an absentee, the property might have been confiscated, but his friends were influential and his known early sympathies for the American cause had helped to preserve this. Certain speculators who had learned of the intention to build the State House on the top of Beacon Hill arranged with the painter's representative, who was his son-in-law, to buy this land, but Copley refused to sign the deed and sent over his son to arrange matters.[42] The latter found it preferable to come to terms with the purchasers, although the artist received three times the price he had paid, the sale left him bitter and his resentment grew with every increase in the value of the land. Fifteen years later, West explained Copley's dejection on the ground of his always ruminating over the loss of a property he had sold for seven thousand pounds and which was then worth one hundred thousand.[43]

The thought of returning to America was often before the painter, who always felt apprehensive about fresh trouble between the two countries.[44] His wife wrote, in 1803, to her married daughter in Boston, "I am certain that we can find an asylum in America, if it should prove difficult to remain, which I hope will not be the case."[45] In his old age Copley, unlike West, had become a disappointed man gnawed by the acidity of his own character and conscious that his talents were declining. When a friend asked him what profession his son intended to follow, he replied, "Anything but a painter. He has my permission to be anything he chooses but that."[46] His own popularity he knew was over and he was repeating the experience of nearly every artist, except West, who reaches old age and whom fashion forsakes—the fate which overtook even Rembrandt. He tried to persuade the King, who did not like him, to sit once more for a portrait, and in order to make the request placed himself conspicuously in a room in the Palace through which George the Third had to pass. Copley asked for permission to say something in private, but the King told him to speak out. Humbly soliciting the favour, the Monarch, whose outspokenness could be brutal, replied, loudly enough for others to hear: "Sit to you for a portrait! What, do you want to make a show of me!" and walked away.[47]

The public also had become indifferent to Copley. His best work were perhaps his battle pieces, yet few of the original subscribers for his print of the *Siege of Gibraltar* took up their subscriptions and two-thirds of all he received went to pay for the engraving. After years passed in comfortable affluence, he found himself reduced in his old age to selling whatever property he had. His home was mortgaged, his son helped to maintain the household, and the artist was under the indignity to borrow money from his son-in-law in Boston.

Copley was to make one last effort to regain the public favour. After West had gained great reputation with *Christ Healing the Sick*, Copley, who thirty-five years before had followed and improved on him as a painter of historical subjects, proposed in his old age to repeat this early success, and copy him in his religious pieces. He therefore attempted sacred subjects, as these had become the fashion of the day, and painted a vast *Resurrection* in the hope that this picture might also be bought by the British Institution.[48] With advancing years his powers, however, had visibly declined. Physically there was a great alteration in his appearance and to his familiars he showed an absent and bewildered manner. His later paintings had become feeble productions and were no longer worthy of his brush. Old age is a curse to those whose faculties are dimmed, and in the year of Waterloo death came as a mercy to Copley.

CHAPTER ELEVEN

John Trumbull's Adventures in London

I

WHEN Gilbert Stuart was a fellow student, under West, along with John Trumbull, and had tried to paint the latter's portrait, he left off, as Trumbull remarked, because "he could make nothing of my damned sallow face." It is even more difficult to make out how Trumbull should have dared to go to London in the midst of the War of Independence. He was the son of the patriot Governor of Connecticut, his brothers were all in the army, and no family had acted more conspicuously on the American side. He himself had taken up arms against England, had served with gallantry and distinction, and been a member of Washington's staff. At the time of his retirement he was a deputy adjutant-general with a colonel's rank on the staff of General Gates. He had resigned his army commission in the middle of a war of which he heartily approved, not, as was said, to study art, but out of resentment at the manner in which he had received promotion from Congress.[1] Like many another man since his day entitled to his country's gratitude, and not without pride in the consciousness of duty well performed, Trumbull suffered acutely from what seemed to him to be a boorish affront. As his friend the historian, William Gordon, wrote to General Gates, he was all the more sensitive on this point because his "heart is somewhat captivated by that bauble—alias bubble—honour."[2]

[357]

Henry Laurens, as President of Congress, was familiar with all the circumstances of the case and considered Trumbull's resignation to have been justified, for "men have a right to punctilio" so long as their insistence did not essentially injure their country.[3] Trumbull's spirited letters, however, had stirred up some feeling among the delegates, who soon after the incident found occasion to express their displeasure in another way. After Trumbull had left the army, he tried to be appointed secretary to one of the diplomatic missions which Congress at this time was despatching, rather haphazardly, to the different capitals of Europe, mainly to encounter rebuffs. Laurens wrote to his friend, the Governor of Connecticut, that if the Colonel were his son he would dissuade him from making any attempt of this kind. But John Trumbull insisted on trying to obtain a secretaryship, which, like every other office in the gift of Congress, had to be balloted for. A lingering resentment left by his outspoken comments was probably not foreign to his failure in obtaining the necessary number of votes.

The late colonel, now in want of an occupation, settled in Lebanon, Connecticut, where he took up drawing. One of his friends who had seen his work, suggested that if he were to practise caricature he could make some of the great figures of the time seem ridiculous,[4] but Trumbull's bent was far too serious for this. Art was an old ambition dating from undergraduate days at Harvard, when in vain he had entreated his father for permission to leave College and study instead under Copley. Now that he had resigned from the army, Trumbull felt independent and, with nothing more pressing to do, and military operations in the North almost at a standstill, except for the venture in Rhode Island in which he took a gallant part as a volunteer, the former soldier thought only about his future profession. Trumbull went to Boston to improve his brush and there rented Smibert's former studio. On its walls hung the copy that the latter had made of Raphael's *Madonna of the Chair*, which the young painter admired without an inkling as to who the picture was by. There was no one in Boston from whom he could learn anything, for art was as non-existent since Copley had left.

After John Temple had met with the rebuff from Congress, he had gone back to his father-in-law's home in Boston. In spite of the failure of his peace mission the late British secret agent was still trying to bring about more amicable relations between England and the United States. As an old friend of Governor Trumbull, with the best of intentions he had persuaded the Governor's son, who complained about the inability to obtain any instruction in Boston, to go to London and study there under West. Eager as the young painter was to do this, he feared lest such a residence might be unsafe because of his well-known connections and his own military record. Temple, however, reassured him, and doubtless pointed out that there were a number of other Americans in the Kingdom either living there, or as visitors, who openly sympathized with the Revolution. It was notorious that many of the colonial Whigs when in England had made no secret of their political feelings. Chief Justice Oliver had once stayed in a Derbyshire inn, where he related having read on the walls of his bedroom the following lines written nearly two years before hostilities began:

> The Eastern Glory is lost: its Power ends
> An Empire rises where the sun descends.

E. G. An American rebel, Sept. 12, 1773, was here.[5]

Temple might have cited as a further example Ralph Izard of Charleston, the future Envoy appointed by Congress to Tuscany. Months after the fighting began, the latter was still residing in London and writing to his bookseller, John Almon, who, like most of the British middle classes, was a warm friend of America, "as to any accommodation that is, I think, out of question."[6] At Bristol dwelt another native of South Carolina, Mr. Eversleigh, a Harvard graduate, whom the loyalist refugee, Samuel Curwen, described as finding "hearty in the cause of America." With the progress of the War a number of these sympathizers had left the British Isles. Thomas Hutchinson, Jr., wrote his brother, at a moment when the prospects of the Revolution appeared gloomy, to say that the very few Americans who remained in London wore long faces and it was becoming a rare thing to meet a Yankee even in the dark.[7] But some still stayed on in England. Temple's offer to arrange for Trumbull to stay in London to study art was, therefore, not so unusual as may appear. With ample confidence in his own influence, which he never undervalued, Bowdoin's son-in-law felt certain that there would be no risk in his friend's residence among the enemy, and offered to obtain special permission for this from the British Government. Soon afterward the secret agent returned to London and wrote from there that he had called on Lord George Germaine on Trumbull's behalf, and frankly explained who the young art student was, and the part he had taken in the Revolution. The Minister assured him that, although no official authorization could be granted, yet if the painter chose to visit London solely to study art, the British Government would take no notice of the fact that he had borne arms against them. Trumbull would be under surveillance and must commit no indiscretion, but so long as he avoided all political activity and confined himself only to painting, he would not be molested.[8]

This intelligent tolerance stands to the credit of a much-abused Minister. The latter's willingness to allow a prominent enemy officer who had fought against Great Britain to reside in London in the midst of a war shows a commendable courage and an indifference to public opinion which to-day could hardly be repeated. Nor did the anomaly of the circumstances in his particular case strike Trumbull until the very moment of his arrest. In eighteenth-century Europe, no democracy had as yet standardized the duties of patriotism. Voltaire could still congratulate Frederick the Great after Rossbach, and the French-born Ligionier could rise to become a British field-marshal, who fought his compatriots. Men felt in general better able to separate their personal activity from that of their nation. Very different ideas, it is true, prevailed in democratic America, but Trumbull believed himself to be covered by the amnesty officially proclaimed the year before by the British Peace Embassy. The painter had resigned his commission, reverted to his status as a private citizen, and ceased to fight against the King, even before the pardon offered to rebels who laid down their arms had been announced. Legally, at least, there was much to say for this view, nor was his claim ever seriously challenged by the British authorities, who arrested him on altogether different grounds. The painter's case offered in fact a remarkable example in law to test the right of an individual, born the subject of a country with which his own was at war, and who had fought against that country, but whose new nationality had not been recognized, to leave his land after an amnesty in order to pursue a peaceful occupation in an enemy state without accepting allegiance to his former King. From every point of view this tangled and complicated question bristled with grave legal difficulties, particularly owing to the still uncertain status of the colonists at this time. The intricacy of its many ramifications was probably among the reasons why Trumbull was never brought to trial. There were enough Englishmen who sympathized with the Revolution not to show some forbearance towards the few Americans in England who, although they had at heart their country's cause, could not successfully be charged with having committed any hostile acts from the time they had laid down their arms. Those who pressed for harsh treatment of the latter were not Englishmen, but loyalists.

Not unnaturally, the refugees had contrasted the tolerant treatment accorded by England to rebel subjects with their own savage persecution in the States, and felt intensely bitter against any Americans in London who favoured independence. Governor Hutchinson noted on April 14, 1779, that three men, whom he mentions by name, all professed subjects of the new State, had appeared publicly and proclaimed their principles without restraint. This was at a time when the estates of Tories who had left America and sought shelter in England were being confiscated in the name of the law and their persons were liable to imprisonment or worse if they returned. Evidence of the greater tolerance shown towards American Revolutionaries in England can also be found in quarters not open to suspicion. In October, 1780, Samuel Huntingdon, a signer of the Declaration of Independence, wrote to Governor Trumbull that he had just talked to a man freshly arrived from London who had seen his son there, as well as a "number of other Americans who had taken an active part in the war and appeared openly in the city and no notice taken of them by authority."[9]

Five months before this letter, John Trumbull had sailed from New London in an armed French merchantman laden with a valuable cargo of sugar and coffee from San Domingo. He went first to Paris, where he saw Franklin, who gave him, as he had given to so many others, a letter for Benjamin West. With France at war, Trumbull crossed to England by Ostend, and sent word of his arrival in London to John Temple, who immediately informed the Secretary of State. The news came like a bombshell to the loyalist refugees, who were amazed to learn that Governor Trumbull's son was in England, and at once apprised Lord George Germaine of their discovery, only to receive from the latter the rebuke that the painter had arrived at three o'clock and he had known it the same day at four, and so long as Trumbull confined himself to art he would not be molested.[10] Next morning the art student presented his letter of introduction to West, who received him with his usual kindness and asked for a specimen of his skill. Having none to offer, West told him to look around the painting room to see if there was anything that he wished to copy, and his selection for this purpose of Raphael's *Madonna*, which he already knew from having seen in Smibert's studio, was regarded as a good omen. After the copy had been finished, West solemnly pronounced Trumbull to be a painter and introduced him to his fellow pupil, Gilbert Stuart.

The former colonel on Washington's staff now became an assiduous art student, though always with an interest in politics, which, considering the peculiarity of his position in the enemy capital, was none too discreetly shown in the letters which he wrote to his father. With more truth than appropriateness the young painter denounced the entire rotten borough system in Parliamentary elections. He was always imbued with the spirit of Connecticut democracy and characterized the English practice as "outrageously ridiculous: the cabals, the palpable corruption, the meanness of intrigue exceeds all my ideas and gives me a much more contemptible opinion that I ever before entertained of the celebrated fabric of British liberty, the mode of election and the inequality of representation are offensive to the very shadow of freedom."[11]

In London the mistaken opinion which Governor Hutchinson had noted in his *Diary* was general at this time that the new Parliament would shortly undo all that the previous one had done, acknowledge American independence, and negotiate an alliance of friendship and commerce with the United States. The painter wrote to his father that the new measures were to be attributed entirely to the spirit of determined resistance shown by Americans and that any relaxation by the States would be followed at once with fresh efforts at oppression. "'Tis the sword only that can give us such a peace as our past glorious struggles have merited. The sword must finish what it has so well begun."[12]

The late colonel had forgotten that he was himself enjoying certain benefits of British liberty in a manner which would not have been possible for an English Tory in democratic Connecticut. Patriotic opinions, highly commendable in Revolutionary America, might be dangerous for an enemy rebel to express in war-time London, when he was supposed to confine himself solely to the study of art, and ought to have had more consideration for the courtesy of a Government tolerant enough to permit his residence in its capital. The painter should also have understood the necessity for extreme prudence in his conduct, as he knew that his presence was bitterly resented by the loyalist refugees, who were all the more infuriated at the indulgence shown to a rabid American because they suspected in this a sign of the Government's growing willingness to make peace. An unforeseen event gave them the opportunity to put an end to this tolerance. In mid-November, 1780, came the news of Arnold's betrayal and of Major André's execution. The feeling of indignation aroused by the latter, in spite of its ample justification under military law, allowed the refugees to throw suspicion on Trumbull and to deal a blow at John Temple, under whose assurance he had come over and whom they particularly detested for his efforts to bring about the recognition of independence. As a former deputy adjutant-general in the American army, Trumbull appeared to be a perfect counterpart to André, who had held the same position in the British forces.[13]

There was resident at this time in London a former American officer, Lieutenant-Colonel John Steel Tyler, a son of Royall Tyler, of Boston, who was a friend of Trumbull's, had arrived with him on the same ship, and lived in the same lodgings. Some loyalist refugees had denounced Tyler as a likely spy, and a warrant was made out for his detention, while further orders were issued by the Under-Secretary, Benjamin Thompson, to arrest another American who dwelt in the same house and who, there were strong reasons to suspect, was the more dangerous man of the two. No name was inserted in the warrant, but the constable was directed to secure Mr. Trumbull's person and papers as well as those of Mr. Tyler.

Fortunately for the latter, warning came in time. A friend who had been dining with some loyalists in Kensington learned from these about the impending arrest and, trumping up an excuse, abandoned the party in order to apprise Tyler. The latter, without returning to his lodgings, and by leaving London at once was able to make good his escape to the Continent. How little foundation existed for the charge that he was a spy may be judged from a letter which Lieutenant-Colonel Tyler, of the Continental Army, then residing in Bordeaux addressed a few months later to apprise Lord George Germaine of his desire to make amends for his former errors, so far as it lay in his power to do this, and to express his repugnance for what he called the existing connections of America, by which he meant the alliance with France. The Revolutionary soldier declared that his greatest ambition was henceforth to serve as an English officer and, if he could be given a command or otherwise employed, he would regard his attention to duty as the best testimony he could offer of his attachment to the British Constitution. Incidentally he asked that a thousand pounds should be sent him to compensate for his American property which would certainly be confiscated by his change of allegiance.[14]

Trumbull, meanwhile, who had been out that evening and had heard nothing about his impending arrest, only returned to his lodgings very late at night. Shortly afterwards, a police officer came to ask for Tyler. The painter supposed at first that his friend might be wanted for debt and was amazed when he learned that the charge was for high treason and that further orders had also been issued to secure him as well, for examination. He was so taken aback by this that later, when recalling the circumstances, he thought he must have looked like a very guilty man, for only then had he realized the "folly and audacity of having placed myself at ease in the lions' den." All the painter's papers were seized, and he was conducted to the Brown Bear Tavern in Drury Lane opposite the police station, where he was locked in a guarded room with barred windows until the following morning when his examination took place.

The sensational arrest of Trumbull attracted much attention. Later, when the news reached America, the historian, William Gordon, wrote to the art student's former chief, General Gates, to say that, although neither Tyler nor Trumbull had played the rascal, they had played the fool. "Trumbull is in safe custody. The Ministry will scarce do anything with him but confine."[15] In London, however, rumours of a kind, not unknown during the late war, were at once current. It was said that letters had been discovered on his person which proved conclusively that well-known men of the Opposition, like the Duke of Richmond and Lord Shelburne, were traitors. Actually only three letters were found, all of which were read as evidence in court. The first was addressed to his father, written at the request of John Temple in order to commend the latter as a friend of the American cause. The second, which led afterwards to many exaggerated reports, was from Franklin's grandson, merely to acknowledge a letter of Trumbull's and convey his grandfather's compliments. The third, but most suspicious of all, was from a certain William White concerning a proposed expedition for which he expected to obtain the equipment "in the kingdom of our dear and great ally." Trumbull insisted that he knew nothing about

White except as a casual acquaintance whom he had met at Vauxhall. The constable testified that he had found only the first letter on Trumbull's person and the other two were in the desk at his residence in George Street. The prisoner, he declared, had behaved like a gentleman and made no attempt to escape. The Bow Street magistrate, Justice Sampson Wright, before whom he was brought, proceeded to question Trumbull with the customary warning that he was under no necessity to answer.[16]

The questions put so angered the painter that he boldly told Justice Wright that evidently the magistrate was more accustomed to the society of pickpockets and highwaymen than to that of gentlemen. With some pride he admitted that, as the son of "him whom you call the rebel Governor of Connecticut," he had served in the rebel army and had the honour of being an aide-de-camp to General Washington. The Governor and the Commander-in-Chief held in their power a greater number of English prisoners than the British had of Americans, and, although they could treat him as they pleased, they ought to remember that their friends in America would be treated in the same way. Trumbull frankly declared in court that he had been deputy adjutant-general until February 22, 1777, and subsequently had sailed for France and been well received by Franklin. He had come to England solely to study painting under Mr. West, to whom he asked for permission to write and who could inform the bench of the manner in which he had passed his time. He considered himself to be protected by the special assurances he had received and the general pardon which had been offered to all rebels by the Peace Embassy in 1778. After making this statement, the painter was shown greater civility by the court and must have created a favourable impression, for the *Morning Post* described the prisoner as having conducted himself throughout the trying scene with a "collected fortitude"[17] becoming to his situation. In his later account of the incident, Trumbull explained to his father that this arrest had been instigated by American loyalists, who persuaded the Ministry that he was a dangerous character and in Franklin's service. The letter from the latter's grandson discovered in his correspondence appeared to substantiate this charge and he was committed to prison on "suspicion of treason." This is also confirmed by Thomas Hutchinson, Jr., who wrote to his brother that a son of Governor Trumbull was confined in Newgate for carrying on a correspondence with Franklin.[18]

The painter was first taken to Bridewell, where he slept that night in the same bed with a highwayman. Next morning he was brought up for a second examination, and, having admitted the crime of bearing arms against the King, he was remanded to confinement. Lord George Gordon's mob had recently demolished nearly all the London prisons except Clerkenwell, and the painter was therefore committed to that jail at a moment when it overflowed with every class of male-factors. The magistrate, when sentencing him apologized for this hardship, and suggested that Trumbull should write to Lord George Germaine, considerately offering to take the letter himself to the Secretary of State. The latter sent a polite word to express regret for what had happened and to tell the painter that as the Government's only object in confining him was his custody, but not his vexation, the Minister was dis-posed to grant him any alleviation possible and the permission to choose any prison he liked, from the Tower down. Far from affluent in his circumstances, Trumbull had discovered the vanity of selecting the Tower for his confinement, as he would have to pay dearly for this honour owing to the exorbitant fees charged to the occupants, an opinion which might have been confirmed by his father's old friend, Henry Laurens, who, imprisoned at the same time, after having been captured off Newfoundland on his way to a diplomatic mission in Holland, was obliged for this privilege to pay his two warders, whom he called "my faithful domestics," nearly a hundred pounds on his release.[19] Instead, the painter learned that he could enjoy the same amenities at a lower cost. Trumbull chose the prison of Tothill Fields, behind Buckingham Palace, mainly because he had heard that the keeper, Mr. Smith, a former butler to His Grace of Northumberland, after having had the charge of ducal silver had been given that of royal prisoners, that he possessed "the manners of a gentleman," and treated those detained with benevolent civility.

This prison consisted of an old, irregular building with a pretty little garden enclosed within the walls, and the painter discovered that he was able to rent a neatly furnished parlour on the ground floor of his keeper's residence for a guinea a week. In these quarters every evening, his jailor, with the unctuous gravity of a ducal butler, called to wish him good night and then performed his sterner duty as a prison warden by locking him in until the following morning. Meals were brought to the painter from a public-house, the Government making him an allowance for a penny's-worth of bread a day, with another penny which he donated to the turnkey for brushing his clothes. In this confinement Trumbull passed his time not too unpleasantly for he was allowed to walk in the garden and had the leisure to copy West's own copy, which the Academician had made many years before, of Correggio's

Saint Jerome at Parma. The imprisonment, as he admitted after his release, was not rigorous. The artist kept health and spirits and was allowed to see his friends.[20] Gilbert Stuart humorously painted his portrait standing behind the prison bars, and greeted his fellow pupil as "Bridewell Jack."

When Benjamin West had received Trumbull's letter written from the prison, he hastened to the Palace to assure the King that his pupil had only been studying art and indulged in no treasonable activities. George the Third is said to have listened attentively and accepted without reserve the explanation given by one of the few men whom he ever trusted. The King expressed sympathy for the anxious moments which Trumbull would have to traverse while he was in the power of the law, with the processes of which even a monarch could not interfere. But he bade West go to see his pupil and assure him that whatever the judges might decree he had his royal word that his life was safe.[21] To his dying day the painter always remembered that Mr. West "has the strongest claims to my gratitude."[22]

John Temple feeling responsible for Trumbull's mishap as it was owing to his advice that he had gone to London, did whatever lay in his power to help, delaying for months his own return to Boston in order to assist his friend. But Temple was at this time himself under a cloud because of his American sympathies, and the painter understood that he had a "hard task to sustain all the sarcasms that were thrown upon him."[23] The refugees hated Temple more than any other man. A paragraph, which appeared in a London newspaper, signed with the latter's initials had referred to Trumbull as an incendiary. The painter, however, regarded this merely as "a villainous trick" of some American loyalist to throw suspicion on his friend.[24] In fact except for West's nephew, the Reverend Isaac Hunt, who helped Trumbull to prepare his petitions, the latter could never forgive the spite with which the refugees continued to display their animosity.

As the *Habeas Corpus* Act had been suspended during the hostilities, Trumbull had found himself unable in his confinement to force a legal trial. In vain he wrote to Lord George Germaine to protest against his imprisonment and to point out that no other charge had been made against him than that of treason committed in America, from which he considered himself fully protected by the amnesty of 1778. This letter, the painter always believed, never got beyond Benjamin Thompson, who, he felt certain, had also prevented West from having an interview with the Minister.[25] Thompson was at that time in sole charge of all American matters and probably took only a strictly official view of the painter's case, though his attitude always left the latter resentful. The Tory Cabinet, unwilling to press the charge of treason which might have been difficult to substantiate, kept the prisoner in suspense without taking a decision. Meanwhile, the painter's friends, prompted by Governor Trumbull's bankers in Amsterdam, the de Neufvilles, took a most active interest in his case and consulted certain of the best-known lawyers of the day like John Dunning and Counsellor John Lee, good Whigs who had successfully defended Admiral Keppel in his sensational lawsuit after Ushant. Both men were of the opinion that as no new charge had been brought the prisoner might ask for a trial safely.[26] Parliament, in fact, had passed certain statutes during the American Revolution that had been renewed from year to year, and which empowered the crown to arrest or to detain persons charged with, or suspected of high treason committed in America or on the high seas, but always with the provision that no person should be punished under this Act for any offence committed within the realm.[27] A prosecution under these statutes would not have been easy, and although Trumbull's arrest in the circumstances can be readily understood, his prolonged confinement without any direct charge being made was only one more blunder committed by an administration which, like others since that time, was little inclined to admit its own mistakes.

Unexpectedly one day Trumbull received the visit of Charles James Fox, who called on him to advise the painter to make a direct request to the Ministers, and said that he would gladly have taken the petition to them himself if he possessed the slightest influence, but he was then no longer even on speaking terms with the members of the Cabinet. He offered, however, to confer with Edmund Burke, and Trumbull, on his advice, wrote to the latter, who was at that time personally unknown to him, complaining of his imprisonment and contrasting his own treatment with that of so many Englishmen in America, who, "although taken in the actual commission of those crimes from which at the worst, I have ceased these four years, are daily indulged with easy parole ... while I am ignominiously imprisoned as a felon." The painter declared that his case was certain to provide an argument to all Americans of the folly of placing any confidence in the promises even of the highest. In a postscript he added, that he had strong reason to suppose that he owed his suffering, not so much to the British Ministry as to "the vindictive and malignant acts of some of my countrymen."[28] When, shortly after this, Joseph Galloway learned of Trumbull's release, he is said to have expressed surprise that he should not have been consulted, which seemed to Benjamin West a clear indication that the influence of the Pennsylvania loyalist was over.

Burke called at once to see Trumbull in his prison and assured him that he would take up his case in the same way as he had lately done for Henry Laurens. The chivalrous Fox visited him again and gave heart to the prisoner but Burke's intervention proved successful and the painter was released on a bond of two hundred pounds, half of which was given by West and the remainder by Copley. Except for the copies of two or three letters to his father, all his papers were returned to him. He was, however, required to leave England within thirty days. He did not wait for this and as soon as he was free, departed for Amsterdam.

From Holland, Trumbull wrote to his father, merely to say that he was in good health. Fearful lest the note should be seized by a British vessel, he added a line to the likely captors requesting as a favour that it be forwarded. A detailed letter despatched to the Governor by a safer route showed that the months in captivity had only strengthened his patriotism. He admitted that he owed his liberation chiefly to Fox and Burke, who were both regarded as pro-American, but added as his personal opinion that even those who called themselves the friends of America were little disposed to acknowledge its independence. He remarked:

"There are few who think liberally and by far the majority would rather push forward though to ruin than give up their insolent ideas of superiority."[29]

II

When John Trumbull had returned to America after seven months' imprisonment, the artist became a contractor for the army and was stationed at Washington's headquarters on the Hudson during the winter of 1782. He was in Philadelphia when the news of peace came. More than ever he wished again to be a painter, and once more argued with his father about the merits of an artistic career till the Governor, after listening attentively, remarked to his son, "you appear to forget, Sir, that Connecticut is not Athens," after which he bowed, withdrew, and never again opened his lips on this subject. The old Governor may have been less displeased with his son's intention than he allowed it to appear. Immediately after peace had been concluded, John Trumbull returned to London carrying a letter from his father to Lord Dartmouth, written principally on behalf of John Temple, but mentioning that his son was going back to improve his "turn of the pencil" which Mr. West had thought worthy of attention, and, although he did not ask for any protection from Lord Dartmouth, he would be glad if the young man could meet with this.

The Governor wrote, also, with becoming gratitude, to Edmund Burke, who had suggested that the painter should take up the study of architecture as being an art more useful in a new nation which would be certain to require many public buildings. Burke's advice was to study under Reynolds as a master, but for personal reasons Trumbull could not do otherwise than return to West, "who for thirty years was more than a father to me." He now worked hard at his art and sat beside Thomas Lawrence at the Academy drawing classes. He painted at this time the portrait of his old friend Colonel Jeremiah Wadsworth, of Hartford, but when he showed this picture to Sir Joshua, instead of a compliment the President of the Royal Academy mortified him by remarking "that coat is bad, Sir, very bad, it is not cloth—it is tin, bent tin," and sadly the young painter had to admit the truth of the criticism.[30]

During the war of independence Colonel Wadsworth had been a contractor for the American and later for the French armies in the United States, having as a partner a certain John Carter, an Englishman, who had married General Schuyler's eldest daughter. When Trumbull resigned from the army, Carter was the official at Albany who had audited his military accounts. To the painter's amazement, he now found the former American officer in the Revolutionary army, residing in London, under his real name of John Barker Church, elected to Parliament as the member from Windsor, and living in great style on the fortune he had made in a war against his own countrymen. Church generously advanced money which enabled the painter to continue his studies and which years afterwards Trumbull repaid.

The late army contractor's extraordinary career, which alternated in residence between England and America, deserves a few words. Of British birth, he had been an auditing officer in the Revolutionary army and became a great friend of Lafayette. The latter had recommended him and Colonel Wadsworth to Rochambeau, who appointed the American and the Englishman as commissaries general to the French army. After the war was over, both men went to Paris, where they were detained for eighteen months while their accounts were being adjusted. Carter then returned to England, assumed once more his real name, which was Church, and bought a fine country place near Windsor. He entertained sumptuously, and at his table Trumbull met Richard Sheridan and other well-known men of the day. Fox and Pitt were frequently his guests, and the former, as his political chief, is also said to have borrowed freely from him, but to have repaid little. Through his early connections, Church knew many French refugees, some of whom like Lauzun had served in the American campaign. Their charm was undeniable and their manners always exquisite even when their morals admitted of no decent doubt, and certain of them to the scandal but admiration of English country neighbours did not sufficiently hide the sinful pleasures which made life in their rural abodes endurable even to impoverished exiles. Church had known Talleyrand well, and when the latter, after exhausting other resources obtained from the sale of his library was suddenly and without warning expelled from England, it was the member from Windsor who advanced the money which permitted the Bishop of Autun to go to America. Church also tried to assist his old friend Lafayette in his unsuccessful attempt to escape from the prison at Olmutz. In 1797, the late member of Parliament returned to New York with his family and a French *chef* named Godcy, who afterwards left his kitchen range for literature to become the founder of the once well-known magazine of that name. During the second phase of his American career, Church was elected to an honorary membership in the Society of the Cincinnati, fought a bloodless duel with Aaron Burr, engaged in some unfortunate mercantile speculation, and lost heavily over the French spoliation claims. In his old age he went back once more, to be received by the Prince Regent and to live in England until his death.[31]

The Marquis de Chastellux, who was a soldier, traveller, philosopher, and a friend of Governor Trumbull, had once suggested that American public buildings ought to be adorned with pictures representing the battles of the War of Independence.[32] Apart from natural pride in a victory which had

[377]

secured freedom the historic importance of the Revolution in establishing a new nation had deeply impressed a generation brought up in the reverence of the republics of antiquity. Already as a boy Trumbull had felt a real veneration for the characters of Brutus and the Scipios, and he discerned in the leaders of the Revolution American heroes of a Roman stamp. He was rightly proud of the part he had taken in the War, and, after meditating lengthily on the best use to which he could put his double experience as a soldier and a painter, the son of the Governor of Connecticut made up his mind to devote himself to representing pictorially the great events in which he had been an actor. The example and precept of West, who at one time had thought of doing this himself exercised a great influence in causing Trumbull to reach this decision. The President of the Royal Academy wisely encouraged his pupil to paint the history of the American Revolution and the *Death of Warren at Bunker Hill* was the first of this series. When the picture was finished West invited some brother artists to a dinner, and Sir Joshua, who was of the party, mistaking the composition for one by his host, congratulated the latter on the merit of the colour. Trumbull could have received no more welcome compliment. This battle piece, later exhibited in Boston, provoked there some criticism for appearing too much to be "the triumph of British valour and humanity,"[33] but it made no such impression on Thomas Jefferson and Mrs. Adams, who saw the picture in London, and praised Trumbull as the first artist who tried to paint for posterity actions which would command the admiration of ages.

It was not unnatural if the painter's historical pictures commemorating American victories over the King's armies, and which are now in the Capitol at Washington, should have given some offence in London. Trumbull, the best of men, never understood the tactlessness of representing in England the series of British defeats in America, any more than he had understood the inappropriateness of criticizing British political conditions. He showed a curious preference to paint in London his pictures of American victories over Englishmen, and persuaded himself that the insufficient success he met with was only because he was a foreigner, without family connection and with the remembrance still rankling of his earlier adventure. To make amends for having represented a series of British disasters he painted the *Sortie from Gibraltar*, which he sold for five hundred guineas to Sir Thomas Baring, and afterwards made the mistake of refusing twelve hundred for another version of the same, hoping to obtain more by exhibiting it and selling the prints. Soldiers had been greatly attracted by this painting, until Lord Hastings, who had served in America, declared at an army dinner that no work of Trumbull ought to be patronized by any British officer.

The painter's real ambition was always to commemorate "the great events of our country's revolution," and he felt immensely proud to have been the only artist who had taken part in the actions which he wished to represent. Trumbull devoted himself wholeheartedly to this plan of depicting the chief actions of the War of Independence in the hope that his compatriots would not blame him for having "squandered uselessly talents from which my country might justly demand more valuable services."[34] It is fortunate for the representation of American history in art that the late Colonel should have risen sufficiently above the anti-artistic prejudices of his age in the United States. His fine sketches of military contemporaries

and his somewhat more turgid paintings are an invaluable
record of the likenesses of the men who participated at the
birth of the Republic. Facing great pecuniary difficulties and
discouragements, he carried out, in a labour of love which
revealed his real talent at its peak, a series of admirable
portrait studies of notable Americans and Frenchmen who
had taken a worthy part in the War of Independence. These
likenesses permitted him to execute larger compositions
but left him unable to proceed with another plan, which
was to engrave the representation of the Revolution.
Washington held Trumbull in high esteem, and tried vainly
to aid him when the painter attempted to persuade Congress
to follow the example of the King of France who was always
a generous subscriber for "all elegant works engraved by his
subjects." Few American politicians have ever regarded art
as a matter worthy of their manly attention, and Congress
engaged in its own controversies offered no help. Trumbull
found almost his only real encouragement from Thomas
Jefferson, then American Minister in Paris, who with the
taste to be expected from his humanities warmly approved
of his friend's purpose. Jefferson had recognized in his compatriot a promising talent and learned with pleasure that his
art had aroused the admiration of French connoisseurs.
His own advice was for Trumbull to study for a time in
Paris, and then proceed to Rome,[35] and to make this easier
the most cultivated of American statesmen offered to employ
the painter, with only nominal duties as his secretary.

When Trumbull returned again to London, he at least
had realized his earlier ambition to be a diplomat. Acting
as secretary to John Jay, sent to negotiate the treaty which
bore his name, the painter committed to memory the text

of that famous document in order to repeat this confidentially to James Monroe in Paris. The feat was useless, because the latter would not hear it, refusing to keep it a secret, as this would have meant a breach of faith with the French Convention.

Trumbull's diplomatic career was a temporary episode, which came to an end with Jay's mission. He remained behind in London and during the French Revolution tried his hand at picture dealing. In the ruin of the *noblesse* and the dispersal of their collections, the painter discerned an advantageous opportunity of obtaining valuable works of art. West supplied him with the money for what he admits was a speculation, and he brought over to England a hundred pictures, purchased with the assistance of a Frenchman named Le Brun, whom Trumbull regarded as the most experienced judge of old masters in Europe. The venture was not successful for the quality of the paintings, sold at auction at Christie's in 1797,[36] did not measure up to expectations.

One other incident which relates to the artist's London life may briefly be mentioned. When the city of Washington was being planned, the Commissioners of Public Buildings addressed themselves to Trumbull to select for them a young architect competent to assist this work. After consulting West and the Court architect, Wyatt, the painter's choice fell on George Hatfield, the brother-in-law of Cosway, the miniaturist, who had just returned after studying in Italy. Hatfield was far too outspoken in his opinions to give satisfaction in the new capital, though in the end he was allowed to build the City Hall in Washington.

Few Americans have ever devoted their lives with greater zeal than Trumbull to exalt his country's glory. But he met with so little encouragement that he found London more congenial as a home than his own country. His reasons for residing abroad are unrecorded. Too proud to complain, introspection was not in his nature, and he lived in an age when men hardly cared to analyse the character of their feelings. He knew only the fact which no patriotism was able to disguise that the artist's life he loved, could be pursued to better advantage in London than in a land where art was still despised and the painter's profession was looked down upon as a frivolous pursuit, "unworthy of a man who possessed more serious talents."[87]

Trumbull had married an Englishwoman and his only son was later to become an officer in the British army. He himself returned to America in 1804, but met with so little success that he sailed again four years afterwards almost on the last ship permitted to leave under the Embargo. The Wests welcomed him, as always, and once again he set up a studio. But he complained that Jefferson's French sympathies made the English feel unfriendly towards Americans, and once more Trumbull realized that he had no family connections and few friends in London. His skill was not impressive enough to overcome the jealousy of other painters and his talent was not enhanced by having to depict the likenesses of indifferent sitters instead of painting martial deeds. Partly owing to his wife's inferior station he was never able to occupy the place in the world of art merited by his character and even by his talent. He attributed his own mediocre success to political prejudice, and admitted that it was only natural if many people believed that they detected in his occupation as an artist the mask of a secret agent. The very few orders he obtained were not enough to keep him out of debt, and his career in London was an unhappy one of patient, but unsuccessful struggle. Trumbull, discouraged, was on the point of again returning to the United States when confounded by the news of the American declaration of hostilities on June 18, 1812. The painter was treated with great civility by the English authorities, but told that war could not be run sentimentally and no exceptions could be made for individuals. Given his choice to reside either at Bath or at Cheltenham, he remarked that he was probably the only American citizen, for both West and Copley had always remained British subjects, who went through two wars with England while residing on English soil. As soon as peace was declared, Trumbull sailed for New York never again to return.

CHAPTER TWELVE

Brief Notes on Three American Artists, Gilbert Stuart, Mather Brown and Patience Wright

I

EVEN to-day it is difficult to think of anyone living through the eventful years which attended the birth of the United States as a nation, without having been stirred to the marrow. Yet, the conflict with the mother country impressed many Americans of that age principally as a disturbing succession of unfortunate events with which they had no intention to be entangled and from the personal inconveniences of which they were eager to escape. Fiery patriots later admitted that, when the Revolution broke out, they were still in a minority, but the same was true of those attached to the Crown. Neither Whigs nor Tories thinking only of their mutual strife paid much attention to the great majority of moderate, peace-loving citizens whose interest lay entirely outside politics, although most of these were subsequently dragooned into partisanship. In times of crisis advocates of reason are shouted down by the violent whose vehement opinions carry far more weight than the placid thoughts of a leaderless, undecided, unadventurous, and frightened majority. The mass of the American population, outside New England and Virginia, who were at first neither on one side nor the other, wanting only to continue their usual occupations and to live undisturbed lives, found themselves obliged either to adopt patriot convictions or else to flee.

[384]

The actual date is unknown and immaterial, but it is usually said that three days before Bunker Hill, Gilbert Stuart had left Boston for London. Like Copley before him, like Mather Brown after him, his great wish was to escape from a conflict which he felt did not concern him, and the issues of which left him entirely indifferent. Stuart, not even a moderate, was a man completely devoid of the slightest interest in politics, and there is no reason to suppose that the alleged Jacobite leanings of his family had anything to do with his apathy towards events in America. No record has been found of any expression of political opinion on his part, nor in fact of sympathy for his country during the stirring years of the Revolution which he passed in London. It cannot even be claimed for Stuart that, like Copley and Trumbull, he felt the compelling wish to paint to distract his thoughts from the trials of his native land.

Perhaps the most gifted of all American artists, Stuart, in his younger days, was an incurable Bohemian, who used his talent mainly when forced to do so by necessity, and then as a means of livelihood. While the War of Independence was being fought, the painter lived in London, almost always in debt even for board and lodging, often it is said, walking the streets, without any definite purpose or lying on his couch for weeks, waiting idly for something to turn up. On one occasion John Trumbull found him in bed apparently ill, though long afterwards, Stuart admitted that his sickness was hunger, and, except for a ship's biscuit, he had not tasted food for a week. Forced by necessity to earn something, he used his musical talent, which was real, to become a church organist at thirty pounds a year. He painted a few portraits, principally of physicians whom he met through the only

cc

friend he possessed then in London, Dr. Benjamin Water-house. With him he tramped the streets, visited art collections, and explored the thieves' quarter.[1] His condition was always miserable. At last he wrote to Benjamin West, then unknown to him, asking for assistance, as he had been "reduced to one miserable meal a day and frequently not even that."[2] The Academician sent him a few guineas to relieve his immediate needs and invited him to call at his house. There were guests to dinner when Stuart arrived, but, as soon as West learned that his visitor was an American, he left the table to welcome the penniless stranger, who for five years remained as pupil and assistant to the highly respectable Court painter. Trumbull has left a description of Stuart at work, dressed in an old black coat with one half torn off the hip and pinned up, looking more like a beggar than a painter.

The years passed in West's painting room were to be the making of Stuart as an artist. For the first time he discovered the incentive to work which caused him gradually to discard some of his more Bohemian habits. By copying Old Masters, he improved his own drawing, which had been defective. At West's house Stuart met also the notable artists of the day like Sir Joshua, whose portrait he painted, although Reynolds remarked that if it was like him he did not know his own appearance. He met there the famous Dr. Johnson, who on hearing that Stuart was an American, complimented him on his English, and asked him where he had learned it, which made the painter reply, with a rudeness worthy of the great doctor himself, that it was not out of his dictionary.[3]

After the Academy Exhibition of 1782, Stuart, who was now favourably known by his skill in portraiture, took a house for himself in order to set up, in Mrs. Hoppner's phrase, "as a great man." His success in London was soon to be second only to that of Reynolds and Gainsborough. William Temple Franklin wrote to his grandfather from London that he intended sitting for his likeness to Stuart, whom West esteemed as the first living portrait painter and declared that his former pupil was able to nail the face to the canvas. The portrait which the latter painted of his master illustrates the aptness of this praise.

Stuart's later career as a painter, has recently been related and does not fall within the purpose of this book.[4] Incurably careless in his life and with a large family to provide for, in spite of the considerable money he earned, as his charges for portraits were only below those of the very greatest, Stuart lived far beyond his means and was always in debt. To escape from his creditors, he moved first to Dublin and later to America, where his return was more patriotically explained as being due to the great admiration he entertained for the character of Washington, whose portrait he desired to paint.

II

"I will not come back to go to the American army or starve at Boston," wrote Mather Brown, a nineteen-year-old boy, to his aunt.[5] After peddling merchandise in New England, he had managed to save enough to support himself for three years, and his greatest ambition was to go to London to study painting under West.

The boy was a grandson of the well-known loyalist preacher in Boston, the Reverend Mather Byles, who had been an intimate friend of Copley, and was one of the very few dissenting ministers on the Tory side. Mather Brown's personal feelings about political matters were, however, just as little Tory as they were patriot. Like Copley, whom he had looked up to from the time when he was a small boy, his sole ambition was to make his way as an artist, and he cared nothing about his country's fate. He had unbounded confidence in himself, considerable Yankee shrewdness, and every intention to keep out of the army. He had already learned how to draw from Gilbert Stuart, who afterward cordially loathed him, and the boy, like Henry Pelham, had made a little money by painting miniatures in Boston. As artists were admittedly a class apart and as nothing was expected from such inferior beings as citizens, no one found it amiss that in the course of a war in which painters took no interest those able to do so should go to England.

Mather Brown first went to Paris in 1780, carrying letters from his clergyman grandfather to Franklin and West. When he arrived in London, both the latter and Copley encouraged him to study art, and West accepted him as a pupil. He obtained an introduction to Lord George Germaine and by the most pushing efforts succeeded beyond expectations in meeting the great of the land. In 1783, he too began to exhibit. He contrived in some way to induce the King and Queen to see his pictures, and wrote home jubilantly that he had spent three weeks at Windsor—probably in West's painting room— and had received a bow from the King. Success came quickly to Mather Brown. Not altogether without some talent, he had unbounded perseverance, unblushing audacity, and had acquired a real trick for portraiture. Delighted with his own rapid achievement, he wrote home to his aunt using a syntax worthy of West himself:

I will let them see if an obscure Yankee boy cannot shine as great as any of them. . . . My ambition shall prove my alliance with Apollo and will produce a new Phenomenon to make the rays of Phiebus (*sic*) shine and rise for the Western Hemisphere.[6]

Mather Brown now set up on his own as a painter, though always retaining a most enthusiastic admiration for West. He also became fashionable for a time and occupied a fine house in Cavendish Square, in London, only a few doors from the one in which Romney lived. Without ever attaining real distinction, Brown's early pictures were conscientious. He worked hard and made a certain name for himself by painting the portraits of many well-known people of the day, even, it was said, though these had omitted to sit for him. His full-length likeness of the Prince of Wales, the future George the Fourth, which hangs at Buckingham Palace, is executed in an easy, mechanical style, as flashily vulgar as is its subject. His pictures, however, attracted some attention, and soon he was able to style himself "Historical Painter to His Majesty and the Duke of York," a title which seemed calculated to increase his reputation and assist him to obtain lucrative commissions from visiting Americans. Mrs. Adams alludes to him in one of her letters, and Charles Bulfinch, the architect, who visited England in 1785, mentions having seen nearly a hundred pictures of his countrymen in the painter's "universally known" rooms. On one side were the portraits of patriots, like Jefferson and Adams, while facing these on the other wall frowned the likenesses of such loyalists as Treasurer Gray and Sir William Pepperell.

Mather Brown never returned to America. For nearly half

a century he painted diligently, first in London and then in the provinces, and his portraits were as regularly sent to the Academy. It is the fate of far more artists than is commonly suspected that, after they themselves are dust and their names have passed into oblivion, their work is later labelled under more advantageous titles. Brown's somewhat vulgar personality and ready-made wholesale commercial style had until lately been forgotten, but many of his productions have since his day passed under the far greater name of Gilbert Stuart. The latter's particular detestation of his erstwhile pupil might have become still more violent if he had ever suspected the trick of fortune which the attributions of future picture dealers were to play on him.

III

Mrs. Patience Mehitabel Wright, best known for her wax portraits, was certainly the oddest personality among early American artists. She was born in 1725, of Quaker parents, at Bordentown, New Jersey, and reputed, on somewhat doubtful ground, to have been John Wesley's niece, which is probably the reason why certain of her verses are preserved in the anthology of the "Bards of Epworth." She had originally tried her talents as a poet, and the following lines lamenting the infelicity of her own married life are cited to illustrate her skill as a versifier and may help to explain certain of the reasons for her husband's neglectfulness:

> Turn Thee at last—my bosom ease
> Or tell me why I cease to please;
> For though thine absence I lament
> When half the lonely night is spent,

Had I not practised every art
To oblige divert and cheer thy heart
I had not asked why dost thou shun
These faithful arms and eager run—
To some obscure unclean retreat
With fiends incarnate glad to meet.[7]

Mr. Wright's too manifest disregard for Mrs. Wright's charms came only after she had borne him two children. Her daughter was to marry the painter, Hoppner, who, after having been brought up at the Palace under royal protection lost this when he took to wife Phœbe Wright. Hoppner, still an unknown artist at this time, was indignant at having been turned out penniless in the street, and attributed his misfortune to Benjamin West. It is difficult to believe this for the latter was never malicious, though he may have disapproved of Mrs. Wright, as she was the only American artist in London never mentioned in connection with him. Yet he helped her son, who before his untimely death, gave great promise as a painter. At the Royal Academy in 1780, Joseph Wright exhibited a portrait of his mother modelling a Charles the First in wax, near which were the heads of George the Third and Queen Charlotte. This was at a moment when the King's unpopularity was extreme and talk of revolution and flight to Hanover was frequently heard. The picture could not fail to occasion sensational comment; Horace Walpole noticed the suggestion, and a contemporary epigram says:

Wright in her lap sustains a trunkless head
And looks a wish—the King was in its stead.[8]

Joseph Wright enjoys another distinction, for at a time when only England and Italy attracted painters from the New

World, he was probably the first American ever to study art in France, and one of West's rare letters written in French recommended the young painter, who came from his native Philadelphia, to "Monsieur Pierre, Peintre du Roi," mentioning to his colleague at the Court of Versailles that Joseph Wright desired to continue his studies in Paris, where his mother enjoyed the patronage of the Duchess of Chartres.[9]

Since 1767 Mrs. Patience Wright had been established in London, and the skill she displayed in modelling wax figures at one time brought the fashionable world to her rooms. She made a famous likeness of Lord Chatham, perhaps the best which exists to-day of that statesman, and which stands among a series of somewhat lurid royal waxen effigies in Westminster Abbey. The King and Queen visited her studio and for a time they felt amused by personal eccentricities which caused her to address the royal couple as George and Charlotte. Later as a zealous Republican, she is said to have scolded the King for making war on her country, and thereby lost Court favour. Ardently American in her sympathies, the legend grew after the War of Independence, inspired doubtless by herself, that the information which she picked up as an amateur spy in the houses of the great rendered immense service to the Revolutionary cause. Mrs. Wright would relate that whenever she had heard of a new commanding officer being appointed, or of a squadron being fitted out, or of anything likely to be useful to "dear America," without anyone suspecting this she found means to transmit the news to Franklin.

When Mrs. Bancroft journeyed to Paris, the Reverend John Vardill, unknown to the spy's mistress had contrived to examine the contents of the correspondence she carried, and reported to the Chief of the Secret Service that she had taken with her a letter, written by Mrs. Wright to Franklin, to inform the Doctor that the "Wicked Ministry" was spreading the report that five thousand Americans had gone over to the British.[10] This was information which no English Government could seriously object to having circulated.

Mrs. Wright was probably only a useful informant in her own estimation. If she really had rendered the services she claimed, Franklin, who was never unappreciative, would hardly have written her later in the way he did, or poked fun at her when he described a friend, who, disinclined to matrimony, had thought of asking Mrs. Wright to make him a wife in wax to place at the head of his table.[11] The Doctor's real feelings came out in his ill-concealed reluctance to see her arrive in Paris. When she wrote to apprise the philosopher of her intention to settle in that capital, he did his utmost to dissuade her. Writing as an old friend, he expressed the pleasure it would be to welcome her, but thought it only proper to mention that there were already in Paris several other artists who modelled in wax (like his friend Mlle. Biheron, famous for her figures), and that it was no longer the taste for persons of fashion to sit for such portraits. Moreover, rent and living in Paris were inordinately expensive. In a postscript came some further objections which he saddled on his grandson whom, of course, she remembered when he was still a saucy little schoolboy; now no longer a small child, his objections were quite as saucy, for the young man had been impudent enough to point out that her life-size wax figures could hardly be packed without danger, and, if she brought them over as passengers in stage-coaches, the cost would be enormous even if they didn't have to be fed. She would also require for

[393]

figures so lifelike that they could be mistaken for living creatures, passports, which cost two guineas and sixpence apiece. Franklin added maliciously that she would pay this without grumbling knowing that the money would not be used against her country.[12]

Franklin's diplomacy, so successful at the Court of Versailles, was wasted on this occasion. Patience Wright was no woman to be deterred by any man's objections even if he was a philosopher and a diplomat. To Paris she went, Franklin notwithstanding, and henceforth every visiting American was left in no doubt of her presence. At the end of the War, Elkanah Watson, who, as a traveller, was himself not devoid of the wish to be conspicuous, described her introduction to him. He had only just arrived in Paris and was giving orders to his servant from the hotel balcony, when he heard a powerful woman's voice scream from an upper story, "Who are you? An American, I hope," and a minute later Mrs. Wright blustered downstairs and approached him with the familiarity of an old friend. He described her as being tall and of sallow complexion, high cheek-bones and keen olive eyes, with the glance of a maniac. She walked with a firm step, straight as an Indian, her appearance corresponding with the originality of her talk.[13]

Mrs. John Adams has also related her visit to this "Queen of Sluts," after she was once more established in London. When she went to see her Mrs. Wright took Mrs. Adams's two hands to express her pleasure at the call and kissed the men who accompanied her, which, with her slatternly appearance, was not at all to their taste. She told the American Envoy's wife that she loved everybody that came from the United States, adding as a hint that Mr. Adams had already been to see her and made her a noble present. In her rooms there was seated an elderly clergyman reading a newspaper, and it was a good ten minutes before visitors discovered that this was only a wax figure.[14]

Among Mrs. Wright's most cherished opinions was a belief that the founders of the United States would be appropriate subjects for her own art. She desired to model a bust of Washington and other likenesses of the American signers of the Treaty of Peace, and wrote to Jefferson, who at the time was in Paris, to enlist his help for this idea on the ground that the more public the honours bestowed on such men by their country, the more this would shame King George. The artist in wax declared that she was prepared to go to any trouble or expense to add her mite, and asked to consult him as how best to honour America by modelling the likenesses of her eminent statesmen. Her letter concluded by mentioning that there was a real risk in sending Washington's portrait to London, owing to the enmity of the government and the espionage of the English police, which had all the folly without the ability of the French.[15]

The habit of addressing epistles to the great was not unfamiliar to Mrs. Wright, and Washington's reply to a letter which she had written him is preserved to-day in the British Museum. Politely non-committal, the Father of his Country wrote to the modeller in wax that if she were to return to America she doubtless would meet with a cordial reception from her numerous friends and that he, too, would be proud to see a person so universally celebrated and on whom Nature had bestowed such rare gifts.[16] For even Washington could occasionally be a politician.

APPENDIX A

Letter of Dr. Edward Bancroft to the
Committee for Foreign Affairs of Congress.
Dated March 31, 1778.

*(The original is in the Continental Congress papers (78 B. II.
447, Congressional Library.) The copy has been obtained through
the courtesy of the Librarian, Dr. Herbert Putnam.)*

Honourable Sirs

In a paper of "instructions, for the Hon. Silas Deane Esqr. Agent for the thirteen United Colonies," dated "Philadelphia 2n. of March 1776," and signed by Benjamin Franklin, Benjamin Harrison, John Dickinson Robert Morris, and John Jay Esqrs. members of the Committee of Congress for secret Correspondence, the following article is contained viz:

"You will endeavour to procure a meeting with Mr. Bancroft, by writing a Letter to him, under Cover to Mr. R. Griffiths at Turnham Green near London, and desiring him to come over to you in France, or Holland, on the score of old acquaintance; from him you may obtain a good deal of information of what is now going forward in England, and settle a mode of continuing a Correspondence. It may be well to remit him a small Bill to defray his Expenses in coming to you, and avoid all Political matters in your Letter to him."

On the receipt of a Letter, written conformably to the preceeding instructions, I set out for France, though in a very ill state of health, and arrived in Paris, a few hours sooner than Mr. Deane—He can most properly inform you, how far I answered the purposes, for which my presence had been desired. Mr. Deane had been also instructed "to obtain an acquaintance with Mr. Garnier, late Chargé des Affaires de France en Angleterre, if in France, or if returned

to England, a Correspondence with him, as a person
extremely intelligent and friendly to our Cause"; and upon
my return, he wrote to Mr. Garnier in England agreeably
to that instruction. But the avowed purpose of Mr. Garnier's
mission there, being to cultivate a good understanding,
between their most Christian and Britannic Majesties, he
thought there might be an impropriety in corresponding
directly with Mr. Deane, though he readily offered to
facilitate, as much as possible my Correspondence with him,
and to give me from time to time, as much information and
advice, as might consist with his Duty to the King his
Master. I embraced and laboured to profit by this obliging
offer. I cultivated this Friendship and obtained the Confidence of Mr. Garnier; I had free, and secret access to him,
at midnight hours, and I not only procured much useful
information from him, but by my own Communications,
made him the means of conveying to his Court, such
sentiments, such intelligence, and such Explications, as
appeared best suited to serve the Cause of America, and
counteract the mischievous artifices, incessantly used
against us, by the British Government. At the same time,
I laboured assiduously in Collecting and Communicating
useful intelligence, first to Mr. Deane, and afterwards to the
Commissioners at Paris; as well as in Executing their
Commissions in England, and generally in promoting the
interests of my Country until the month of March 1777,
when certain Circumstances, having drawn on me the
particular suspicions of the British Ministry, and in the
Opinion of all my friends, rendered it unsafe for me to stay
any longer in that Kingdom, I came over to this City, and
have since endeavoured to make myself useful to the

Commissioners, and my Country, as far as my confined opportunities would permit.

As, the Congress had thought proper, without my solicitation, or knowledge, to notice me in this manner, and had thereby led me into embarrassments, I flattered myself that their notice of me, would not have been entirely withdrawn, at least without some misconduct on my part, (which I think cannot be pretended), and that I should have been thought worthy, of some regular Employment. But twelve months having now passed since I left England, and there being no appearance of anything but neglect, towards me, on the part of Congress, it seems expedient that I should turn my attention from Public Business to my own private Concerns; and having determined immediately to do this, it only remains for me to desire that you Sirs, will be pleased to communicate to Congress, my sincere Thanks, for the Honour which their Committee formerly did me. I shall ever remember it with gratitude, and without complaining of the neglect, which has succeeded, and which many causes may have concurred in producing. I have not chosen to practice those means of self advancement, which are usually employed: wishing that in our Country, no public Trust or Employment might ever be given, but from Considerations of Public advantage, I have courted no interests, nor asked anything of any man—I have not even written to any person since Mr. Deane's arrival here, because I would not incur the suspicion of communicating the Secrets, or misrepresenting the Conduct of those, especially commissioned by Congress, nor of exaggerating my own little services, which I thought it belonged to others to describe. How they have been described or whether any accounts of them have come to your hands after the failing of so many Dispatches, you Sirs will best know . . . I have also been so long absent from my Native Country, that I am much less known in it, than in that which I have lately renounced. My maturer years have been almost all passed in England. There my Talents, such as they are, had been employed, and frequently employed in the Cause of my Country. There I had acquired some share of Litterary Reputation, had been unanimously elected into the Royal Society, and had been honoured with the Friendship of many worthy and of some very illustrious men; But being at the same time almost a stranger in America, I am neither surprised nor offended at the neglect which has been shewn me.

I sincerely rejoice at the happy situation of our affairs and at the means of Deliverance from our Enemies with which Mr. Deane Returns.

I have the Honour to be with profound Respect
Honourable Sirs
By your most Humble and most Devoted Servant
Edwd. Bancroft.

To the Hon. Committee
of Congress for Foreign Affairs.

APPENDIX B

Letter of John Adams to Alderman William Lee
intercepted by the Post Office

(Public Record Office: London. C.O. 5/134)

(1.) Extract.
William Lee, Esqr.   Philad. 4th Oct. : 1775.
Tower Hill.

The two Armies at Boston are likely to remain inactive the remainder of the season. It is not the Policy of the Provincials to attack the Enemy in their Lines; and the regular Officers freely acknowledged they are too weak to attempt ours. It is certain they generally dislike the service and wish to be recalled. The strength of Gage's Fortifications do not indicate the Conqueror, whilst Genl. Washington has been able to spare 1,200 men for the Canada Expedition. We have just received by the August Packet, Genl. Gage's account of the Battle of Charlestown, the Errors of which you must be able readily to discern, from the public accounts in the Newspapers. It may be plainly seen on the face of his Letter; for he says, the Provincials were discovered entrenching themselves by Day-break, and the Detachmt. must have marched after dark, under cover of the Night; so that, considering the length of Day-light at that Season, the whole Provincial Intrenchments, which he magnifies as Cannon-proof, etc., must have been the work of a few hours. The Truth is, it was performed in 3 Hours, and was a little Earth thrown up, not sufficient to protect 300 Men, and the best part of the Provincial Army was in open Ground. There was but 700 of our Men engaged, and had the commanding Officer of the Body of reserve marched over the Causeway, and joined the Provincials who were engaged, it is thought, the Regulars would have been entirely cut off. But the Consequences of the

Affair speak distinctly, and shew that it was far from a Victory since they did not pursue 50 yards, and from that Time to the present, have been actually besieged.

You will see by the enclosed News-paper, how far our Canada Armies have advanced. We are anxious for their fate, as they are not the best accoutred or disciplined; but they are filled with that spirit and Confidence that so universally prevail through-out America, the best Substitutes for Discipline. The Congress are sitting here and now they are joined by the Delegates from Georgia, the representation of America is completed. As they keep their Deliberations secret, I can't inform you of what at present employs their Attention, but believe they have little Business before them, and are waiting to know what Measures will be pursued at home. God grant they may be such as will open a Door for finishing this un-natural Contest! The Congress, like all aggregate Bodies, being composed of Men of different Tempers and Complexions, there will no doubt be some variety of Sentiment as to means; their Ends are perfectly the same. We cannot in this Country conceive that there are Men in England so infatuated, as seriously to suspect the Congress, or people here, of a Wish to erect ourselves into an independent State. If such an Idea really obtains amongst those at the Helm of Affairs, one Hour's residence in America would eradicate it. I never met one Individual so inclined, but it is universally disavowed. Whatever Views the Delegates from the Massachusetts may have, inspired by a keen Sense of Miseries their Country has endured, they have never disclosed Sentiments favourable to an Independancy on Great-Britain [*sic*.]. They know too well, such an Attempt would be likely to create Disunion. I may venture to assure you, that the Temper of the Congress leans towards Moderation, and could it meet with a Disposition to Peace on the other side of the Water, matters would easily be adjusted; but it must be such a Peace as brings with it Security; without which, this Country is determined to risque everything, and endure everything. Were the right of Taxation internally and externally and of internal Legislation given up, we should agree to a full Legislation in commercial Matters. As to mere Articles of News, the Papers will give you fuller Information, than what can be comprized within the compass of a Letter. I send this by a Vessel which put in here by Stress of Weather. All Communication is cut off with Europe, except by the Packet, and a Governmt. Conveyance is not an eligible one. We expect soon to have one of our own.

J. A.

(Endorsed) Philad., 4th Octr. 1775.

Extract of a letter from J. A. to Wm. Lee Esqr.

APPENDIX C

Memorial of John Vardill
16 November 1783

(Original in Public Record Office, London)
A.O. (Audit Office) 12/20 (pp. 22-29)

To the Honourable The Commissioners appointed by Act of Parliament for enquiring into the losses and Services of the American Loyalists.

The Memorial of John Vardill.

Sheweth.

That he is a Native of New York, and was late Professor of Natural Law, and Moral Philosophy in King's Collidge, and Assistant Preacher and Lecturer in the Episcopal Churches and Chapels in that City. He has been long obnoxious to the Rebels from his uniform opposition to their Measures; from his Writings in Defence of the British Church and Government against the Perodical Papers called "The American Whig"; from his vindication of the English Universities and Education in general, in a Pamphlett 1772 in Answer to the Address of Dr. Witherspoon, President of the College of New Jersey, and now Member of the Congress; and from some Publications in 1773 sign'd Poplicola, recommending an Application to Parliament by their legal Assemblies and Councils instead of a Congress and Non-importation Agreement.

Came to London for Ordination 1774 and on the Death of Dr. Ogilvie at New York, was chosen by the Vestry Unanimously his Successor as Assistant Preacher and Lecturer in the Churches and Chapels at New York: had leave of absence to further and hasten the Grant of a Charter, then under the consideration of the Privy Council, to constitute the College of New York a University: wrote and published a number of Periodical Pieces in defence of Government under the Signature of Corrolænus, for which

[411]

he received the thanks and promises of Patronage of Government. He at the same time drew up at the desire of the American Minister, an Acct. of the State of America, and his opinion of the best Plan for the Settlement of the Dispute; He promoted greatly by his letters the Petition from a detachment of the Assembly of New York from the general Union, furnished Government with much and valuable information by an extensive correspondence with Congress Leaders, as well as with Loyalists; among the former of whom were Messrs. Jay, Robt. Livingston, Gouverneur Morris, and James Duane of the Congress; Egbert Benson, Atty. General: Robt. Harper: Sir James Jay, and John Jones of the Legislature of New York, and John Parke Custis, Son-in-Law to Gen. Washington and a Pupil of your Memorialist. One effect among others of this correspondence was to secure to Government the Interest of two Members of the Congress by the promise of the Office of Judges in America: but the negotiation was quashed by the unexpected fray at Lexington in April 1775.

In consequence of these and such like services and to give the Loyalists at New York a Proof of the Attention and Rewards which would follow their Zeal and Loyalty Administration were pleased to appoint him Regius Professor of Divinity at King's College, and he was ordered to acquaint the President and College with this instance of Royal Patronage, and that the Establishment of the Professorship and his appointment should make a clause in the Charter then to be granted. The Intelligence was accordingly inserted in the New York Gazette of 1775, but the National Disappointments which ensued have prevented the grant of that Charter.

[412]

APPENDIX C

In 1775 the Rebels having gained the ascendancy at New York, and being much incensed by Letters against him from London, and by their knowlidge of his Character and Conduct in General, he could not return to New York with any safety, and Government was therefore pleased to give him his present Allowance of £200 per Ann. with the most direct and explicit Promise, that he should be no loser by his Loyalty and Services, and that the Allowance should be other ways provided for, or able to return to New York with Honour and Advantage to them and himself, Relying on this, instead of returning into the Country or employing himself in the Line of his Profession he devoted his time, from 1775 to 1781 to the Service of Government: and not to mention various Periodical pieces and Pamphlets which he wrote, or furnished Materials for, as well as Intelligence supplied from an extensive American Correspondence; waving these and hoping that the necessity will apologize for this free Communication:

In 1777 your Memorialist detected a Gentleman in London employed by Dr. Franklin, among other purposes, to purchase Cutters for Packet Boats, in which he and a Capt. Nicholson were to sail from France to America. Your Memorialist perswaded him to unbosom himself, and at the desire of the late Lord Suffolk went down with Col. Smith after him to Dover; where, after obtaining a full Discovery the Captain was engaged to proceed to France, to furnish all the Intelligence he could collect and to deliver the Letters from time to time committed to him. This he faithfully did for two years, whereby many vessels bound to America, were taken and much useful Information obtain'd A Gentleman of distinction was also sent over to him to direct and

[413]

receive Information and he had proceeded (thro the Captain) very far in a Negotiation for Peace with Dr. Franklin: but the capture of Burgoyne blasted it.

Your Memorialist having also discovered that a Mistress of Dr. Bancroft Secy. to Dr. Franklin, was about to leave London for Paris, he formed an Acquaintance with her, and found as he suspected, that she had Letters to convey from the Factions in this Country, on which he proposed a Plan, and procured a Person to accompany her to Brighthelmston who there obtained a coppy of the most Material Contents of the Letters, for the use of Government.

Hearing about the same time, that an American Vessel was taken and brought into Portsmouth by a Mutiny of the Sailors, and finding that the Captain was an Acquaintance, your Memorialist invited him to his House, and led him to Confess that he was bound to Amsterdam, that he had a number of Letters (come from the Board of War at Boston) to People in Holland, France and England These he delivered to your Memorialist who gave them to Mr. Eden by which means, among other particulars Government was inform'd of the Articles most wanted by Congress, of the Houses and persons with whom they corresponded and of the Ships employed for the purpose.

In 1777 Your Memorialist also met accidentally in London with an American Fellow Student a Gentleman of Birth, Fortune and Considerable confidence with Dr. Franklin, who after much perswasion and promise, confess'd that he was here on Congress Bussiness, had brought Letters from Dr. Franklin and others at Paris, and was about to return with some from hence, he was prevaild on by your Memorialist to disclose them and for a Certain Reward to continue

[414]

his Residence at Paris and to give all the Information he could to Lord Stormont, occasionally visiting this Country to convey Letters to and from Paris. This Gentleman often dined with Dr. Franklin and was intimate with all the American Leaders. He among other things informed Government of the fictious Titles and Directions, under which the Rebel Correspondents have received their Letters.

These Services were not without Expence to your Memorialist and in one Instance endangered his Life, and drew on him the hatred of many of his Countrymen, especy. the Trimmers, and false Loyalists as a Reward for these and other Services, Governmt was pleased to give him an immediate appointment, by Warrant in 1777 (the Charter being unavoidably postponed) to the Regius Profes.sorship of Divinity with a full promise, and purpose of granting him at the same time, a direct, certain and permanent Provision for Life, by annexing to it a Salary of £200 per Ann. But thro' the Changes and Misfortunes of the Times, this Engagement has not yet been filfill'd.

In 1778 at the request of One of the Commissrs. then Embarking for America, he drew up an Account of the Characters of the leading Rebels and Loyalists and supplied him with Letters of Introduction to Messrs. Jay, Livingston, Duane and Morris, of the Congress; and to Messrs. Benson, Harper, Jones and Custis, who had great Influence in the Rebel States.

In 1779 he went down to Yorkshire and opposed the Association in a Series of Paper's call'd "The Alarm" and sign'd *Cassandra*, which he caused to be printed and circulated thro' the Counties. For these he had the thanks of the

Nobility and Gentlemen of the County, and a Letter of high approbation from a Distinguish'd Person in Administration.

In 1780 he also published a Pamphlet against the Associations; and assisted in writing another entitled "The Declaration and Address, from the Loyalists to the People of America, which was extensively Circulated thro' the Colonies; not to mention that for three years, he supplied (without Reward) a Morning Paper with Paragraphs and Essays, in support of Governmt.

Your Memorialist has lost by his Loyalty, by the Services above recited, and others of the same nature, and by the Unfortunate issue of the War, his Income as Professor of Natural Law and Moral Philosophy at King's College, £100 stg. Ecclusively of Fees for Private Pupils, which from his Station and Establish'd Charactor, would have been numerous: and the use of Chambers, a Cellar, Yard and Garden. The Salary as Assistant Minister and Lecturer in the Church at New York £200 stg. not to mention that he was next in order to the Rector, and would have succeeded (as was the established Rule) on his Death or Removal. The Salary which Government engaged to annex to his Regius Professorship £200 stg.

He has a Wife and Daughter, and an increasing family.

His Father has an Estate at New York, the Yearly Rent of which was about £220 consisting of Houses and Lots of Ground. But as your Memost. cannot precisely asertain and prove the Fact, and is also uncertain whether the Rebels will (after the Evacuation of New York) confiscate it or not he must be silent on the Subject.

Having thus brefly stated his Services and Losses, Your Memost. therefore prays, that his Case may be taken into your Consideration in Order that your Memorialist may be enabled, under your Report, to receive such Aid and Relief as his Services and Loses may be found to deserve.

Novr. 16th 1783.

APPENDIX D

Note on the Spy, Van Zandt, alias George Lupton

THE MISPLACED confidence shown so often by Deane and Franklin was principally due to the difficulty they found in creating a proper organization, from among the very few Americans abroad. The inconvenience of what John Adams called "militia diplomacy," unavoidable as circumstances rendered this, was never more convincingly shown than in the experiences of the first American agents in Paris. Silas Deane was particularly unfortunate in his judgment of men. When rumours reached him about the son of a very respectable New Yorker, Jacobus Van Zandt, being the British spy he was, Deane wrote the father to express relief on learning that his son had got into debt, as this seemed to give a lie to the allegation.[1]

Van Zandt, while on a visit in London, had been induced to become a spy by the Rev. John Vardill. The clergyman, in his later memorial, described Lupton, which was the name Van Zandt went under, as being a man of good family. The latter often spoke of himself as a gentleman born, a circumstance which made him considerably increase his demands for money. After his brother, who had been fighting in the American army, was taken prisoner by General Howe, the spy solicited better treatment for him, adding that "these unhappy times have placed brothers against brothers, and fathers against sons."[2] Later, when Van Zandt proposed to return to America, he expressed the curious wish to go with his character cleared, and wrote to the Chief of the Secret Service in London that if any rumour of what he had done should reach his father, he would lose every shilling he had in the world.[3]

In order to obtain information, Van Zandt had passed himself off in Paris as a patriotic American business man who remained abroad while waiting for advice from home. This subterfuge could not be continued indefinitely, and he devised an ingenious scheme to divert suspicion, and at the same time to ascertain the fate of different vessels, by shipping his effects in half a dozen bottoms and then insuring these. He asked £500 for the purpose, and William Eden, the Chief of the British Secret Service, found the idea of sufficient merit to send him £200.[4] The spy also picked up a good deal of useful intelligence in the ports. He found out that English muskets, cleared for Bilbao, had actually been shipped to America,[5] and discovered the preparation of privateers at Dunkirk and the particulars of vessels fitted out at Bordeaux which they were still in time to intercept. Lupton confirmed reports, received also from other sources, that the American Commissioners' dispatches would be forwarded through Captain Hynson, and ascertained the channel of Deane's communications with people in England which the latter had sent under cover to agents in Amsterdam. At one time, the spy actually succeeded in being employed as a messenger to carry the American Commissioners' instructions to the seaports. At Nantes he had found sixty or seventy Americans on whom he called as a compatriot, and had made friends with Franklin's nephew, Jonathan Williams, who was in charge of all shipments. He learned that eighty thousand stands of arms, with pistols, swords, and uniforms, ostensibly cleared for Martinique, were all going to the Revolutionary Army. This journey had been expensive, but the spy pointed out to William Eden, when making his report, that intelligence of this kind could not be obtained by anybody.[6]

Lupton was also an intimate friend of William Carmichael, the wild young secretary of the American Commission, who intended at one time to go to St. Petersburg, for, having heard of the Empress Catherine's fancy for handsome men, he thought that she might find "curiosity in an American."[7] Carmichael spoke without restraint to Van Zandt, especially after a bottle of champagne, "which sets him chatting like a madman and completely off his guard,"[8] never suspecting that all his chatter would at once be reported to the head of the British Secret Service. At one time Carmichael had thought of carrying on a peace negotiation of his own, unknown to Deane and Franklin, whom he complacently regarded as being quite unfitted for their task. Carmichael's plan to bring about a reconciliation without actual independence was to start with a press campaign in England, which would point out the folly of war, while publishing, at the same time, the details of French and Spanish preparations.[9]

Occasionally the American spies would meet together in London. The Reverend John Vardill, who was in charge of local activities in the capital, reported on December 12, 1777, that Dr. Bancroft had arrived and announced that he and Van Zandt would visit Mr. Eden as soon as was convenient.[10] The latter, however, desired to call only at night, not daring to appear in Downing Street by daylight. When he learned that Lord North had spoken to David Hartley, the future British Peace Commissioner, regarding Dr. Bancroft's activities, Van Zandt was filled with terror, and begged Eden to entreat Lord North to deny any knowledge of him, and to burn all his correspondence, a wish which remained unfulfilled, for the original of this letter may still be read at the British Museum.

NOTES AND REFERENCES

Chapter One

1. MS. letter, March 31, 1778. Library of Congress, Washington. *Continental Congress Papers*, 78, B. II, 447. Printed in Appendix A.
2. Royal Society, *Letters and Papers*, VI, Nos. 111–12.
3. See Appendix A.
4. Franklin, Writings (edited by Smyth) VII, 233. Letter to David Hartley, Feb. 22, 1779.
5. A copy of the letter is in the possession of his great-granddaughter, Mrs. Bancroft Vidal, whose kindness in giving me information regarding her ancestor I take pleasure in acknowledging.
6. Public Record Office (henceforth designated as P.R.O.), S.P. 44/265, p. 377 *sq.*
7. P.R.O., F.O. 4, f.189 *sq.* (A considerable portion of the text of this memorial is published by S. F. Bemis in his valuable article in the *Am. Hist. Rev.*, vol. 29, p. 493 *sq.*)
8. *Edward Bancroft's Narrative of Silas Deane*, published by P. L. Ford. Brooklyn Historical Printing Club, 1891. (Also reproduced in Stevens, *Facsimiles*, 890.)
9. *Deane Papers*, I, 240 *sq.*, Sept. 13, 1776.
10. Bancroft to T. Walpole, Nov. 3, 1777; B. F. Stevens, *Facsimiles of Manuscripts in European Archives Relating to America* (hereafter referred to as S.F.), No. 289.
11. *Deane Papers*, I, 242.
12. *Ibid.*, I, 250.
13. A scientist of note who had gone to England in 1773 to solicit aid for an Academy at Newark, Delaware. He returned to America after the Declaration of Independence and was later elected as a delegate from North Carolina to the Continental Congress.
14. *Deane Papers*, I, 288, 290.
15. P.R.O., A.O. 13, Bundle 54. See also Appendix C.
16. MS. letter, March 31, 1778. Appendix A.
17. *Deane Papers*, I, 243; Sept. 13, 1776.
18. *Ibid.*, II, 24, March 16, 1777.
19. Hutchinson, *Diary and Letters*, II, 141, 144.
20. *Deane Papers*, III, 180.

21. *Ibid.*, 152, 201.
22. Memorandum on American Public Men, 1778, prepared for William Eden. S.F., 487.
23. Adams, *Works*, III, 150.
24. Letter of Favier to Vergennes, no date, end of 1777. S.F. 1812.
25. Information kindly communicated by Miss Mildred L. Saunders, Archivist, Dartmouth College.
26. Letter to Eden, Dec. 17, 1777. S.F. 231.
27. P.R.O., A.O. 13. Memorial of Paul Wentworth, March 23, 1784.
28. Franklin, *Writings*, VI, 303: *Dartmouth Papers*, Hist. MSS. Comm., 11th Report, App. V, p. 373.
29 Letter to W. Eden, Dec. 12, 1777. In the five years he had been in the Government service he had spent £2437. S.F. 315.
30. Letter of Dec. 17, 1777. S.F. 1781.
31. Letter to William Eden, May 11, 1777. S.F. 156.
32. *Ibid.*, Jan. 4, 1778. S.F. 331.
33. *Royal Inst. MSS.*, Hist. MSS. Comm. I, 94. S.F. 218.
34. *Add MS.* 34414, f. 335. All manuscripts, unless otherwise stated, are in the British Museum. Letter of Nov. 8, 1777.
35. Lord Suffolk to W. Eden, July 21, 1777. S.F. 477.
36. Wentworth to Eden, Nov. 21, 1777. S.F. 220.
37. The manuscript of this contract is reproduced in Stevens's *Facsimiles*, 235, from the *Auckland Papers*, and also in Franklin's *Writings*, X. 311.
38. *Add. MSS.* 34413, f. 20; June 18, 1777.
39. *Ibid.*, 34414, f. 27; June 27, 1777.
40. *Ibid.*, f. 234; Oct. 15, 1777.
41. Letter of March 31, 1778. See Appendix A.
42. Wentworth to Eden, Nov. 16, 1777. S.F. 218.
43. *Add. MSS.* 34414, f. 361 *sq.*
44. *Corresp., George III*, (Edited by Fortescue), III, 495.
45. *Add. MSS.* 34414, f. 380; Nov. 21, 1777.
46. *Ibid.*, f. 195; Sept. 29, 1777.
47. *Corresp. George III*, IV, 19, No. 2168; the King to Lord North, Jan. 16, 1778. See also *ibid*, III, 2067; IV, 2132.
48. *Add. MSS.* 34415, f. 296, March 27, 1778. S.F. 342.
49. Adams, *Diary*, April 21, 1778; *Works*, III, 138, 141.
50. *Add. MSS.* 34414, f. 195 *sq.*; Sept. 29, 1777.
51. *Corresp. George III*, III, 481; Sept. 27, 1777.

52. *Ibid.*, 532; the King to Lord North, Dec. 31, 1777.

53. P.R.O., C.O. 5/134. The letter is reprinted in Appendix B.

54. Letter to John Randolph, Aug. 25, 1776. *Works* (Edited by Ford), I, 484.

55. M. C. Tyler in *Am. Hist. Rev.*, I, 42 *sq.*

56. *Add. MSS.* 34414, 207, 333; letter of Oct. 16, 1777.

57. *Add. MSS.* 34414, f. 58, July 17, 1777.

58. An interesting account of this negotiation from which the writer has greatly benefited is contained in an article by S. W. Bemis, 'British Secret Service and the French-American Alliance,' *Am. Hist. Rev.*, vol. 29, p. 493 *sq.*

59. Eden to Wentworth, Dec. 6, 1777. S.F. 484.

60. *Ibid.*, Dec. 5, 1777, S.F.483.

61. Letter of Nov. 1, 1777. S.F. 288.

62. *Add. MSS.* 34414, f. 433 *sq.* Dec. 17, 1777.

63. This was an accepted opinion. "Jealousy and suspicion of those in trust are leading traits in the American character." Memorandum, at the end of a letter written in Philadelphia. Dec. 11, 1766. (No signature.) *Add. MSS.* 20733, f. 145 v.

64. *Add. MSS.* 34414, f. 452, *sq.*

65. Letter to Elbridge Gerry, July 9, 1778. *Works*, III, 177 *sq*,

66. Wentworth to Eden, Dec. 25, 1777. S.F. 321.

67. Letters to Eden, end of December, 1777. S.F. 321, 723.

68. *Ibid.*, Jan. 1, 1778. S.F. 768.

69. Favier to Vergennes, Jan. 10, 1778. S.F. 1832.

70. *Ibid.*, Jan. 2, 1778. S.F. 1818.

71. *Ibid.* S.F. 1818, 1833.

72. T. B. Scott, *American Secretaries of State*, I, 17.

73. *Corresp. George III*, III, 519. Lord North to the King, Dec. 23, 1777.

74. *Ibid.*, IV, 14; Jan. 13, 1778.

75. Eden to Wentworth, wrongly dated Jan. 2, 1777—should be 1778. S.F. 488.

76. Wentworth to Eden, Dec. 28, 1777. S.F. 322.

77. *Ibid.* No date, but early in 1778. S.F. 325.

78. *Deane Papers*, IV, 99. See also Lee's Letter to John Adams, Sept. 19, 1799. In George L. Clark's *Silas Deane* (1913), the real problem offered by Deane is hardly discussed and Paul Wentworth is not mentioned. Nor does C. Van Tyne in his *American Revolution* express an opinion as to Deane's conduct.

79. *Ibid.*, II, 329; to Jonathan Williams, Jan. 13, 1778.
80. *Add. MSS.* 34414, f. 43–f. 176.
81. *Ibid.*, 34413, f. 164, Jan. 25, 1778.
82. *Corresp. George III*, IV, 29, No. 2181; Lord North to the King, Jan. 30, 1778.
83. *Ibid.*, IV, 150.
84. *Ibid.*, IV, 189, No. 2210; the King to Lord North, March 9, 1778.
85. *Ibid.*, V, 200 *sq.*; The King to Lord North, March 3, 1781.
86. *Dict. of Am. Nat. Biog.*, article on Silas Deane.
87. *Corresp. George III*, V, 255; July 19, 1781.
88. *Ibid.*, V, 262; Aug. 7, 1781.
89. *Deane Papers*, V, 184.
90. *Ibid.*, 70.
91. *Ibid.* 482, 489, 494, *sq.*
92. *Add. MSS.* 34414, f. 182, See also f. 333; Nov. 8, 1777.
93. Letter, Jan. 22, 1778. Harvard College Library MSS.
94. Harvard MSS., Feb. 9, 1779.
95. Doniol, Histoire de la participation de la France à l' établissement des Etats Unis (5 vols. 1887-1899), III, 169.
96. *Works*, III, 138, 191.
97. Lecky. *England in the Eighteenth Century*, VI, 432. (Lecky himself had no suspicion about Bancroft being a spy.)
98. See also Franklin, *Writings*, IX, 50.
99. P.R.O., F.O. 4, f. 13 *sq.*; letter of Nov. 18, 1783.
100. *Ibid.* f. 183, f. 185; Sept. 16, 1784.
101. *Ibid.*
102. I owe this information to the kindness of his great-granddaughter, Mrs. Bancroft Vidal.

Chapter Two

1. Letter of Jonathan Boucher to George Washington. *Letters of Georg Washington* (edited by W. C. Ford, 1899), p. 45.
2. Dec. 22, 1774. Quoted by A. Morgan Dix, *History of Trinity Church* (New York, 1898), p. 365.
3. P.R.O., A.O. 13/67.
4. *Ibid.* 12/20. Printed in Appendix C.
5. *Ibid.*

6. See Appendix C. See also S.F. 339.
7. See Appendix C.
8. P.R.O., A.O. 12/20 Appendix C.
9. This chapter was completed before the writer had seen William Bell Clarke's scholarly book on Lambert Wickes (New Haven, 1932), which relates from a different angle Hynson's part in the theft of Franklin's papers.
10. *Deane Papers*, II, 256.
11. Elizabeth Jamp to J. Hynson, Feb. 12, 1777. S.F. 14.
12. Vardill to Hynson, Feb. 13, 1777. S.F. 17.
13. J. Vardill to Lord North, Feb. 10, 1777, S.F. 12.
14. Feb. 9, 1777. S.F. 53.
15. In 1778, the figures were £79,000; in 1779, £86,000; in 1780, £80,000. S.F. 2024.
16. *Add. MSS.* 34414, f. 265, Oct. 27, 1777.
17. *Add. MSS.* 34413, f. 396 *sq.*; April 14, 1777.
18. *Ibid.* f. 410 *sq.*, April, 1777.
19. Memorandum of April 6, 1777. S.F. 249.
20. *Add. MSS.* 34413, f. 401, April 10, 1777.
21. P.R.O., A.O. 12/20.
22. *Add. MSS.* 34414, f. 29; June 28, 1777.
23. *Ibid.* f. 255 *sq.*
24. S.F. 248.
25. *Add. MSS.* 34414 f. 239 *sq.*; Oct. 20, 1777.
26. Wm. Knox to W. Eden, Dec. 22, 1777. S.F. 319.
27. P.R.O., A.O. 13/67.
28. Vardill to Eden, Feb. 6, 1778. S.F. 339.
29. *Ibid.* April 11, 1778. S.F. 438.
30. *Deane Papers*, II, 203, Oct. 26, 1777. (This letter was sent to Eden. *Add. MSS.* 34414 f. 261.)
31. *Ibid.* II, 199. Oct. 24, 1777.
32. *Ibid.* III, 347.
33. *Ibid.* II, 314 *sq.*
34. *Ibid.* III, 220 *sq.*
35. *Ibid.* II, 256; Nov. 28, 1777.
36. *Ibid.* V, 347 *sq.*
37. Dec. 1777. S.F. 312.
38. P.R.O., Treasury, 50/20.
39. Vol. 81, p. 672.

1. Beaumarchais to Vergennes, Jan. 1, 1778. Printed in Doniol, II, 686.
2. *Add. MSS.* 34414, f. 338.
3. *Corresp. George III*, IV, 350 *sq.*, June 11, 1779.
4. *Add. MSS.* 34414, f. 338.
5. *Letters on the American War* (London, 1778), 34.
6. *Ibid.* 28, 34.
7. *Ibid.* 38 *sq.*
8. *Add. MSS*, 34414, f. 356 *sq.*
9. *Ibid.* 34415, f. 177 *sq.*
10. *Ibid.* f. 339 *sq.*
11. *Clare College* (Cambridge, 1928), I, 173 *sq.*
12. S.F. 426.
13. Letter of March 4, 1778. *Proc. Mass. Hist. Soc.* 2nd ser. X, 418 *sq.*
14. *Add. MSS.* 34415, f. 398.
15. *Ibid.* June 15, 1778.
16. *Ibid.* 500, June 18, 1778.
17. *Annual Register*, 1778, p. 216 *sq.*
18. *Selwyn and his Corresp.* III, 299.
19. *Annual Register*, 1778, p. 292.
20. *Corresp. George III*, IV, 286.
21. Bowdoin-Temple Papers, *Proc. Mass. Hist. Soc.*, 1897, 6th.ser. IX, 19.
22. *Ibid.*, 21.
23. Letter of Benjamin Hallowell to John Pownall, Sept. 29, 1773. S.F. 2029.
24. P.R.O., T. 1/622.
25. *Bowdoin-Temple Papers*, 283; Dec. 4, 1771.
26. *Ibid.* 281.
27. *Ibid.* 378, Oct. 13, 1774.
28. *Ibid.* 359; March 15, 1774.
29. *Diary and Letters* (2 vols., London, 1883–86), I, 279.
30. *Warren-Adams Letters* (Mass. Hist. Soc. Coll.), II, 250.
31. *Add. MSS*, 34415, f. 334. S.F. 424.
32. *Bowdoin-Temple Papers*, 420; letter of David Hartley, May 22, 1778.
33. *Diary and Letters*, II, 238.
34. *Journal of Congress*, XII, 858.
35. S. Adams, *Writings*, IV, 54, *sq.*, Sept. 3, 1778.
36. *Ibid.*, IV, 101; see also Wharton, *Dip. Corr.* I, 665 *sq.*

NOTES AND REFERENCES

37. *Ibid.*, and letter to John Winthrop, Dec. 21, 1778.
38. *Bowdoin-Temple Papers*, 426; letter of Sept. 21, 1778.
39. *Ibid.*, Nov. 7, 1778, 429.
40. See Chapter XI.
41. *Autobiography*, 58.
42. *Warren-Adams Letters*, II, 63; Nov. 5, 1778.
43. *Bowdoin-Temple Papers*, 427. [The endorsements are published in the *Papers*.]
44. *Writings*, IV, 95 *sq.*; Dec. 13, 1778.
45. See *Letters of Members of Congress*, III, 533; William Whipple to Joseph Bartlett, Dec. 14, 1778.
46. *Writings*, IV, 101 *sq.*; Dec. 21, 1778.
47. *Ibid.*, 95 *sq.*; Letter to Mrs. Adams, Dec. 13, 1778.
48. Doniol, IV, 29 *sq.*; Gérard to Vergennes, Dec. 12, 1778.
49. *Ibid.*, 51, Dec. 6, 1778.
50. *Ibid.*, 52 *sq.*; Dec. 7, 1778.
51. *Ibid.*, 57; Dec. 10, 1778.
52. *Ibid.*, 29, note *sq.*
53. *Writings*, IV, 99 *sq.*; letter to James Bowdoin, Dec. 19, 1778.
54. *Deane Papers*, III, 79.
55. *Bowdoin-Temple Papers*, 433; letter of May 7, 1779.
56. *Ibid.*, 458.
57. *Ibid.* 434 *sq.*
58. *Bowdoin-Temple Papers*, 458, 484.
59. *Ibid.*, 454.
60. Dec. 6, 1780; in *Bowdoin-Temple Papers*, 445 *sq.*
61. *The Remembrancer*, 1781, Part I, 78 *sq.*; *Ibid.*, 1780, Part II, 376.
62. Trumbull, *Autobiography*, 329, 338.
63. *Ibid.*, 338.
64. *Letters of Members of Congress* (edited by E. C. Burnett), V: 79, James Lovell to Sam Adams, March 17, 1780; 96, Thomas McKean to Richard H. Lee, March 25, 1780.
65. *Bowdoin-Temple Papers*, 456 *sq.*
66. Wharton, *Dip. Corr.* IV, 638; letter of Aug. 16, 1781.
67. *Bowdoin-Temple Papers*, 485; Sept. 27, 1782.
68. *Ibid.*, 2d ser., VI (1907), 15; March 5, 1783.
69. *Ibid.*, 28; Samuel Dexter to Temple, Dec. 13, 1783.
70. William Gordon to John Adams, Sept. 7, 1782. *Proc. Mass. Hist. Soc.*, vol. 63, p. 470.

[433]   FF

71. *Bowdoin-Temple Papers*, 2d ser. 10 *sq.*; Oct. 20, 1783.
72. *Ibid.*, 7 *sq.*; Oct. 1, 1783.
73. William Gordon to George Washington, *Proc. Mass. Hist. Soc.*, vol. 63, p. 517.
74. *Bowdoin-Temple Papers*, 2d ser., 37, 40 *sq.*
75. P.R.O., F.O. 4, June 29, 1785.
76. Letter of April 24, 1785; *Warren-Adams Letters*, II, 250.

Chapter Four

1. G. E. Ellis, *Memoirs of Count Rumford* (London, 1876) I, 8 *sq.* The biography, which is contained in the first volume of his collected works is invaluable for the documents and letters it contains.
2. *Ibid.*, 185 *sq.*; letter to Timothy Walker, Aug 14, 1775.
3. *Ibid.*, 100.
4. This information appears in Mr. French's book *General Gage's Informers* (University of Michigan Press). See also Randolph G. Adams, *The Papers of Lord George Germaine* (Ann Arbor, 1928), p. 18.
5. E. Alfred Jones, *Loyalists of Massachusetts* (London, 1930), 275.
6. David Hartley, *Letters on the American War*, 3.
7. *Stopford Sackville MSS.*, Hist. MSS. Comm. II, 13 *sq.*
8. *Diary and Letters*, II, 289, 337.
9. *Stopford Sackville MSS.*, II; letter of Aug. 16, 1785.
10. H. E. Egerton, *The Royal Commission on the Losses and Services of American Loyalists*, 53 *sq.* (Roxburghe Club, 1915).
11. Samuel Curwen, *Journal and Letters* (edited by G. A. Ward, 1842), 316, 322.
12. *Royal Inst. MSS.*, Sept. 30, 1781.
13. *Stopford Sackville MSS.* II, 249.
14. P.R.O., H.O. 42/2.
15. *Royal Inst. MSS.* II; Feb. 24, 1782.
16. *Ibid.*, Jan. 29, 1782.
17. P.R.O., H.O. 42/2.
18. *Stopford Sackville MSS.* II; Aug. 6, 1782.
19. Ellis, I, 137.
20. *Stopford Sackville MSS.* II; Aug. 6, 1782.

21. Memorial to Sir G. Carleton, March 14, 1783; printed in Ellis, Appendix I, 671.
22 P.R.O., H.O. 42/2; also *Winslow Papers*, 88 (edited by W. O. Raymond, New Brunswick Hist. Soc. 1901); letter to Lord North, June 8, 1783.
23. *Royal Inst. MSS.* IV, 204; *Winslow Papers*, 104.
24. P.R.O., H.O. 42/2.
25. *Corresp. George III*, No. 4412; the King to Lord North, July 10, 1783.
26. *Winslow Papers*, 104; letter of July 8, 1783.
27. *Ibid.* 130; letter to Ed. Winslow, Sept. 10, 1783.
28. A biography of Benjamin Thompson is now in preparation by Mr. and Mrs. Charles D. Lowry, of Evanston, Illinois.
29. *Winslow Papers*, 169 *sq.*; letters of March 7, 1784.
30. *Ibid.* 195; letter of April 22, 1784.
31. *Works*, V, 232 *sq.*
32. *Ibid.* V, 258.
33. *Ibid.* 261 *sq.*
34. Bence Jones, *The Royal Institution* (London, 1871), 62; letter of Lord Grenville, Sept. 14, 1798.
35. Ellis, I, 209; letter of Jan. 18, 1793.
36. *Ibid.* 97, 290.
37. *Ibid.* 212; Jan. 26, 1796.
38. *Ibid.* 347.
39. *Ibid.* 351; letter of Dec. 8, 1798.
40. John Adams, *Works*, X, 660; letter of June 24, 1799.
41. *Add. MSS.* 34045; letter of Jan. 26, 1799.
42. Bence Jones, 70; Ellis, I, 337.
43. *Royal Inst. MSS.*; letter of April 12, 1798.
44. *Add. MSS* 34045; letter of Jan. 26, 1799.
45. Bence Jones, 57.
46. Ellis, 524; letter of March 12, 1804.
47. *Royal Inst. MSS*; letter of April 30, 1802.
48. Ellis, I, 257.
49. *Add. MSS.* 33542, f. 214.
50. Bence Jones, 85.
51. Ellis, I, 558.
52. *Ibid.* 550.
53. *Ibid.* 562.
54. *Ibid.* 561; letter of April 12, 1808.

Chapter Five

1. See James K. Hosmer—Thomas Hutchinson, Boston, 1896; and articles on Hutchinson by George E. Ellis in the *Atlantic Monthly,* May, 1884, and Oct. 1886.
2. Johns Adams, *Diary,* March 17, 1766; Works VI, p. 189.
3. Letter of T. Hutchinson, Aug. 30, 1765; printed in Stark, *Loyalists of Massachusetts* 154.
4. Thomas Hutchinson, *Diary and Letters* (2 vols., London 1883–86), I, 290; Nov. 9, 1774.
5. *Ibid.* I, 116.
6. Adams, *Works,* X, 194, 231.
7. *Diary and Letters,* I, 188.
8. Stark, *Loyalists of Massachusetts,* 128.
9. Hutchinson, *Diary and Letters,* I, 108.
10. *Diary;* Aug. 31, 1777.
11. *Egerton MSS.* 2659, f. 110; *Diary and Letters,* I, 275.
12. *Corresp. George III* (edited by Fortescue), III, 116.
13. *Works,* X, 261 *sq.*
14. *Diary,* letters I, 128.
15. *Egerton MSS.* 2659, f. 11 *sq.*
16. No. 177, New Bond Street.
17. *Egerton MSS.* 2659, f. 109.
18. Letters of James Murray, *Loyalist, Boston* (1901), 257.
19. Letter to Eden, July 21, 1777. S.F. 477.
20. *Diary and Letters,* I, 378; Feb. 17, 1775.
21. *Ibid.* 201; Aug. 3, 1774.
22. *Ibid.* 245; Sept. 21, 1774.
23. *Diary and Letters,* 230 *sq.;* Aug. 25, 1774.
24. *Add. MSS.* 35427, f. 22; June 24, 1775.
25. *Diary and Letters,* I, 185; July 9, 1774.
26. *Add. MSS.* 35427, f.i., Nov. 2, 1774, *sqq.* contains the letters written by Governor Hutchinson to Lord Hardwicke.
27. *Ibid.* f. 3; Nov. 21, 1774.
28. *Ibid.* f. 4; Jan. 4, 1775.
29. *Diary and Letters,* I 297; Nov. 19, 1775.
30. *Egerton MSS.* 2659, f. 141; March 3, 1775.
31. *Diary and Letters,* I. 284.
32. *Egerton MSS.* 2661, f. 48; letter to Sir W. Pepperell, Aug. 15, 1774.

33. *Diary and Letters*, I, 283; Nov. 1, 1774.
34. *Ibid.* 393; Feb. 22, 1775.
35. *Egerton MSS*, 2659, f. 141.
36. *Add. MSS.* 35427, f. 19.
37. *Ibid.* f. 21; June 17, 1775.
38. *Diary and Letters*; June 10, 1775.
39. *Ibid.* I, 459; June 1, 1775.
40. *Add. MSS.* 35427, f. 149; Oct. 10, 1778.
41. *Ibid.* f. 24, v.
42. *Ibid.* f. 49; Oct. 18, 1775.
43. *Ibid.* f. 32; July 26, 1775.
44. *Ibid.* f. 33.
45. Among the articles in the inventory at Milton figures a set of the *Marriage à la Mode*, a silver epergne weighing 144 ounces, and thirty-five dozen old Madeira.
46. Reprinted in *Proc. Mass. Hist. Soc.* XVII, 301.
47. *Egerton MSS.* 2659, f. 161, 27; June, 1775.
48. Stark, *Loyalists of Massachusetts*, 174.
49. *Ibid.* See also *Proc. Mass. Hist. Soc.* May, 1895, 163.
50. *Add. MSS.* 35427, f. 47. See also *Diary and Letters*; Oct. 11, 1775.
51. *Ibid.* f. 51.
52. *Ibid.* f. 114.
53. *Egerton MSS.* 2659, f. 189; Dec. 7, 1775.
54. *Add. MSS.* 35427, f. 123; Sept. 1, 1776.
55. *Ibid.* f. 118; letter of Oct. 9, 1776.
56. *Ibid.* f. 128; letter of Feb. 13, 1777.
57. *Ibid.* f. 139; letter of Aug. 22, 1777.
58. *Ibid.* f. 141; letter of Aug. 31, 1778.
59. *Ibid.* ff. 154, 164; Nov. 27, 1778; Jan. 25, 1779.
60. *Ibid.* f. 185; May 31, 1779.
61. *Ibid.* f. 193; Aug. 23, 1779.
62. *Diary and Letters*, II, 136; Feb. 13, 1777.
63. *Egerton MSS.* 2661, f. 71.
64. *Diary*, II, 290; Oct. 11, 1779.
65. *Egerton MSS.* 2659, f. 134.
66. *Diary and Letters*, II, 274 *sq.*; Aug. 29, 1779.
67. *Diary and Letters*, II, 272; Aug. 19, 1779.
68. *Egerton MSS.* 2659, f. 334, 338.
69. *Egerton MSS.* 2659, f. 292.

70. Letter of June 17, 1780.
71. *Egerton MSS.* 2660, ff. 63, 97; letters of May 18, 1788, and April 20, 1790.

Chapter Six

1. *Works*, X, 63, 110.
2. H. E. Egerton, *Causes of the American Revolution*, 178.
3. See Lorenzo Sabine, *The American Loyalist* (1847); J. T. Stark, *Loyalists of Massachusetts*; E. Alfred Jones, *Massachusetts Loyalists* 1930; C. H. Van Tyne, *The Loyalists*, etc. (1902); Egerton Ryerson, *The Loyalists of America* (2 vols. 1880); A. C. Flick, *Loyalism in New York* (1901), etcetera
4. *Works*, X, 197, 231.
5. E. Alfred Jones, *Loyalists of Massachusetts* (London, 1930), Introduction, viii.
6. *Egerton MSS.* 2671, ff. 66, 84.
7. Letter printed in *Proc. Mass. Hist. Soc.*, 2d ser., X, 413, 418.
8. *Egerton MSS.* 2671, ff. 66, 87.
9. *Letters of a Loyalist Lady*, 70 *sq.*
10. The Reverend Joshua W. Weekes; quoted by E. A. Jones, *op. cit.* Introduction.
11. Quoted by Sabine, *The American Loyalists*, 18.
12. *Proc. Mass. Hist. Soc.* 2d ser. X, 413–418.
13. Jonathan Boucher, Jan. 8, 1776; *Maryland Hist. Mag.* vol. 8, p. 344.
14. Letter of Aug. 16, 1784.
15. T. Jefferson to John Randolph, Aug. 25, 1776. *Works* (edited by Ford), I, 484.
16. S. Curwen, *Journal and Letters* (edited by S. A. Ward, London, 1842); Dec. 18, 1776.
17. *Egerton MSS.* 2672, f. 5.
18. *Ibid.*; June 13, 1776.
19. *Proc. Mass. Hist. Soc.* 2d ser. X, 418 *sq.*
20. *Ibid.*
21. *Winslow Papers*, 13; letter to Edw. Winslow, Jan. 10, 1776.
22. S. Quincy, *Letters*, 1777; *Proc. Mass. Hist. Soc.* XIX, 211 *sq.*
23. See Wilbur H. Siebert, *The Flight of the American Loyalists* (Columbus, 1911).

24. S. Quincy, *Letters*, p. 211 *sq.*

25. Edw. Oxnard, *Diary*. Printed in *New Eng. Hist. and Gen. Reg.* XXVI (1872), 175 *sq.*

26. Samuel Curwen, *Journal and Letters* (London, 1845), 207.

27. Hutchinson, *Diary and Letters*, II, 240.

28. P.R.O., H.O. Dom. 42/1, quoted in *Clare College* (Cambridge, 1928), I, 173.

29. Sabine, 265; see also M. C. Tyler, *Literary History of the American Revolution*, II, 287 *sq.*

30. *Egerton MSS.*, 199 *sq.*

31. Burnett, *Letters of Members of Congress*, II, 200; Jan. 1, 1777.

32. Hutchinson, *Diary and Letters*, II, 228 *sq.*

33. *Letters to a Nobleman* (1779), 29. See also the anonymous *Considerations upon the American Enquiry* (London, 1779). For General Sir William Howe's opinion of Galloway see his *Observations upon a Pamphlet* (1780), 41.

34. Curwen, letter to Wm. Browne, Aug. 31, 1775.

35. *Diary*, June 21, 1776.

36. Curwen, Letter to Isaac Smith, June 6, 1776; Charles Russell, June 10, 1776.

37. Hutchinson, *Diary and Letters*, II, 239, Jan. 10, 1779.

38. Curwen, 74; Aug. 24, 1776.

39. Letter of Henry Hulton, Commissioner of Customs in Boston; *Letters of a Loyalist Lady* (1927), 98.

40. Curwen, Dec. 18, 1776.

41. *Ibid.*; Dec. 8, 1776.

42. *Ibid.* 106. *Add. MSS.* 20733, f. 141; J. Wharton to John Almon, March 20, 1777.

43. *Ibid.* 179; letter to George Russell, March 16, 1778.

44. See Hutchinson, *Diary*, II, 227; Dec. 7, 1778.

45. Curwen, 207 *sq*; letter of Judge Sewall, Dec. 18, 1778.

46. *Ibid.* 326; Nov. 22, 1781.

47. *Egerton MSS.* 2659, f. 352.

48. *Letters of James Murray, Loyalist*, 289.

49. Peter Van Schaack to his brother; letter of Feb. 19, 1783.

50. Curwen, 373; letter to Andrew Dalglish, March 17, 1783.

51. *Egerton MSS.* 2660, f. 21 v. See letter of Elisha Hutchinson, July 27, 1782.

52. Curwen; letter to R. Ward, Aug. 11, 1783.

53. Wm. Pynchon to S. Curwen, Jan. 2, 1784.
54. Wm. Pynchon to S. Curwen, March 2, 1784.
55. Curwen, 408; Sewall to Curwen, June 28, 1784.
56. Curwen, *Journal*, Sept. 25, 1784.

Chapter Seven

1. J. Boucher; letter printed in *Maryland Hist. Mag.* vol. 9, p. 237.
2. S.F. 1129 (Aug. 20, 1778); also S.F. 1128.
3. Stark, *Loyalists of Massachusetts*, 55.
4. Curwen, 216; letter to F. Sewall, March 6, 1779.
5. Printed in Sabine, 525. Other memorials are reprinted in E. Alfred Jones's scholarly work, *The Loyalists of Massachusetts* (London, 1930), Appendix, 307 *sq.*
6. Sabine, 70.
7. Siebert, *Flight of the Loyalists*, 19.
8. E. A. Jones, 123.
9. MS. letter which in Oct., 1931, was in possession of Henry Sotheran, London.
10. Lord E. Fitzmaurice, *Life of Lord Shelburne*, III, 182, 189.
11. Writings, IX, 175; letter of March 5, 1784.
12. *Works*, IX, 516.
13. Fitzmaurice, *Shelburne*, III, 291, 301; Sabine, 98 *sq.*
14. Quoted by C. H. Van Tyne, *Loyalists of the American Revolution* (1902), 288.
15. *The Case and Claim of the American Loyalists* (London, 1783).
16. *Winslow Papers*, 174.
17. Hutchinson, *Diary and Letters*, II, 372; letter from Pelham Winslow, Dec. 1, 1781.
18. *Egerton MSS.* 2660; letter to Elisha Hutchinson, July 27, 1784.
19. E. A. Jones, 132.
20. Franklin, *Works*, X, 401.
21. Printed in Curwen, 444.
22. *Ibid.* 385; see letter to John Tummins, Aug. 4, 1783.
23. Sabine, 103.
24. *Letters of David Colden, Loyalist* (1783, edited by E. A. Jones), *Am. Hist. Rev.* XXV, 83 *sq.*
25. Letter of May 6, 1780, printed by Sabine, 98, footnote.

NOTES AND REFERENCES

26. Van Tyne, 290.
27. *Winslow Papers*, 350; *Hist. MSS. Comm. Royal Inst.* IV, 155.
28. A. G. Bradley, *The United Empire Loyalists* (London, 1932), 124 *sq.*
29. Papers, 1781–83 (Roxburghe Club); letter to Lord George Germaine of Dec. 23, 1781.
30. For an account of the work of the Commission see John Eardley Wilmot's book on the subject, London, 1815.
31. Winslow Papers, 198; Colonel Beverley Robinson to Edward Winslow, April 29, 1784.
32. Alex. C. Flicke, *Loyalists in New York*, 202.
33. J. T. Adams, *New England in the Republic*, 73; see also H. E. Egerton, *American Revolution*, 174.
34. H. E. Egerton, 158.
35. See A. G. Bradley, *The United Empire Loyalists*, 271.

Chapter Eight

1. *Almon's Remembrancer* (1775), 101, 128, 305.
2. See Wharton, *Dipl. Corr.* I, 614.
3. *Diary and Letters*, II, 148; see also article by W. H. Siebert, *Proc. Mass. Hist. Soc.* (1912), 409.
4. *Letters of James Murray, Loyalist* (Boston, 1901), 254, 261.
5. Ernest Barker, *Burke and Bristol* (Bristol, 1931), 21.
6. *Commerce of Rhode Island* (Mass. Hist. Soc. Publ.), I, 139, 146.
7. See Dora M. Clark's excellent work on *British Opinion and the American Revolution* (1930), 95.
8. Burke, *Works*, II, 236.
9. *Dartmouth Papers*, II, 296.
10. Barker, 75.
11. *Diary and Letters*, I, 347; Jan. 10, 1775.
12. H. C. Van Schaack, *Peter Cruger* (New York, 1859), 13.
13. *Parl. Hist.*, vol. 18, 64 *sq.*
14. *Ibid.* 227 *sq.*
15. *Diary and Letters*, I, 368; Feb. 2, 1775.
16. *Parl. Hist.*, vol. 18, p. 644 *sq.*
17. Van Schaack, *Cruger*, 21.
18. Printed in S.F. 454.
19. *Add. MSS.* 20733; letter of Sept. 21, 1775.

20. *Writings* (edited by Smyth), VI, 460; July 30, 1776.

21. P.R.O., C.O./134, Nov. 3, 1775.

22. *Ibid.*; letter of Jacob Walton, Nov. 1, 1775.

23. Letter to Lord Temple, Sept. 24, 1777.

24. *Parl. Hist.*, vol. 18, p. 1148 *sq.*

25. *Ibid.*, vol. 19, p. 584 *sq.*

26. *Add. MSS.* 34415, f. 15. Major Skene was in the Chair; the others were "Krugher" (Cruger), Livius, who was secretary, Vardill, Green, Williams, Boyd, Williamson, White, "late Sullivan's A.D.C." (Austin?), Traill and Miner. (Letter to William Eden, Jan. 1, 1778.) (S. F. 768.)

27. Published in *The Remembrancer*, 1781, Part I, 233.

28. Barker, 127.

29. *The Remembrancer*, 231.

30. *Observations on the Mode of Electing Representatives in Parliament, by Mr. Dawes of the Inner Temple* (Bristol and London, 1784), 37–42.

31. *Ibid.*

32. P.R.O., A.O. 20, f. 276.

33. *Ibid.* A.O. 13/67; Sept. 9, 1779; A.O. 20 f. 276.

34. *Ibid.* 103, f. 73.

35. *Ibid.* A.O. 20, f. 276.

36. Letter of Sept. 17, 1782. Printed in H. C. Van Schaack, *Life of Peter Van Schaack.*

37. Van Schaack, *Life of Peter Van Schaak*, 104.

38. *Ibid.* 333.

39. *Works*, III, 137.

40. *Maryland Hist. Mag.*, vol. 9, p. 233.

41. *Add. MSS.* 20733, f. 75; letter to John Almon, Oct. 9, 1775.

42. *Egerton MSS.* 2671, f. 44, v, f. 84.

43. Sam Adams, *Works*, IV, 238; letter to J. Scollay, Dec. 30, 1780.

44. J. Adams, *Works*, X, 241; letter to William Tudor.

45. Hutchinson, *Diary and Letters*, I, 183; July 5, 1777.

46. *Ibid.* I, 220.

47. Franklin, V, 220, 205; VI, 348.

48. *Parl. Hist.* vol. 19, p. 526; Dec. 2, 1777.

49. *Pownall Memorial* (1783), 47.

50. *Parl. Hist.*, vol. 18, p. 892; Nov. 8, 1775.

51. *Ibid.*

52. *Ibid.* vol. 19, p. 526 *sq.*

53. *Ibid.* 934; March 17, 1778.
54. *Ibid.* 731; Feb. 10, 1778.
55. *Travels*, I, 262–69.
56. Letter to Sir H. Mann, May 6, 1770.
57. *Parl. Hist.*, vol. 19, p. 702; Feb. 6, 1778.
58. *Ibid.* p. 138; May 6, 1778.
59. *Ibid.* vol. 21, pp. 582, 627.
60. See *Thomas Pownall*, by Charles A. W. Pownall (London, 1908), 425 *sq.*
61. *Memorial*, 55 *sq.*
62. Joseph Quincey, *History of Harvard College*, 707.
63. *Bowdoin-Temple Papers*, *Proc. Mass. Hist. Soc.*, 7th ser., VI, 1 *sq.*
64. *Ibid.* 21; letter of Nov. 20, 1783.
65. *Ibid.* 27, 32.
66. *Ibid.* 39.

Chapter Nine

1. *Penn. Mag. of Hist. and Biog.*, Jan. 1908; article by Charles H. Hart.
2. Letter of July 20, 1798, reprinted in the same magazine, XVIII, 221.
3. Now in the National Portrait Gallery, London.
4. *Ann. Reg.* (1820), 1167.
5. W. Dunlap, *History of the Arts of Design in the United States*, I, 60.
6. See West's "Discourse to the Students of the Royal Academy," delivered shortly after his election as President in 1792.
7. Mme d'Arblay—*Letters* (Edit. Ward) II, 35.
8. See W. T. Whitley, *Gilbert Stuart*, 42.
9. H. Clifford Smith, *Buckingham Palace* (1931), 182.
10. George Ticknor, *Life and Letters*, I, 63.
11. S. Curwen, *Diary*, April 10, 1776.
12. Galt, II, 195.
13. Whitley, *Artists and Their Times*, II, 73.
14. Leigh Hunt, *Autobiography* (Edit. London, 1850), 124.
15. W. Dunlap, I, 127.
16. *Copley-Pelham Letters*, 118 *sq.*
17. Galt, II, 71.
18. Quoted by M. C. Tyler, *Am. Hist. Rev.* I, 42 *sq.*
19. Trumbull, *Autobiography*, 312.

20. Farington, *Diary*, July 13, 1813, and told also to S. F. B. Morse.
21. *Ibid.* I, 279.
22. Elkanah Watson, *Memoirs* (1861), 202.
23. Letter printed in *Penn. Mag. of Hist. and Biog.*, Jan. 1908.
24. Leigh Hunt, *Autobiography*, 17 *sq.*
25. Published in *Penn. Mag. of Hist. and Biog.* II, 36 *sq.*
26. J. T. Smith, *Nollekens and His Times* (1926), II, 301.
27. Dunlap, I, 70.
28. Quoted by Whitley, *Artists*, II, 56.
29. *Add. MSS.* 36593, f. 390.
30. Letter to W. Rawle, Sept. 21, 1805; published in *Penn. Mag. of Hist. and Biog.* XIII, 482.
31. Whitley, II, 49.
32. Galt, II, 196.
33. W. Hazlitt, *Conversations with James Northcote* (London, 1830), 133.
34. Farington, Nov. 19, 1804.
35. *Ibid.* Dec. 8, 1798.
36. *Ibid.* I, 279.
37. *Ibid.* Dec. 14, 1804; Jan. 6, 1805.
38. *Egerton MSS.* 2182; letter to the Reverend William Douglas, Sept. 1797.
39. Farington, April 13, 1806.
40. Duff Cooper, *Talleyrand*, p. 132; Cunningham, *Lives* (1830), II, 51.
41. *Add. MSS.* 36297, f. 29 *sq.*
42. Farington, April 6, 1810.
43. *Ibid.* May 23, 1811.
44. S. F. B. Morse, *Letters and Journals* (edited by E. L. Morse, Boston, 1914), I, 47.
45. Letter of B. West to the Dilettante Society.
46. *Works* (edited by Coleridge), I, 466.
47. *Ann. Reg.* (1820), 1173.
48. S. F. B. Morse, I, 68.
49. Whitley, *Artists*, I, 123.
50. Farington, June 17, 1813.
51. Galt, I, 190.
52. *Letters and Journals*, I, 63, 69.
53. Farington, Sept. 3, 1819.
54. *Ann. Reg.* (1820), 87.
55. Benj. R. Haydon, *Memoirs* (London, 1853), II, 146, note.

NOTES AND REFERENCES

Chapter Ten

1. *Add. MSS.* 36593, f. 53 v; letter to Caleb Whitefoord, Dec. 7, 1763.
2. *Writings*, IX, 45; letter to Ian Ingenhousz.
3. *Add. MSS.* 23775; letter of John Smibert, March 15, 1744; also April 6, 1749.
4. *Bowdoin-Temple Papers, Proc. Mass. Hist. Soc.* 6th ser., IX, 84.
5. S. F. B. Morse, *Letters and Journals* (edited by E. L. Morse, Boston, 1914), I, 46; letter to Mr. and Mrs. Jarvis, Sept. 17, 1811.
6. Quoted by James T. Adams, *New England the Republic*, 72, from *National Arithmetick or Observations on the Finances of Massachusetts* (1786).
7. *Copley-Pelham Correspondence*, 65. *Mass. Hist. Soc. Coll.* (1914). (All quotations from Copley, unless otherwise stated, are from this correspondence.)
8. *Ibid.* 51, 63; Copley to West, Nov. 12, 1766; Copley to F. M. Newton, Nov. 23, 1767.
9. *Copley-Pelham Correspondence*, John Morgan to l'abbé Grant, Nov. 24, 1773.
10. *Copley-Pelham Correspondence*, 47 *sq.*; Copley to Peter Pelham, Sept. 12, 1766.
11. *Ibid.* 41 *sq.*; R. G. Bruce to Copley, Aug. 4, 1766.
12. *Ibid.* 82 *sq.*; John Greenwood to Copley, March 23, 1770.
13. *Ibid.* 71 *sq.*; Myles Cooper to Copley, Aug. 5, 1768.
14. *Ibid.* 95; John Wilkes to N. Barber, Sept. 21, 1770.
15. *Ibid.* 97 *sq.*; Copley to B. West, Nov. 27, 1770.
16. *Ibid.* 36; Copley to R. G. Bruce, Sept. 10, 1765.
17. *Ibid.* 211 *sq.*; Copley to J. and I. W. Clarke, Dec. 1, 1773.
18. *Ibid.* 218; Copley to J. W. Clarke, April 26, 1774.
19. *Ibid.* 192; J. Clarke to Copley, Dec. 20, 1772.
20. *Ibid.* 221; P.R.O., C.O. 5/38-9; letter from John Small, June 9, 1774.
21. *Ibid.* 340; Copley to Henry Pelham from Parma, June 25, 1775.
22. *Ibid.* 301; Copley to H. Pelham, March 14, 1775.
23. *Ibid.* 332; Copley to his mother, June 25, 1775.
24. *Ibid.* 348 *sq.*; Copley to H. Pelham, Aug. 6, 1775.
25. *Ibid.* 83; H. Pelham to Paul Revere, March 29, 1770.
26. *Ibid.* 233; H. Pelham to Copley, July 17, 1774.
27. *Ibid.* 322; H. Pelham to Copley, March 16, 1775.
28. M. B. Amory, *Copley* (Boston, 1882), 42.

29. P.R.O., C.O. 5/38–39; Sept. 16, 1775; *Corresp.* 357 *sq.*
30. Curwen, April 1, 1776.
31. Letter of Dec. 4, 1779, quoted by Amery, 42.
32. See Paul L. Ford, article in *Atlantic Monthly*, April, 1893, 499 *sq.*
33. *Egerton MSS.* 2659, f. 336 v.
34. Quoted by W. T. Whitley, *Artists in England*, 169.
35. Letter to Mrs. Adams, Aug. 21, 1776.
36. Amory, 104.
37. This house, No. 25, has been entirely rebuilt.
38. *Diary*, Dec. 23, 1807.
39. W. T. Whitley, *Artists and their Times*, II, 48.
40. W. T. Whitley, *Gilbert Stuart*, 78.
41. Amory, 142 *sq.*; letter of Feb. 27, 1796. Other quotations from young Copley's letters are taken from this book.
42. Letter of Jan. 2, 1796.
43. Farington, Nov. 30, 1811.
44. Amory, 192; letter of Oct. 22, 1800.
45. *Ibid.* 241; letter of Oct. 12, 1803.
46. Quoted by Whitley, *Artists and Their Times*, II, 230.
47. Farington, June 17, 1806.
48. Farington, May 20, 1811.

Chapter Eleven

1. *Letters of Members of Congress* (edited by E. C. Burnett, Washington) II, *passim*; III, 14.
2. *Proc. Mass. Hist. Soc.* 323; Aug. 5–12, 1776.
3. *Letters of Members of Congress*, IV, 440, 462. Wm. Gordon to General Gates, Aug. 13, 1777.
4. *Proc. Mass. Hist. Soc.* XIII, 354.
5. *Egerton MSS.* 2672.
6. *Add. MSS.* 20733; Aug. 4, 1776.
7. *Egerton MSS.* 2659, f. 228; Aug. 20, 1778.
8. J. Trumbull, *Autobiography* (1871), 58 *sq.*
9. *Trumbull Papers*, IV, 177.
10. *Autobiography*, 66.
11. *Trumbull Papers*, IV, 137; letter of Sept. 12, 1780.
12. *Ibid.*

13. *Autobiography* 68 *sq.*
14. P.R.O., C.O. 5/144; Aug. 6, 1781. (Trumbull calls him "Major" Tyler.)
15. *Proc. Mass. Hist. Soc.* vol. 63, 455.
16. Almon, *Remembrancer*, 1780, Part II, 376.
17. Quoted by Whitley, *Artists and Their Times*, II, 109.
18. *Egerton MSS.* 2659, f. 318; Nov. 23, 1780.
19. D. V. Wallace, *Henry Laurens* (1915), 381.
20. *Trumbull Papers*, IV, 238.
21. *Autobiography*, 76.
22. *Ibid.* 317.
23. *Bowdoin-Temple Papers, Proc. Mass. Hist. Soc.* 6th Ser. IX, 453.
24. *Autobiography*, 332.
25. *Ibid.* 318.
26. *Trumbull Papers*, IV, 222.
27. 17 George III, ch. 9.
28. *Autobiography*, 323.
29. *Trumbull Papers*, IV, 245.
30. *Autobiography*, 92.
31. See article on J.B. Church in *Journal of American History* 1908. Many of his letters are in the New York Public Library.
32. Chastellux, *Voyages dans l'Amérique* (1791), II, 299.
33. Dunlap, II, 30.
34. *Autobiography.* Letter to Thomas Jefferson, Jan. 11, 1789.
35. Jefferson, *Works*, V, 272, 299.
36. Farington, Feb. 14, 1797.
37. *Autobiography*, 158.

Chapter Twelve

1. Dunlap, *History of the Arts of Design in the United States*, I, 202–07.
2. Lawrence Park, *Gilbert Stuart* (New York, 1926), I, 30.
3. Dunlap, I, 219.
4. W. T. Whitley, *Gilbert Stuart* (Harvard University Press, 1932). See also by the same writer *Artists and Their Friends*, II, 96. Mr. Whitley has discovered many new facts regarding Stuart's career as a portrait painter.

5. Letter of June 19, 1780, cited by F. W. Coburn, article on Mather Brown, *Art in America*, April, 1932, to whom the writer desires to express his obligation for most of the facts contained in this brief notice.
6. Printed by Coburn, article cited.
7. Printed in *The Bards of Epworth; or, Poetic Gems from the Wesley Cabinet.*
8. Quoted by Whitley, *Artists*, II, 55.
9. Letter of Dec. 7, 1781. Printed in *Penn. Mag. of Hist. and Biog.* Jan., 1908.
10. *Add. MSS.* 34413, f. 422 *sq.*; report by John Vardill.
11. Franklin, *Writings*, X, 583.
12. Letter of May 4, 1779.
13. Elkanah Watson, *Memoirs* (1861), 137.
14. Mrs. Abigail Adams, *Letters* (1848), 177.
15. Letter of Aug. 4, 1785; printed in Dunlap, I, 155.
16. *Add. MSS.* 12099; letter of Jan. 30, 1785.

Appendix D

1. *Deane Papers*, II, 366. Feb. 16, 1778.
2. *Add. MSS.* 34414, f. 180. See S.F. 265.
3. *Ibid.* 34415, f. 90, Jan. 28, 1778.
4. *Ibid.* 34414, f. 25; June 27, 1777. S.F. 173.
5. *Ibid.* 34413, f. 416 v.; April 10, 1777.
6. *Ibid.* 34414, f. 116; Aug. 20, 1777. See S.F. 187.
7. *Ibid.* 34413, f. 456.
8. *Ibid.* 34414, f. 28.
9. *Ibid.* 34414, f. 298, Nov. 1, 1777.
10. *Ibid.* 34414, ff. 422, 428.

INDEX

INDEX

Boucher, Rev. Jonathan, loyalist refugee, 226; on "friends of America," 267; warning to Washington, 306

Bowdoin, James, father-in-law of John Temple, 83, 91, 108; annoyed at treatment of Temple, 92; testimony to Temple, 100–1; attacked by Temple's enemies, 109; correspondent of Govr. Pownall, 276–7; refuses military rank to Govr. Pownall, 278; member of Arts Society in Boston, 1767, 328

Boydell, engraver, 328

Boy with the Squirrel, by John Copley, 331

Brickdale, unsuccessful against Henry Cruger, 249

Bristol, centre of English intercourse with America, 246; petition for repeal of Stamp Act, 247

Bristol Gazette, 249

British Claims Commission, 210

British command in America, incapacity of, 181

British compensation to loyalists, 241 *sqq.*

British delay in leaving America, 238

British garrisons in America, 232

British Government, effort to enlist Hessian mercenaries, 3; ignorance of American situation, 79; incompetence of, 181–2, 190; instructions to Richard Oswald, 232; relations with American Colonies undefined, 245

British Imperialism, 245

British Institution, founded by Benjamin West, 320

British Secret Service, under Wm. Eden, 59; informed of Bancroft's "gossip," 12

British subjects, problem of American-born, 261

Bromfield, Miss Sally, friend of Henry Pelham, 346

Bromley, author of *History of the Fine Arts*, 314

Brown, Mather, student under Benjamin West, 311; career, 387 *sqq.*; ambitions, 387–8; in Paris, 388; under West, 388; advised by Copley, 388; success, 388; portraits, 389; "Historical Painter to His Majesty and the Duke of York," 389; pictures sold as Gilbert Stuart's, 390

Bulfinch, Charles, and Mather Brown, 389

Bunker Hill, significance to Americans, 27; effect of on Govr. Hutchinson's opinion, 175

Burgoyne, effect of surrender at Saratoga, 28–9, 70, 256, 273

Burke, Edmund, 169, friend of John Temple, 103; denunciation of peace proposals for loyalists, 233; invited to stand for Bristol, 248; defines duties of an M.P. to electors, 248; despises Govr. Pownall, 271; Benjamin West of his circle, 295; John Trumbull's appeal to, 373; visit to Trumbull in prison, 374; advice to Trumbull on career, 375–6

Burr, Aaron, duel with John Barker Church, 377

Bute, Lord, Commission to John Greenwood for collection of pictures, 333

Byles, Rev. Mather, friend of Copley, grandfather of Mather Brown, 387 *sqq.*

Byron, Lord, satire on Benjamin West, 321

Cabanis, physician, 149

Camden, Lord, friend of Bancroft, 9; of Temple, 100

Canada, proposed cession to U.S., 231; agents sent to investigate claims of refugees, 240; loyalists in, 243; loyalist position in 1812, 243–4; expedition in reported by John Adams, 405–6

Canada, British, founding of by Loyalists, 243

Canterbury, Archbp. of, courtesy to Govr. Hutchinson, 183

Cape Breton Island, loyalists exiled to, 238

Carleton, Sir Guy, 129

Carleton, General, dismisses Indian troops, 178–9; British C.-in-C. in New York, 1783, 238

Carlisle, Lord, Member of Peace Embassy, 77; repudiation of private negotiations of Johnstone, 81

Carmarthen, Lord, Secretary of State, 1784, 7; Foreign Secretary, 112

Carmichael, Edward, disloyal secretary of Silas Deane, 21; sent back to

INDEX

[453]

INDEX

306; his admiration for John Copley, 350; headquarters on the Hudson River, 375; esteem for John Trumbull, 380; and Mrs. Patience Wright, 395

Waterhouse, Dr. Benjamin, friend of Gilbert Stuart, 385–6

Watson, Elkanah, in London, 350; and Mrs. Patience Wright in Paris, 394

Watson, Col. George, Mandamus Counsellor, friend of John Copley, 336

Wedderburn, Solicitor-General, 5; Attorney-General,80; John Temple's criticism, 102

Weekes, Rev. Dr., on American intimidation of loyalists, 195

Wentworth, Governor, friend of Count Rumford, 115

Wentworth, Paul, knowledge of Bancroft's activities, 8; American loyalist, 14; "friend" and "foe" of John Adams, 15 *sqq.*; career, 16 *sqq.*; in service of British Govt., 18; "The Master Spy," 18 *sqq.*; M.P., 1780, 20; in Paris to discover attitude of Spain, 22; difficulties with Bancroft, 23; excellence of his information, 26; great effort to prevent French intervention, Dec., 1777, 28 *sqq.*; secret terms offered to Benjamin Franklin and Deane, 1777, 28; proposals for negotiations with America, 29; in Paris to discover terms on which America would treat for peace,Dec., 1777, 30; plan of reconciliation, 31 *sqq.*; failure to understand revolutionary psychology, 32; watched by French secret service, 1778, 33 *sqq.*; reaction to French suspicions, 33, 34; his "explanations" to Favier, 35, 36; J. L. Favier, 35 *sqq.*; reports of attempted negotiations, 1777–8, 38–9; contribution to Silas Deane's downfall, 40 *sqq.*; proposals to Deane, 41; death in Surinam, 44; information to Lord Suffolk on Lafayette and Hynson, 60–1; payment of £200 and promise of £200 a year to Hynson, 65; to Paris to negotiate peace terms with Deane, 70; advice neglected, 75; mission in Paris, 257; references to Henry Cruger, 258; M.P., 1780, 259; plan for Peace Commission divulged, 272

West, Benjamin, lost allegorical sketch, 241–2; Court painter, 283 *sqq.*; summary of career, 283; why he was "made a painter," 284–5; painting in Philadelphia, 285; in New York, 286; opportunity to travel, 286–7; arrival in Rome, 286–7; "American savage" in Rome, 288 *sqq.*; portrait by Angelica Kauffman, 290; his acquaintances in Rome, 290–1; arrival in London, Aug., 1763, 291; his lodgings in London, 291; becoming famous, 292–3; pictures create sensation in 1764, 294; refusal of Lord Rockingham's commission, 296; his stainless purity and business instinct, 296–7; his adaptability to Court life, 298; and foundation of Royal Academy, 300; reception of *Death of Wolfe*, 301; paintings for Windsor, 302; and proposal to paint panels for St. Paul's Cathedral, 302; pictures of Revealed Religion, 302 *sqq.*; painter by Royal Appointment 1772, 305; proposal for American Revolutionary pictures, 308; helpful to Americans in England, 308 *sqq.*; shelter for family of Leigh Hunt, 309; his life in London, 1777 to 1820, 310 *sqq.*; his house in Newman Street, 310; his help to other artists, 311; instruction of students, 311; painting *Lear and Cordelia*, 312; pall-bearer for Sir Joshua Reynolds, 312; President R.A., 312; his *Hagar and Ishmael*, 312; his "vulgar" use of English, 313; his illiteracy, 313–4; decrease of popularity, 316; feeling jealousy of his contemporaries, 315–6; in Paris, 317–8; admiration for Napoleon, 317; resignation as P.R.A., 318; re-elected P.R.A., 1805, 318; Annuity stopped by Court, 1811, 319; his rally after 1811, 320; *The Crucifixion* and *Christ Rejected*, 320–1; *Christ Healing the Sick*, 320–1; Anniversary dinner, 1814, 322; takes on English nationality, 1813, 322–3; death, 1820, 323; his collection of great paintings, 324; sale of paintings, 1829–40, 324–5; funeral, 324; on U.S. art,

INDEX

330; advice and help to John Copley, 322 *sqq.*; hospitality to Copley, 338; effect of Italy, 339–40; no warm friendship with Copley, 346–7; stands bail for John Trumbull, 347; explanation of Copley's dejection, 1811, 354; Trumbull introduced, 363; intervention with George III for Trumbull, 371; portrait by G. Stuart, 387; help for Joseph Wright, 391; bail for Trumbull, 374; Trumbull's return, 375; kindness to G. Stuart, 386

West, Mrs. B., formally visited by Mrs. John Copley, 346–7

West, "Father" of Benjamin, arrival in London, 295

West Indies, break with England feared, 74; refugees, 225

Weymouth, Lord, Secretary of State, help given to Bancroft, 8

Whateley, duel with Temple, 85

Whigs, opinions on American independence, 86; increase in New York, 196

Whistler, 352

White, William, suspected letter in John Trumbull's papers, 367–8

Wickes, Lambert, 56

Wild, Jonathan, highwayman, 84

Wilkes, John, admiration for Copley's work, 334

Wilkins, Isaac, of New York, divided loyalties, 199

William IV (Prince William Henry) in America, 129

Williams, Jonathan, nephew of Franklin, correspondent of Silas Deane, 67; in charge of shipments, 422

Williamson, Dr. (of Philadelphia), accused by Bancroft as British spy, 10, 427

Wilmot, John Eardley, M.P., to examine claims of refugees, 240

Winslow, Edward, loyalist in Halifax, 134

Winthrop, Dr., Prof. of Philosophy, testimony to Temple, 94; friend of Temple, 98–9, 100

Witherspoon, Dr., controversy with Vardill, 52, 411

Woburn, America, Rumford's connection with, 138

Wolfe, General, 250

Worcester Resolution, 19 May, 1783, denunciation of loyalist exiles, 236–7

Wright, Joseph, son of Mrs. P. M. Wright, 391; student of art in France, 381–2

Wright, Mr., husband of Mrs. P. M. Wright, 391

Wright, Mrs. Patience Mahitabel, wax portraitist, 390 *sqq.*; birth and parentage, 390; her verses, 390–1; model of Lord Chatham, 392; a zealous republican, 392; her activities as a *soi-disant* spy, 393; and Franklin, 393–4; in Paris, 394; and Mrs. John Adams, 394–5; desire to model founders of U.S., 395; on English police, 395

Wright, Phœbe, wife of Hoppner, 391

Wright, Justice Sampson, and John Trumbull, 368

Wyatt, Sir James, Court architect at Windsor, 304–5; hated by Benjamin West, 314–5; appointed P.R.A., his failure, 318; Court architect and John Trumbull, 381

Yorktown, surrender of Cornwallis at, 220